CROATIA

DALMATIAN COAST

DUBROVNIK • SPLIT • THE ISLANDS

JANE FOSTER
PIERS LETCHER

www.bradtguides.com

Bradt Guides Ltd, UK
The Globe Pequot Press Inc, USA

Bradt GUIDES

TRAVEL TAKEN SERIOUSLY

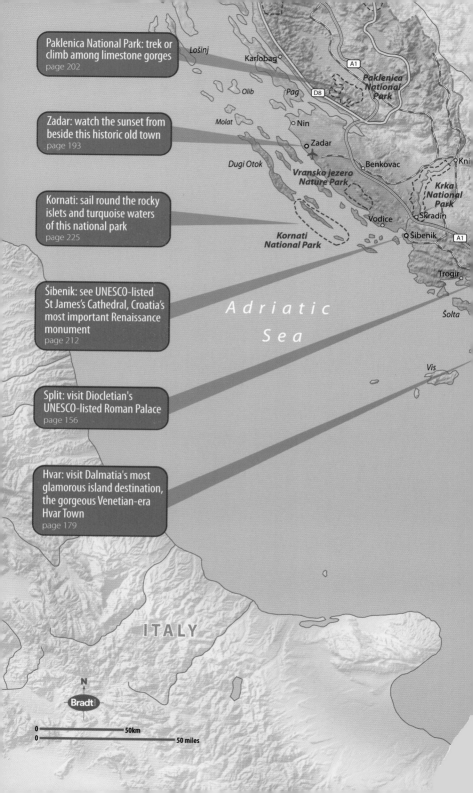

Paklenica National Park: trek or climb among limestone gorges
page 202

Zadar: watch the sunset from beside this historic old town
page 193

Kornati: sail round the rocky islets and turquoise waters of this national park
page 225

Šibenik: see UNESCO-listed St James's Cathedral, Croatia's most important Renaissance monument
page 212

Split: visit Diocletian's UNESCO-listed Roman Palace
page 156

Hvar: visit Dalmatia's most glamorous island destination, the gorgeous Venetian-era Hvar Town
page 179

Lošinj
Karlobag
A1
Paklenica National Park
Olib
Pag
D8
Molat
Nin
Zadar
Dugi Otok
Benkovac
Kni
Vransko jezero Nature Park
Krka National Park
Vodice
Skradin
Kornati National Park
Šibenik
A1

Adriatic Sea

Trogir
Šolta

Vis

ITALY

N

Bradt

0   50km
0   50 miles

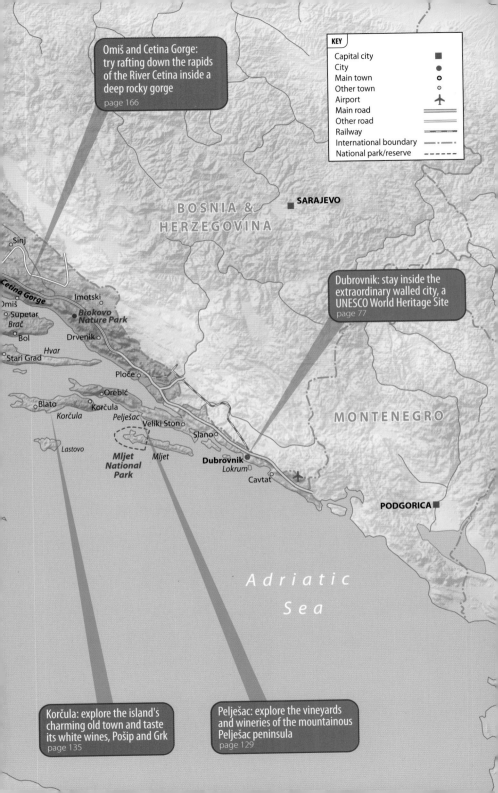

Omiš and Cetina Gorge: try rafting down the rapids of the River Cetina inside a deep rocky gorge
page 166

KEY
Capital city ■
City ●
Main town ◉
Other town ○
Airport ✈
Main road
Other road
Railway
International boundary
National park/reserve

BOSNIA & HERZEGOVINA

■ SARAJEVO

Dubrovnik: stay inside the extraordinary walled city, a UNESCO World Heritage Site
page 77

Sinj

Cetina Gorge

Imotski

Omiš

Supetar

Brač

Bol

Biokovo
Nature Park

Drvenik

Hvar

Stari Grad

Ploče

Orebić

Blato

Korčula

Korčula

Pelješac

Veliki Ston

Slano

Lastovo

Mljet
National
Park

Mljet

Dubrovnik

Lokrum

Cavtat

MONTENEGRO

■ **PODGORICA**

A d r i a t i c

S e a

Korčula: explore the island's charming old town and taste its white wines, Pošip and Grk
page 135

Pelješac: explore the vineyards and wineries of the mountainous Pelješac peninsula
page 129

DALMATIAN COAST
DON'T MISS...

NATIONAL PARKS
One of Dalmatia's four national parks, Krka features a river gorge with dense woodland and spectacular waterfalls, like these viewed from Skradinski buk PAGE 215
(I/D)

UNESCO WORLD HERITAGE SITES
Dalmatia boasts a wealth of UNESCO World Heritage Sites, among them Diocletian's Palace in Split, centred on the Roman peristyle (pictured) PAGE 156
(KF/S)

WINE AND VINEYARDS
Steep vineyards on Hvar's south coast enjoy maximum sunshine, ideal for producing the region's robust red wines PAGES 50 & 178
(AB/S)

WATERSPORTS AND ADVENTURE ACTIVITIES
The Dalmatian coast is a great destination for watersports and outdoor enthusiasts; pictured, sea kayaking at the foot of Dubrovnik's Lovrijenac Fortress PAGE 60
(OD/S)

BEACHES
A swathe of fine pebbles shaded by pine trees, Punta Rata on the Makarska Riviera is one of the region's top beaches PAGE 166
(X/S)

DALMATIAN COAST
IN COLOUR

above
(I/S)   Joined to the mainland by two bridges, the UNESCO-listed island town of Trogir is delightfully car-free PAGE 161

below
(T/S)   Medieval Korčula Town sits compact on a fortified peninsula PAGE 135

Vast walls, complete with fortresses, towers and crenellations surround Dubrovnik's red-roofed old town PAGE 77

above
(Ma/D)

Ivan Meštrović's statue of Marko Marulić presides over Voćni trg (Fruit Square) in Split's old town PAGE 158

right
(D/S)

The colourful fishing harbour at Sali, on Dugi Otok PAGE 227

below
(X/S)

AUTHOR

Jane Foster is a British freelance travel writer originating from the Yorkshire Dales and now based in Split on the Dalmatian coast. She writes primarily about Croatia, a country she has explored extensively, both for pleasure and for work, as well as neighbouring Montenegro. She is the Croatia and Dubrovnik expert for the *Daily Telegraph* travel section, and has also contributed articles to various other publications, including *Conde Nast Travel*, *National Geographic Traveller*, *Food and Travel* and *Decanter* wine magazine.

AUTHOR'S STORY

I slipped into travel writing sideways, after completing a degree in architecture at Oxford Polytechnic, followed by a year of work experience at a studio in Rome. While in Italy, I became interested in switching to art criticism but, not having much writing experience, took an internship at the Associated Press and helped research Italy stories for *The Guardian*. One thing led to another and I ended up moving to Croatia in 1998. Here the idea of travel writing popped up – all the old guidebooks were titled *Yugoslavia*, a country that no longer existed as such, and the first tourists were already returning to the coast.

Having now lived in Dalmatia for almost two decades (with an interlude in Greece from 2003 to 2011), I've written several guidebooks – my first shot was a short Croatia and Slovenia section for *Thomas Cook Europe by Rail*. Already, when studying architecture, I often made journeys across Europe to visit notable buildings, museums and galleries, and regarded travel as a formative experience. Nowadays, with the ever-increasing problem of overtourism, I try to focus on sustainable projects where possible, such as agrotourism. It has been an honour to take on this new guidebook with Bradt Guides – I've always respected Piers Letcher's writing and his knowledge of history of art, so I hope this new Bradt guide to the Dalmatian Coast will do justice to his original, excellent, *Croatia*, also published by Bradt.

First edition published October 2024
Bradt Travel Guides Ltd
31a High Street, Chesham, Buckinghamshire, HP5 1BW, England
www.bradtguides.com
Print edition published in the USA by The Globe Pequot Press Inc,
PO Box 480, Guilford, Connecticut 06437-0480

Text copyright © Bradt Travel Guides Ltd, 2024
Maps copyright © Bradt Travel Guides Ltd, 2024; includes map data ©
OpenStreetMap contributors
Photographs copyright © Individual photographers, 2024 (see below)
Project Manager: Susannah Lord
Cover research: Pepi Bluck, Perfect Picture

ISBN: 9781804692349

British Library Cataloguing in Publication Data
A catalogue record for this book is available from the British Library

Photographs 4Corners images: Johanna Huber (JH/4C); Dreamstime: Boris
Stromar (BS/D), Donyanedomam (D/D), Happywindow (H/D), Ilijaaa (I/D),
Martinbreza (Ma/D), Michaldziedziak (Mi/D), Xbrchx (X/D); Shutterstock.com:
Ajan Alen (AA/S), Alena Brozova (AB/S), canadastock (C/S), Dreamer4787 (D/S),
goran_safarek (GS/S), Inu (I/S), Julija Ogrodowski (JO/S), Kirk Fisher (KF/S),
mezzotint (M/S), Michael Paschos (MPa/S), Miroslav Posavec (MPo/S), Nenad
Nedomacki (NN/S), ninopavisic (N/S), OldskoolDesign (OD/S), Phant (P/S),
Renata Sedmakova (RS/S), trabantos (T/S), Vaidotas Grybauskas (VG/S), xbrchx
(X/S), zhukovvvlad (Z/S)

Front cover Beach on the Makarska Riviera (JH/4C)
Back cover, clockwise from top left A vineyard on Vis Island (X/S), Trogir old town
(I/S), chamois, Biokovo (GS/S)
Title page, clockwise from top left Cycling by Lake Vrana (GS/S), sailing near
Zadar's waterfont (X/D), Korčula's medieval old town (T/S), sheep on Pag
Island (H/D)

Maps David McCutcheon FBCart.S. FRGS

Typeset by Ian Spick, Bradt Travel Guides Ltd
Production managed by Imprint Press; printed in India
Digital conversion by www.dataworks.co.in

CONTRIBUTORS

Born and educated in the UK, **Piers Letcher** has lived in France for 40 years. He has published many books, more than a thousand newspaper and magazine articles and hundreds of photographs. He is currently a freelance writer, specialising in science and technology, and a travel photographer. Piers is the author of *Eccentric France* and *Dubrovnik: The Bradt City Guide*, and co-author of *Zagreb: The Bradt City Guide* and several editions of the Bradt guide to Croatia.

Rudolf Abraham (w rudolfabraham.com) is an award-winning travel writer, photographer and guidebook author specialising in Croatia and central and southeast Europe. He first visited Croatia in 1998, lived in Zagreb for two years, and continues to spend several weeks a year in his favourite country in Europe. He is the author of more than dozen books including the first English-language guide to hiking in Croatia back in 2004, and has contributed to around 40 more. He co-authored the Bradt guide to Istria, has updated three editions of the Bradt guide to Croatia, and his work is published widely in magazines including *Family Traveller*, *National Geographic Traveller* and *Wanderlust*. When not in London or travelling for work, there's a good chance you'll find Rudolf on a small island on the Croatian Adriatic.

FEEDBACK REQUEST

At Bradt Guides we're aware that guidebooks start to go out of date on the day they're published – and that you, our readers, are out there in the field doing research of your own. You'll find out before us when a fine new family-run hotel opens or a favourite restaurant changes hands and goes downhill. So why not tell us about your experiences? Contact us on 01753 893444 or e info@bradtguides.com. We will forward emails to the author who may post updates on the Bradt website at w bradtguides.com/updates. Alternatively, you can add a review of the book to Amazon, or share your adventures with us on Facebook, Twitter or Instagram (@BradtGuides).

Acknowledgements

For this first edition of Bradt's *Dalmatian Coast*, I thank the Croatian National Tourist Board, which has helped me several times in the past to arrange research trips. I also thank Šibenik Tourist Board for organising my visit to St Nicholas Fortress, and the Meštrović Gallery for ensuring that I was well received at the Meštrović Mausoleum and the Church of the Holy Redeemer in Otavice. And, of course, the Zlarin Coral Centre for showing me their marvellous work on the thought-provoking plastic-free island of Zlarin.

Regarding help with wonderful accommodation during my travels, I thank Mason Rose and Adriatic Luxury hotels in Dubrovnik, and Marc van Bloemen, also in Dubrovnik; Ivana Pačić Unković and the Lešić Dimitri Palace in Korčula; and Marzia Marti and Sunčani Hvar in Hvar. On the island of Vis, thanks are due to Filip Prelec and Lana Schmidt for showing me the geotrails of Vis Geopark; and on the island of Pag, Pag Outdoor for introducing me to their hiking and cycling trails.

Finally, I thank Zoran Pejović in Split and Saša Sobot in Dubrovnik for keeping me up to date on the best new restaurants, bars and wineries Dalmatia has to offer.

LIST OF MAPS

Contents

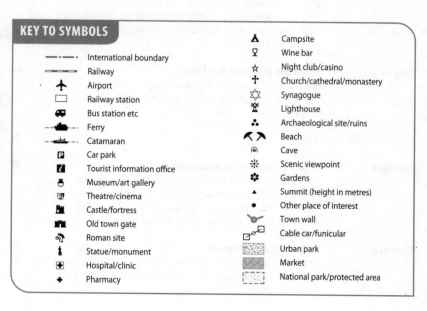

KEY TO SYMBOLS

— · — · — International boundary
════════ Railway
✈ Airport
▭ Railway station
🚌 Bus station etc
— ⛴ — · Ferry
— ⛴ — · Catamaran
🅿 Car park
🛈 Tourist information office
🏛 Museum/art gallery
🎭 Theatre/cinema
🏰 Castle/fortress
🏯 Old town gate
🏺 Roman site
🗿 Statue/monument
✚ Hospital/clinic
✚ Pharmacy

🛆 Campsite
⚱ Wine bar
☆ Night club/casino
✝ Church/cathedral/monastery
✡ Synagogue
🗼 Lighthouse
∴ Archaeological site/ruins
↖↗ Beach
⌂ Cave
❄ Scenic viewpoint
❀ Gardens
▲ Summit (height in metres)
● Other place of interest
⌣ Town wall
⛊ Cable car/funicular
▦ Urban park
▨ Market
▩ National park/protected area

Introduction

A region of sublime natural beauty, Dalmatia combines a rugged mountainous coast with the deep blue waters of the Adriatic and literally dozens of glorious pine-scented rocky islands. Cultural highlights include the mainland port city of Dubrovnik, with its mighty medieval walls protecting a delightful old town of stone-paved alleys and noble Baroque buildings; and Split, centring on Diocletian's Palace, a vast waterside residence built as a palatial retirement home for the eponymous Roman Emperor, now the heart of the city. Both Dubrovnik and Split are UNESCO World Heritage Sites.

In contrast to these grand mainland port cities, on the islands you'll find smaller but equally alluring settlements, such as Hvar Town and Korčula Town, built by the Venetians, who used them to service and supply their galleys on their voyages to the East. Imposing hillside fortresses, handsome churches with graceful belltowers and mysterious monasteries with cloistered courtyards abound as you explore Dalmatia, bearing witness to historic ties with the Republic of Venice, which ruled the region from around 1420 to 1797.

But the first people to spend their holidays in Dalmatia were probably the Romans. Archaeologists have uncovered several *villae rusticae* (on Hvar, Mljet, Pag and Dugi Otok, to name but a few), where privileged Romans kept vineyards and olive groves, no doubt enjoying the gentle sea breeze on balmy summer evenings, while drinking a toast to Bacchus. Later, in the early 20th century, wealthy Central Europeans would alight in Dalmatia on convalescence, to relish the warm climate, therapeutic waters and bracing sea air, thus leading to the establishment of the region's first hotels. Nowadays, most visitors come here for cultural sightseeing, watersports (especially sailing) and adventure activities.

Indeed, Dalmatia's dramatic and varied landscapes, and sunny Mediterranean climate, make it a superb setting for outdoor pursuits. In Bol, on Brač's south coast, you can try windsurfing near the gorgeous Zlatni Rat beach, or hire a bike and pedal up to Vidova Gora, the highest peak on all the islands, for stunning panoramic views over the shimmering Adriatic. On Pag, with its arid limestone interior inhabited by hardy little sheep, you might join a full-moon night-time hiking tour along craggy stone trails, or hire a kayak and paddle along its meandering shores. Aboard a sailing boat you can explore the pristine waters and uninhabited rocky islets of Kornati National Park (look out for dolphins, peregrine falcons and eagle owls), while climbers will relish the challenging steep rocky cliffs and verdant gorges of Paklenica National Park.

Wherever you go, but especially on the islands, you'll find local traditions and eccentricities. On Hvar and Korčula, be sure to taste their wines, made from unique indigenous grape varieties, such as Bogdanuša and Pošip. On Pag, feast on tender lamb and salty sheep's cheese; on Vis, enjoy some of the most authentic seafood dishes at rustic waterside eateries; and, on the Pelješac peninsula, taste oysters, plucked directly from the waters of Mali Ston Bay. Whatever route you choose, you can expect a warm welcome from locals, who are proud and happy to share their love of their magnificent land and islands with visitors.

HOW TO USE THIS GUIDE

AUTHOR'S FAVOURITES Finding genuinely characterful accommodation or that unmissable off-the-beaten-track café can be difficult, so the author has chosen a few of her favourite places throughout the country to point you in the right direction. These 'author's favourites' are marked with a ✳.

PRICE CODES Throughout this guide we have used price codes to indicate the cost of those places to stay and eat listed in the guide, as follows:

Accommodation price codes Prices are based on the price of a standard double room (hotel, pension, etc) in high season (Jul–Aug); expect prices to drop by around 10–15% in June/September and considerably more off season.

Exclusive	€€€€€	over €320
Upmarket	€€€€	€160–320
Mid-range	€€€	€80–160
Budget	€€	€40–80
Shoestring	€	less than €40

Restaurant price codes Prices are based on the average price of a main course.

€€€€€	over €30
€€€€	€20–30
€€€	€10–20
€€	€5–10
€€	less than €5

MAPS

Keys and symbols Maps include alphabetical keys covering the locations of those places to stay, eat or drink that are featured in the book. Note that regional maps may not show all hotels and restaurants in the area: other establishments may be located in towns shown on the map.

Grids and grid references Some maps use gridlines to allow easy location of sites. Map grid references are listed in square brackets after the name of the place or site of interest in the text, with page number followed by grid number, eg: [84 C3].

Part One

GENERAL INFORMATION

DALMATIA AT A GLANCE

Location
Size 12,158km²
Language Croatian
Population 796,370 (2021 census)
GDP per capita €20,001 (World Bank 2024 figures from Croatia as a whole, not just Dalmatia)
Life expectancy 76 years (men), 82 years (women)
Religion Roman Catholic (78.97%); Orthodox Christian (3.32%); Muslim (1.32%); other (0.26%) (2021 census, figures from Croatia as a whole, not just Dalmatia)
Regional capital Split
Other main cities and towns Zadar, Šibenik, Dubrovnik
Climate Mediterranean
Time GMT + 1
Currency Euro (€)
Exchange rate £1 = €1.18, US$1 = €0.92 (July 2024)
International telephone code +385
Electrical voltage 230V
Public holidays 1 January (New Year's Day); 6 January (Epiphany); 3 February (St Blaise's Day, Dubrovnik only); Easter (20 April 2025, 5 April 2026, 28 March 2027); 1 May (Labour Day); 7 May (St Domnius' Day, Split only); 30 May (Statehood Day); Corpus Christi (60 days after Easter Sunday, and taken seriously in Croatia. Corpus Christi falls on 19 June 2025, 4 June 2026, 27 May 2027); 22 June (Day of Antifascist Struggle); 5 August (Homeland Thanksgiving Day); 15 August (Assumption of the Virgin Mary); 1 November (All Saints' Day); 18 November (Remembrance Day for Victims of the Homeland War); 25 and 26 December (Christmas).

1

Background Information

GEOGRAPHY

Dalmatia is perhaps most famous for its enormous – relative to its size – coastline and wealth of islands, but away from the beaches, it's also geographically diverse. A long ridge of mountains – or rather series of ridges, peaking at Dinara – stretches from the northwest to the southeast of the region. The Adriatic islands can also be surprisingly mountainous, with peaks up to 778m (Brač), and Hvar, Vis, Korčula and Mljet all rising to over 500m.

The coast and islands are Dalmatia's natural selling point when it comes to tourism. It has an astonishing 1,200km of indented mainland coast as well as 79 islands (the largest being Brač, Pag and Hvar) and some 500 islets.

CLIMATE

If you're seeking an escape from a wet winter, then Dalmatia is probably not for you – most of the rain here falls in the cooler months, making it chilly and damp inland but drippy along the coast. Outside the long, dry summers, Dalmatia is wetter than you might think, but the humid winters are more than compensated for by warm, early springs, hot, dry summers and prolonged autumns.

Dalmatia enjoys a Mediterranean climate. Down at sea level, the **coast and islands** have wet, mild winters and long, hot and very dry summers. Daily averages range from 5 to 10°C in winter and from 25 to 30°C in summer, though almost never exceed 35°C – and daily maximums in Dubrovnik never fall below 12°C. The coast gets most of its precipitation in the autumn, with 377mm falling in Dubrovnik from October to December, but only 10mm of rainfall expected in Split in July. However, that's not to say that it won't rain during the summer months – August occasionally sees severe storms and flooding in some areas of the Dalmatian coast and islands – though such conditions are thankfully quite rare.

The sea is, for many, the main attraction, so you should remember that it cools down to a chilly 12°C at Split in winter, although from mid-June to early September, it stays above 20°C, making for pleasant swimming (especially in August, when the water reaches its maximum temperature of 27°C).

There's also no shortage of sunshine on the Adriatic – Zadar is pleased with its 2,558 hours annually, while Brač brags about its 2,700 sunny hours per year, and Hvar claims to have more hours of sunshine than anywhere else on the coast. Bring plenty of suncream. Up in the mainland mountains, though, the weather is surprisingly unpredictable all year round, so plan accordingly. Snow can fall in any month of the year at 1,700m, and terrible hail can fall as late as June on the Velebit massif at 1,200m, just a few kilometres inland from the coast. In winter, it has even been known to snow in coastal resorts like Split and Trogir.

The geological term 'karst' came from the rock formations of neighbouring Slovenia (Kras) and is now used to describe any similar terrain – very useful as that includes most of the limestone mountains along Croatia's coast and on its islands.

Karst is grey, wild and very dry. It is formed by the absorption of water into porous limestone, which then corrodes and finally erodes the harder limestone underneath – this, combined with a history of earthquakes, is the geological reason for the shape of the Adriatic and its islands.

Young karst is typically characterised by small fissures in the rock, while more developed areas contain long underground caves, rivers that appear from the rock and then disappear again almost immediately, and highly porous limestone that is completely dry only a few minutes after rain has fallen. Karst is irregularly sculptured into sharp and wild shapes and is extremely abrasive.

Croatia's karst was once almost entirely covered in vegetation, but large parts, particularly along the coast and on the islands, were deforested (the Venetians, in particular, needed a lot of wood) and then lost their soil from wind, erosion and overgrazing. This is known as naked karst and can be seen at its most spectacular and barren on the island of Pag and on some of the islands of the Kornati archipelago. It's incredibly poor land, on which it seems unlikely that anything could survive – but people do live here and somehow eke out a living from the wilderness.

When an underground cave collapses, the surface is flattened, and soil gradually accumulates. Usually, this is then cleared of rocks, walled in, and cultivated. One of the hazards of this type of field (known as polje) is that they don't always drain as quickly as they fill up, creating lakes of a few days' or weeks' duration. Every so often, you'll be surprised by a boat at the edge of a field or pasture, even in the mountains. It's also the reason why you'll never see houses built on the polje itself, but always to one side.

NATURAL HISTORY AND CONSERVATION

Croatia is blessed with unpolluted lakes, spectacular limestone scenery and the cleanest coastline on the Mediterranean. During Tito's days, Yugoslavia embarked on a progressive programme of tourist development and although some of the resorts along the coast might be considered a little overdeveloped, there's also a wealth of national parks and other protected areas.

FLORA AND FAUNA In the remoter forests of the interior and the inland national parks, there are still bears and wolves at large, though you're unlikely to see them – bears are notoriously cautious, while wolves only come down from the mountains to raid villages for scraps during the depths of winter. Wild boar, however, are still common, even on the islands (it's a culinary speciality on Pelješac and Korčula). You might also be lucky enough to see chamois and mouflon in the mountains in Dalmatia. But you're more likely to see eagles than griffon vultures.

Snakes are reasonably common, but there are very few that are poisonous (admittedly, one of these, the nose-horned viper or *poskok*, is very poisonous), and the old saying is worth repeating: they're much more frightened of you than you are of them. Snakes will mostly avoid regularly walked paths or roads, but if you're heading across country, it's as well to wear sensible shoes or boots.

You'll see a number of charming species of lizard if you're out walking or even sightseeing – they love to bask on warm stone the moment the sun's shining. Look out, too, for frogs if you're near water, and several varieties of toad peculiar to the woods which grow on limestone mountains. Martens, wild cats and squirrels also live in these forests, but they're pretty shy.

From early summer onwards, Dalmatia features several species of butterfly you won't see often in the UK – look out for swallowtails in the mountains, white admirals on the islands, and hosts of butterflies of all species if you're here in late spring or early summer.

Literally dozens of species of flora and fauna are protected in Croatia, many of them living in Dalmatia. Most endangered of all is the fast-disappearing Mediterranean monk seal, which used to live in a cave off the south coast of Biševo, near Vis. Although now considered geographically extinct in Dalmatia, a monk seal was spotted in Mljet National Park in 2022. These elegant dark brown seals grow to around 2.4m in length and weigh up to 300kg or more. There are also a surprising number of dolphins along the Dalmatian coast, notably around the Kornati archipelago, as well as further south, near Vis, Korčula and Lastovo. Look out for them if you're sailing in remote waters – they sometimes follow boats.

Croatia's flora is also delightful. Along the coast and on the islands, you'll find aromatic wild herbs and abundant oleander. In the woods and forests, there's a wide variety of plants and trees ranging from orchids to holm oak to pine and beech, while higher up in the mountains, you'll find beautiful summer pastures, home to tiny flowers and fragrant herbs.

As the summer wears on, the colours fade and everything dries out, leaving an arid impression across much of the region, which doesn't really wear off until the leaves change to their superb autumnal colours.

ENVIRONMENTAL ISSUES In spite of the long-standing promotion of ecotourism, the creation and maintenance of a whole crop of national parks and protected areas (page 6), and its pride in having the cleanest waters of the Mediterranean, Dalmatia hasn't entirely escaped the blights of the modern world. Coastal pollution from industrial and domestic waste has been experienced in some areas, and new roads continue to chew a path through forests on mountains such as Velebit.

Much more significant, in environmental terms, however, was the destruction of both infrastructure and natural resources by the civil strife of the early 1990s. In spite of the quick repairs in tourist centres like Dubrovnik, it will take some time before the damage is entirely fixed in rural Lika.

Fire is a major environmental hazard – a landscape that quickly absorbs what little water there is and a hot, dry summer is a recipe for accidental combustion. And gusty winds can mean that fire soon gets out of control. The starting of any fire in Dalmatia in summer is strongly discouraged and forbidden in the national parks. If you're going to be barbecuing, do so carefully, and be sure you have what it takes to put the flames out if things get out of control.

Dalmatia is also strongly exposed to one other environmental risk: earthquakes. A major and active earthquake fault network runs through Italy and the Balkans, and it was an earthquake in 1667 that killed more than 5,000 people in Dubrovnik and levelled most of the public buildings.

The most recent serious earthquake in Dalmatia occurred in 1996, with its epicentre in the area of Slano and Ston, 50km up the coast from Dubrovnik.

The historical town of Ston – now famous for its excellent oysters – was almost completely destroyed. Although there were no fatalities, around 2,000 people in the area lost their homes to the earthquake damage.

NATIONAL PARKS, NATURE PARKS AND OTHER PROTECTED AREAS Croatia has an impressive range of national parks, nature parks and other protected areas. Below, you'll find a summary of what's on offer – more detail can be found in the relevant chapters.

National parks Dalmatia has four national parks.

Kornati archipelago This is a scattered group of 147 uninhabited islands, islets and reefs south of Zadar; 89 of the islands were declared a national park in 1980. Popular with the yachting community, it's relatively difficult to access for other visitors to Croatia but is nonetheless one of the most striking national parks, with sheer cliffs, unusually indented coastlines, clear seas and no water sources at all. See page 225.

Krka River and waterfalls The Krka River runs from Knin to Skradin, just inland from Šibenik. The park – mainly visited by boat – features stunning karst scenery of lakes, waterfalls, canyons and deep forests. At the river's widest point, you'll find a lovely Franciscan monastery on an island. See page 215.

Mljet The western part of the island of Mljet, between Korčula and Dubrovnik, has been designated a national park with good reason. Home to Europe's only wild mongooses, lush vegetation, and a former monastery on an island on one of two saltwater lakes, Mljet is a delight. See page 122.

Paklenica This pair of fabulous limestone gorges runs up from the sea into the Velebit massif not far from Zadar. Popular with Croatian climbers and walkers, it offers hiking from the merely gentle to the seriously strenuous. See page 202.

Nature parks Dalmatia also boasts six designated nature parks.

Biokovo This is the name of the massif overhanging the Makarska Riviera between Split and Dubrovnik, and although it's a hard walk to the summit, it offers the most breathtaking views out over the islands of Brač and Hvar. See page 168.

Dinara Croatia's newest nature park, designated in 2021, encompasses Dalmatia's highest mountain, east of Knin, close to the border with Bosnia & Herzegovina. See page 215.

Lastovsko Otočje Far out to sea, south of Mljet, this nature park comprises the islands of the Lastovo archipelago. See page 144.

Telašćica Bordering on the northern end of the Kornati archipelago and hogging the cleft-stick inlet at the southern end of Dugi Otok (Long Island), Telašćica has Croatia's biggest cliffs, rising a dramatic 180m out of the sea. It's naturally popular with anyone lucky enough to be on a sailing holiday. See page 227.

Velebit Stretching for more than 100km from Senj to Zadar, the 2,000km² Velebit Park includes both the Paklenica and North Velebit national parks, the

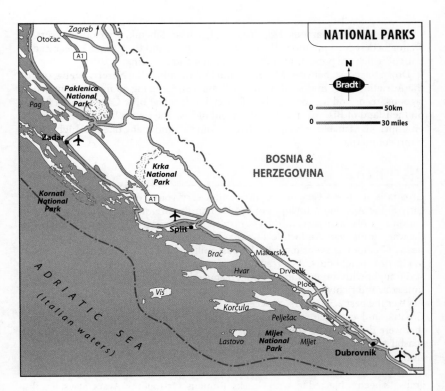

N

Bradt

0 ————————— 50km
0 ————————— 30 miles

Zagreb

Otočac

A1

Paklenica
National
Park

Pag

Zadar

Krka
National
Park

BOSNIA &
HERZEGOVINA

Kornati
National
Park

A1

Split

Brač

Makarska

Hvar

Drvenik

Ploče

Vis

Korčula

Peljašac

Lastovo

Mljet
National
Park

Mljet

Dubrovnik

A D R I A T I C S E A
(Italian waters)

latter being home to the **Velebitski Botanički Vrt** botanical gardens and the strictly protected Hajdučki Kukovi nature reserve. The gardens, established in 1967, are some of the remotest in Croatia, being situated at around 1,500m in the most inaccessible part of the Velebit, and feature flora unique to the region. See page 202.

Vransko Jezero Between Zadar and Šibenik, in northern Dalmatia, lies Croatia's largest natural lake, famous for its mix of sea and freshwater fish, and an ornithological reserve, which is home to a wide variety of wading birds and a colony of rare purple herons. See page 201.

Other protected areas This section wouldn't be complete without a brief mention of some of Croatia's other protected areas.

Probably the most famous – and the one you may have seen photographed from the air – is **Zlatni Rat** (Golden Cape), at Bol on the island of Brač, one of the most impressive beaches on the Adriatic. The 600m spit of fine gravel, backed by pine forests, changes shape according to the sea currents and seasonal winds.

In addition, Dalmatia now has two geoparks. The **Geopark Biokovo Imotski Lakes** lies inland from Makarska, near Imotski. It encompasses the **Red and Blue Lakes** (Crveno Jezero and Modro Jezero), a pair of unusually deep water-filled holes in the karst. The bottom of Red Lake is only 19m above sea level, with a depth varying from 280 to 320m, and Blue Lake really is blue. By contrast, the **Vis Archipelago Geopark** lies out to sea, around Vis, highlighting the island's unusual rock formations.

Apart from the famous Krka (page 215) near Šibenik, two other rivers in Dalmatia deserve a mention. The Cetina, near Omiš, and the Zrmanja, near Zadar, both of which are popular for rafting, kayaking and canoeing.

Down the coast, between Makarska and Dubrovnik, is the **Neretva Delta**, one of the Adriatic's most important waterfowl reserves, featuring swampy salt marshes, lagoons, reeds and meadows. Also of special note is the **Blue Cave** (Modra Špilja) on the island of Biševo, off the western end of Vis. The cave – like the Blue Grotto on Capri – is visitable only by boat (from Komiža), and many rate it as highly as its Capri counterpart.

HISTORY

Croatia is at once a very old country and a very young one. Inhabited since the early Stone Age and a linchpin of the Roman Empire, it only became a modern nation in 1991, and parts of the country were still under UN control – following the war – until 1998. And while it was a respectable kingdom of its own in medieval times, Croatia has spent most of the past millennium attached to (or subjugated by) its near neighbours. As a result, the country's history is unbelievably turbulent and fraught with foreign intervention, plagued by constant strife from pre-Roman times on, and richly textured with assassinations, intrigues, piracy and treachery.

Over the past 2,500 years, a succession of empires invaded, annexed or occupied Croatia, and each left its mark. For example, islands along the Adriatic coast that were deforested by the Venetians in the 18th century are still barren, yet the coastal towns and cities wouldn't be half as lovely if it weren't for the Venetian Gothic architecture.

Croatian independence today is remarkable given the sheer number of land grabs it's been subjected to, with Greeks, Romans, Ostrogoths, Avars, Slavs, Franks, Byzantines, Venetians, Hungarians, Tartars, Austrians, French, Italians, Turks, Germans and Serbs all having had their eye on a piece of the Croatian action.

Which is hardly surprising: the Adriatic has been the most practical trade route between Europe and the East since trade began there around 3,000 years ago. Croatia has also been a buffer zone between east and west and between north and south for centuries. Here, we will look more specifically at Dalmatia and also reference what was happening in other regions of Croatia to complete the puzzle.

ILLYRIANS, GREEKS AND ROMANS In spite of lots of early Stone Age finds, recorded history in Croatia starts with the Illyrians, a group of tribes that shared techniques for building and burying their dead, but not much else, it seems. In fact, Dalmatia is named after the Delmatae tribe, while Istria was named after the Histri. By the 6th century BC, the Illyrian tribes were trading with the ancient Greeks and within two centuries, the Greeks had established colonies in the area, notably at Pharos (now Stari Grad, on the island of Hvar), at Lumbarda on Korčula, in Trogir, and on the island of Vis.

By 229BC, the Greeks were calling on Rome to help them in their quest to dominate the Illyrians, and the Romans pitched in with enthusiasm – though it took them more than two centuries to complete the job. In AD9, five years before becoming emperor, Tiberius finally annexed the area for Rome, thereby becoming the first (and last, until 1918) person to unify this bit of the Balkans.

Under Roman rule, the Balkans – and Dalmatia in particular – prospered, providing the empire with troops and provisions and receiving the protection of a major world power in return, setting something of a pattern for the region. The

Romans built (or reinforced) many of the existing settlements, with their principal cities being Pola (Pula) in Istria and Jadera (Zadar) and Salona (Solin) in Dalmatia. As was their wont, they also constructed summer palaces along the coast and on the islands and reinforced trade links all the way from Pula to Cavtat.

The most famous Dalmatians to make it big at this time were the three who went on to become Roman emperors, most notably Diocletian, who ruled from AD284 to AD305 – an astonishingly long period given that more than a dozen emperors had come and gone in the generation before he came to power. Diocletian ruled from Nicomedia (now Izmít, in Turkey) but started building himself a fabulously swanky retirement home just along the coast from his native Salona within months of taking the purple. Diocletian's Palace in Split remains one of Croatia's most impressive monuments, with its corridors today being streets and its rooms entire houses.

In AD293, Diocletian partitioned the empire into the western and eastern parts, with the River Drina being the boundary, thus sealing Croatia's fate forever as a province on the front line. Diocletian's frontier ran through the cities of Budva and Belgrade, and a rough approximation of this can still be seen on maps today, marking the eastern border of Slavonia in Croatia and running down the eastern side of Bosnia & Herzegovina and Albania. Everything east of this line ultimately became Byzantium and Orthodox, while everything west became part of Rome (and the eventual Holy Roman Empire) and Catholic. The division is also clearly visible today in the use of the Latin alphabet to the west and Cyrillic to the east.

Diocletian abdicated in AD305 and retired to Split, spending the last 11 years of his life in palatial splendour, rousing himself only to have Christians thrown to the lions; having tolerated the religion for most of his reign, he spent the rest of his life in the relentless persecution of it.

ARRIVAL OF THE SLAVS The Roman Empire imploded in the 5th century, leaving the way clear for invasions by Huns, Goths, Vlachs, Avars, Bulgars and – most importantly for this guide – Slavs.

One group of Slavs, coming from what is now Poland, was the Croats. They conquered Roman Pannonia (now roughly the area known as Slavonia) and much of Dalmatia, and drove the inhabitants from the Dalmatian capital, Salona, to the nearby islands of Šolta, Brač, Hvar, Vis and Korčula.

During the same period, other Slavic ethnic groups, the Slovenes and the Serbs, settled the areas roughly corresponding to Slovenia and Serbia.

After a series of tussles with the Franks, Avars and Byzantines, the Croats finally managed to unite Dalmatian and Pannonian Croatia in AD925, under the crown of King Tomislav. For more than a century, the kingdom prospered, with the greatest Croatian king being Petar Krešimir IV, who ruled over Bosnia, Slavonia and the Dalmatian towns and islands from 1058 to 1074.

Byzantium and Venice were already encroaching on the southern and northern coastlands, however, and Hungary soon captured most of the interior, driving a corridor through to the sea by 1089. After the death of King Stjepan II in 1091, it all fell apart. A decade later, in 1102, the Hungarian King Kalman knocked together the heads of the 12 most powerful Croatian clans, persuading them to sign up to the Pacta Conventa, under which they would accept the Hungarian monarch's rule, but were able to maintain Croatia's traditions and customs. Amazingly, the treaty held until 1918.

VENETIANS, AUSTRO-HUNGARIANS AND THE ILLYRIAN PROVINCES Over the next 700 years, Croatian history largely depended on which of its neighbours was

Most people dressing for work in the morning don't spare a thought for Croatia – which is a pity, as the ubiquitous tie they put on not only originated there but is also named after the country.

The origins of one of fashion's most durable accessories date back to the Thirty Years War in Europe, which ran from 1618 to 1648. The story goes that Croatian mercenaries of the period wore a colourful silk scarf tied around the neck. Some of their number were stationed in Paris and were presented to the court (whether that of Louis XIII, who died in 1643, or Louis XIV, who succeeded him, is debatable), triggering off a copycat craze for cravats – the word coming from dressing *à la Croat* (or *Hrvat*, in Croatian).

During the dandyish reign of Louis XIV, the wearing of cravats by French men became widespread, and the new fashion soon spread right across Europe – indeed, the French word *'cravate'* exists in one form or another in almost every European language, from *gravata* in Greek to *krawatte* in German.

Today, across the whole world the tie is considered a basic part of business attire, though for the most part probably not the enormously expensive long and floppy silk scarves favoured by Croatian soldiers, but the rather more sober ties launched in England at the end of the 19th century.

the most powerful at the time, with Hungary/Austria driving down from the north, the Ottoman Empire steaming in from the southeast, and Venice ever expansive from its corner of the Adriatic. Venice needed a string of harbour towns along the Adriatic for servicing her merchant ships on journeys to the East, and almost all of Dalmatia (except Ragusa) came under Venice from 1420 to 1797. Much of Dalmatia's architectural heritage dates from this period, with the mainland coast and islands still looking remarkably Venetian today.

During the 16th century, Austria created the Krajina (a military frontier) as a buffer against the advance of the Ottoman Turks, and Serbs who had escaped Ottoman rule were given land in the Krajina in exchange for military service. This included Lika, the inland region behind Velebit mountains, bordering North Dalmatia.

In 1558, the Croatian and Slavonian diets were united, and Zagreb became Croatia's capital.

RAGUSA At the same time, another city, Ragusa (present-day Dubrovnik), was at the height of its fame and power. Between 1358 and 1808, Ragusa was one of the most important – and independent – of the Dalmatian cities, fending off unwanted interference by successfully paying off the Ottoman Turks and the Hungarians. Ragusa's territory expanded beyond the city to include the Pelješac peninsula to the northwest and the Konavle Valley to the southeast, as well as the islands of Mljet and Lastovo.

THE ILLYRIAN PROVINCES Venice and Ragusa alike were swept aside by Napoleon, who created the Illyrian Provinces (1809–1814), a region running down the coast, all the way from Trieste and Slovenia in the north to Dubrovnik in the south. The region was administered by Marshal Marmont and, for a few years, benefitted from the French passion for building roads, fortifying towns and encouraging the local south Slav culture – in a bid to create a buffer against undue Russian and Austro-Hungarian ambitions. 'Though Marmont was a self-satisfied prig, he was an extremely competent and honourable man, and he loved Dalmatia,' as Rebecca West (author of *Black Lamb and Grey Falcon: A Journey through Yugoslavia*) so succinctly put it when she came through in 1937.

AUSTRO-HUNGARIANS It was for nought; Napoleon fell, and Habsburg rule over Croatia was restored in 1815, this time incorporating Dalmatia. This is why you will see some rather nice Vienna Secession buildings in Split.

The Kingdom of Croatia, Slavonia and Dalmatia continued under Austro-Hungarian rule until the 525th anniversary of the Ottoman defeat of Lazar, last of the independent Serbian rulers, at the battle of Kosovo Polje in 1389.

On that day (28 June 1914), Archduke Franz Ferdinand, heir to the Austro-Hungarian Empire – in a remarkable display of hubris, given that it was a day of national mourning – ignored all warnings and paid an official visit to Sarajevo. And with his wife, Sophie Chotek, was shot dead by a 19-year-old student called Gavrilo Princip, thus kicking off World War I. Austria had long been looking to declare war on Serbia, and this provided the perfect excuse. Russia took offence; Germany supported Austria; Britain and France piled in with Russia; and the world's bloodiest war to date was underway.

THE KINGDOM OF THE SERBS, CROATS AND SLOVENES Aware that the Austro-Hungarian Empire was going to come out of the war at best badly diminished, Slovenia and Croatia threw in their lot with Serbia in 1918, resulting in the creation of the Kingdom of Serbs, Croats and Slovenes, under the Crown of Serbian King Petar I from the dynastic Karađorđević family.

Petar was succeeded on his death, three years later, by his son, King Aleksandar I, in the face of increasing irritation by the Croats that they had so little power in Belgrade. The Croatian Republican Peasant Party, led by firebrand Stjepan Radić, had won local elections in 1920, but this wasn't of any use to the party in the capital.

Tension remained high through the 1920s until, on 20 June 1928, Radić was shot in Belgrade's parliamentary chamber by a Montenegrin deputy. Six weeks later, Radić died, and more than 100,000 turned up to his funeral in Zagreb. The king suspended parliament 'reluctantly' at the beginning of 1929 and established a dictatorship in its place, promising to restore democracy once unity had been achieved. In October of that year, however, he did finally manage to put diplomats and letter-writers out of their misery by changing the country's name to the much more manageable Yugoslavia – Land of the South Slavs.

So much for the good news: 1929 also saw the founding of the Ustaše by Ante Pavelić, a party dedicated to the violent overthrow of the Yugoslav state, and one that would later have a dramatic effect on Croatia's future.

Croatian national sentiment continued to run high, and, in 1934, King Aleksandar, aged 46, was assassinated in Marseille in a plot sponsored by the Ustaše but executed by a Macedonian with Italian support. Aleksandar's death left the ill-equipped Prince Petar to run the country – aged only 11. His uncle, Prince Pavle, was drafted in to help, but Yugoslavia was in no state to prosper. And war was once again on the horizon.

WORLD WAR II By the time World War II broke out – not the Balkans' fault this time around – the country was in a mess. The Ustaše fascists wanted independence for Croatia, Macedonia was trying to secede, and only the Yugoslav Communist Party, founded in 1919 and outlawed nine years later, had any countrywide support.

Yugoslavia managed to remain neutral for the first year and a half of the war but increasing Axis pressure resulted in Prince Pavle signing a pact on 25 March 1941, aligning Yugoslavia with fascist Germany and Italy, in spite of his personal pro-British sentiments. Two days later, a group of air force officers, backed by both the communists and the Orthodox Church, staged a coup d'état, deposed Prince Pavle and installed King Petar II, now aged 17½, in his place.

The pact was annulled, and Yugoslavia reaffirmed its neutrality; Hitler responded by bombing Belgrade on 6 April. On the same day, massive German and Italian armies entered the country, and Yugoslavia capitulated ten days later. King Petar II escaped to London with the Yugoslav government and set up house in Claridge's, never to return to his former kingdom.

THE USTAŠE Once Yugoslavia had thrown in the towel in 1941, the Ustaše declared the Independent State of Croatia (Nezavisna Država Hrvatska, NDH), leaving the rest of Yugoslavia to be carved up between Germany, Hungary, Bulgaria and Italy. Much of Dalmatia came under Italian occupation until Mussolini capitulated in 1943, then the German Nazis moved in.

From the start, the Ustaše tried to clear the Serbs out of Croatia. When this proved impossible, they set up concentration camps in north Croatia, the most notorious being Jasenovac, about 100km south of Zagreb. The camps were used from 1942 to 1945 to eliminate not just Serbs but also religious minorities (including thousands of Jews) and political opponents of the Ustaše, and reports are that they were as bad as the more notorious German camps, such as Auschwitz.

Nobody will ever know for sure how many people were killed by the Ustaše, but it's now thought that between 300,000 and 400,000 Serbs were killed in total, with 40,000–50,000 being murdered at Jasenovac alone.

THE RESISTANCE After the fall of Yugoslavia in April 1941, resistance was immediately organised, but divided into two fiercely opposed groups, the Četniks and the partisans. The royalist, pro-Serbian, Četniks supported the government in exile in London and hated just about everybody else – Croats (both Ustaše and resistance), Germans, Italians and communists.

As anti-Germans, the Četniks were aided at first by the Allies, but they were regarded with distrust by many Yugoslavs. The partisans, on the other hand, led by Josip Broz 'Tito', were the army of the Communist Party. Although only 42,000 strong at the outset, their effective resistance and daring attacks earned them wide support from communists and non-communists alike. Many Dalmatians joined the partisans, and they were the driving force in liberating the region in 1944.

When the end of the war was close, Ustaše founder Ante Pavelić mobilised large numbers of Croat reservists and civilians and persuaded them to go to Bleiburg, in Austria (the British HQ), to surrender to the Allies. The British, to whom they surrendered, immediately handed them back (against American orders) to Tito's troops, who had some shot and buried in mass graves on the spot and marched the rest to the other end of Yugoslavia along what Croats now call the Križni Put (Way of the Cross). Contemporary Croatian history tells us that at least 50,000 died along the way. Ante Pavelić wasn't one of them: he escaped to South America (Pavelić and many of his closest allies were helped by Argentina's leader, Juan Peron, who offered them blank passports) and then on to Franco's Spain, where he died in 1959.

Yugoslavia paid a terrible price during World War II, with more than a tenth of its citizens being killed. Among them were at least 300,000 Croats, 300,000 partisans and nearly 400,000 Bosnians. But the resistance had successfully tied up enormous numbers of Axis soldiers, and it's quite possible that the Allies couldn't have won the war without Yugoslavia.

With the help of the British (aid was transferred from the Četniks to the partisans in 1943) and the Red Army, Belgrade was finally liberated in 1944 and, by 1945, a provisional government, in temporary accord with the government in exile, was in force.

TITO AND A NON-ALIGNED YUGOSLAVIA Post-war elections not surprisingly gave the communists 90% of the vote. That gave the government the freedom to set up on the lines adopted by Stalinist Russia and to embark on an experiment with collectivisation.

Stalin, however, was wary of Yugoslavia, as it was the only country in the Eastern Bloc to have made its way entirely independently. And indeed, in 1948, Tito broke with the Cominform, the economic ground base for the countries allied to the Soviet Union. This declaration of non-alignment was arguably the greatest political act of Tito's career, allowing Yugoslavia to develop its own brand of communism. Yugoslavia was not part of the Eastern Bloc, and people here are rightly offended if you think it was.

Tito's was a brave political move, for sure, but it brought hard times for Yugoslavia in the 1950s, starting with an economic blockade by the Soviet Union. Credits from the West and the launch of mass tourism in the 1960s saved the country, however. Tito introduced the idea of workers' self-management, putting the country's hospitals, schools and factories in the hands of those who staffed them, allowing competition within the framework of communism, and proving popular and successful during the 1960s and 1970s. Visit the Red History Museum (page 114) in Dubrovnik to learn more about life in Yugoslavia.

In an attempt to solve Yugoslavia's nationalist problems, Tito had also decentralised the state itself, giving each of the six republics complete control over its internal affairs. While Tito lived, this was a remarkably effective strategy, mainly because he was ruthless in suppressing opposition. Croatian writers and intellectuals issued a declaration in 1967 stating that Croatian was a different language from Serbian, and Croatian Serbs quickly counter-declared their right to be taught in Serbian. But Tito would have none of it and was quick to quash the so-called 'Croatian Spring' in 1971.

After being declared President for Life in 1974, Tito died in 1980, three days before his 88th birthday. His body made one more trip around the country in the Blue Train made famous during the early post-war days when he toured the country tirelessly promoting his programme of Brotherhood and Unity. This time it was mourners who lined the tracks in their thousands, and it's difficult now to conjure up just how important Tito's funeral was. It still stands as one of the best attended ever, from an international perspective, with official mourners coming from more than 120 countries, including four kings, 32 presidents and other heads of state, 22 prime ministers, and more than 100 representatives or secretaries of communist and workers' parties.

POST-TITO Like so many singularly powerful men, Tito left his country with a weak succession. Each of the republics would, in theory, get a year as head man, but without Tito's personal charisma and unifying strength, it was never going to work. It wasn't long before the old problems of nationalism, unfair distribution of wealth between the republics, and corruption in government resurfaced.

On to this scene arrived Slobodan Milošević, who rapidly gained popularity in Serbia after defending Serb protestors against mostly ethnic Albanian police in Kosovo in 1987. Two years later, on 28 June 1989 – that date, again (page 11) – Milošević addressed a million Serbs at Kosovo Polje and was elected President of Serbia in the autumn.

This was the beginning of the end for a united Yugoslavia. Milošević's talk of an ethnically pure Greater Serbia was never going to sit well with Slovenes, Croats, Bosnians, Macedonians – or indeed most Kosovars.

WAR – AND CROATIAN INDEPENDENCE
The fall of the Berlin Wall in 1989 and the collapse of communist governments across Europe encouraged several republics, led by Slovenia and Croatia, to try to change the political structure of Yugoslavia.

In 1990, led by former army general and dissident (some would prefer revisionist) historian Franjo Tuđman, the Croatian Democratic Union (HDZ) won elections. Once in power, the HDZ pushed parliament to drop the word 'Socialist' from the Croatian republic's name, and the red star was quietly removed from public symbols. The HDZ also put Croatia's 600,000 Serbs on the defensive by changing their status from 'constituent nation' in Croatia to 'national minority', and many Serbs in government lost their jobs. The HDZ didn't improve matters by making itself an easy target for Serb propaganda, party members playing straight into Serb hands by attempting to rehabilitate the Ustaše or by saying that the numbers of people killed at Jasenovac were inflated.

At the same time, most of the republics tried to negotiate a transition to a confederation, on the Swiss model, but this went completely against the Milošević view of a Greater Serbia, with money and power concentrated in Belgrade. As a result, the rebellious republics raised their sights, aiming for independent statehood instead. Trouble was inevitable.

During the summer of 1990, encouraged by Belgrade into fearing real danger, Croatia's Serbs (armed by the Yugoslav People's Army, the JNA) declared an autonomous region around Knin, 50km inland from Šibenik in North Dalmatia. Croatian police helicopters, sent in to sort out the trouble, were soon scuttled by Yugoslav Air Force MIGs. Tension continued to mount until March 1991, when Knin paramilitaries took control of the Plitvice Lakes, resulting in the first casualties of the conflict.

Slovenia, meanwhile, had unilaterally decided to declare independence on 25 June 1991, so Croatia declared independence on the same day – after a referendum held in May had delivered a 94% verdict in favour of a sovereign and independent Croatian state. Milošević immediately sent tanks into Ljubljana in Slovenia and to the Italian and Austrian borders. The world sat up and took notice, and the EU introduced sanctions; within a week, Serbia realised it didn't stand a chance (with Italy and Austria so close), and the war in Slovenia was over. Within a month, the army had left the country – though it only retreated as far as Croatia, and later distributed many weapons to the local Serb population.

Croatia, with a significant Serb minority, wasn't as fortunate as Slovenia. As soon as it proclaimed independence, the Serbs countered by proclaiming the independent state of Republika Srpska Krajina (RSK) within Croatia, declaring loyalty to Belgrade and Milošević (the commander of the army), and choosing Knin as its capital.

In six months at the end of 1991 – with the help of the JNA and heavy fighting, bombardments and air strikes – the Serbs ethnically 'cleansed' several inland areas of Croatia, reawakening memories of the brutality of the 1940s. Thousands of Croats were forced to leave their homes, and many were killed by the JNA or loosely associated paramilitary forces.

Many inland towns were besieged and bombarded for months, with wholesale destruction and local suffering involved. Worst of all was the siege of Vukovar (in eastern Croatia), which ended with appalling atrocities being carried out on the local Croatian population. Dubrovnik was also besieged, suffering huge damage and considerable loss of life.

Local industry across the country was effectively destroyed, and Croatia was paralysed by the RSK, which controlled most of the country's oil resources, the land routes to the Dalmatian coastal cities, and the main access road from Zagreb into Slavonia. The tourist trade – one of Croatia's main sources of foreign earnings – came to a complete halt.

By the time the UN was able to broker a ceasefire in January 1992, thousands of people had died, tens of thousands of homes had been destroyed, and Croatia had hundreds of thousands of local refugees, placing a huge burden on the main cities. Only then did the European Union (in spite of French and British reluctance) recognise Slovenian and Croatian independence. In May, after amending its constitution to protect minority groups and human rights, Croatia joined the United Nations.

It was not a happy country, however. Croatia was all but impossible to administrate with its newly fragmented borders, and from 1994, it lobbied hard, against intense European opposition, to end the UN policing of the ceasefire line. Failing on that front, it took matters into its own hands. From June 1995, Croatia 'liberated' the Krajina in a series of lightning assaults, first reclaiming the main road into Slavonia and then focusing on the main part of the RSK in August.

In just three days, fuelled both by fear and by propaganda from Belgrade, most of the civilian Serb population fled the land they had lived on for centuries, in perhaps the biggest example of ethnic cleansing in the war so far. The leaders of the RSK launched rocket attacks on Zagreb and Sisak as a parting shot before retreating to Serbia. In the vacuum left in the Krajina, however, Serb houses across the RSK were looted and destroyed while the authorities turned a blind eye.

The December 1995 Dayton Peace Agreement finally helped to restore stability to the region, reinforced at the end of 1996 by the signing of a peace treaty between Croatia and Yugoslavia, although the last bit of eastern Slavonia that was still in Serb hands was only returned to Croatia, under UN supervision, in January 1998.

A vast reconstruction programme has meant that most houses have now been rebuilt, and Serbs have been encouraged to return – though nobody's sure quite how many have actually done so. What is clear is that with so much bloodshed, anguish and suffering across the region, reconciliation has been a painful process.

Nowadays, there is increased awareness of the wrongs committed by all sides, and political dialogue and tolerance between Croatia and Serbia has improved enormously.

GOVERNMENT AND POLITICS

Independence brought Croatia a new constitution and a new political system that – as the Ministry of Foreign and European Affairs says on its website (w mvep.gov. hr/en) – is now 'democratic and based on a respect for human rights, law, national equality, social justice and multiple political parties'. The last part is certainly true enough, with a bewildering array of three- and four-letter acronyms to deal with. At the elections in the year 2000, following the death of Franjo Tuđman, more than 4,000 candidates from 55 political parties stood for office. As Rebecca West said witheringly when she was here in 1937: 'There is no end to political disputation in Croatia. None.'

Croatia's independence also brought it a new flag, known locally, irreverently, as the 'zoo' – above the chequerboard of the main flag are the old coats of arms from the regions, featuring Dalmatia's three crowned leopards, Istria's goat and Slavonia's marten.

Croatia's legislature consists of a parliament, the Sabor, with 151 MPs elected for a four-year period. Croatia's second president, the popular centrist Stjepan (Stipe) Mesić – a former Secretary of the HDZ who was also Croatia's first prime minister in 1990 – was in office from 2000 to 2010.

Like Tuđman, Mesić had also been condemned in the repression of the 'Croatian Spring' in 1971 and served a one-year jail sentence. Later, however, he went on to be elected to the Sabor (parliament), the body from which Yugoslav presidents were appointed in rotation, following Tito's death in 1980. As a result, Mesić also became the last president of a united Yugoslavia until his resignation in December 1991.

In 1994, disagreeing with the HDZ policy on Bosnia & Herzegovina – Tuđman still appeared keen to carve it up between Serbia and Croatia – Mesić left the party and set up the rival Croatian Independent Democrats (HND). Three years later, he joined the Croatian People's Party (HNS) and became the HNS executive vice president.

In the parliamentary elections of 2003, the HDZ saw a return to form, winning 66 of the 151 seats available in the Sabor and forming a government via an informal coalition with other smaller parties, with Ivo Sanader as prime minister. Quite suddenly, in July 2009, Ivo Sanader resigned – he has since been at the centre of a major scandal involving the 'disappearance' of vast amounts of government funds during his time in office – and Jadranka Kosor, Croatia's first female prime minister, was elected in his place. Mesić was succeeded by the SDP candidate Ivo Josipović, who became president in February 2010. A former lawyer (and lecturer at Zagreb's Academy of Music), Josipović had earlier been a member of the SDP, though he left politics in 1994 before returning as an independent MP in 2003 and renewing his membership of the SDP in 2008. Jadranka Kosor was succeeded as prime minister by the SDP's Zoran Milanović (who holds a master's degree in EU law from the Flemish University in Brussels) in 2011.

Josipović lost the presidential election of January 2015, which saw the HDZ's Kolinda Grabar-Kitarović voted in as Croatia's new president – the first woman to hold this office. Grabar-Kitarović was formerly Minister of Foreign Affairs from 2005 to 2008, Croatian Ambassador to the United States from 2008 to 2011, and Assistant Secretary General for Public Diplomacy for NATO from 2011 to 2014.

Croatia joined NATO in 2009 and, after long anticipation, finally joined the EU in the summer of 2013. This brought a new sense of stability, both within the country and when viewed from the outside. Investment increased in many sectors, and a sense of prosperity came into being, at least for some people.

In 2016, the HDZ came back into power (this time with a slightly less ultra-conservative image) with Andrej Plenković as prime minister. In 2020, Zoran Milanović (former SDP prime minister) replaced Kolinda Grabar-Kitarović as president.

Croatia joined the Schengen area and the Eurozone on 1 January 2023.

The April 2024 general election resulted in a hung parliament, after which the HDZ managed to retain their hold on power by forming a coalition with right-wing nationalist populist DP (Domovinski pokret – Homeland Movement).

ECONOMY

Progress towards economic reform after the war in the 1990s was hampered by coalition politics, but significant reform in recent years has since led to EU membership (in 2013), and the huge boom in tourism over the past two decades has helped ensure that the economy is now in better shape than it has been for years.

Inflation was 0.2% in 2015 (down from 6% in 2008), and GDP per capita in 2014 was estimated at €10,561 – still under half that in the UK or France. The average net salary had risen to 5,697kn (around €750) per month in 2015, though unemployment stood at 16.1%, a figure which had risen due to the global downturn in 2009. In 2023, average monthly net salary was €1,148, and unemployment stood at 6.5%.

Croatia adopted the euro on 1 January 2023.

TOURISM The driving force behind the Croatian economy – especially in Dalmatia – is tourism. In the year 2000, revenue from tourism finally exceeded the 1990 figures for the first time. Tourism accounts for 20% of Croatian GDP – in 2023, it brought in a revenue of some €14.45 billion.

In 1990, some 3.5 million tourist nights were spent in Dubrovnik – more than 814,000 of them by the British. The following year, people stayed away in droves. Since 1998, however, the recovery has been rapid and continuous, and the number of tourist nights in Croatia as a whole has rocketed.

The vast majority of tourists in Croatia are foreign visitors (around 90%), mainly coming in search of sea and sunshine. The most numerous among them in 2023 were Germans (23.6 million nights) and Slovenians (10.6 million nights), with the UK some way down the list but climbing steadily with 3.7 million nights.

Over the last two decades, tourism facilities have improved enormously. Many old hotels have been renovated, and new hotels, several with impressive contemporary design, have opened. New restaurants have added vegetarian options, and some specialise in Creative Mediterranean and even fusion cuisine. Rather than pursuing the typical Mediterranean sea-and-sunshine formula, Dalmatia is now developing experiential tourism, as well as a sustainable approach, with sectors such as agritourism, adventure sports, and wine and gastronomy offering visitors insight into the local way of life.

In fact, destinations such as Dubrovnik and Split have become so popular they now suffer from overtourism during peak season (July–August). The biggest problem (literally) is cruise ships, which disembark tens of thousands of extra visitors daily, overwhelming diminutive historic centres with large tour groups leading to congestion. Low-cost flights and Airbnb also contribute to enormous influxes of visitors each summer, when locals are massively outnumbered.

In 2020–21, Covid-19 imposed a real challenge to tourism, especially in Dalmatia, which lies further from Central Europe than Istria, where visitors from neighbouring countries could still arrive easily by car. Dubrovnik especially saw a massive slump in visitor numbers. On the plus side, Croatian authorities dealt admirably with trying to keep people safe, provide reliable information and offer testing.

In 2023, Croatia received 20.6 million tourist arrivals and 108 million tourist nights, returning to a similar level of pre-pandemic figures from 2019.

PEOPLE

During the war of the 1990s, many people were displaced, and the ethnic demographic changed following the exodus of hundreds of thousands of Serbs in 1995.

In the 1991 census, around three-quarters of people considered themselves Croats, while 12.2% said they were Serbs. A decade later, the 2001 census showed that almost 90% of people thought of themselves as Croats, while Serbs only accounted for 4.5% of the population. In the 2021 census, the gap had increased a little more, with 91.6% Croats and 3.2% Serbs.

What's more, the population has been dropping steadily, from 4.78 million in 1991, down to 4.28 million in 2011 and down further to 3.87 million in 2021. This is partly due to an ageing population and a drop in birth rates, as well as a large number of young Croats migrating to other European countries, mainly Germany and Ireland.

Over the last few years, Croatia has seen an influx of migratory workers from Nepal and Thailand, many of whom are employed in the tourism sector, as well as refugees from Ukraine.

However they describe themselves, the people of Croatia are largely warm, hospitable and generous, though, inevitably, this varies from place to place and person to person. In the interior, and especially in the national parks and nature reserves, people tend to have more time for you, whereas, along the coast, you might sometimes find a certain brusqueness, especially at the height of the season. But in Dalmatia, as everywhere, you'll find that if you treat them right, people on the whole will treat you right, too.

LANGUAGE

The official language is Croatian, written using the Latin alphabet. Though comparatively unfamiliar to most, it is not as difficult as it might seem – it's a phonetic language, for a start, so letters are always pronounced in the same way (unlike English) – and it's well worth making the effort to learn a few words and phrases. English is widely spoken on the coast and in major tourist centres – less so off the beaten track. The Dalmatian dialect borrows from Venetian, so if you speak Italian, you will recognise a few words. See page 230 for more details and vocabulary.

RELIGION

In the 2011 census, some 87.8% of the population labelled themselves as Roman Catholics (up from three-quarters in 1991) – by 2021, that had dropped to 79%. Catholicism has long been tied to national identity here – it's as much a statement against Tito's brand of socialism or Serbia's Orthodox Church as it is a credo in itself. As a result, church attendance was hugely popular in the first years of Croatian independence, though it has tailed off somewhat in recent years.

Outside of church service times, there are often people worshipping privately at the bigger churches and cathedrals, and their peace and privacy should, of course, be respected. Smaller churches – and even some of the bigger ones – may well be closed outside the periods immediately before and after mass.

Beyond Catholicism, in 2021, 3.3% of the population declared themselves Orthodox Christians, while Muslims accounted for 1.3% of the population.

EDUCATION

Children in Croatia, and by definition Dalmatia, begin school at the age of six or seven, attending primary school (*osnovna škola*) and then from age 14 secondary school (*srednja škola*). Secondary schools can take the form of *gimnazija* (similar to a grammar school), vocational or art schools. In recent years, the secondary school leaving examination (*matura*) has started to replace entrance exams at some universities. Dalmatia has universities in Zadar, Split and Dubrovnik, and there are also a fair number of polytechnics and other accredited schools of higher education. The standard is high, and the syllabus demanding – as anyone who has worked their way through the reading lists for literature courses will happily tell you.

CULTURE

ARCHITECTURE Thousands of years of foreign occupiers have left Dalmatia with an impressive architectural heritage, ranging from Greek and Roman ruins to a wealth of delightful Venetian harbour towns and several fine Vienna Secession buildings from the brief period under Austro-Hungary. See the individual chapters for specific sights (and sites). Regarding modern architecture, in 2018, MoMA in New York hosted the 'Toward a Concrete Utopia: Architecture in Yugoslavia 1948–1980' exhibition, which examined Yugoslav architecture, including several examples of buildings in Dalmatia. Around the same time, HRT (Croatian Radio Television) aired the excellent *Betonski Spavači*, a series in three episodes (2016, 2019 and 2023) reassessing modern architecture from the Yugoslav period. In many ways, it symbolises the acceptance that some things that came out of Yugoslavia were actually rather good, including design with a collective social conscience.

ART There are very few Dalmatian artists who are well known outside the country, the most famous probably being the sculptor Ivan Meštrović (page 160), whose works you can see in Split, Drniš and Cavtat. Anyone with an interest in painting would do well to also look up turn-of-the-century artists Vlaho Bukovac, honoured at the Bukovac House (page 116) in Cavtat, and Emanuel Vidović, whose moody paintings you can see at the Vidović Gallery (page 160) in Split. Also be sure to explore the vibrant modern paintings of the Dubrovnik colourists, Ivo Dulčić, Antun Masle and Đuro Pulitika, at the Dulčić Masle Pulitika Gallery (page 110) in Dubrovnik.

Painter Ignjat Job also originated from Dubrovnik and is sometimes referred to as the Croatian van Gogh. Two rooms are dedicated to his expressionist canvases, inspired by Dalmatian landscape and customs, at the Dešković Gallery (page 178) in Bol on Brač.

MUSIC What you will probably remember best from a visit to Dalmatia is *klapa*, the quite beautiful Dalmatian a cappella singing, often performed impromptu in outdoor spaces at night. One of the most likely places to hear it is in the domed vestibule (page 157) just off the peristyle within Diocletian's Palace in Split. There is also an annual Festival of Dalmatian Klapa held in Omiš (page 166) each July. Tito's communist government was unusual in encouraging people to retain their folk tradition and, as a result, most of the popular tourist destinations – notably Dubrovnik and Split, and many of the islands – have summer music festivals that highlight the best in folk songs and dancing, along with jazz and classical music. Recently, Dalmatia has also started hosting a number of open-air music festivals featuring local and foreign musicians. These range from big mainstream electronic spectacles at Zrće beach in Novalja (page 52) on Pag to smaller, more alternative events, such as the Ship Festival in Šibenik and the Vrlika Lake Festival near Drniš.

LITERATURE AND THEATRE For people here, their most notable writer is Marko Marulić (1450–1524), the Father of Croatian Literature, from Split. You can see a statue of him in Split on Voćni trg (page 158). His best-known piece, *Judita*, was an epic poem and the first work to be published in Croatian. It has been adapted for theatre – look out for performances at the Split Summer Festival. Another noted writer is Petar Hektorović (1487–1572) from Hvar – he wrote *Fishing and Fishermen's Talk* while living at the lovely Tvrdalj in Stari Grad (page 186). In Dubrovnik, Renaissance writer Marin Držić (1508–67) is best known for his comedy *Dundo Maroje*, often performed at the Dubrovnik Summer Festival. The Držić House (page 107) is open to the public.

Returning to Split, journalist and screenwriter Miljenko Smoje (1923–1995) is still much loved for his satirical works in the local dialect and two TV series, *Malo Misto* (1969–71) and *Velo Misto* (1979–81). You can see a statue of him (erected in 2023) overlooking Matejuško fishing harbour in Split.

INTANGIBLE CULTURAL HERITAGE Dalmatia now has six traditions inscribed on the **UNESCO Intangible Cultural Heritage List**, including lacemaking on the islands of Hvar and Pag, the Procession of the Cross on Hvar, Klapa multipart singing, the Nijemo Kolo silent circle dance of the Dalmatian hinterland, the Festivity of St Blaise in Dubrovnik, and the Sinjska Alka (page 52).

2

Practical Information

WHEN TO VISIT

Most Dalmatians recommend September as being the best month to be on the coast or visit the islands. The weather is sunny, the school holidays are over, and the sea is still easily warm enough for swimming. June, too, is absolutely gorgeous, with the sea just right for swimming and all the hotels and restaurants up and running, fresh and ready for the season ahead. Note, though, that there's an increasing tendency for accommodation and catamarans to fill up as June progresses. October is also fine, but by November the sunshine hours are down and the rainfall hours up.

September and June are the best months for walkers and cyclists, closely followed by October and May. Earlier than May, you might find it damp in the lowlands and freezing higher up; later than October, and you run the risk of being caught by the first snows on Velebit and Biokovo.

Yachting, sailing and motor-cruising have a season running from the beginning of May to the first week of October. Outside this period, charters won't be possible, and you'll find the weather, in any case, less pleasant, with a more frequent gale force *bura* (the cold, dry, gusty northeasterly wind).

July and August are easily the most popular months with all types of visitor, so you may want to leave well alone. These are the months when you'll be competing for rooms with several million others, and if you're travelling by car, you'll find parking a hassle and queues for the car ferries measured in hours. That said, July and August are easily the best months for being on the beach, and Croatia's coastal nightlife only really comes alive in summer. And there are plenty of open-air cultural highlights, too, with concerts, plays, dance and opera hosted at the Dubrovnik and Split summer festivals.

If you're not bothered by the damp and cold, winter is a great time for cultural exploration – the coast and islands are deserted, and you'll have museums and churches to yourself. Even Dubrovnik's city walls can be quite lonesome but gloriously sunny in winter. Waiters and hoteliers will be delighted you're there rather than hassled by the next customer, and while you may have to wait a day for the next ferry, you won't have to queue. Finally, if you're planning winter trips to any islands, especially the smaller and remoter ones, bear in mind that from November until Easter, they're simply not expecting you. That means accommodation can be hard or impossible to find and restaurants may be closed for the duration – even such otherwise popular spots as Hvar Town – so check ahead before you catch the ferry.

HIGHLIGHTS

SCENIC INTEREST For wild karst scenery right on the seashore, you can't beat the Velebit massif, at its most accessible in Paklenica National Park, which has well-marked trails for all grades of walking. Less rugged scenery, with woodland punctuated by falling water, is provided by Krka National Park, where the River Krka carves its way through a canyon close to Šibenik.

Offshore, the island of Mljet is outstanding, with its twin saltwater lakes and roaming mongooses, while if you have no time to do anything at all, you'll still have time to take the 10-minute ride from Dubrovnik to the island of Lokrum. The country's most famous beach is Zlatni Rat, near Bol, on the island of Brač; though if it's sand and not shingle you're after, then head to Šunj on the island of Lopud, and if you have your own boat, you'll find the exquisite Kornati archipelago irresistible.

WILDLIFE AND BOTANY In the Velebit mountains, you'll find chamois and mouflon, along with red, fallow and roe deer, and wolves and bears (though you are unlikely to encounter them close up).

Ornithologists are spoiled for choice, from the waterfowl and wading birds on the Neretva Delta, south of Split, and Vransko Jezero, near Zadar, to the peregrine falcons and eagle owls of the Kornati archipelago.

Botanists, for their part, can head up to the remote Velebitski Botanički Vrt gardens and their unique mountain flora.

BY BOAT Croatia's section of the Adriatic is a sailor's paradise, with more than a thousand islands to choose from, and spectacular scenery all along the way. And Dalmatia is home to Croatia's loveliest islands. Remote uninhabited islets compete with the charm of historic towns like Hvar and Korčula on the islands and Split and Zadar along the coast. With a boat, you can sail alongside Croatia's most spectacular cliffs at Telašćica (on the island of Dugi Otok) or lose yourself among the islets and hidden coves of the Kornati. And there are few greater pleasures than being thrown a mooring line from a private jetty belonging to a tiny restaurant, with an evening of eating, drinking and music ahead of you.

ART AND ARCHITECTURE For many visitors, one of the highlights of Dalmatia is the Venetian Gothic architecture of towns along the coast and islands. Add one-offs like Roman Split, medieval Dubrovnik and Renaissance Šibenik, and you'll find yourself having to pick and choose – or come back again next year. Dalmatia's place at the crossroads of Europe means you can find anything here, from Greek and Roman ruins to Vienna Secession villas, from fortified monasteries to Venetian loggias and from Romanesque churches to medieval frescoes.

PUBLIC TRANSPORT Almost everything in this guide can be reached on public transport, which in Dalmatia mostly means by the regular catamarans and inexpensive ferries, or by bus. A good train service runs from Zagreb down to Split but doesn't go as far as Dubrovnik. Some parts of the mountains, obviously, are a whole lot easier to reach by car than by bus; but having a car won't solve all your problems, as queuing to board ferries to the islands can be pretty hard going, not to mention finding parking once you reach your destination. If you can't easily reach something on public transport, we'll tell you in the text.

SUGGESTED ITINERARIES

WEEKEND TRIP For a weekend break, the top of your list should really be Dubrovnik, which you'll find has more than enough to keep you busy for at least

This list isn't in any particular order but represents the places we've been most taken with on Croatia's Dalmatian coast.

DUBROVNIK Clichéd, over-busy and over-priced (relatively speaking, anyway), there's still nowhere else on earth like Dubrovnik. Walk a circuit of the city walls and fall in love with Dalmatia. See page 77.

DIOCLETIAN'S PALACE, SPLIT Spreading out from the peristyle, the streets of the old town of Split were once palatial corridors and the houses huge reception rooms for the former Roman emperor in retirement. It's difficult not to be captivated. See page 156.

ŠIBENIK CATHEDRAL Šibenik itself is lovely, but the 15th-/16th-century cathedral here – Croatia's most important Renaissance monument – is terrific. It's also home to Pelegrini, widely considered Dalmatia's (and Croatia's) top restaurant. See page 212.

KORČULA Many visitors' favourite island, with its medieval-walled capital sitting pretty on a tiny peninsula and nearby vineyards producing indigenous white wines, Pošip and Grk. See page 135.

KORNATI For sailing enthusiasts, nothing beats chartering a private yacht and exploring the wild, rocky, uninhabited islets and turquoise waters of the Kornati archipelago. A true escape. See page 225.

CETINA GORGE The River Cetina snakes its way down towards Omiš on the Adriatic, passing over a series of rapids and providing superb conditions for rafting, kayaking and canyoning. See page 166.

HVAR Dalmatia's most glamorous island destination, Hvar Town is a huddle of gorgeous Venetian-era stone buildings concealing cocktail bars, boho-chic seafood restaurants and gift shops. See page 178.

two to three days – if not longer. Alternatively, you could take advantage of budget fares to Split or Zadar, which might just give you enough time to visit one of the Dalmatian islands as well.

ONE WEEK A one-week visit would give you enough time to base yourself on the coast, either in Dubrovnik, Split or Zadar, visiting several of the islands. Budget flights make it easy to fly into one city and out of another, with two single tickets not necessarily costing any more than a return – so you can potentially cover a two-region section of the mainland coast (ie: south Dalmatia to central Dalmatia, or central Dalmatia to north Dalmatia).

TWO TO THREE WEEKS If you have two or three weeks, you can see quite a bit of Dalmatia without having to rush – although there's always the temptation to rent an apartment and spend a whole week in one place. In either case, you can work your way up or down the coast, making the most of the excellent ferry and catamaran

BIOKOVO Overhanging the Makarska Riviera, Biokovo is Croatia's answer to Cape Town's Table Mountain, offering fabulous views out over the islands of Brač and Hvar. See page 168.

LOKRUM This is a haven, just a short boat ride away from the bustle of Dubrovnik, offering rocks to swim from, woods to picnic in, and a small café set in a ruined Benedictine monastery. See page 113.

KRKA RIVER AND FALLS Several sets of travertine waterfalls you can walk over, across and around, a monastery on an island in the river, and boat trips up and down make Krka a delight. See page 215.

TROGIR The traffic-free old town of Trogir is one of the most charming on the whole Adriatic coast. A medieval island settlement, it's astonishingly well preserved and deserving of its classification as a UNESCO World Heritage Site. See page 161.

PELJEŠAC PENINSULA Wild and rugged, this one is for wine lovers – terraced vineyards on Pelješac's steep seaward slopes produce the outstanding Dingač red wine, and many wineries are open for tastings. See page 129.

ZADAR Dalmatia's former capital (before Split took over), Zadar is packed with impressive Romanesque churches and two excellent museums – the Archaeological Museum and the Museum of Ancient Glass. See page 193.

PAKLENICA NATIONAL PARK Twin karst canyons running up from the sea into the Velebit massif offer some of the best and most accessible walking, hiking and climbing in Croatia. See page 202.

MLJET Lush vegetation, an abandoned monastery on an islet on a lake on an island, Europe's only wild mongooses and relatively few visitors make Mljet a treasure not to be missed. See page 122.

network. A two- or three-week stay also gives you plenty of scope to include a decent hiking trip on Velebit.

ONE MONTH Those with a month in Dalmatia should count themselves lucky indeed, and, as with a two- or three-week visit, can divide their time between travelling along the coast and islands, and exploring the mountains and river canyons of the interior.

TOURIST INFORMATION

Croatia has an active national tourist board and dozens of tourist organisations locally, so there's usually no shortage of information available.

The Croatian National Tourist Board is an excellent source of information and can provide you with maps, brochures and accommodation details. The website w croatia.hr is a great place to start, but if you don't have easy access to the internet,

Arguably the best beach in Dalmatia is that hidden cove you discover all by yourself – however, here are five of the best sand/shingle beaches the mainland coast and islands have to offer, all of them well-known and extremely popular.

ZLATNI RAT (GOLDEN CAPE) Possibly Croatia's most iconic beach, a long spit of fine shingle at Bol on the island of Brač (page 176).

SAKARUN A pale sand/shingle and pebble beach on Dugi otok (page 227).

ŠUNJ Nice little sand/shingle beach on the island of Lopud (page 120).

PUNTA RATA A swathe of fine pebbles backed by fragrant Aleppo pines affording natural shade in Brela (page 166).

BANJE Immediately outside Dubrovnik's city walls, this sand-and-pebble beach gets madly crowded but offers the chance of a swim while sightseeing (page 100).

you may want to contact one of the offices listed below for information. Note that these are the only English-language offices. For a full list of European regional offices, see **w** croatia.hr.

Once in Croatia, you're likely to find that some tourist or information offices – in reality and on the map – are actually closer to travel agents; they'll be keen to help you find accommodation and arrange excursions but may not be so useful when it comes to maps or finding local information. Official tourist information offices are listed throughout this guide.

Head office Croatian National Tourist Board, Iblerov trg 10/IV, 10000 Zagreb; **w** croatia.hr
UK office Croatian National Tourist Office, New King's Hse, 136–144 New King's Rd, London SW6 4LZ; **w** croatia.hr

USA office Croatian National Tourist Office Inc, 33 Irving Place, New York 1003, PO Box 2651 10108; **w** croatia.hr

TOUR OPERATORS

There's a long history of package tourism as well as independent travel from the UK to Croatia, and there are plenty of operators to choose from – beyond those listed opposite, it's worth seeing what your local travel agent has to offer, as well as visiting **w** visit-croatia.co.uk/index.php/tour-operators-croatia.

A growing number of North American operators now include Dalmatia in package tours. You can contact the New York office of the **Croatia National Tourist Board** (☏ +1 212 279 8672), though a quicker route to a Dalmatian holiday is often simply to contact one of the UK operators listed opposite. It's also a good idea to check what's available at your local travel agent, since new tour itineraries are being developed all the time to meet evolving demand.

There are a number of well-established tour operators within Croatia who can organise holidays from abroad; some can even help arrange the travel to and from your home country. For local experts, you may want to try one of the operators listed here.

CROATIA

Katarina Line 📞+385 51 603 400; **w** katarina-line.com. Specialises in mini-cruises on small boats (max 38 persons), with plenty of options in Dalmatia.

My Luxoria 📞+385 91 295 5551; **w** myluxoria.com. Šibenik-based company specialising in villa rentals, with dozens of properties in Dalmatia.

Secret Dalmatia 📞+385 91 567 1604; **w** secretdalmatia.com. Luxury travel agency specialising in unique high-end experiences in Dalmatia.

UK

Activities Abroad 📞01670 789991; **w** activitiesabroad.com. Offering family & adult activity holidays in Croatia, & perfect for those wanting to get close to Dalmatia's nature.

Activity Yachting 📞01243 641304; **w** activityyachting.com. Small company offering sailing holidays in Croatia, notably Dalmatia, mainly based on the flotilla concept.

Balkan Holidays 📞020 7543 5555; **w** balkanholidays.co.uk. Has a wide variety of package destinations on offer along the coast & on the islands.

Cycling Croatia 📞020 3286 5980; **w** cyclingcroatia.com. Cycling tours (both guided & self-guided), including a 5-night Split-to-Dubrovnik tour, taking you across the islands.

Croatia Gems 📞0117 409 0850; **w** croatiagems.com. Hand-picked villas & apartments.

Croatian Villas 📞020 8888 6655; **w** croatianvillas.com. Offering a wide selection of villas & apartments in good locations, & specialists in multi-centre holidays within Dalmatia, Croatia & neighbouring countries.

First Choice **w** firstchoice.co.uk. Covers most of the world, including Dalmatia; part of the TUI group.

Freedom Treks 📞01273 224066; **w** freedomtreks.co.uk. Specialists in cycling holidays, including a Split-to-Dubrovnik boat & bike tour.

Green World Holidays 📞01926 330223; **w** greenworldholidays.com. Offers family adventure holidays, including rafting down the Cetina & exploring the island of Brač.

Headwater Holidays 📞01606 720199; **w** headwater.com. Specialises in walking & cycling holidays, including Dalmatia.

Nautilus Yachting 📞01732 867445; **w** nautilusyachting.com. Well-established company offering good learning-to-sail & flotilla holidays.

Peter Sommer Travels 📞01600 888220; **w** petersommer.com. Cultural tours & gulet cruises led by experts such as archaeologists, including several choices in Dalmatia.

Ramble Worldwide 📞01707 537200; **w** rambleworldwide.co.uk. Specialists in walking holidays, including a popular Dubrovnik coast & islands tour.

Responsible Travel 📞01273 823700; **w** responsibletravel.com. Active & outdoor specialist.

Saga Holidays 📞0808 189 8814; **w** holiday.saga.co.uk. Aimed at the over-50s, Saga has a range of Dalmatian destinations on offer along the coast & a loyal following.

Sunvil 📞0208 568 4499; **w** sunvil.co.uk. Offers tailor-made holidays to Azores, Dalmatian Coast, Greece & more.

Trafalgar Tours 📞0808 281 1126; **w** trafalgar.com. Ranks among the world's largest & best-known tour operators.

TravelLocal **w** travellocal.com. A UK-based website where you can book direct with selected local travel companies, allowing you to communicate with a ground operator without having to go through a 3rd-party travel operator or agent. Your booking with the local company has full financial protection, but note that travel to the destination is not included. Member of ABTA, ASTA.

TUI 📞0203 451 2688; **w** tui.co.uk. The world's largest leisure, travel & tourism company.

USA

Friendly Planet Travel 📞+1 800 555 5765; **w** friendlyplanet.com. Efficient family-run Philadelphia-based operator with an emphasis on upper-end hotels & luxury coach touring.

Homeric Tours 📞+1 800 223 5570 (within the US), +1 212 753 1100 (outside the US);

w homerictours.com. A Mediterranean-focused operator founded in 1969.
Kutrubes Travel ✆ 617 426 5668; **w** kutrubestravel.com. Family-run, Boston-based outfit specialising in the Balkans. Offers a 10-day Paddle Croatia Adventure, taking you around the islets near Šibenik by sea kayak.

RED TAPE

PASSPORTS AND VISAS Nationals of most English-speaking and EU countries only need a valid passport to visit Croatia for up to three months within a six-month period starting from the first day of entry. If you want to stay for longer, you'll need to apply for a temporary residence permit (*privremeni borovak*) at the Croatian embassy in your home country. This is supposed to take up to 12 weeks, but don't be surprised if it takes almost as many months.

Full details of who does and does not need a visa for Croatia, as well as up-to-date addresses and phone numbers of all the Croatia diplomatic missions worldwide – and foreign diplomatic missions in Croatia – can be found on the Ministry of Foreign and European Affairs' website (**w** mvep.gov.hr).

Make sure you keep your passport with you at all times, as the failure to produce an identity document for a police officer can incur a fine or imprisonment – although having said this, if it's behind the reception desk at your hotel you're hardly likely to get into any trouble.

POLICE REGISTRATION The Law on Aliens governs the stay of foreigners in the country. It is essentially based on the old Yugoslav law and is similar in all the former Yugoslav republics. Under Article 150, a foreigner must be registered with the police at the latest within 48 hours of arriving in Croatia. If you are staying in a hotel or other licensed accommodation, the hotelier will do this for you and must register you within 24 hours of your arrival at the hotel. The hotel will fill out the necessary *potvrda* (certificate) for you, and you need do nothing except provide your passport for your identification details. You are entitled to keep your section of the potvrda (normally returned with your passport at the end of your stay). It is advisable to keep your copy because, if you can't prove your official registration for any part of your stay in Croatia, you could be subject to deportation and a restriction on your return to Croatia.

If you are staying in private accommodation, with friends or in your own home bought in Croatia, you or your host must complete the registration within 24 hours of arrival at the accommodation; this should be done at the nearest tourist office if there is one in the local town, or at the nearest police station. Registration is included in the tourist tax per day and varies from place to place and the time of year. This is included in your accommodation costs if you are renting. Foreigner homeowners in Croatia staying in their own home (*koriščenje nekretnine*) are exempt from the tourist tax outside the peak tourism season (15 Jun–15 Sep) and pay a reduced tourist tax during the peak tourism season. If, as a homeowner, you will be using your property a lot during the summer season, you can pay a reduced lump sum for the entire period, saving you the hassle of going in and out of the tourist office. This will register you in the country for 90 days, however, and you will then not be able to return for a further three months. You will need to bring proof of your ownership of the property in order to qualify for home ownership exemptions/reductions to the tourist tax.

In the unlikely case that you first read this section while waiting for a delayed bus after you've already been in Croatia a while and therefore have not yet registered, you'll find that most unregistered tourists will probably get away with just a discretionary warning. Application of the law is, however, much stricter. The Law on Aliens is available on the Ministry of Interior's website (**w** mup.hr).

CUSTOMS There are no restrictions on the personal belongings you can bring into Croatia, though the government recommends you declare big-ticket items (boats, expensive camera or film equipment, etc) to be sure of being able to re-export them hassle-free. Crossing into or out of Croatia in your own non-Balkan registered vehicle, it's incredibly rare to be stopped or seriously questioned for any length of time, however.

Standard customs allowances apply for duty-free – 200 cigarettes, 1 litre of spirits and 4 litres of table wine per person. If you're taking your pets, make sure they have an international veterinary certificate showing that it's been at least two weeks, but not more than six months, since they've had their rabies shot.

You can take as much foreign currency as you want in and out of the country (though you're expected to declare amounts larger than €10,000). For goods purchased in Croatia costing over €100, you can claim a VAT refund on the way out of the country on presentation of the PDV-P 'tax cheque' the merchant will have given you for this purpose – but it can be a giddyingly long procedure. Any questions you have can be answered by the helpful staff at the Customs Administration in Zagreb (☏01 209 9120 (general information); **w** carina.gov.hr).

DRONES Note that you need an EU Drone Certificate before flying a drone in Croatia. Do not fly your drone over people on the beach.

EMBASSIES

There is a useful list of contact details for **Croatian diplomatic missions** abroad at **w** mvep.gov.hr/en – click 'Embassies and Consulates'.

Most English-speaking countries have **embassies or consulates** in the capital, Zagreb, while the UK also has consulates in Dubrovnik and Split. For a comprehensive click-through list of all embassies and consulates in Croatia, go to **w** mvep.gov.hr/en and click 'Embassies and Consulates'.

GETTING THERE AND AWAY

There are five main ways of travelling to Croatia: plane, train, bus, car or boat. You could also arrive on foot, by bicycle or by hitching a lift (but see page 43).

BY AIR
From the UK Flying to Dalmatia is easily the quickest way of arriving. A whole slew of budget airlines flies direct to Dalmatia from all over the UK, including Belfast, Birmingham, Bristol, East Midlands, Edinburgh, Glasgow, Leeds-Bradford, Liverpool, Manchester, Newcastle, and various London airports. However, these routes operate during the summer (April–October) only, and routes and timetables tend to change, so check the websites.

If you're planning a visit between November and March, you'll need to fly to Zagreb (2hrs from London) and then proceed down to Dalmatia. Both Croatia Airlines (**w** croatiaairlines.hr) and British Airways (**w** britishairways.com) fly to Zagreb all year. Expect to pay anything between £200 and £600 for a scheduled return flight, including taxes.

You can also shop around for flights through sites such as w whichbudget.com, as well as UK sites such as w cheapflights.co.uk, w lastminute.co.uk, w opodo.co.uk and w skyscanner.net, or US sites like w expedia.com. But don't automatically assume that these are always the cheapest – these sites don't necessarily include fares from low-cost carriers or charter operators, where the cheapest fares are found on the company's own websites.

easyJet w easyjet.com. To Split, Zadar & Dubrovnik.

Jet2 w jet2.com. To Split & Dubrovnik.

Ryanair w ryanair.com. To Zadar & Dubrovnik.

TUI w tui.co.uk. To Dubrovnik & Split.

Wizz Air w wizzair.com. To Split & Dubrovnik.

From outside Europe
United Airlines flies direct from New York–Newark to Dubrovnik from mid-May to mid-September, and Air Transat flies from Toronto to Zagreb from May to September. There are no direct flights from Australia or New Zealand, but most airlines will be able to route you through a European hub, usually in conjunction with Croatia Airlines. Pricewise, the best deals are generally to be found by choosing to route your Europe-bound flight through one of the hubs served by low-cost carriers such as easyJet or Ryanair.

If you're having trouble finding a reasonably priced flight through the usual channels (newspapers, travel agents, etc), there are a number of alternatives. One is to take a package tour – see the list of tour operators on page 27. If you want to sort out your own accommodation, some operators will be happy to arrange a 'flights-only' package for you. Even if this isn't the case, it can sometimes still work out cheaper to book yourself on a package and then not use the entire accommodation segment – though if you do this, you should check the conditions very carefully to ensure you still have a return flight home. Charter operators flying to Croatia from the UK are listed above.

BY RAIL
The train is a slow and difficult way of getting to Croatia, and not significantly cheaper than the plane. The journey from London to Zagreb takes over 24 hours non-stop and involves at least three or four changes – you can then reach Split by train from Zagreb, but there's no railway to Dubrovnik. But if you're a train lover, have access to a cheap ticket or are planning on stopping off at various places on the way, it's nonetheless a great way of travelling. An excellent resource for planning rail travel across Europe is the Man at Seat 61 (w seat61.com).

If you're roving around Europe, Croatia can be included on an InterRail (w raileurope.co.uk) or a Eurail pass (bought outside Europe – see w eurail.com) – and InterRail tickets, once the privilege of those under 26, are now available to all age groups. International connections come in to Zagreb from Ljubljana (2½hrs), Belgrade (6–7hrs), Budapest (6hrs), Munich (10hrs), Innsbruck, Salzburg and Vienna (9, 7 & 6½hrs).

BY BUS
Long-distance coaches operate between most cities in Europe, but it's a long journey (London to Zagreb takes between 30 & 40hrs), and buses aren't as cheap as they used to be (sample fares, without student discount, range from £160 upwards). That said, if you can get a discount, this may be a viable way to go – though if you're going to forego the convenience of a direct flight, the train is obviously a much more pleasant option for a long trans-European journey. A vast range of bus-related websites are available from w budgettravel.com, while from the UK, Flixbus (w flixbus.co.uk) is the principal operator.

BY CAR In spite of the long drive (London to Zagreb is 1,640km by road; London to Dubrovnik 2,175km) and the expense (tolls and fuel in Europe are pricey), having your own car in Croatia can certainly be an advantage, especially if you're travelling as a family, or planning on moving around a great deal and wanting to visit remote places. Unless you're wedded to the idea of touring in your own vehicle, it can be much more cost-effective to rent a car once you get there rather than take your own, and all the big companies have agencies in the main cities and airports. If you're doing this, make sure you book the car before you arrive in Croatia, as it's much more expensive once you get there if you haven't reserved ahead. Note that traffic on the coast – and on the motorways between Zagreb and the coast, especially at weekends – can be extremely busy in the summer.

If you do decide to drive all the way, you'll find a good motorway between Ljubljana and Zagreb (though the tolls in Slovenia are surprisingly expensive), and good motorways from Zagreb to the coast, making Dalmatia a whole lot faster to get to than it used to be. The motorway now runs (almost) all the way to Dubrovnik.

An alternative – slower, but with its merits – is to drive down through Italy and then take the overnight car ferry across from Ancona to Split. At around €105 for the passage (small car + driver), it's pricier than coming through Slovenia and Croatia – especially if you take a cabin – but it does mean you can take a break in Italy on the way. If you're doing this in summer, it's essential to have a ferry booking – Italians simply love Croatia and tend to bring their cars with them. See below and page 43 for details of ferry routes.

In truth, however, if you're only going to main tourist centres – especially in high season, when coastal traffic can be terrible – why not just forget about driving altogether and stick to public transport?

BY BOAT You can travel across and up and down the Adriatic on one of the many ferries and catamarans that ply the Dalmatian coast. Note that Dubrovnik and Split are well connected by several fast daily catamarans in summer (none in winter), while Split and Zadar are not connected by boat, so you'll need to travel by road. The ferries are a slow but very attractive way of getting around and a reminder of the only way people travelled any distance here as recently as the 1930s. Catamarans are faster but much more expensive and less fun.

There are now several companies plying the Adriatic between Italy and Croatia, including: Jadrolinija (w jadrolinija.hr) between Ancona and Split (overnight; all year), Ancona and Zadar (overnight; summer-only), and Bari and Dubrovnik (as of 2024 a daytime crossing; summer-only); and SNAV from Ancona to Split.

International ferries aren't especially cheap, with a typical passenger fare (without a cabin) across the Adriatic in summer starting at €44 pp, plus port taxes – see the previous section for details of the various ferry companies operating between Italy and Croatia. If you're travelling down through Italy by train and planning to cross the Adriatic from Ancona, make sure you leave plenty of time to arrive from the main train station to the port – once here, you now have to go through a rather complicated book-in procedure, which involves a short bus ride from the ferry terminal. And if you're coming via Bari airport, bear in mind that the seaport is a long way away, and you'll need to factor in moderately expensive taxi rides (or inconvenient buses).

Ferry travel is the only way to get between the coast and islands (with the exception of a couple of islands connected to the mainland by road bridge), and the main centres are well connected all year round, though ferries are generally more frequent in summer. If you're on foot, there's no need to book (on the whole; fast catamaran routes are an exception), and the short-hop ferries are inexpensive.

One of the most attractive ways of seeing the Adriatic and the Dalmatian coast and islands, of course, is from your own – or a chartered – boat. There is an extensive network of around 50 marinas offering literally thousands of berths, while a whole raft of companies offers charters, from skippered motor launches to self-sail yachts. Prices vary enormously depending on what you're looking for (page 61), and you should book well ahead, as it's becoming increasingly popular.

HEALTH   *with Dr Daniel Campion*

PREPARATIONS It is always important to purchase proper health insurance prior to travel, in case of a medical emergency. Check that your policy adequately covers the activities you'll be doing in Croatia (diving, hiking in the mountains), and that you can be flown home if necessary.

Travellers from EEA countries or Switzerland can use their EHIC in Croatia, which allows access to public healthcare on the same basis as citizens. Normally, hospital treatment and some other medical and dental treatments are free. If you are travelling from the UK, you should apply for a UK Global Health Insurance Card (GHIC) before setting off – this will cover state healthcare in Croatia, but not private treatment. Prescribed medicines are not free and are often no cheaper than they would be at home. Bring any drugs or devices relating to existing medical conditions with you.

If you use needles for any reason, you should bring a doctor's note explaining why. It's a good idea to bring along a small first-aid kit. This could include sticking plasters (band-aids), antiseptic cream, painkillers (ibuprofen or paracetamol), loperamide and rehydration salts in case of diarrhoea, high-factor sunscreen, insect repellent, antifungal cream (eg: clotrimazole), tweezers, condoms or femidoms and a digital thermometer. You can top up your supplies of these at any pharmacy.

Vaccinations There are no legal requirements for vaccination to enter Croatia, but most doctors would advise immunisation against diphtheria, tetanus and polio (given as an all-in-one ten-yearly vaccine), and for high-risk travellers hepatitis A too. For longer trips (four weeks or more), or for those working in the medical field or with children, vaccination against hepatitis B is worth considering. Similarly, a course of rabies injections is advisable for travellers at highest risk, such as those working with animals or travelling remotely for extended periods.

Travel clinics and health information A full list of current travel clinic websites worldwide is available on w istm.org. For other journey preparation information, consult w travelhealthpro.org.uk (UK) or w wwwnc.cdc.gov/travel (USA). All advice found online should be used in conjunction with expert advice received prior to or during travel.

HEALTHCARE If you have a pre-existing medical condition, are pregnant or are travelling with children, then you may wish to establish where high-quality healthcare facilities are in Dalmatia before arriving (see above). Larger hotels and tour company representatives are often able to assist, but, failing that, contact the nearest British embassy or consulate for advice. For minor treatments, a visit to one of the ubiquitous pharmacies (*ljekarna*) should sort you out, and there's very often someone who speaks some English. For more serious problems, get yourself to a clinic or hospital (*klinika* or *bolnica*).

MEDICAL PROBLEMS

Mountain health Prevention being far better than cure, walkers and hikers should be familiar with first aid – or at the very least carry a booklet covering the basics. It's especially important to know how to deal with injuries and hypothermia. If you're in real trouble, call the police or alert the mountain rescue service (page 206).

Hypothermia is responsible for the deaths of more walkers, hikers and climbers than any other cause. It occurs when the body loses heat faster than it can be generated, and the commonest cause is a combination of wet or inadequate clothing, and cold wind. It's easily avoided by making sure you always have a waterproof, a sweater or fleece, and a survival bag with you – even if you're hiking with only a daypack. If one of your group shows signs of hypothermia – uncomfortable shivering, followed by drowsiness or confusion – it's essential that he or she is warmed up immediately. Exercise is not the way to do this. Wrap them in warm clothing, or even better a sleeping bag, then increase blood-sugar levels with food and hot, sweet drinks.

Regarding **injury**, again, prevention is better than cure. Try to avoid walking or climbing beyond your limits – the majority of accidents happen when you're tired. If scrambling or bouldering, avoid using your knees or elbows, and keep at least three points of contact with the rock (two hands and a foot, or vice versa). In the event of being injured, use surgical tape for cuts that would normally be stitched, and then bind the wound laterally with zinc-oxide tape. If you're going a long way off the trail, take an inflatable splint.

Ticks and mosquitoes Travellers planning to go rambling or trekking through forests during the spring–autumn period are at risk of **tick-borne encephalitis**. This is uncommon in Dalmatia; ticks are more prevalent in northern Croatia. The ticks that transmit this potentially fatal disease live in long grass and overhanging tree branches. Precautions include wearing long trousers tucked into boots, and a hat. Using tick repellents and checking for ticks at the end of the day can also help. If you do find ticks, remove them as soon as possible (see below) and go to a doctor for treatment. Pre-exposure vaccine is available in the UK: two doses, two weeks

TICK REMOVAL

Ticks should ideally be removed complete, and as soon as possible, to reduce the chance of infection. You can use special tick tweezers, which can be bought in good travel shops; or failing this, with your fingernails, grasp the tick as close to your body as possible, and pull it away steadily and firmly at right angles to your skin without jerking or twisting. Applying irritants (eg: Olbas oil) or lit cigarettes is to be discouraged as a means of removal since they can cause the ticks to regurgitate and therefore increase the risk of disease. Once the tick is removed, if possible douse the wound with alcohol (any spirit will do), soap and water, or iodine. If you are travelling with small children, remember to check their heads, and particularly behind the ears, for ticks. Spreading redness around the bite and/or fever and/or aching joints after a tick bite imply that you have an infection that requires antibiotic treatment. In this case seek medical advice.

apart provide good protection if time is short. However, it's still important to seek medical help in the event of a tick bite.

From May onwards, you should think about protecting yourself against **mosquitoes**. First detected in 2004, the invasive *Aedes* tiger mosquito which can transmit dengue and other viruses is now well established in Croatia; occasional locally acquired cases of dengue fever have been reported. Along the coast and on the islands it helps to have a plug-in repellent (with a screw-in bottle of fluid; the ones that take tablets aren't effective). You can buy these anywhere mosquitoes are present. It is also wise to use insect repellents containing DEET or Icaridin whenever you are outside of your accommodation.

Rabies The most recent case of rabies in Croatia (in a fox) dates back to 2014 – since then there have been no confirmed cases of rabies in wild or domestic animals. As neighbouring countries may have less effective control measures, exposure to wild animals such as foxes could still be a risk. Rabies is spread by the saliva of any mammal, including bats. If you are bitten, scratched or licked over an open wound then wash the wound with soap and running water and apply an antiseptic – even alcohol will do. This helps stop the rabies virus entering the body and will guard against other wound infections. Go as soon as possible to a doctor for treatment. You should still seek treatment even if you have had the pre-exposure course, but it does make treatment easier and less expensive than if you have not. Pre-exposure vaccinations for rabies are particularly important if you intend to have contact with animals and/or are likely to be more than 24 hours away from medical help. Ideally three doses should be taken over a minimum of 21 days.

If you think you have been exposed, then post-exposure prophylaxis should be given as soon as possible, though it is never too late to seek help, as the incubation period for rabies can be very long. Those who have not been immunised will need a full course of injections. A blood product called rabies immunoglobulin (RIG) may also be recommended. This is expensive and may be hard to find – another reason why pre-exposure vaccination should be encouraged.

Tell the doctor if you have had a pre-exposure vaccine, as this should change the treatment you receive. And remember that, if you develop rabies, mortality is 100% and death from rabies is probably one of the worst ways to go.

Snake bites In the extremely unlikely event of being bitten by a snake, try not to panic, as a racing heart speeds up the spread of venom – much easier said than done, of course. Many 'traditional' first-aid techniques do more harm than good. If possible, splint the bitten limb then transport the victim to hospital immediately.

Leptospirosis Fans of caving, rafting and canyoning should be aware of this dangerous bacterial infection. Leptospirosis is caught by swimming in rivers contaminated with the urine of infected animals. Symptoms include a sudden fever, headache, jaundice and muscle aches, between 2 and 26 days after exposure. If you get these symptoms, seek medical advice. It can be treated with antibiotics; the earlier the better.

Scuba-diving injuries Certified scuba divers should always dive conservatively and within recreational dive limits. Decompression sickness can be avoided by ascending slowly and making safety stops at 5m. Signs and symptoms of decompression sickness include tingling or numbness in extremities, aching joints, rashes, headaches, dizziness and nausea. If affected, request 100% pure oxygen and seek medical assistance. Decompression sickness can be fatal and, while the most severe symptoms become apparent within the first 2 hours of surfacing, problems can emerge up to 24 hours after diving. Allow your dive crew to help and advise you: they are trained in managing dive emergencies. Hyperbaric chambers are located in Zadar and Dubrovnik.

Dubrovnik – Poliklinika Marin Med Ante Starčevića 45, Dubrovnik; ☏020 400 500; w marin-med.com/hyperbaric-chamber

Zadar – Poliklinika Marin Med Ljudevita Posavskog 7, Zadar; ☏023 551 111; w marin-med. com/hyperbaric-chamber

DRINKING WATER Tap water throughout Dalmatia is good and perfectly safe to drink. In the mountains, rivers and streams should be treated with caution. Use chlorine-based water purification tablets if you're off the beaten track, or equip yourself with a filter bottle such as AquaPure.

SAFETY

Croatia is safer and freer of crime than most other EU countries, and Dalmatia is especially safe, though the normal precautions you'd apply at home apply here, too – don't be showy with money, jewellery or flashy possessions, and avoid the seedier or ill-lit parts of cities at night. Pickpockets have started operating in the busier tourist destinations in summer. But you're more likely to be robbed by fellow travellers than Croats, so be especially careful in hostels, campsites and overnight trains or buses, and keep your valuables close to you and separate from the rest of your luggage.

Car theft, however, is prevalent, and foreign-registered cars – and especially expensive foreign-registered cars, such as Audis, BMWs and Mercedes – are attractive to thieves. Generally speaking, you wouldn't expect problems along the coast, though be careful where you leave your car in any big city.

You'll see lots of police around, and they have rather fearsome powers – freedom of dissension shouldn't be taken for granted. The police carry out occasional spot checks on locals and foreigners alike for identification, so make sure you have your passport or identity card with you at all times. Otherwise, you'll find the police friendly and helpful, though few speak much English. Note that antisocial behaviour is not tolerated in Dalmatia. Due to a rise in unruly drunken young tourists, the vast majority of whom are English-speaking, hefty fines are now imposed for public disturbances, such as fighting, verbal abuse, climbing on monuments, walking through towns in swimwear, and urinating, defecating or vomiting in public spaces.

If you're driving, keep to the speed limit. There are an astonishing number of speed traps – especially along the Magistrala, the old coastal road running all the way from Zadar to Dubrovnik. If you're stopped for a traffic violation, you may find the police negotiate a lower penalty with you – the heavier fine for speeding, for example, may be traded down to the lower fine (payable in cash) for not wearing your seat belt.

EMERGENCY NUMBERS

European emergency number ☏112
Police ☏192
Fire service ☏193
Ambulance ☏194
Search and rescue at sea ☏195

If you do get closely involved with the police, stay courteous, even (especially) when it's difficult to do so. Stand, rather than sit, if you can (it puts you on an even footing) and establish eye contact – if you can do so without being brazen or offensive about it. Some people recommend shaking hands with officialdom, but it depends very much on the circumstances. Wait until an interpreter arrives (or anyone who understands you clearly) rather than be misunderstood, though this may not happen on the same day. And remember that you can be held at a police station for up to 24 hours without being charged. Your consulate will be informed of your arrest, normally within the first day.

MINEFIELDS Along the frontlines of the war of the early 1990s – and that means in about a third of Croatia – minefields were laid down, and a handful still haven't been completely cleared. Most are clearly marked off with barbed wire and skull-and-crossbones signs saying 'Mine,' and it would be plainly stupid to explore further. Not every minefield is labelled, however. If you see villages that seem to have been abandoned for decades, or fields that haven't been cultivated for a long while, there's an unlikely but real risk of uncleared mines, and it's best to leave well alone.

There is still a danger of uncleared mines in north Dalmatia, notably in parts of southern Velebit and Paklenica – all the more reason to carry a decent map or guidebook.

And if you're travelling in the former war zone – in areas inland from Zadar – it's wise to stick to roads and tracks that carry regular traffic or to marked footpaths in the countryside.

WOMEN TRAVELLERS

Dalmatia is safe for women travellers, though, like anywhere with a big influx of holidaymakers, it has its fair share of both local and foreign men on the make. This tends to come in the form of courteous persistence rather than aggression and is usually easily rebuffed. Speaking firmly – in any language – should make your intentions clear.

People dress here the same way as they do anywhere in Europe, so there's nothing to worry about as far as dressing modestly is concerned – though wandering around churches in beachwear is likely to offend. If you want to get your kit off, head for the nearest naturist beach (usually marked FKK) – you won't be pestered.

LGBTQIA+ TRAVELLERS

Homosexuality may have been legalised a generation ago in Croatia, but you won't find people particularly tolerant or open about it in Dalmatia.

Most activity is still very much underground, and even in Dubrovnik, one of Croatia's most tolerant and liberal cities, there is only a small LGBTQIA+ scene. Elsewhere, same-sex couples (men in particular) can still raise eyebrows (or even hackles) when checking into hotels, though, as everywhere, younger people tend to be more tolerant.

TRAVELLING WITH KIDS

Though perhaps not as child-friendly as the UK in terms of facilities at museums, etc, Dalmatia is nevertheless a great place to travel with kids, who will love the endless coastline, warm sea, ferry-hopping and mountainous ice creams. You'll find decent playgrounds (*igralište*) in most towns or cities of any size and a whole slew of bouncy castles on the coast. Dubrovnik has a decent aquarium, and there's the chance to see dolphins off some of the islands (especially around the Kornati). Many of the larger resorts, notably a couple of Valamar hotels on the Lapad peninsula in Dubrovnik, have special facilities for families with children.

TRAVELLING WITH A DISABILITY

Croatia has done a great deal to introduce active programmes and legislation to support those with disabilities. Dalmatia's main airports are accessible, with ramps and lifts where needed, and good disabled toilets. Accessing ferries and catamarans can be challenging, but you'll usually find that the crew will be happy to help anyone with limited mobility.

Most of the better hotels are equipped for guests with mobility problems, though note that some establishments in protected historic buildings have not been permitted to install lifts.

In Dubrovnik, there's no disabled access to the famous city walls, but you can get in and around most of the old town with no major problems – though the crowds at particularly busy times of year (or day) can be oppressive if you're a wheelchair-user.

Access for people with disabilities in other cities and tourist destinations is generally pretty good, but obviously less easy where there are cobbled streets and stone stairways in old towns or through the narrow streets and lanes of hilltop villages.

There are disabled parking spaces across the region, and these are generally well respected, particularly following a campaign based around the immediate towing away of improperly parked vehicles combined with signs carrying the message 'If you take my place, take my disability'.

The UK's **gov.uk** website (w gov.uk/government/publications/disabled-travellers/disability-and-travel-abroad) has a downloadable guide giving general advice and practical information for travellers with a disability (and their companions) preparing for overseas travel. The **Society for Accessible Travel and Hospitality** (w sath.org) also provides some general information. The website **Wheelmap** (w wheelmap.org) has an interactive global map showing accessible and partially accessible properties, including museums, hotels and restaurants.

WHAT TO TAKE

The best way to pack for anywhere – and Dalmatia is no exception – is to set out all the things you think you'll need and then take only about a third of it. How much you eventually end up taking will depend to a large extent on whether you have your own transport (everyone takes more in their own car) and whether or not you're planning on camping (camping comes with a list of irreducibles; page 38). But be realistic, especially if you're going to have to carry all your own stuff – what feels like an easy 15kg pack in your living room can be more like a sack of rocks halfway up a mountainside or even getting from the bus station to a hotel in the heat of summer.

If you're coming to Dalmatia for a beach holiday, it's worth remembering that the majority of the beaches are rocks or pebbles, so if you have sensitive feet bring appropriate beach footwear – along with the usual hat, sunglasses, suncream, etc. Summer evenings along the coast can be cool but are rarely cold, so a light sweater should be sufficient; but if you're coming here in winter, bring warm clothes, especially if you're going inland or into the mountains.

Don't forget the usual range of documents you'll need – passport, tickets, cash, insurance papers, credit card, driving licence – and something to carry them in. A belt bag or pouch is practical but also draws attention to where you're keeping your valuables. Far better is a zipped pocket for the essentials, whether that's in a daypack or trousers, but it's a personal choice.

And bring any books you want to read – except in the major cities and tourist centres, you'll have trouble finding much more than yesterday's papers.

Also, bring spare glasses if you wear them, along with any special medicines you need. You may also find it handy to have a tube of travel detergent with you for washing your smalls, and a travel alarm for those early starts. And last but not least, if you're bringing any electrical appliances – even just a camera and a phone charger – remember an adaptor. Electricity comes in the European standard size and shape, at 220V and 50Hz, and twin round-pinned plugs are used.

WALKERS AND HIKERS Walkers and hikers need adequate clothes from the ground up, so make sure you have decent footwear – light, waterproof boots with good ankle support and a strong sole can make the difference between comfort and misery. But bring another pair of lighter, more flexible shoes or sandals, too, as you can get seriously fed up with wearing boots night and day. Proper hiking socks, while expensive, are worth every penny, but, again, make sure you have alternatives, not just for washing, but for those evenings out or for travelling to and from your hiking destination.

For hiking in the mountains, you'll need hard-wearing trousers, especially if you come into contact with karst. Jeans are tough but useless in the mountains, as they're heavy and uncomfortable when wet and take ages to dry. Unless you're travelling in winter, you'll also need shorts, as it can warm up quickly during the day.

Take a variety of tops, so you can wear more thin layers rather than fewer thicker ones, and don't forget the all-important fleece and waterproof jacket (Goretex or similar material). It's definitely worth spending more on these last items – breathable, workable clothes are the difference between being warm and dry and cold and wet. In the summer – in fact, for all but winter use – bring a waterproof jacket that packs small, such as the nifty little Minimus made by Montane (w montane.com), which is lightweight, waterproof, incredibly breathable, and packs down to the size of an apple.

If you're using a rucksack as your main luggage you might prefer to go for tall and narrow rather than short and wide – not only is this easier for walking, but it's also a whole lot more manageable for going through doorways and along narrow corridors. Outside pockets can be useful but are also just another zip to break.

Whatever your luggage, make sure you also have a good daypack, with adequate space for everything you might need on a full day's walk – extra clothing, survival bag, water bottle(s), food, camera, maps, compass, penknife, medical kit, sunglasses, etc. If you're going high into the steeper national parks (notably Paklenica), you should definitely have walking poles or a stick with you, as the paths can be slippery. The best sort are retractable poles, which can fit into your main bag or pack when checking your bag in at the airport.

CAMPING It sounds obvious, but if you're camping, take a tent that's easy to pitch (and practise at home before you leave) – trying to assemble an unfamiliar model on a windy and rainy night is suffering itself. Bring tent sealant and repair material; both are hard to find outside rare specialist shops.

What you have in the way of a sleeping bag and sleeping mat will define the shape of your nights – and, again, it's worth testing these before you leave home. Buy a down-filled bag if you can afford it, as they're warmer and more comfortable in use, and more compact when rolled, although care should be taken to keep them dry, as they lose their insulating properties when wet and take a long time to dry. Having said that, if you're camping on the coast in the summer, anything but the lightest summer bag is likely to feel unbearably hot.

It can be worth dispensing with cooking materials, eating utensils and prepacked food altogether. Given that freelance camping is illegal, you're generally going to be close to both restaurants and supermarkets, and in summer three hot meals a day are not essential. Again, it's a personal choice, but the business of finding fuel, the weight and bulk, and the overriding cheapness and cheerfulness of cafés and restaurants take away the necessity of doing your own cooking while camping in Croatia.

MONEY AND BUDGETING

MONEY Since 1 January 2023, Croatia's currency has been the **euro** (€).

Major **credit cards** (notably Visa, Eurocard/MasterCard and American Express) are accepted by most big hotels, restaurants and shops, though away from the coast, their use isn't ubiquitous – and if you're staying in private rooms (page 46), you'll find cash is king. Credit and debit cards can also be used for raiding cash dispensers (ATMs) – widespread on the mainland and main islands, less so on the smaller islands. Note that you'll get much better rates at ATMs belonging to Croatian banks (such as OTP banka, Zagrebačka banka and Erste) than at those set up by private international companies (notably Euronet, which has installed ATMs in historic façades in popular tourist destinations in Dalmatia). Such companies charge higher provisions and give less favourable exchange rates.

Most people use **ATMs and exchange offices** to get euros these days, but money can still be brought in the form of travellers' cheques, which are a safe way to travel and are worth the small commission you pay for the peace of mind – though changing them is a greater hassle than just turning up at an ATM. You lose about the same percentage of your money if you use a credit card, but it's easier to keep track of cheques. American Express cheques are still the most widely used, easily recognised and most quickly refunded in case of loss or theft, and your local bank will issue them to you (though you may have to insist).

Finally, have enough money/resources with you – having money wired to you from home is an expensive hassle.

BUDGETING How much you'll spend will depend mostly on what level of luxury you're looking for and, to some extent, on the season and where you're going.

Camping and using public transport are going to cost a lot less, obviously, than staying in swanky hotels and cabbing it around town. That said, Croatia is neither particularly cheap nor expensive – broadly speaking, you should expect to pay about the same as in western Europe. Hotel accommodation and restaurants are, on average, slightly cheaper than in the UK, but about the same as in France – though house wine can be considerably cheaper than in either. Supermarket prices are slightly higher than they would be in the UK.

After the cost of getting to Croatia, your biggest single expense will be **accommodation**. Expect to pay €60–120 per night for a double room in private accommodation in summer, while doubles in hotels start at around €80 and rise beyond €500. Single rooms are relatively scarce, but when available go for about 70% of the cost of a double. Off season along the coast, those establishments (both hotels and private rooms) that don't close up altogether will discount by up to 20% in spring and autumn, and as much as 50% in winter.

For a couple, daily **food and drink** costs from around €60 for picnic food bought in supermarkets and maybe eating out once a day in a cheap restaurant or pizzeria, to €240 for breakfast in a café and lunch and dinner with wine in more upmarket restaurants. An average *konoba* or grill-type restaurant meal for two, with salad, risotto or grilled meat and wine, averages around €30 a head. A good quality fish dinner on the Adriatic, on the other hand, can easily set two of you back €200 or more. White fish (sea bass, sea bream, etc) is priced by weight – around a hefty €100 per kilo is not unusual – whereas dark-fleshed fish such as mackerel is much cheaper (not to mention more nutritious and usually more sustainable).

Public transport is inexpensive, with a Dubrovnik city bus ticket costing €1.73. Typical long-distance bus fares in 2024 were €20–30 for the ride from Dubrovnik to Split and €16–20 for Split to Zadar.

If you're really eking out the cash (camping or basic private rooms, picnic food), you could get away with a budget of €40 per person per day. Twice that would get you into nicer private rooms and cheap restaurants, while €200 would buy you a nice holiday, but not fish every day. For that, and upper-end hotels in luxury destinations such as Dubrovnik and Hvar Town, you'd need to count on around €400 per person per day.

Entry fees for attractions are reasonably inexpensive but in a constant state of flux, so haven't been specifically included with each site here – in 2024, however, you could expect to pay anything from €5 to visit some of the smaller museums and galleries, to €35 to walk around the walls of Dubrovnik. Entry to the national parks in summer ranges from €10 (Paklenica) to €40 (Krka).

Tipping A service charge isn't included in your restaurant bill, so – assuming the service has been good – it's appropriate to round up the bill to the nearest €10 or so (although waiting staff in places like Dubrovnik increasingly expect 10%). Don't be afraid not to tip if you think the service has been terrible, but equally, don't be too stingy or extravagant – people appreciate a little extra since they're generally less well off than their customers, but leaving a huge tip can tend to rub it in (as well as spoil things for future diners). Taxi drivers the world over expect fares to be rounded up, and Dalmatia is no exception.

GETTING AROUND

You can get around Croatia by plane, train, bus, car, bicycle and hitchhiking – or on foot – and around the Adriatic by ferry, or on your own (or a rented) boat. There's a train from Zagreb to Split, but rail connections are non-existent along the Dalmatian coast, where you'll find yourself on the ubiquitous buses or ferries and catamarans. Public transport is regular, effective and good value for money, but can be slow and is sometimes overcrowded – notably in summer.

BY AIR Croatia Airlines' (**w** croatiaairlines.hr) domestic flights are pretty good value, and a great way of getting from one end of the country to the other, especially if you've already seen it all from the bus. A one-way, online fare from Zagreb to Dubrovnik went for as little as €106 in March 2024; the flight takes around 55 minutes, compared with the 10–12-hour, around €25 bus ride. Buy tickets online at the website, but if you're planning on flying in summer, make sure you book well ahead and bear in mind that if you do so from a travel agent outside Croatia, the price could be considerably higher.

BY RAIL Trains cover the route from Zagreb down to Split in Dalmatia, stopping at Knin en route. They're about the same price as buses or slightly cheaper for any given distance, but can be faster (inter-city, *brzi*) or slower (local trains, *putnički*). Trains can get very crowded, especially in summer, and are prone to delays. Local trains (the ones not marked in red on timetables) are usually much less crowded and much less punctual. The line between Zagreb and Split has reduced the journey time between the two cities to around 6 hours 45 minutes (daytime) or 8hrs 30 minutes (night sleeper train).

For all trains, buy tickets in advance (unless there's no ticket office); you'll pay a surcharge if you wait until you're on board. *Dolazak* means arrivals, while both *odlazak* and *polazak* mean departures. *Blagajna* is where you buy your tickets.

Zagreb and Split railway stations have lockers where you can store bags and cases, costing €2 a day for a small- or medium-sized locker or €3 for a big locker. Both stations also have a manned left-luggage facility, working approximately from 06.00 to 21.30 daily.

You'll find all the timetables on the Croatia Railways Passenger Transport website (**w** hzpp.hr).

BY BUS The bus network is wide-ranging, reliable and regular, though there are fewer bus companies than there were before Covid-19, and prices have increased. Buses offer the best way of coming into contact with local people and are the only way of travelling on public transport along the mainland coast and on the islands. The hourly average speed clocks in at about 45km/h on the coast, though much faster on motorways (for example, between Split and Zadar). Prices and speeds vary quite a bit depending on the route and the time of year. Buses that go on ferries to the islands include the ferry fare in the cost of the ticket.

On major routes – such as Split to Dubrovnik or Zadar, for example – buses leave almost every hour in peak season; in more remote areas, they may only run once or twice a day, or even once or twice a week, to coincide with local needs.

If a bus originates in the town you're leaving from, you can buy tickets and make reservations at the bus station, and you should do this a day or more ahead if you can. Otherwise, buy tickets online. If it's last minute, you can try waiting for the bus to arrive and pay the driver as you get on; but that depends on whether there are spare places.

Luggage is stored in the holds under the bus, and you'll pay a small supplement (often around €1) for this. The price seems to be entirely arbitrary and provides you with paltry insurance, but even so it's an amount sufficiently large for the bus company not to want to lose, however, so your luggage should be guarded safely.

If your bus breaks down – it happens – the chances are someone will be called to come and repair it on the roadside, and if necessary, you'll be transferred to another bus – in which case, you should obviously take all your bags with you.

Buses stop every 2 hours or so for a *pausa*, and the conductor shouts out the duration of this above the din: *pet, deset, petnaest* and *dvadeset minuta* are the commonest break lengths (5, 10, 15 and 20mins). These invariably occur where you can grab a quick drink/snack/meal, and use a toilet. Watch the driver and you won't go far wrong but be warned that the bus will go without you if you've made a mistake. Buses sometimes change drivers at these stops.

Online information is generally reliable between larger towns. But one problem you may encounter is localised information, meaning that if you have to change buses to get to your destination, you may not be able to find out the timings for the second part of the journey before you get there. There's not much you can do about this.

For bus timetables, see w getbybus.com. If travelling to/from Zagreb, see the excellent w akz.hr, or to/from Split, w ak-split.hr.

BY CAR The most comfortable and often quickest way of travelling is by car, and sometimes it's the only way to get somewhere really remote. Road quality has improved enormously since 1991, and there are now several good sections of motorway open – you'll pay tolls on these, though they're not excessive. The most expensive stretch, the 380km from Zagreb to Split (Dugopolje exit), costs €24. For more on Croatian motorways and tolls see w hac.hr. Fuel costs around €1.50 per litre.

Inland and on the islands, the roads are less well maintained than you'd expect in western Europe (and often unpaved in really remote areas), while along the coast, the single-lane Magistrala, running from Rijeka to Dubrovnik, inevitably clogs up in summer with holiday traffic – though the opening of the new motorway from Zagreb to Zadar and Split has alleviated the problem to some extent. In fact, the fast road extends nearly all the way to Dubrovnik now, with just a few stretches still to be completed.

Street parking in cities is a non-starter (pay instead for public parking), and parking anywhere along the coast can be a major hassle in high season.

You may find Dalmatian drivers rather ambitious – to the extent that blind corners and oncoming traffic aren't seen as a natural impediment to overtaking – but don't be competitive; the omnipresent (and omnipotent) traffic police are quick to keep drivers in line with steep fines and worse. Speed limits – 50km/h in built-up areas, 90km/h out of town (locally variable; keep your eyes peeled), and 130km/h on the motorway – are strictly enforced.

In the event of an accident or breakdown, you can call the Croatian Automobile Club's hotline (↘1987; w hak.hr). If you see someone else in need of assistance, you're legally obliged to stop and help. And remember: it's illegal for passengers under the influence of alcohol or children under 12 to sit in the front of the car; the blood alcohol limit is 0.05%, or zero for drivers under the age of 24; all passengers must wear seat belts; it's illegal to drive while using a mobile phone; and in winter (late Oct–late Mar), headlights must be on at all times.

To source car parts or fix problems, your first port of call should be a petrol station – these are usually open from dawn until dusk, though on some main roads and in big cities there are 24-hour outlets. Try to ensure your car is roadworthy and insured against fatal breakdown, however. Although parts are in better supply and repairs more quickly effected than they used to be, it can still be an expensive and time-consuming business.

Car hire Car hire in Dalmatia isn't especially expensive as long as you book ahead from outside the country – count on spending from €350 a week with full insurance and unlimited mileage. The major companies are represented in all the main population centres and the most popular tourist destinations, as well as at airports, and increasingly don't hit you for a huge penalty if you pick up and drop off at different places. There are some good, cheap local companies as well.

BY BICYCLE Sadly, the main roads of mainland Dalmatia are still not very cycle-friendly. Courtesy is in short supply, traffic density is too high for comfort, and along the coast, there isn't even the alternative of small roads or cycle paths to choose from. You should do anything you possibly can to avoid the Magistrala (the old coastal road from Zadar to Dubrovnik) – it's not just busy but downright dangerous, particularly in summer.

One way of doing this is to be clever with ferries and the islands, which are absolutely superb for cyclists. Central Dalmatia, in particular, has taken an excellent initiative in publishing a great series of maps entitled 'Central Dalmatia by Bike' (w dalmatia-bike.com), which covers the islands of Šolta, Brač, Hvar and Vis, with suggested routes and route profiles provided. Other good cycling maps include the HGSS map of Brač.

Cycle touring can also be a great way of visiting the islands and remains an excellent way of getting to meet local people. There are innumerable little Dalmatian villages connected by roads that aren't even on the map because they don't carry any traffic, but you do need to be good at navigating and well-provisioned, as road signs are in short supply. Make sure you have decent off-road tyres, too, as surfaces are highly variable (and often gravel rather than tar). The 4x4 tracks and forest roads of Velebit are a good place for mountain biking, as is the island of Pag, and the Kabal Peninsula on Hvar.

BY FERRY There are few experiences more pleasant than a ferry ride on the Adriatic, and in Dalmatia they're plentiful, economical, regular and reliable. Most domestic services are run by state-owned Jadrolinija (w jadrolinija. hr), though in summer, other local operators provide supplementary services, mainly catamarans.

Services vary from the roll-on, roll-off ferries used for very short hops between the coast and the nearest islands, to fast catamarans, to the huge ferries, complete with cabins, that cross the Adriatic from Split to Ancona and Dubrovnik to Bari.

Local ferries are inexpensive – typical passenger fares are usually between €5.50 and €10.50, with prices dropping around 20% in the low season. Sample (high season) Jadrolinija ferry passenger fares include: €6.25 Split–Supetar; €8.10 Split–Stari Grad; and €8.25 Split–Vis. Catamaran prices are notably higher: expect to pay €20 Split–Bol (Krilo catamaran); €30 Split–Korčula (Krilo catamaran); and a whopping €50 Split–Dubrovnik (Krilo catamaran).

Taking your car to the islands needn't break the bank. Sample prices are: €25.05 Split–Supetar; €47.25 Split–Vis; and €45.80 Split–Stari Grad. Travelling with trailers and camper vans are more expensive.

However, many of the islands have perfectly serviceable local bus routes, and it's worth asking yourself whether taking your own car to the islands is really necessary, given the stress of queuing to board ferries and find parking, not to mention causing unnecessary pollution.

BY BOAT If you have a basic motorboat licence, you can hire a small engine-powered boat for a few hours to explore the nearby coast and islets while on holiday. Boats are generally available in seaside destinations close to small islets, such as Korčula Town, which lies opposite the Korčula archipelago, and Hvar Town looking on to the Pakleni islets. Expect to pay around €70–100 per day (approx 09.00–19.00) for a small boat. If you don't have a licence, you can still rent a dinghy (rowing boat without an engine) or a kayak.

For full-blown sailing holidays, see page 60.

HITCHHIKING Definitely not a recommended option. Tourists are unlikely to pick you up, and locals tend to be travelling very short distances.

WALKING AND HIKING Walking is the slowest but most interesting way of getting around – you could follow in the footsteps of Patrick Leigh Fermor, who walked from the Hook of Holland to Constantinople in 18 months in 1933 and 1934. Plan on taking more money than he did, though – he survived on a pound a week.

Dalmatia is ideally suited to the walker, with lots of national parks and nature reserves, and marked trails that range from the gentle stroll to the strenuous hike. A network of local and national walking, climbing and mountain associations keeps the paths in good repair, and staffs and maintains the mountain huts and lodges.

Hiking in the Velebit karst is a lot like walking in the Alps or the Dolomites. Even though Velebit is considerably lower, it shares the fairly hard climate, and there's generally not much surface water around, winter or summer. You need the right equipment and plenty of food and water with you if you're hiking here, but it is some of the most rewarding walking you'll ever do.

If you're going to focus on walking, Rudolf Abraham's or Sandra Bardwell's books (page 238) may be of interest – they have a whole range of hikes from the easy to the demanding, covering most of the coast and islands.

Mountain safety Up in the mountains, in regions where the regular emergency services don't operate, you can call on the help of Croatia's mountain rescue service, the GSS (Gorska Služba Spašavanja; w gss.hr), if you're in real trouble. Like mountain rescue people anywhere, the volunteers who staff the service won't be amused if you call them out for no good reason but will willingly risk life and limb to bring you to safety if needed.

You can reach the GSS through the nearest information point or by calling the European emergency number (☏ 112). You can also contact the GSS through the head office of the Croatian Mountaineering Association (Hrvatski Planinarski Savez, or HPS; ☏ 01 482 3624; w hps.hr). If you're well equipped with enough clothing, food, water, maps and a compass, the chances are, you won't need to make that call.

Marked trails Most of the trails in the national parks and nature reserves are well-marked using a painted red circle with a white dot in the middle or two red lines separated by a white line. The markings are maintained by local hiking and mountaineering associations and are usually very clear, but if you're in a remote or rarely accessed part of the mountains, then you may find markings worn or damaged, especially if there's no mountain lodge nearby. Occasionally, you'll find trails where trees have been cut down, leaving the way ahead uncertain – try to make sure you have a local map (see below) and a compass with you in any case.

MAPS The national tourist board can provide you with a useful reversible 1:1,000,000 (1cm = 10km) road map/tourist map that is good for situating yourself and planning an itinerary and is perfectly acceptable for most users.

Hired cars generally come with GPS navigation for road trips, and most visitors will also have GPS on their mobile phones. However, note that in remote locations, especially on the islands, mapping can be a little unreliable, and it is often quicker and easier to ask locals for directions.

More detail – at a higher price – is provided by Freytag and Berndt's 1:250,000 Croatia/Slovenia road atlases or the separate maps covering the various parts of the country, available from the Austrian publisher in 1:250,000, 1:500,000 and 1:600,000 sections. Two chunks of the Dalmatian coast are even covered at 1:100,000.

Kümmerly and Frey, the Swiss publisher, also does a reasonable 1:500,000 map covering Slovenia, Croatia and Bosnia & Herzegovina; Belletti Editore has a similar offering, but only covering Croatia and Slovenia; and Nelles has a good driving map of the Croatian Adriatic Coast with Istria at 1:225,000 and the rest of the coast at 1:525,000 and includes town plans for the main centres. You may also see the Hungarian Cartographia (1:850,000) on offer, but it's not great, to be honest.

Far and away the best map for drivers is the 1:300,000 two-sided map of 'Bosnia Erzegovina', which is published by Studio FMB Bologna – it covers all of Croatia except eastern Slavonia and is a good deal more accurate than any of the others, though unfolding it and turning it over on the move is no joke, as it's enormous.

Finally, there's a pretty good 1:100,000 scale map of Istria published by Bruno Fachin Editore in Trieste, which also includes the most accurate map of the island of Krk I've ever seen.

None of these, of course, is of much use for walkers or hikers looking to stretch their legs in the national parks or nature reserves. The best hiking maps by far are the detailed local (usually 1:25,000) maps published by the HGSS (w hgss.hr), SMAND (w smand.hr) and national park offices. These cover most of the main hiking areas (Velebit, Gorski Kotar, Bjelolasica, Biokovo, Medvednica, etc), as well as an increasing number of the islands (Cres, Lošinj, Rab, Brač, Hvar, Vis, Lastovo, Mljet). They are available through some of the larger bookshops in Zagreb and other main cities, stores selling hiking equipment (such as IGLU Sport in Split and Starigrad Paklenica), as well as some of the larger bookshops, and usually sell for about €6–8. Hiking maps produced by local tourist offices are generally far less detailed and therefore much less useful if you actually try to hike with them. An exception is the local hiking map produced by the Baška tourist office, which is excellent, extremely detailed and accurate.

There is also a good series of maps published under the Trsat Polo imprint of the Geodetski zavod Slovinje (Slovenian Institute of Surveyors), which covers the whole coast at 1:100,000, with separate maps for Istria, Kvarner and Dalmatia 1–4. They're available in most Croatian bookshops. The series is aimed at sailors and drivers and includes plans of the marinas, as well as sea and mooring guidance, along with contours and clearly marked footpaths – however, the latter are in general *not* accurate, and for hiking you really should not use these but stick with the SMAND and HGSS maps.

If you're planning a walking holiday, it's also well worth getting hold of Rudolf Abraham's books *The Islands of Croatia* and *Walks and Treks in Croatia* or Sandra Bardwell's *Croatia: 9 Car Tours, 70 Long and Short Walks* (page 238). The former is the most recent of these, covering day walks on the islands and is the only book which includes sections of the relevant HGSS and SMAND maps. The latter two cover a range of walks on the coast and islands.

Town and city plans are generally available cheaply or for free at local tourist offices and will get you around the main sights, though they may not be all that much help if it's a particular street address you're looking for.

ACCOMMODATION

Thanks to its popularity with tourists in the 1970s and 80s, Dalmatia has a good supply of accommodation, coming in a range of flavours – private rooms and apartments, hotels, family-run pensions and B&Bs, farmsteads (agritourism), campsites, hostels and mountain lodges.

Private rooms and apartments offer the best value for money, but if you're in the mood to splash out, there's little to beat a cosy boutique hotel in a renovated historic building. Most hotels on the Dalmatian coast and islands were built in the tourist boom of the 1970s, though almost all have now been renovated and upgraded since

the war of the early 1990s, and there's a whole wealth of smaller, smarter hotels and
swish five-star establishments opening up around the country.

Hotel accommodation and campsites in the main resorts fill up fast in summer,
so you need to reserve well ahead of time. Turning up on the fly in high season in
Hvar Town can be a disappointing experience.

These days there are also several hostels to choose from, providing another good
budget option.

In a category all of its own, you could also choose to holiday in a lighthouse, of
which there are 11. Several of these are in utterly remote locations, atop tiny rocky
islets immersed in an endless blue of sea and sky. Pictures and descriptions are
available at **w** croatia.hr or **w** lighthouses-croatia.com – for further information
and bookings, you should contact Hrvoje Mandekić at Plovput (✆ 021 390 609;
e turizam@plovput.hr.

PRIVATE ROOMS/APARTMENTS Anywhere that sees regular tourists has a supply
of private rooms (*privatne sobe*) and apartments (*apartmani*) available, and for
most independent travellers these represent the best-value accommodation
option. They are the equivalent of B&Bs in the UK (though usually without
breakfast), and are generally clean, comfortable and friendly. Apartments
generally have basic kitchenettes, so you can prepare snacks, making them ideal
for families with kids. Most also have either a balcony or terrace for sitting out.
Their big advantage over hotels – other than reduced cost (many private rooms
go for around €60 a night in shoulder season) – is that they offer you a chance
to meet local people though, in the most popular places, families are starting
to insulate themselves from their lodgers, and even use private companies to
manage their rooms and apartments. Note that some charge more for stays of
three nights or fewer.

Rooms can be found online (or sometimes through the local tourist office if it's
a last-minute decision).

Private rooms and apartments are classified by the local tourist office and come
in five categories, ranging from one-star to five-star, with the level of comfort
and price increasing with the number of stars. Apartments can be great value for
families or small groups but check how many beds have been crammed into each
room before you book. More expensive apartments tend to be better located rather
than roomier.

Inland from the coast, there's also a healthy move towards eco- or agritourism,
with rooms being available in farmhouses and small villages. This is a nascent trend
and not yet fully established but look out for signs if you're in the countryside.

Finally, with both private rooms and apartments, don't be afraid to say no if you don't like the look of the place. A couple of good places to look for private rooms and apartments are **w** gdjenamore.com and **w** apartmanija.hr.

HOTELS Croatia's numerous hotels are classified by the standard international one-to five-star system, though at the lower end, they don't represent very good value for money when compared with the better private rooms, which generally cost around half the price of the worst hotel in any particular town.

Many establishments are still of the large, modern and functional variety, though there is an increasing number of smaller, family-run hotels and top-end five-star places appearing. The smaller boutique hotels are often the nicest places to stay and offer more personalised service, though rooms need to be booked well in advance. Most of the bigger hotels – which is where you're likely to be if you're on a package – have been substantially upgraded since 1995, and many have good sports facilities and spas.

Breakfast is almost invariably included in the room price and ranges from rolls, butter and jam to a full buffet and à la carte dishes cooked to order, with a strong correlation between the quality of the food and the number of stars. You can save a fair amount of money by opting for half or full board – the supplement is usually only small, €10–20 – but bear in mind, you'd be limiting yourself to eating meals in the hotel rather than getting out and about.

CAMPING In a country with fine weather and beautiful countryside, camping ought to be the ideal option. It ought to be, but it isn't always. Campsites are not especially cheap (usually not far behind a private room), and sites are often huge and far removed from easy access by public transport. Some of the places you're most likely to visit – notably Split – don't have campsites at all. (There is a campsite called Camping Split (**w** campingsplit.com), but it actually lies in Stobreč, 7km east of Split city centre.)

The explanation is a simple one – camping is mainly aimed at northern Europeans with their own transport, who drive down to Dalmatia for a week or two and set up a temporary base on the beach, often in a big, modern caravette. And if that's what you want to do, then you'll find Dalmatia's campsites friendly, clean and very well equipped. Expect to pay upwards of €35 a night for two people, a pitch and a parking space at an *autokamp*. Glamping is also becoming steadily more popular, and you'll find comfortable wooden cabins and spacious safari tents at some sites. Visit the official Croatian Camping Union website (**w** camping.hr) to find a full list of sites, facilities and prices.

Freelance camping in Croatia is illegal and, if you're caught, you'll be subject to an immediate and fairly hefty fine. If you're off the beaten track and camping independently, however, then please, please don't let it be you that starts off the forest fire. Many areas of Dalmatia, especially on the islands, have no free water supply, and fires are a major hazard – so much so that in some areas, even smoking is forbidden (in a country that is smoking-mad). Huge areas of forest – and more than one mountain lodge – have been devastated by fire.

YOUTH HOSTELS Dalmatia has only two officially recognised youth hostels (**w** hfhs.hr), but with summer prices averaging under €30 a head, it can be easily the most economical option for single travellers (if you're in Zadar or Dubrovnik). In recent years, a new breed of smart, user-friendly hostels has started springing up all over the place (Zadar, Split, Dubrovnik, Hvar Town, to name just a few places), which, in many cases, offer several double rooms with en suites. For two or more people travelling together, however, private accommodation can still be both more convenient – no daytime lockout, for example – and competitive in price, so shop around. Though be aware that some hostels have turned into party bases and can get rowdy.

MOUNTAIN LODGES Croatia has more than 100 mountain huts and lodges, around 30 of which are in Dalmatia, with facilities ranging from the basic (roof and walls) to the positively hotel-like. They're excellent value for money and are usually run by the local mountain associations under the auspices of the Croatian Mountaineering Association (Hrvatski Planinarski Savez, HPS, Kozarčeva 22, Zagreb; \01 482 3624; w hps.hr/info/planinarske-kuce), where you'll find a full list of the accommodation available, along with altitudes and contact numbers. You can also ask at the various park offices around the country.

Huts usually fall into the following three categories: *planinarskil/dom* (staffed mountain hut), *planinarska kuća* (hut open only by prior arrangement), and *sklonište* (basic unstaffed shelter, usually open all year).

EATING AND DRINKING

What you eat and drink in Dalmatia will depend on where you are – on the mainland coast and the islands, fresh seafood prevails, but if you move inland, you'll find lots of roast lamb and other meat specialities on the menu. Each micro-region has its own wines and beers to be proud of, and everywhere you go, you'll find a range of fearsome spirits designed to warm the cockles and cement friendships.

FOOD If you're in a hotel, then breakfast of some sort will invariably be included in the price – usually in the form of a self-service buffet, with the quality and variety of fare on offer closely correlating to the number of stars.

If you're in a private room, you can rely on cafés and cake shops (*slastičarnice*) to sell you pastries and cakes for breakfast, and if you're outside the most touristed areas, you may still find *burek*, a pastry filled with cheese (*sa sirom*), meat (*sa mesom*) and just occasionally spinach (*špinat*). Burek is cheap, filling and usually delicious – if occasionally too greasy for comfort.

Bakeries (*pekarnica*) sell a wide variety of bread (though occasionally only powdery white rolls and plain loaves) and sometimes offer ready-made sandwiches (*sendvići*) available with cheese (*sir*) or ham (*šunka*) fillings. Street markets (*tržnica*) will provide you with the usual fare for picnics, and you can ask for sandwiches to be made up to order at (most) deli counters in supermarkets (*samospluge*) – just

RESTAURANT PRICE CODES	
Price brackets have been used for restaurant listings throughout this guide, based on the average price of a main course:	
€€€€€	over €30
€€€€	€20–30
€€€	€10–20
€€	€5–10
€	less than €5

point at the type of bread you want filled, say '*sendvić*' and point at your choice of filling to go inside.

Pizzerias are the next step up the food chain and represent great value for money – though on the coast and islands, you can expect them to be significantly more expensive than inland. Pizza here is close to what you get in Italy, with a thin crust and a variety of toppings. Pizzerias also tend to do good (and keenly priced) pasta dishes – though some diners may consider Dalmatian pasta a little over-cooked and soggy.

Restaurants (*restoran, konoba* or *gostiona*) tend to focus on meat and/or fish dishes. Meat isn't especially exciting, though the local lamb can be truly excellent. Fish, for its part, is ubiquitous and delicious – but can turn out to be pricey. For most white fish, you'll pay by the raw weight, and a decent-sized fish for two can come in at as much as €80 on its own. Whitebait, blue fish (sardines, mackerel, etc) and squid are, on the other hand, a lot cheaper.

Shellfish is especially popular on the coast, with steamed mussels on many menus and cockles appearing in pasta dishes and starters, and you can get great oysters in the south (from Ston). You may also see lobster on the menu – but mind the price tag, as it comes in at around €200/kg (and watch out for mistranslations; crayfish is often billed as lobster). Finally, you'll see plenty of *škampi* (grilled or cooked in a tomato '*buzara*' sauce, though you may get shrimp rather than scampi or king prawns) and *crni rižot* (literally black risotto) on offer; the latter is a delicious, pungent dish, made with cuttlefish ink, and though popular, it's not to everyone's taste.

You'll see the term *ispod peka* on many menus – this is a delicious traditional method of cooking octopus or lamb by slow roasting it under an iron bowl over hot coals. You'll also see lots of *pršut*, Croatia's answer to Italy's prosciutto, and pronounced (and produced) in almost exactly the same way. The air-dried ham is a Dalmatian speciality and practically melts in the mouth when sliced thinly enough.

Of course, if you're **vegetarian**, pršut, like much else on the menu, is a non-starter – indeed, it's a non-main and a non-dessert, too. However, vegetarian options have improved greatly in recent years, and there are now some excellent vegetarian and vegan restaurants to choose from, such as Urban & Veggie (Dubrovnik; page 96) and Pandora GreenBox (Split; page 154). A good place to search for vegetarian and/or vegan dining options is w happycow.net/europe/croatia. Even where restaurants don't offer specific vegetarian options, you can always get a cheese omelette (*omlet sa sirom*), a meat-free pasta dish or a pizza, along with a range of salads. There are also a number of homemade cheeses, which vary from the tastily pungent to the surprisingly bland (though these, like most cheeses, will in most cases be made with rennet, which will, of course, be off the menu for strict vegetarians). A must-try is the slightly salty, hard sheep cheese from the island of Pag, *Paški sir* (page 219).

For basic restaurant vocabulary, see page 234.

DRINK The most important thing you need to know is that you can drink the water – all publicly supplied water is safe unless it explicitly says otherwise. The next piece of good news for drinkers is that alcohol is pretty inexpensive when compared to northern Europe, with a bottle of beer (0.5l, in a refundable glass bottle) costing around €1.20 in a supermarket and a half-litre of draught beer (*pivo*) costing anything from €4–6, depending on the establishment, in a café or bar. Premium imported brands, such as Guinness, go for a little more, but local beers are just great, regular favourites being Ožujsko (from Zagreb) and Karlovačko (from Karlovac) – beer is the drink of choice in north Croatia, while wine predominates in Dalmatia. Craft beer has become quite a thing throughout the country – the success of the Dubrovnik Beer Company (page 97) being an example.

Wine Croatia, and especially Dalmatia, makes lots of wine (*vino*), and the quality continues to improve. Almost the entire production is guzzled down domestically, however, so you're very unlikely to see it on the supermarket shelves at home – though reds have long been imported into Germany, and Istrian whites are increasingly making an appearance in the UK. Equally, you won't see much in the way of non-local wine on menus or in the shops, so you're pretty much obliged to go the Croatian way. On a hot summer day in Dalmatia, it's normal to order a refreshing *bevanda* (half white wine, half water) rather than beer.

Dalmatia is known for reds made from the Plavac mali grape (in central and south Dalmatia, especially on Pelješac, Hvar and Brač) and Babić (in the Šibenik area). Native whites include Pošip and Grk (on Korčula), Debit (around Šibenik), Bogdanuša (Hvar), Vugava (Vis) and Dubrovačka malvasija (Konavle Valley, south of Dubrovnik). Many wineries are open for tours and tastings through summer (some of the best are listed in regional chapters here), and this is undoubtedly the most enjoyable and fairest way to purchase wines directly from the producer.

In shops, you can pay anything from €4–60 for a bottle, while in most pizzerias and restaurants, a litre of the house red or white goes for €14–20, and bottled wines start at around €24 and head rapidly up from there. Swankier establishments don't always sell house wine (it's worth asking, however, even if it's not on the menu), and you can easily find yourself spending upwards of €40 a bottle. If given a choice, it's worth making the effort to try some of the local white Dubrovačka Malvasija in Dubrovnik, Pošip or Grk from Korčula, Bogdanuša from Hvar, or Vugava from Vis. If you like your reds, try the sublime Dingač, which is made from Plavac mali grapes grown on the Pelješac peninsula – but prepare to pay upwards of €24 a bottle in a supermarket or €50 in a restaurant.

Spirits (*rakija*) Spirits are common, dangerous, and fairly cheap. In supermarkets, you'll find rakija (a spirit based on distilled grapes, flavoured with either herbs, fruit, nuts or honey) at around €12–14 a one-litre bottle. A favourite in Dalmatia is *travarica*, a rakija featuring a lot of alcohol and a combination of herbs such as sage, fennel, thyme, rosemary and St John's wort. Other types include *medica* (flavoured with honey), *orahovac* (walnut) and *šlivovica* (plum). You can also buy rakija directly from local producers, and you'll find various local specialities, such as *rogačica*, made from *rogač* (carob) on Vis. The quality of spirits varies enormously and can't usually be determined from the label – price is a reasonable (but far from infallible) indicator.

Friendships, business deals and meetings are all cemented with rakija, and it's surprising how often you'll find yourself expected to down lethal drinks. If you don't drink at all, it's not a bad idea to come up with a plausible reason why not (health is always a reliable standby), as Croatians tend to be suspicious of anyone who won't join in.

Soft drinks In marked contrast to the abundance of alcoholic choices, there are surprisingly few soft drinks available. Cola is, of course, mind-numbingly popular, and bottles of sweet fizzy orange are ubiquitous – look out for Pipi, produced in Split and sold in retro orange-and-turquoise bottles and cans. In the most popular tourist spots along the coast, there's a better range of drinks now available – largely due to the presence of Italians here – but otherwise, the most exotic thing you'll find will be the delicious homemade lemonade sometimes available with your morning pastry.

Coffee and tea Coffee is as popular here as everywhere, and in cafés tends to be excellent – though what you'll be served with breakfast in the lower-end hotels can be frankly disgusting. At home, most families drink dark, sweet, gritty *Turksa kava* (Turkish coffee), though in cafés, Italian espresso is the norm. Tea is most often *šipak* (rosehip) and is drunk with lemon and sometimes honey. Ordinary 'English' tea is known as black tea (*crni čaj*) or Indian tea (*Indijski čaj*), but don't expect to find anything you'll be able to stand a spoon in unless you bring your own. Tea and coffee will cost anything from €1.50 to €4 in a café, depending on the upmarketness (or otherwise) of the establishment. If you want a latte-style coffee, ask for a *bijela kava*; for decaf – increasingly available – ask for *bez kofeina*.

PUBLIC HOLIDAYS AND FESTIVALS

Croatia has the usual mix of religious and secular public holidays, as well as innumerable feast days, folk festivals and annual cultural events. Specifics are covered in the relevant sections, but the national holidays and a few of the festivals are included here.

NATIONAL HOLIDAYS You should expect banks and shops to be closed on Croatia's national holidays, which fall as follows:

1 January	New Year's Day
3 February	St Blaise's Day
Easter	20 April 2025, 5 April 2026, 28 March 2027
1 May	International Workers' Day
30 May	Statehood Day
Corpus Christi	60 days after Easter Sunday, and taken seriously in Croatia, with processions and lots of first communions. Corpus Christi falls on 19 June 2025, 4 June 2026, 27 May 2027
22 June	Day of Antifascist Struggle
5 August	Homeland Thanksgiving Day
15 August	Assumption of the Virgin Mary
1 November	All Saints' Day
18 November	Remembrance Day for Vukovar
25–26 December	Christmas

FESTIVALS Dalmatia's robust Catholic heritage was built on the back of a strong pagan culture, and you'll find lots of the festivals and celebrations here owing more than a little to each. The calendar of festivities is based around both Christian (Easter, Corpus Christi, saints' days) and seasonal (spring, solstices, harvest) events, with Dalmatians ready and willing to celebrate them all.

On religious holidays and feast days – not to mention the local patron saint's day – villagers and townspeople will hold processions, masses and major celebrations, and they're a great thing to be a part of if you're in the neighbourhood.

There are also innumerable festivals relating to the business of survival on the land or sea. Most seaside towns, villages and ports have at least one annual fisherman's festival (where the sea is treated with the usual mix of fear and due respect and blessed by the local priest).

Pretty much every island and town along the coast now has a 'cultural summer' and 'musical nights' which keep things lively once the sun's gone down, with Dubrovnik's summer festival being the largest and most famous. Classical music concerts, theatre productions and folk-dance performances are held most evenings in the old town through six weeks of July and August, and the festival culminates in spectacular fireworks. Split Summer Festival sees similar events around the same time, including impressive opera performances on the Roman peristyle.

The festival year kicks off (or closes, depending on your viewpoint) with the **New Year's Regatta** on the island of Hvar, held annually and running from 28 to 31 December, featuring seriously competitive dinghy racing.

Things are reasonably quiet from then until 3 February, St Blaise's Day in Dubrovnik, which sees the old town crowded with locals (some in traditional folk costumes) and a religious procession. Soon after, the wildly popular carnival season gets underway in February, culminating on **Shrove Tuesday** – or sometimes on the weekend before. Masked parades can be found in many Dalmatian towns, but Dubrovnik takes the biscuit for the biggest and most showy event.

Split celebrates St Domnius' Day on 7 May (a local holiday) with a religious procession and stands selling basketwork and wooden kitchenware on the Riva (seafront promenade).

Film festivals and open-air summer cinema kick off in June. In Split, the Mediterranean Film Festival (**w** fmfs.hr) sees nine days of open-air screenings above Bačvice Bay.

June also sees the beginning of the **open-air music festival** season. You'll find several big electronic music festivals taking place through summer at Zrće beach in Novalja on Pag and at The Garden in Tisno (between Šibenik and Zadar). Split hosts **Ultra Europe** for three nights in early July when locals lucky enough to have a house on one of the islands board the first ferry out of town – if you want to enjoy Split's historic monuments and easy-going vibe, this is not the time to visit. On a more traditional note, Omiš hosts the Festival of Dalmatian Klapa from late June into early July.

On the first Sunday in August, 18th-century-uniformed cavalrymen charge around the town of Sinj, inland from Split, on horseback with lances, in the colourful **Sinjska Alka** festival (**w** alka.hr), which celebrates the town's 1715 victory over an army of Turks.

Throughout July and August, you'll have the chance to see the **Moreška** sword dance performed on the island of Korčula, which continues a tradition dating back at least 1,000 years.

In the autumn, once the harvest is in, the biggest festival is **All Saints' Day**, when every graveyard and cemetery in Dalmatia becomes a mass of flowers and flickering candles. The year then closes with **Christmas**, which is much as you'd expect, though a big fish rather than a turkey is the thing to have during the main celebration on **Christmas Eve**.

SHOPPING

Dalmatia is not a great place for bargain hunters, with prices for most goods pretty much in line with those across the EU, though you'll find an unbelievable number of stores selling sunglasses (especially in Split) and boutiques selling beachwear, both at prices a wee bit lower than in London or Milan. If you've forgotten to bring something with you, it'll be fairly easy to replace, but you're probably not going to need to buy extra suitcases for all the things you bought here on the cheap. Shops generally open from 08.00 until 20.00, with larger supermarkets staying open until 22.00 in summer. Most smaller shops close on Sundays.

PDV (VAT) Purchase tax (PDV, or VAT) is set at a flat rate of 25% on all goods except essentials and books. In theory, non-EU citizens can get this reimbursed on single-ticket items costing over €100, but you have to really want the money. Fill in the PDV-P form at the point of sale and get it stamped so that when you leave Croatia (or the EU if you are travelling onwards to other EU countries), you can have the goods, receipts and forms certified by the Customs Service at the airport at your last stop before flying out of the EU – not a process for the impatient. The purchase must be in its original packaging and should have been bought within the last three months. If the Customs Service are satisfied, you will be given back the refund in cash. Some refund services, depending on the airport of your departure, may require you to mail back the documents upon your return home, and you will then have a lengthy wait before receiving the refund.

It's worth the hassle, of course, on really big-ticket items, but bear in mind when you're bringing goods back into your home country, you may, in any case, be subject to import duties or asked to prove you've actually paid the VAT.

BOOKS If you run out of holiday reading along the mainland coast, you shouldn't have too much trouble finding something to read, though expect to pay about 20% over the cover price. On the islands, it's a different matter, so pack accordingly.

MUSIC If you get hooked on the local music – and it happens – make sure you buy before you leave the country. There's a whole Croatian pop and rock music scene, as well as traditional folk music and the curiously popular 'turbofolk', but even in an online world, Croatian music is pretty hard to come by once you're out of the country. CDs are about the same price (that's full price, not discounted) as in most of the EU.

HANDICRAFTS AND DESIGN ITEMS When Rebecca West travelled round Croatia in 1937, she spent a good part of her trip buying up antique peasant costumes, noting that fewer and fewer people were wearing them. This trend has continued unabated to the present day, meaning you're unlikely to see traditional dress at anything other than folk festivals or weddings. The beautifully embroidered waistcoats and skirts are still being made, but with a few exceptions mostly fill a tourist need.

By contrast, contemporary Croatian design is looking up. While travelling around Dalmatia, you'll find plenty of small shops selling works by local artists, designers and craftspeople – paintings, etchings, ceramics, objects made from local stone, and jewellery. You'll also find some chic items of clothing and accessories by up-and-coming young designers. One of the nicest places to shop for all these items is the Life According to KAWA concept store (ℹ️ KAWA.LIFE8) in Dubrovnik.

NATURAL COSMETICS In Dalmatia, you'll also find nicely packaged cosmetics, including soaps, and face and body creams, made from natural essential oils and wild herbs. Some of the best include Sapunoteka (from Šibenik) and Brač Fini Sapuni (from Brač), with fragrances recalling hot summer days on the islands.

WINE A few bottles of Dalmatian wine make a perfect souvenir or present to bring home. Note that prices in airports are rather steep, so if you have a suitcase booked into the hold, you're better off buying wine at local shops or directly from producers. Most wineries can also arrange to have your bottles boxed and sent home so you do not need to carry them.

ARTS AND ENTERTAINMENT

With more than a nod to Austria in the north and Italy to the west, Croats love going to the theatre, and there are excellent productions to be seen at the professional theatres in Dalmatia, notably in Split and Dubrovnik.

The **Croatian National Theatre** in Split sees dozens of performances annually, in a season that runs all year except July–August and includes excellent **ballet**, **opera** and **theatre** productions in a mix of premieres and revivals. Theatre productions tend to be in Croatian, but all opera is put on in the original language, and, of course, ballet is universal. Tickets can be hard to get (though some are kept aside for sale on the day), partly because – by the standards of most countries, and especially for opera – they're inexpensive, costing around €4–24 apiece. The current programme can be found in English on the theatre's website at w hnk-split.hr.

Croats are also great **cinema**-goers. Fortunately for English-speakers, most of the films are subtitled rather than dubbed and range from Hollywood box office hits to art films (the latter being especially prevalent at the open-air summer cinemas on the coast and islands). This makes going to the cinema easy enough, and tickets are cheap, but you'll be lucky to find films made outside the USA/UK that you'll be able to understand without good language skills.

Croatia has more than its fair share of **concerts** and **festivals**, too. See page 51, as well as individual entries throughout the guide, for more information.

Most towns of any size have at least one **museum** or **gallery**, though the quality of these varies greatly – there are few modern art galleries, for example (though Split's and Dubrovnik's are excellent). Mostly, too, galleries and museums reflect Dalmatia's long history of attachment to one empire or another, so you'll see a lot of Austro-Hungarian and Venetian influences in the art and architecture. The most notable exception is the sculptor Ivan Meštrović, whose work you'll see everywhere, and in particular at the Meštrović Gallery in Split.

OPENING TIMES

Croats are industrious and hardworking but like to knock off early and enjoy the evening. So, you'll find people up at dawn, and many offices and shops open from 07.30 or even 07.00, but you may well find businesses shut after 16.00. Supermarkets and pharmacies have fairly long hours and tend to be open all day, while smaller shops may take an extended lunch hour.

Generally speaking, things tend to be open when they're needed – if there's a real demand, then it'll be met. You'll find **tourist agencies** in the main resorts open from early in the morning until late at night, seven days a week, in summer, but probably only open in the morning and on weekdays for the rest of the year.

Museums are usually closed at least one day a week – normally Monday but see individual listings for details. **Restaurants** generally serve lunch between noon and 15.00, and dinner from 18.00 to 22.00, though cheaper places like pizzerias, and almost everywhere on the coast in summer, will have more extended hours. Unusually for Europe, **banks** are often open from 07.00 to 19.00 on weekdays and until 13.00 on Saturdays.

Many **churches** – even some of the bigger ones – are only opened for services, and the periods just before and after them. The tourist office can sometimes help you find the person with the key if there's something you absolutely must see.

MEDIA AND COMMUNICATIONS

For a country of fewer than 3.9 million people, Croatia has a surprisingly vigorous and wide-ranging press. It is also a very internet-friendly country.

MEDIA The dominant media provider is Croatian Radio and Television, HRT, which attracts an audience in excess of 2 million a day to its four TV channels and national and local radio stations. HRT 1 and 2 produce the usual mix of news, documentaries, films, serials, game shows and sports, HRT 3 shows cultural programmes, films and documentaries, and HRT 4 is dedicated almost exclusively to news. Note that films and documentaries are shown in the original version (often English) with Croatian subtitles, so they can be accessible even if you do not speak Croatian. The website, at **w** hrt.hr, has an English-language sitemap that will help you find the various web-streamed audio services on offer.

The most popular national daily newspapers are *Jutarnji list* (**w** jutarnji.hr) and *Večernji list* (**w** vecernji.hr), published in Zagreb, while two of the most prominent magazines are *Globus* (**w** jutarnji.hr/globus) and *Nacional* (**w** nacional.hr). In Dalmatia, the most popular daily newspaper is *Slobodna Dalmacija* (**w** slobodnadalmacija.hr) published in Split. In the 1990s, the satirical weekly *Feral Tribune*, which even used a fake *Herald Tribune* masthead, originally a supplement to *Slobodna Dalmacija*, and also published in Split, was a regular thorn in the side of the Tuđman government.

For news in English, the internet is your best bet, either by going through paper-specific websites like **w** guardian.co.uk or by tuning in directly to the BBC or another English-language news provider (**w** news.bbc.co.uk, **w** cnn.com, **w** abcnews.go.com, etc). Alternatively, you can tune in to the BBC World Service through the internet or – if you're lucky – catch one of the intermittent English-language news bulletins on HRT radio. In the bigger centres, you can pick up the main English papers a day or two (or more) out of date.

POST Post offices (*pošta*, or HPT) in the main cities have long opening hours, usually from 07.00–19.00 (or 08.00–20.00) Monday to Friday, and until 13.00 on Saturdays, but on the islands, most work shorter hours, limited to 08.00–14.00 Monday to Friday. Letters take up to five days to arrive from Croatia to other European countries or up to 12 days to countries beyond Europe. Prices for sending parcels vary depending on the weight and destination. Don't seal them until you've given the cashier time to check you're not posting bombs or contraband. If you send anything valuable, you may have to pay duty on it when you get home.

If you want mail sent to you, have it addressed to Poste Restante, Pošta, postcode, town name. It will be delivered to the town's main post office if there's more than one – and remember you'll need a photo ID, such as a passport, to recover your mail. If your family name is underlined and/or in capitals, your mail is more likely to be filed correctly – but if there's nothing for you, it's always worth asking them to look under your first name as well. Incoming post takes around five days from most European destinations and about 12 days from North America – but can be quicker, or indeed slower.

Stamps (*marke*) are also sold at newsstands, tobacconists and anywhere you can buy postcards, which can save you queuing at the post office. It now costs €1.70 to send a postcard or a letter to anywhere in Europe, the USA, Australia or New Zealand.

For branch locations and other information, see **w** posta.hr.

TELEPHONE Croatia's phone network is good and reliable. The international access code is 00, so for international calls, simply dial 00 (or +) followed by your country code, followed by the local phone number (without the leading zero in most cases, but not in Italy or Russia, for example).

The international code for calls into Croatia is +385. Area codes within Croatia are, for the most part, refreshingly simple, covering large geographical areas. Dubrovnik and south Dalmatia use the 020 area code; Split and central Dalmatia are 021; the Šibenik area and part of north Dalmatia are 022; and Zadar and the rest of north Dalmatia is 023. There is one notable anomaly – the island of Pag is cut in two, served by 023 in the south and 053 in the north. The codes are included at the beginning of each chapter.

Partial privatisation of the former state-owned telephone operator Hrvatski Telekom (HT) has seen the company rebranded as T-Com/T-Mobile by majority shareholder Deutsche Telekom (w hrvatskitelekom.hr).

One final word – like everywhere else in the world, you should aim to avoid calling long distance or international from your hotel room. Tariffs for fixed and mobile calls may have fallen, but hotel rates certainly haven't. The cost of a 15-minute call home from a decent hotel room can spoil your entire trip.

Mobile phones There are five mobile operators in Croatia: A1, Bonbon, Hrvatski Telekom (aka T-Mobile), Telemach and Tomato. The network is comprehensive, and the local operators have roaming agreements with their foreign counterparts, so you'll almost certainly find your own phone works just fine. With Croatia now part of the EU, calls and texts within the EU cost the same as they would for EU nationals at home (and therefore will be included in their provider's monthly allowance), but with the UK out, thanks to Brexit, that does not necessarily apply to visitors using British mobile providers. Check with your provider before travelling.

Otherwise, if you're not from and calling within the EU, using your own mobile for international calls will be expensive. Remember if you're calling your travelling companions that you need to make an international call: to dial a UK-registered mobile being used in Croatia, for example, you need to dial 0044 or +44 first.

If you're going to be glued to the phone, one option is to buy a local prepaid subscription and then top up your SIM card as needed. Not only is a local prepaid number convenient for your outgoing calls, but it also means you can easily be called from home. Local SIM cards become deactivated if not used for three months, so if you come to Croatia every year (for example) and don't use the SIM card in between (and why would you), you'll need to get a new one each year.

A local SIM card (T-Mobile, Telemach, etc) costs very little, and the price will include a certain amount of prepaid credit, which can easily be topped up when needed at many supermarkets and kiosks, as well as mobile phone shops.

INTERNET Internet uptake has been rapid in Croatia, and there's an enormous amount of information now available online. You'll find an increasing number of major towns offering free Wi-Fi across the city centre, practically all hotels and hostels have free Wi-Fi, and even on the most remote islands, many cafés and bars offer Wi-Fi for their customers.

CULTURAL ETIQUETTE

All visitors have an effect not just on a country but on its people, too. There are plenty of arguments for and against this that don't need to be enumerated here – suffice to say that it's worth considering both the environmental and sociological effects of your visit.

INTERACTING WITH LOCAL PEOPLE Croatia has been affected hugely by tourism, which has brought an improved standard of living to the country as a whole and to hundreds of thousands of individuals along the Dalmatian coast and on the islands. Tourism has also destroyed a way of life that was poorer and harsher and yet is often fondly remembered for its generosity and humanity. Your surly, inattentive waiter at the dog-end of the summer season is probably dreaming of being the fisherman his father was – even though he knows how hard a fisherman's life really is. *Yugonostalgija* is understandable when you consider that everyone was guaranteed a good free education and decent health care, and homelessness was unheard of.

Away from the tourist spots – especially in the mountains, in smaller communities inland and on the islands – there are plenty of opportunities to build bridges between foreigners and local people. Take the time to talk to those you meet, show people what life's like back home (photographs and postcards say more than words ever can, even if you do speak the language) and share in a cup of coffee or a drink and a cigarette, if invited.

In Croatia as a whole – and especially in the parts of the country directly affected, such as Zadar and Dubrovnik – it's a good idea not to discuss the recent war. It's a conversational minefield, and the last thing you want is to step on a conversational landmine. Even with a population that's now over 90% Croat, you won't always know immediately whether you're talking to a Croat or a Serb and, even if you are sure, opinions are sufficiently divergent to be dangerous. Many families have mixed marriages somewhere down the line, and some family relationships were irreparably damaged by the war. The only really safe thing you can say, if you're asked directly, is that you're pleased it's all over.

ENVIRONMENT Croatia's environment is in good shape (page 4), so don't spoil it – preserving it is in everyone's interest.

The biggest impact you personally can have on the environment is to start a fire. There's almost nothing that can be done once a fire's out of control in Dalmatia's drier areas in summer, especially when the wind picks up, so be especially careful here. Unless there's a plentiful supply of water nearby, in fact, it's advisable to avoid fires, or even naked flames, altogether. If you smoke, stub out cigarette butts properly.

Litter, by comparison, is a question of environmental pollution and ugliness. Paper tissues take months to deteriorate, tin cans take around 100 years, and plastic bottles need some 450 years to decompose. Do not leave trash on beaches or throw non-biodegradable material in the sea. Take your litter with you – and if you collect any you find along the way, take that, too. Recycling bins, separating plastic, paper, glass, general rubbish and biodegradable waste, are now placed in various locations in all the main towns and even most smaller villages. Rubbish disposal is a massive problem on the islands, so don't make it worse.

Tap water is of high quality, so invest in a drinking flask and refill it at cafés, rather than buying water in plastic bottles. Buy tote bags instead of using plastic bags. Be like Zlarin (page 213), Croatia's first plastic-free island.

DRESS/NATURISM In summer, you won't look out of place in shorts and a T-shirt, but you won't be able to visit churches if you're too skimpily dressed – there are signs outside churches along the coast and islands giving you a pretty good idea of the dress code. Seaside topless sunbathing won't offend, but you shouldn't really be anywhere off the beach in your swimsuit (or, indeed, out of it). Indeed, following a surge in bad behaviour by drunken young tourists (mainly Brits and Australians), hefty fines of €150–300 are now issued in Split and Dubrovnik, and on Hvar, for walking through town in swimwear.

Nonetheless, Dalmatia is the main homing ground for the great European naturist – hundreds of thousands of (very well-behaved) nudists come here every year just to get their kit off. There are several naturist campsites, and many coastal towns have a dedicated beach. Just look out for the FKK signs if you're interested. Dalmatia's also one of the few places where you can go on a naturist sailing holiday. Mind your tackle.

SMOKING Non-smokers beware: with more than a million smokers (and one of Europe's highest rates of lung cancer), Croatia is one of the last bastions of the 40-a-day habit.

However, in May 2009, Croatia introduced a ban on smoking in indoor public spaces – including cafés, bars and restaurants. Needless to say, this was a vast improvement, but it caused such an uproar (among café owners and smokers) that it was at least partially revoked, the ruling now being that bars and cafés smaller than 50m² that do not serve food have the choice of whether to be smoking or non-smoking (guess which most choose), whereas larger establishments (again, not serving food) may only have a smoking area (less than 30% of the total area) if it is properly ventilated. Restaurants at least seem destined to remain smoke-free – though the nice terrace outside, which is obviously where you'll want to sit, won't be.

Most of the upper-end hotels now have a no-smoking policy in rooms, though you can smoke on your balcony. Likewise, the bars and restaurants in these hotels – and some of the more upmarket establishments – have smoke-free sections.

DRUGS Illegal drugs are best avoided in Croatia. The penalties are stiff and harsher still for smuggling – don't be tempted or tricked into carrying anything across borders. Split, in particular, has something of a reputation with the authorities for being part of a drugs corridor from Asia to the West, so be especially vigilant, and – without excessive paranoia – make sure you know exactly what's in your bags.

TRAVELLING POSITIVELY

After travelling in Dalmatia (and possibly even before you go), you may want to do something for the region – the obvious way you can help is through voluntary work.

VOLUNTARY WORK There are a number of well-established voluntary programmes operating in Dalmatia. They're all popular, and you need to book well ahead if you want to participate. Mainly, you'll find opportunities to help with marine conservation and cleaning up beaches. Look up Volunteer World (w volunteerworld.com) for details. More specifically, local organisations, notably national parks and nature parks, are listed here:

Blue World Institute w blue-world.org/get-involved/volunteer. Occasionally needs volunteers & interns to help with research into dolphins off the islands of Murter & Vis.
Kornati National Park w parkovihrvatske.hr/en/the-kornati-dolphinographer. Needs people to monitor bottlenose dolphins in summer & to catch & ring Caspian gulls in spring.
Krka National Park w parkovihrvatske.hr/en/archaeological-associate. Needs archaeological associates to help with research in summer, as well as riverbank waste collectors & indigenous species habitat protectors.
Lastovo Islands Nature Park w parkovihrvatske.hr/en/the-lastovo-cleaner.

Needs people to help clean up marine debris on the beaches of the archipelago in summer.
Mljet National Park w parkovihrvatske.hr/en/cleaner-of-the-mljet-coves. Needs people to help clean the coves of rubbish from the sea in spring.
Telašćića Nature Park w parkovihrvatske.hr/en/eco-patrol-team-telascica. Needs people to help with eco-patrolling, ie: cleaning up coves of floating rubbish & sorting waste for recycling in summer, as well as dry-stone wall builders & olive tree cultivators.
Vransko Jezero Nature Park w parkovihrvatske.hr/en/dry-stone-wall-buildermeadow-keeper. Needs dry-stone wall builders & meadow keepers in summer.

3

Sports and Adventure Activities

Dalmatia is a great destination for sports and adventure activities. The deep blue Adriatic makes a gorgeous venue for sailing, scuba diving, windsurfing, kitesurfing and sea kayaking. On the mainland, several rocky gorges, carved by rivers which tumble over falls and rapids, provide ideal conditions for rafting and canyoning, while Dalmatia's rugged limestone cliffs offer a true challenge to rock climbers.

SAILING

There's really no better way of seeing Dalmatia's wealth of islands than by sailing boat. Once you've covered the costs associated with the boat (and most likely a skipper), a sailing holiday is (or can be) quite reasonable, with the only significant outlays being food, drink and mooring expenses.

Dalmatia's main yacht charter base is in Split, and the most popular stretch of coast and islands lies between Split and Dubrovnik. It's rather similar to sailing in Greece, but with shorter distances between the islands, better equipped and more hospitable marinas, and wonderfully picturesque villages and fortified historical towns. And a slightly lower-key nightlife, unless you're on Hvar.

SAILING EXPERIENCE The type of sailing holiday you embark on will depend, at least to some extent, on your level of experience. Those who have not sailed before might join a group of more experienced friends or family, but bear in mind that a week on board in a confined space can strain even close friendships, so choose carefully. Once you're on board, the captain's word really is final.

Alternatively, you might start by taking a sailing course. For an idea of prices, a six-day learning-to-sail Competent Crew Sail course with Split-based Ultra Sailing (w ultra-sailing.hr) costs from around €750 per person (excluding accommodation and food).

If you're at an intermediate level, and at least one member of your crew is reasonably experienced, then sailing in a flotilla (a group of boats led by an expert skipper) is an excellent way of improving your sailing skills while not having to worry too much about navigation or the *bura* (that gusty northeasterly wind). Flotilla boats generally take six and eight people each, and as you'll be sailing with other boats, you'll get to meet the other sailors, too.

The requirements for renting a boat are strict. Sailing is a tremendous activity, but it is also potentially hazardous. If you do not have the necessary skills, you will need to hire a local skipper. Not only will they captain your boat, but they will also provide insider knowledge, guiding you to hidden coves and authentic local eateries. Expect to pay €230–350 per day for the services of a skipper.

CHARTERS There are literally hundreds of charter companies to choose from and thousands of vessels, both sailing boats (monohull and catamarans) and motorboats. Almost all charters run one-week, from Saturday afternoon (boats are normally available from 17.00) to the following Saturday morning (boats generally need to return to base by 18.00 on the Friday evening, with disembarkation the next morning by 09.00).

Price depends on model, size, capacity and season. In peak season (Jul–Aug) in the summer of 2024, you could expect to pay €4,600 per week for a six-berth Beneteau Oceanis 41 sailing boat or €4,900 per week for an eight-berth Beneteau Oceanis 45 chartered in Split. All in all, the price of a cabin for two works out similar to the cost of a double room in a mid-range hotel.

ROUTES The location of your charter base will obviously decide the waters you'll be sailing in. However, note that you'll need to be flexible about your exact route, depending on changeable weather conditions and prevailing winds – take your skipper's advice on this. Depending on your particular interests, such as scuba diving, hiking or wine-tasting, your skipper will plan a route to include the activities you'd like to try along the way.

If you hire a boat from Split (or nearby Trogir or Kaštela), a one-week sailing holiday would typically take in the Central Dalmatian islands of Brač, Hvar, Vis and Šolta. From Dubrovnik, you could expect to explore the South Dalmatian Elaphiti islands, the Pelješac peninsula, Korčula and Mljet. From Šibenik, you could see Skradin and Krka NP, Murter, the islets of Kornati NP, and Zlarin. And from Zadar (or nearby Biograd), you might explore Ugljan, Dugi Otok and Telašćica Nature Park, and the islets of Kornati National Park.

Note that some charter companies can accommodate one-way routes such as Split–Dubrovnik, though you normally have to pay a surcharge if you leave the boat in a different charter base from the one where you originally collected it.

MOORING The Dalmatian coast and islands host dozens of sailing marinas. The biggest company, Adriatic Croatia International Club (known everywhere as ACI), runs 23 marinas, 14 of which are in Dalmatia, and has an excellent website (w aci-marinas.com) listing fees, locations and facilities.

Marinas tend to be well equipped, and most offer good technical and repair services, hot showers and laundry facilities, and have a restaurant, café and shop selling basic provisions. An alternative to marinas is mooring 'stern-to' in the smaller harbours (such as Hvar Town or Vis Town). You can also find mooring lines in some sheltered bays, while remoter restaurants (for example, in the Kornati) put out mooring lines to encourage sailing crews ashore. Harbours and bays are sometimes free but can charge variable fees depending on the length of the boat (expect to pay between €4 and €13 per metre), how much jetty you're occupying, and facilities available (such as water and electricity). The alternative is dropping anchor in a sheltered bay – this is free everywhere except in national parks.

PROVISIONS AND EATING OUT Keeping yourself in food and drink should not be a problem. You can stock up on speciality items in supermarkets in towns, but you will also find plenty of green markets and small shops in the villages on the islands. If there has been a prolonged spell of bad weather and there isn't a ferry service, you may find it hard to get bread or fresh fruit, but it's very unlikely to affect you during the summer sailing season.

Restaurants, especially on the smaller islands, tend to be good value, with local wines and seafood highly recommended, and you're more likely to find the homely *konoba* (low-key restaurant) here than on the mainland. In fact, some of the best seafood eateries are run by an owner-cook who is also a fisherman, in which case you can't go wrong. Your skipper will be able to recommend reliable eateries.

WATER AND FUEL Watering and fuelling is not usually a problem, with all marinas and most ports having abundant supplies of both, though you may have to scout around to find the right person responsible for supplying water to boats. Some islands, however, have no water supply of their own, so do not expect to fill up here. Your skipper will know more about this.

CHARTS AND GUIDES Dalmatian waters are well charted, and Croatian, English, German and Italian charts are available. When you hire a boat, it will already be supplied with all the necessary maps and charts.

Highly recommended comes the *Adriatic Pilot*, which is now in its eighth edition (published in 2020). This 500-page nautical guide to the Adriatic comes in at £39.50, well worth the expense, and is available through Amazon.

WINDS If you're sailing outside the summer months, you'll need to keep a weather eye out for the *bura* (fresh, dry northeasterly) and the *jugo* (a warm, humid, east-southeasterly, accompanied by heavy clouds and rain). Once winter's over, you can expect lighter winds and better weather, though during July and August storms are more frequent, and during September winds strengthen again.

Summer is characterised by the prevailing *mistral*, which is no relation of the Provençal horror. The mistral here is a sailor's dream, a fair-weather wind that springs up locally late morning, strengthens until the early afternoon and then dies down at sunset.

The summer bura is more localised and much less persistent than the winter version, springing up in sudden squalls and capable of gale-force strength, particularly in the Velebit Channel. Fortunately, it's very reliably forecast, so listen carefully to the weather bulletins on the radio and head for a well-sheltered port if a bura's on the way.

The summer jugo is also mostly a local wind. Be warned it can switch quickly to a bura – something to be borne in mind if you're in a mooring exposed to the northeast.

WEATHER FORECASTS/SAFETY Marinas always have the latest forecasts available, but Dalmatia also has two coastal radio stations that broadcast excellent weather reports – particularly for the bura – and warning announcements in both Croatian and English, several times a day (see opposite). They receive radio-telephone messages round the clock and re-broadcast these, so stay tuned to whichever station is nearest.

After the weather, the coastal radio stations broadcast nautical warning messages, with information on obstacles to navigation, lighthouse failures, prohibited areas, etc. Continuous weather forecasts are also issued by harbour offices and at w meteo.hr.

During the day, you can usually contact marinas on VHF channel 17, while harbourmasters' offices are on channel 10. Harbourmasters tend to have their own patrol boats, which can be used to help boats in distress, and (as elsewhere) they can also call on the help of any suitable ship in the vicinity, including foreign boats.

For a list of harbourmasters' offices and port authorities, with contact details, see w mmpi.gov.hr.

Dubrovnik Radio VHF channels 04, 07, 28, 85; at ☺ 06.20, 13.20, 20.20 & 01.20.

Split Radio VHF channels 07, 21, 23, 28, 81, 84; at ☺ 05.45, 12.45, 19.45 & 00.45

DIVING *Original text by Thammy Evans*

With almost 1,200km of mainland coast, Dalmatia hosts 79 islands and literally dozens of islets and reefs, home to some stunning marine wildlife, beautiful underwater vistas, as well as wrecks dating from 3–4BC to World War II and later. The island of Vis has the highest concentration of wrecks (both ships and planes) and is a compact location for diving, with excellent visibility.

Thousands of divers visit Dalmatian underwater sites annually, as diving here is easily accessible and offers warm waters from May to October. Water temperature averages 21–29°C at the surface during summer and 7–10°C in the winter. At 20–30m, the water temperature remains a constant 16–19°C from the summer until the end of the diving season in November. Visibility is best in spring, autumn and winter when summer plankton and spawning algae clouds are completely absent.

Home of the International Centre for Underwater Archaeology (ICUA; w icua. hr), opened in Zadar in 2007, Dalmatia is leading the world marine community in conservation and preservation. It is also an excellent place to start an interest in wreck diving. Numerous sites lie close to the coast and in PADI open water or advanced open-water dive depths (up to 30m). Many dive centres along the coast offer diving courses at all levels, and some offer wreck diving speciality courses. At the end of this section, you'll find five of some of the best introductory wreck and cave dives in the region.

PLANNING THE DIVE
Dive costs and packages Diving costs with a dive centre range from €30 for a beach dive to €60 for a boat dive. Many places will do packages, such as a discount for two dives in a day or up to ten dives in a week, sometimes with limitless shore dives.

All the dive centres offer diving courses at most levels, usually in PADI (Professional Association of Diving Instructors) or with SSI (Scuba Schools International). Again, prices vary, so it is worth comparing websites for up-to-date prices: a Discover Scuba afternoon comes to around €135, while a PADI Open Water Diver (OWD) course is around €395.

Rules and regulations As with elsewhere around the world, diving in Dalmatian waters is regulated by several laws. These are overseen by the Croatian Diving Federation (Hrvatski Ronilački Savez; w diving-hrs.hr), which grants diving concessions to qualified centres, clubs and individuals. Qualified individuals wanting to dive independently of the dive centres and local clubs must apply for a concession via the local harbourmaster.

Wreck-salvage laws in Croatia are very strict and very simple: nothing may be removed from a wreck. All battlefield casualty wrecks in Croatian waters are war graves and thus also deemed cultural monuments. Diving to most Croatian wrecks therefore also requires a special permit, which usually costs €10 and is organised by the local dive centre that has permission to take divers there. Not every dive centre is allowed to go to every wreck.

The Adriatic is a rich, fascinating, and unique body of seawater. It is unique largely because no more than 4% of the water flow of the northern Adriatic around the Istrian peninsula escapes into the southern Adriatic (beyond Dubrovnik). Over 75% of the Adriatic's water flow, which is anti-clockwise, recycles around at Split. On its way around, the water flow picks up more polluted waters from the eastern Adriatic coast and organic matter from the main Mediterranean basin and mineralises it through a system of combination with the clean karst-rock waters from Croatian rivers.

As a result of all this, the Adriatic is home to over 70% of all the fish species to be found in the whole Mediterranean, and more than 30 of these are found only in the eastern Adriatic owing to the karst rock formations of the region and their abundance of fresh spring water. Seven of the species of fish found in the Adriatic are endemic to the waters (ie: found nowhere else in the world). Sadly, however, overfishing in the last 50 years threatens the extinction of 64 fish species found in the Adriatic.

COMMON SIGHTINGS Crabs, moray eels, goby, cleaner shrimp and lobsters are very common. Other commonly sighted species include:

Soft corals (Alcyonacea) Soft corals, particularly gorgonian sea fans and sea whips, are common in waters with higher nutrient value (and therefore lower visibility) where they filter-feed off plankton as well as through some photosynthesis in a symbiotic relationship with algae. A large gorgonian colony can be over a metre high and wide but only some 10cm thick. They will be oriented across the current to maximise access to food. Those unable to photosynthesise are more brightly coloured.

Damselfish (*Chromis chromis*) Juvenile damselfish are deep lightning blue in colour and only 2–3cm in length. Shoals of 20 or 30 are common at 3–4m. Adults are dark brown or black.

European conger eel (*Conger conger*) The European conger eel, like the moray eel family, is found in cracks and crevices. European congers are grey, while moray species tend to be more colourful. Neither species is poisonous or dangerous unless provoked (although the flesh of morays, if eaten, can be poisonous if the eel itself has eaten something else poisonous). The European conger can grow up to 3m in length (morays up to 4m).

Bearded fireworm (*Hermodice carunculata*) Growing up to 15cm long, bearded fireworms are poisonous to touch, causing sharp irritation where bristles enter the skin, and there have been reports of dizziness and nausea in severe cases. Bristles can be successfully extracted using sticking plaster, and the irritation can be relieved by applying neat alcohol or white spirit.

Nudibranchia These amazing tiny shell-less molluscs, often only 1cm long, are abundant for those with the patience to see them. A torch helps in order to highlight their colours in lower visibility. *Flabellina affinis* (fuchsia pink) and *Janolus christatus* (electric blue) are especially common.

PROTECTED FLORA AND FAUNA

Mediterranean killifish (*Aphanius fasciatus*) The Mediterranean killifish, also known as the South European toothcarp, is a locally protected species more abundant elsewhere in the Mediterranean. It is becoming rare in Croatia due to the destruction of its preferred lagoon habitat.

Orange stony corals (*Asteroides callycularis*) Orange stony corals are best seen on a night dive when their colours show up brightly in a torch's rays, and when these primitive animals feed on the likes of tiny brine shrimp.

Loggerhead turtle (*Caretta caretta*) The loggerhead turtle is an extremely rare sight along the built-up and shallow shores of the northern Adriatic, but the clean waters of the eastern Adriatic are their preferred choice.

Black tree coral (*Gerardia savaglia*) Sometimes better known as 'black' tree coral, this fast-growing branchy primitive animal is beige-yellow when alive and leaves behind a brown-black skeleton. Found below 15m depth and as low as 120m, it has been a popular souvenir, leading to its destruction.

Long-snouted seahorse (*Hippocampus ramulosus*) The long-snouted seahorse, like all seahorses, is a protected species. It is particularly vulnerable because of its commercial value in traditional Chinese medicine (to counter weak constitution in children, adult male impotence and bed-wetting!) and for aquariums, for which more than 25 million are caught wild every year. Slow moving because of their tiny fins, the creatures are very shy and tend to hide in sea grass, which they cling to with their tails to prevent being swept off by sea currents. Seahorses have been seen at various dive sites around the Dalmatian islands. In some instances, they have been known to grow up to 15cm in length.

Long-armed purple starfish (*Ophidiaster ophidianus*) The long-armed purple starfish grows to 15–40cm in length. Usually found below depths of 5m, they can sometimes appear red or orange.

Noble pen shell or fan mussel (*Pinna nobilis*) This is the largest bivalve mollusc in the Mediterranean and can grow up to 1m in height. Often found among seagrass at shallow depths. Take great care not to touch it, so watch your buoyancy in its vicinity.

Neptune grass (*Posidonia oceanic*) Endemic to the Mediterranean, Neptune grass only grows in very clean waters. It is thus on the decline. It tends to grow in meadows on sandy beds and can reach up to 1.5m in height. Lesser Neptune grass (*Cymodocea nodosa*) is also protected but can be found outside the Mediterranean.

Orange puffball or golf ball sponge (*Tethya aurantiacum*) This sea sponge looks exactly like an orange. This is a charming quote by Barnes, Fox and Ruppert (2004): 'Some are known to be able to move at speeds of between 1mm and 4mm per day'.

Wildlife and natural habitats are also protected. A permit is required to dive around some national parks, such as the Kornati archipelago. Some of the dive centres which have permission and permits to dive at restricted sites are listed in this chapter.

Equipment All diving centres will have the basic equipment that you find in most dive centres around the world, and in Croatia they tend to be in good condition. Female wetsuits are increasingly common, but female BCDs (buoyancy control devices) are rare, as are BCDs with integrated weight systems. Even in the summer, diving is usually done in a 5mm full wetsuit, with boots and strap fins. Only some centres have Nitrox, and fewer still have Trimix. An increasing number of dive centres now sell a small range of diving equipment; otherwise, you can find several dedicated stores along the coast (but note that prices in Croatia will often be more expensive than the big specialist diving stores elsewhere in the world). One of the best is Di-Nautika in Split.

Di-Nautika Uvala Baluni bb, Split; 021 322 005; w di-nautika.hr. In the ACI sailing marina, this little shop is the showcase of its bigger version on the east side of town on Kralja Zvonimira 85. Offers a good range of equipment for both recreational diving & fishing as well as professional diving trades. Also services equipment.

Safety Diving safely is the responsibility of every diver. In general, if you've not dived for three years or more, most dive centres will want you to do a refamiliarisation dive or scuba tune-up with an instructor (for around €80). If you've not been diving over the winter or for a year or so, your first dive of the season should always be a check dive, especially if you have your own equipment, to ensure that you and your equipment work as you expect them to. Check dives are usually done from the shore in front of the dive centre, as these are the cheapest, and it is easy to go back to the centre if something's not working.

For more information regarding health and safety for divers, see page 34.

Wreck diving With hundreds of shipwrecks strewn along the coast, Dubrovnik is a great place to go wreck diving. Most sites are within 90–100 minutes' boat ride from a dive centre, and many lie within Dalmatia's stated recreational dive limit (40m). That said, diving at 20m+ in Dalmatia is not like diving in the clear blue waters of the tropics or off Egypt, Malta or some of the Pacific islands. Planning the dive and diving the plan is essential in waters that can have low visibility, even when you are outside of the wreck. Navigational and decompression skills are a must, as is a Nitrox qualification if you want to stay down long enough to make the descent worthwhile.

As a result of the higher skill set required to dive wrecks, most centres will require that you are qualified to at least CMAS 2* level (equivalent to PADI Rescue Diver, SSI Advanced Open Water Diver (AOWD) +40 dives or having taken the BSAC Dive Leader course even if you have not qualified with all the dives). Many will also require that you show a current (within the last year) fit-to-dive medical certificate. If you have not got one from your usual doctor, these sometimes can be obtained through a private doctor in Croatia. Your dive centre will be able to tell you where if there are any indications that you need one.

If the dives listed at the end of this chapter whet your appetite, there are even bigger, better, deeper dives for you techies out there, including the 150m Columbia near Dubrovnik and numerous American B-24 Liberator fighter planes around the island of Vis. Most recently, a very rare Junkers Ju 87 Stuka was found off the island of Žirje by the Croatian Department of Underwater Archaeology.

DIVING CENTRES There are dozens of diving centres in Dalmatia. The ones listed below, arranged from northwest to southeast, are chosen for their spread along the coast and for access to some of the best dive sites. Most dive centres are open from May to September unless otherwise listed. Key staff at the centres all speak English (as well as Croatian, German and Italian). For those wanting to know more about diving for the people with mobility issues, see **w** iahd-adriatic.org.

Najada diving Murter, Murter Island; **m** 098 169 3107; **w** najada.com. Najada have a contract with Kornati National Park (page 228), meaning they can run dives at 9 sites in these protected waters. They also have 4 apartments to rent at the dive centre on Murter. Offer PADI & SSI courses.

Aqualis Dive Center Hvar Hvar, Hvar Island; **m** 091 620 5847; **w** hvardiving.com. Founded by a Hungarian couple, Aqualis offer dives to several superb sites, including the Kampanel seawall & reef, filled with red gorgonians. They also specialise in diving for people with mobility issues & are recognised by the International Association of Handicapped Divers (IAHD). Offer PADI, SSI freediving & IAHD courses.

Trogir Diving Center Pod Luka 1, Okrug Gornji; **** 021 886 299; **m** 091 524 1856; **w** trogirdivingcenter.com. Northwest of Split, near the ancient town of Trogir, this diving centre is popular, not least because it also has its own on-site tavern cooking excellent food for centre divers only, including b/fast, lunch & dinner if required. With 4 boats, the choice of dives for the day is wide. Offer CMAS courses only. Nitrox available.

ISSA Diving Center Komiža, Vis Island; **** 021 713 651; **m** 091 201 2731; **w** scubadiving.hr) ISSA Diving Centre is a haven for wreck divers as it is located on the most wreck-abundant island in Croatia. As a result, it is fully equipped for technical diving & offers TDI, as well as SDI diving courses. The centre has 3 boats at its disposal & offers Nitrox & Trimix.

B-24 Diving Center Komiža, Vis Island; **m** 091 766 1415; **w** diving-croatia.hr. Another Komiža-based centre offering dives to several nearby wrecks & caves, B-24 is run by Veljano Zanki, freediving world champion, & specialises in both scuba diving & freediving. Offers PADI, SDI & TDI courses.

Diving Center Blue Planet Masarykov put 20, Dubrovnik; **m** 091 899 0973; **w** blueplanet-diving.com. Based at the Hotel Dubrovnik Palace on Lapad, Blue Planet run dives to the wreck *Taranto* (next to Grebeni islet, just a 10min boat ride from the centre), sunk by an underwater mine in 1943, & the nearby Sveti Andrija islet, as well as various sea caves, walls & reefs. Offer PADI courses.

TOP FOUR DIVE SITES IN DALMATIA
1 *Vassilios*

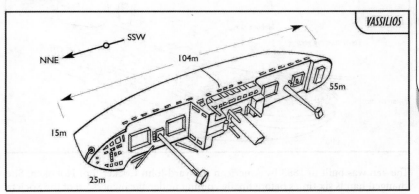

Description	104m cargo ship sunk by its own crew
Depth	25–55m
Location	Near Vis island, 43°00′24″N, 16°03′56″E
Difficulty	CMAS 2*, AOWD
Visibility	usually good even in summer
Dive centres	ISSA, B-24

The *Vassilios* has an interesting history. It was built by Nitta Ship Builders in Osaka, Japan for the US Shipping Board (USSB), and its construction was completed in 1920. Originally named *Eastern Temple*, it was sold to a Greek cargo company in 1938, when it was used to transport coal bought by fascist Italy from coal mines in Wales to supplement the coal already being mined in nearby Istria. On one of her regular voyages from Swansea to Venice, her rudder failed just off Vis on 19 March 1939 while navigating up the Adriatic. Hitting the shore, she quickly sank, but all the crew survived. It was not uncommon in those days for owners to sink their own ships in order to collect insurance money. At the time, the ship was worth almost 8 million Royal Yugoslav dinar, with 1.25 million dinars of Welsh coal aboard.

The wreck is so close to the coast, just 25m from the Rt Stupišće lighthouse, that it can be dived from the shore. Most diving expeditions come by boat, however, and anchor just off the lighthouse. From there, a descent to 15m starts to reveal this huge vessel below, with the starboard side of the bow reached at 25m. The ship lies completely on her port side. Her interior is easy to access through the bulkheads and corroded deck, with chinks of light coming through the increasingly corroded hull. Her cargo of coal is difficult to discern as it is now so covered in sediment, but the coal and many other items on the ship can still be seen.

This is a big ship to dive, so Nitrox or Trimix is recommended for advanced divers to increase bottom time and shorten decompression time. It is a great dive for novice technical divers with the usually good visibility of the northeastern Adriatic. Open-water divers can also get much out of the dive from the starboard side of the ship.

2 *Teti*

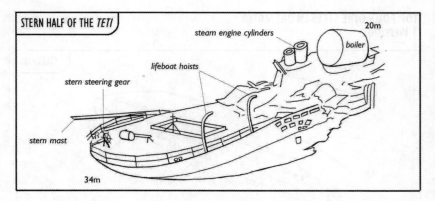

The *Teti* was built in 1883 by American shipyard John Cockerill of Hoboken. She changed hands six times before finally coming under the ownership of the Societa

Description	72m cargo steamboat, which ran aground in 1930
Depth	10–34m
Location	Off Mali Barjak, near Vis, 44°56'4"N, 13°34'7"E
Difficulty	OWD
Visibility	usually very good
Dive centres	ISSA, B-24

Italiana Navigazione Trasporti e Armamenti Ravenna of Italy. Transporting granite roadblocks from Komiza itself on Vis as part of the Italian industrialisation effort of the 1930s, the ship ran aground in very bad weather on 23 May 1930 on the rocky shores of the island of Mali Barjak. The incident is well-documented in the local archives due to the rescue efforts of the local islanders, who saved all the crew and were officially thanked by the Kingdom of Italy for their bravery.

With the wrecked bow of the boat lying in only 10m of water and the almost intact stern gradually descending to 34m, this is an excellent introduction to the thrills of wreck diving. The relatively low depth of the boat allows for a reasonable bottom time on air for those without a Nitrox qualification, and there is usually little current, making for easy diving. Visibility is almost always very good, and the ship is small enough that almost the entire boat can be seen from one end or the other, and the whole ship can be explored in one dive (although subsequent dives are always interesting). Descent to and ascent from the wreck is directly down and up the gradient of the shoreline, making it additionally easy to find your dive boat in the event of separation.

The steam boiler and engine cylinder can be explored, and the rear steering wheel, completely intact and thoroughly barnacled, makes for excellent photo opportunities. For those with AOWD and enough experience, the cargo area of the stern can be entered through the bulkhead and exited through an additional port hatch further down the stern.

3 *S57* Torpedo Boat

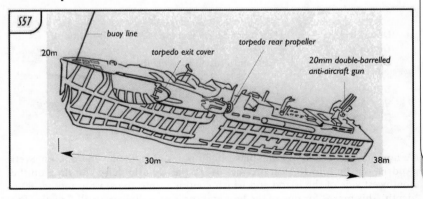

Schnellboot torpedo boats were common in World War II. Their design is testimony to the idiom 'necessity is the mother of ingenuity'. After World War I, Germany's re-industrialisation was curbed in the Treaty of Versailles in an effort to ensure that she did not build excessive war-fighting capabilities. However, this only resulted in

Description	S57 German torpedo boat wreck
Depth	20–38m
Location	Near Žuljana on the Pelješac peninsula, 42°51'21"N, E 17°29'37"E
Difficulty	CMAS 2*, AOWD
Visibility	low in summer, better in winter
Dive centre	Blue Planet Diving Aquarius

effective and efficient developments under different circumstances. Instead of big and obvious, Germany went for small and fast. The resulting *schnellboote* (known as 'E-boats' in English) were less than 35m in length, with high sides and of lightweight construction (steel frame with a mahogany hull). Armed with torpedoes fired from two ports on either side of the bow, they were fast and deadly. They were also quick to make in only four months, aiding their proliferation.

The *Schnellboot-57* first saw service in October 1940 in the North Sea. She was transferred to duties in the Adriatic in early 1944. During the early morning of 19 August that year, she was engaged in a battle with British motor torpedo boats (MTBs). *S57* was hit and caught alight. Neither the crew nor those of her accompanying schnellboote could put out the fire. So having towed her in vain as far as the shores of Pelješac, her crew detonated an explosive in her hull, which broke her bottom, and she sank.

The *S57* is well-preserved. There is much to see from the outside through her metal frame, which is no longer cased in its wooden hull, having rotted early on. Of particular interest to most are her remaining torpedoes, anti-aircraft guns and the bridge control panel. Only three dive centres (page 67) have the permits to dive this site.

Further information on Schnellboote can be found at w bmpt.org.uk/boats/S130/index4.htm.

4 Sveti Andrija

Description	Steep cliff dive below the island's high lighthouse
Depth	3–80m
Location	Sveti Andrija island, near Dubrovnik, 42°38'08"N, 17°57'03"E
Difficulty	OWD
Visibility	excellent
Dive centre	Blue Planet Diving Aquarius

A number of Croatia's islands have lighthouses atop them. The one on Sveti Andrija was built in 1873. It presides over a particularly sharp cliff drop on the southwest side of the island and which continues into the sea for another 80m depth. This makes for one of the best and sheerest wall dives in all Croatia. The wall is a firework of colour and activity, although you'll need a torch at lower depths. Rare red gorgonian coral grows here, as well as Clavelina red sea potatoes and other Mediterranean sponges. With the greater depths available immediately below, the location is host to larger fish, such as greater amberjack, groupers and the odd ray. Closer to the wall are shoals of electric-blue baby damselfish in early summer and pink swallowtail sea perch. At 12m depth, a small cave in the wall makes for a convenient first decompression stop for those who have gone deep.

Other lighthouse-topped dives, which are even more spectacular but more difficult to access, are Sušac and Palagruža. Sušac is only 13 nautical miles from Lastovo but 19 nautical miles from the nearest harbour. Here an inland lake surrounded on all sides by high cliff walls can only be accessed underwater. Palagruža, at 37 nautical miles from Vis, is Croatia's southernmost land point. Although the Palagruža islands stand tall like towers, the water at their feet is a mere 10m, making them a warm harbour for an abundance of fish. The lighthouse here provides accommodation (w lighthouses-croatia.com). Diving these locations is an adventure for the journey there itself and, once there, their remote nature offers wildlife opportunities that are hard to find closer to the mainland coast. Arranging diving here is also difficult and expensive because of the long travel times. Try ISSA and B-24 for arrangements.

WINDSURFING

The Dalmatian coast has several locations ideal for windsurfing. With a bit of practice, surfing is fairly easy to master, regardless of age or fitness level. But you do need the right wind. For beginners, gentle winds of around 5–7 knots are best, while more experienced surfers will enjoy the challenge of gusts of up to 25 knots. In Dalmatia, you'll be dealing with three main types of wind on the Adriatic: the chilly dry *bura* (northeasterly), the warm damp *jugo* (southern) and the summer thermal mistral (which blows off the sea towards the land in the afternoon). Various companies offer surfing instruction and equipment rental – all you need to bring is swimwear, a towel and suncream. Expect to pay around €200 for a 6-hour beginner's course. Once you feel safe to go it alone, board rental costs €25–50 per hour, depending on the type of board and the destination. Note that besides windsurfing, kitesurfing is also growing in popularity here.

TOP FOUR WINDSURFING LOCATIONS IN DALMATIA

1 Bol On the south coast of Brač, Bol (page 176) is Croatia's top windsurfing destination, hosting various national and international championships. In summer, conditions are suitable for beginners in the morning, with a gentle eastern wind. During the afternoon, the mistral wind speeds up in the sea channel between Brač and Hvar, making the sea surface choppy with no swell, offering plenty of fun for experienced surfers.

2 Viganj On the Pelješac peninsula close to Orebić, Viganj (page 135) is another well-known surfing destination. Like Bol, it gives on to a sea channel (this time between Pelješac and Korčula), exposing it to the thermal mistral, which accelerates during the afternoon. Mornings are calmer, with steady wind and almost flat water.

3 Nin Close to Zadar, at Nin (page 200), the warm shallow Nin lagoon offers good conditions for both windsurfing and kitesurfing. In summer, expect a light-to-moderate mistral wind here. Occasionally, the bura also picks up, but it tends to be gustier and wilder in spring and autumn.

4 Neretva Delta Close to Ploče, halfway between Dubrovnik and Split, the Neretva Delta (page 129) also has ideal conditions for kitesurfing and kiteboarding. Each summer, warm shallow water and stable thermal winds, plus prices that are lower than other Dalmatian seaside destinations, attract an ever-increasing number of surfers.

SEA KAYAKING

Ideally for sea kayaking, you want several small islands grouped close together so you can paddle between them and explore their coasts and coves. Sea kayaking is easy to learn. Beginners might start in a double kayak led by a more experienced paddler. Various providers offer kayaking tours and rentals. Expect to pay around €50 for a 3-hour beginner's course and €60–80 per person for a half-day guided kayaking tour. If you want to paddle around independently, rental costs around €15 per hour for a single kayak or €25 for a double kayak. Bring a flask of water, swimwear, a hat, a towel and suncream. Everything else will be provided. Note that besides kayaking, SUPs (stand-up paddle boards) are very popular here.

TOP FOUR SEA KAYAKING LOCATIONS IN DALMATIA
1 Elaphiti islands Close to Dubrovnik, the tiny car-free Elaphiti (page 118) are much loved by sea kayakers. Various Dubrovnik-based providers, such as Outdoor Croatia (w outdoorcroatia.com), run guided tours around the crystal-clear waters of Koločep, Lopud and Šipan, with time for swimming and snorkelling included.

2 Pakleni islets Opposite Hvar Town on the island of Hvar, the pine-scented Pakleni islets (page 185) offer an escape from the crowds. Here you can explore rocky shores and hidden pebble coves with providers such as Hvar Sea Kayaking (w hvar-seakayaking.com), who arrange sunset tours.

3 Korčula archipelago Opposite Korčula Town (page 135) on the island of Korčula, the turquoise waters of these tiny islets are best explored by sea kayak. Contact Korčula Outdoor (w korcula-outdoor.com).

4 Zadar archipelago Close to Zadar (page 193), the small islands of Molat, Ist and Zverinac can be explored on multi-day kayaking tours with Malik Adventures (w malikadventures.com).

RAFTING AND CANYONING

Rafts used on rivers in Dalmatia are basically inflatable open rubber boats steered by oars. Organised group rafting trips normally see 6–8 passengers per raft, captained by an experienced skipper. Rafting here over gentle rapids is very safe and suitable for anyone from 8–80 years old, so long as they know how to swim. Bring swimwear, trainers and a towel – you'll be given a life jacket and helmet. Between spring and autumn, river temperatures are 14–19°C. Expect to pay around €35–50 per person for a half-day guided rafting trip.

Canyoning is an exhilarating experience, suitable for anyone over the age of 8. You'll be given a wetsuit, lifejacket and helmet. Following a guide, you will wade, scramble, jump and dive through rapids and swim through pools. Extreme canyoning involves the additional challenge of abseiling with ropes and, for this, the minimum age is 16.

TOP RAFTING AND CANYONING LOCATIONS IN DALMATIA

Cetina Canyon The source of the River Cetina lies in the foothills of the Dinaric Alps. Towards the end of its journey, the Cetina passes through a dramatic verdant rocky canyon over a series of waterfalls and rapids to meet the sea at Omiš (page 166) near Split. It is Dalmatia's top rafting destination. The most popular route runs 10km, beginning from the village of Zadvarje, in the deepest part of the canyon. Most adventure sports providers can arrange transport from Split (at an additional cost), and some also offer canoe safari, canyoning and extreme canyoning here.

Zrmanja Canyon Running down through a rocky canyon to Novigrad, close to Zadar, the emerald-green River Zrmanja (page 209) cascades towards the sea. Organised rafting trips usually run 12km from Kaštel Žegarksi to Muškovci. Most adventure sports providers can arrange transport from Zadar (additional cost), and some also offer canoe safari and canyoning here.

ROCK CLIMBING

Rock climbing (aka free climbing) is physically demanding and requires strength, agility and endurance. Climbers use their hands and feet to ascend steep cliffs, wearing harnesses and using ropes and pre-placed bolts. Meanwhile, a partner remains on the ground, also wearing a harness and holding the rope, so that if the climber slips, they will not fall far but will remain suspended.

Dalmatia's top location for rock climbing is the Velika Paklenica gorge in Paklenica National Park (page 202), with over 500 marked routes ranging in difficulty from Grade 3 to 9a. Paklenica's best-known rock face is Anića Kuk, which offers several routes of up to 350m, attracting climbers from all over the world.

You'll also find some good rock faces, complete with marked climbing routes, inside the Cetina Canyon near Omiš (page 166). This is a good option for beginners, with shorter routes of 10–30m high.

Expect to pay around €60 for a 2-hour climbing trip or €80 for a 3-hour trip in the company of an instructor. You'll be supplied with climbing shoes, a harness and a helmet. The minimum age stipulation varies from 8 to 12 years old.

74

Part Two

THE GUIDE

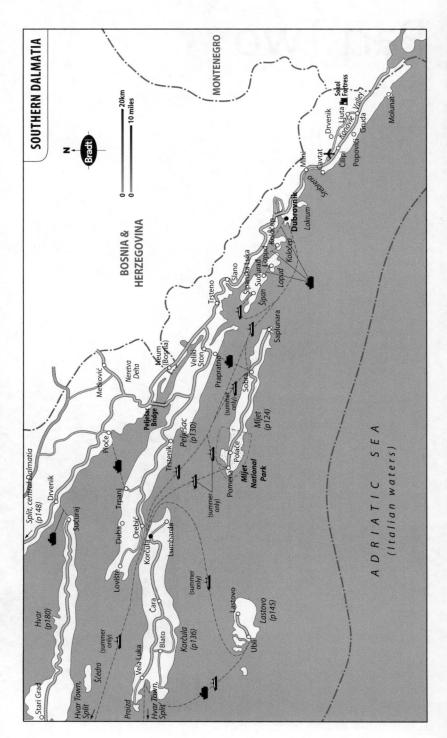

MONTENEGRO

Sokol
Fortress

Drvenik

Ljuta
Konavle
Valley

Čilipi
Popovići Gruda

Molunat

Mlini
Cavtat

Srebreno

BOSNIA &
HERZEGOVINA

Dubrovnik

Lokrum

Trsteno

Slano

Šipanska Luka

Sudurad
Šipan Lopud
Koločep

Lopud
Koločep

Metković

Neum
(Bosnia)

Nereva
Delta

Veliki
Ston

Prapratno

Saplunara

Ploče

Pelješac
Bridge

Trstenik

Pelješac (p130)

Sobra

(summer
only)

Mljet
(p124)

Drvenik

Trpanj

Dubo

Orebić

Pomena Polače

Mljet
National
Park

(summer
only)

Split, central Dalmatia
(p148)

Sučuraj

Lovište

Korčula

Lumbarda

(summer
only)

Hvar (p180)

Šćedro

Čara

Korčula (p136)

Lastovo

Lastovo (p145)

Stari Grad

Vela Luka

Blato

Proizd

Ubli

Hvar Town,
Split

Hvar Town,
Split

ADRIATIC SEA
(Italian waters)

SOUTHERN DALMATIA

N

Bradt

0   20km
0   10 miles

4

Dubrovnik and Southern Dalmatia

Telephone code 020 (+385 20 from abroad)

The biggest draw in southern Dalmatia is the extraordinary walled city of **Dubrovnik**, but the area is unusually rich in other sights as well, and – in spite of some of the Adriatic's cleanest waters – there are fewer resorts and package destinations on the islands here than further north. The islands range from the tiny car-free **Elaphiti (Koločep, Lopud** and **Šipan)** and the densely wooded and sparsely populated **Mljet** (one-third of which is a national park) to popular culture-rich **Korčula**, remote **Lastovo**, and Dubrovnik's own back garden, **Lokrum**. Onshore, there's the long, straggly wine-growing peninsula of **Pelješac**, with oyster-rich **Ston** at its base, while against the Bosnian border, you'll find the wetlands of the **Neretva Delta**.

DUBROVNIK

Dubrovnik is an extraordinary place. Vast walls, up to 25m high, come complete with fortresses, towers, crenellations and a guards' walkway along the entire 2km extent. The walls encircle an incredible stone-built, red-roofed city, which juts out into the clearest, cleanest blue-green waters of the Adriatic. The streets are paved with time-polished pale marble, with the town's harmony owing as much to the 17th-century rebuilding programme following the Great Earthquake in 1667 as it does to Dubrovnik's remarkable history, stretching back well over 1,000 years.

Of course, Byron's 'Pearl of the Adriatic' is no secret, with over 1 million tourist arrivals in 2023 (not counting nautical data), and even more coming in for the day on some 470 foreign cruise ships in the same year. Nevertheless, the city copes admirably with the influxes, and you'll find a place full of sedate cafés, bars and restaurants, wonderful architecture, intriguing museums, atmospheric churches and a world-famous summer festival. The entire old city is a UNESCO World Heritage Site.

As if that weren't enough, Dubrovnik is blessed with an especially kind climate. Winter daily maximums rarely fall below 12°C, the sun shines reliably right through the summer, and there are plenty of beaches, with swimming popular from May to October. The city even has its own perfect forested island, Lokrum, just a few hundred metres offshore.

HISTORY Although some Roman, Illyrian and early Christian remains have been found in Dubrovnik, it was only at the beginning of the 7th century that the area was permanently settled. Survivors from the Roman colony at Salona (near Split), which had been taken over by avaricious Avars, teamed up with the remnants of the colony at Epidaurus (now Cavtat), which had been ravaged by Slavs, and settled on the rocky outcrop which is now part of the old town south of Stradun. Doubtless scarred by their recent experiences, they started building fortifications right away – and kept on doing so until the 16th century. They called their town **Ragusa**, which first shows up in print in the year AD667.

Slavs, meanwhile, settled on the lower slopes of **Mount Srđ**, across the marshy channel that would become Stradun. Over the centuries, the populations mixed, the channel was filled in, and the city walls grew to encompass both parts of the settlement. But even today, there's a clear distinction between the steep narrow streets leading uphill from Stradun to the north and the palaces, churches and open squares that characterise the rest of the city to the south. To their dying day (which we'll get to in a little while), Ragusan patricians insisted they could trace their lineage back to Roman rather than Slav ancestors.

After switching between Byzantium and Venice and back again, and even throwing in its lot with the Normans on a couple of occasions at the end of the 11th century, Ragusa finally recognised that Venice was top dog in the Adriatic in 1205 and remained under Venetian sovereignty until 1358. It nonetheless kept its own currency and continued to develop its own institutions and culture.

Ragusa was also becoming a trading state of increasing importance, capitalising on its fortunate position between north and south and east and west. By the early 13th century, favourable trading agreements were in place with many of the Italian city-states and far inland into the Balkans. Over the years, it developed a strong seafaring tradition, with trade routes eventually established all the way to Spain, Portugal and England. Dubrovnik sailors were even on board Columbus's ships when they discovered the West Indies in 1492.

Back at home, the early 14th century saw a number of important developments. After a huge fire destroyed most of the city in 1296, a new urban plan was developed. Dominicans and Franciscans were allowed inside the city walls for the first time on condition that they defended the two main land gates at either end of Stradun – where you'll still find their respective monasteries and churches today.

WHAT'S IN A NAME?

For most of its extensive history – right from the 7th century through to 1918, in fact – Dubrovnik was known as Ragusa. The name was changed to Dubrovnik (according to Rebecca West, at least) only because Ragusa sounded too Italian by half.

The truth, as usual, is somewhat more complicated. Dubrovnik was originally not one place but two, divided by what's now the main street, Stradun. On the seaward side, which was originally almost an island, was Ragusa, populated by people of Roman origin. On the landward side, populated by Slavs, was Dubrovnik. Given that the nobles all came (or claimed to come) from Roman stock, Ragusa was the name which stuck – until the city was incorporated into the newly founded Kingdom of Serbs, Croats and Slovenes after World War I.

The name Ragusa is thought to be a corruption of the Greek word *lausa*, meaning rock, while the name Dubrovnik comes from the Croatian word for oak woods, *dubrava* – which were once plentiful on the hills above the town before being cut down and used to build Dubrovnik's impressive fleet of ships. (A fleet of ships that gave us another word, incidentally – argosy, a variant on the name Ragusa.)

The city's first hospital was inaugurated in 1347, but a seriously nasty dose of the plague all too quickly followed in 1348, which reduced the population by 8,000. Soon, however, Dubrovnik was ready for its '**Golden Age**', which began when it escaped Venice's grasp in 1358 by formally becoming part of the Hungarian–Croatian kingdom. In exchange for paying Hungary 500 ducats a year, however, and providing armed forces when called upon to do so, the republic was allowed to do pretty much whatever it liked.

The first thing it liked to do, it seemed, was to frogmarch the Venetian rector, Marco Saranzo, off on to his state galley, thereby kicking off the best part of 500 years of tension between the two republics – a situation only resolved when Napoleon dissolved La Serenissima in 1797.

In 1365, just seven years after sorting things out with Hungary, Dubrovnik signed a treaty with Sultan Murat I – again with a 500-ducat-per-year price tag – which allowed the republic free-trading status across the whole of the occupied territories of the Ottoman Empire. By monopolising large chunks of the trade to and from the interior, Dubrovnik became hugely wealthy. Dubrovnik had freedom, liberty and independence – but it was *Libertas* (the republic's long-standing motto) bought with gold.

With money came territory, and during the Golden Age Dubrovnik's lands stretched from the town of Neum to the north (now in Bosnia) all the way to Sutorina, on the Bay of Kotor, to the south (now in Montenegro), a distance of around 120km. It included the Elaphiti islands (Koločep, Lopud and Šipan), the islands of Mljet and Lastovo, and the Pelješac peninsula.

At the beginning of the 15th century, the remaining wooden houses in the town were demolished and rebuilt in stone. This was not so much for aesthetic reasons as to prevent fires from spreading. With many potential enemies, Dubrovnik had large stockpiles of munitions that had an unfortunate habit of going off – the Rector's Palace was destroyed by fire and explosions twice within a generation, in 1435 and again in 1463.

The 15th century also saw Dubrovnik flourishing as a haven of liberalism. It offered asylum to refugees, including Jews, at times when many other cities turned them away at the gate. In 1416, slavery was definitively abolished, over 400 years ahead of Britain (1833) and America (1863). Many slaves subsequently had their freedom bought for them by Ragusan nobles. A public health service was in place as early as 1432, while the principle of education for all was established three years later, along with one of Europe's first orphanages and a free retirement home for the poor and elderly (it's still running, but no longer free).

The republic's wealth was also put to good use in a major building programme. The city walls were reinforced and defensive fortresses and towers constructed along their length. Onofrio della Cava, a bright engineer and architect from Naples, spent the six years to 1444 putting in place a sophisticated water supply (including an 8km aqueduct), which still works today and powers the two Onofrio Fountains on Stradun. In 1468, Stradun itself was repaved with marble, and in 1516, work began on the Customs House (formerly called the Divona and now known as the Sponza Palace).

Tragically, an earthquake destroyed most of the city in 1520, and the plague returned in force in 1528, leaving 20,000 dead.

By the end of the 1520s, the Turks had pretty much defeated Hungary, and Dubrovnik was quick to change its allegiance from the Hungarian king to the Turkish sultan – now agreeing to pay an annual tribute of 12,500 ducats to keep the peace (that's inflation for you). The money was taken to the Sublime Porte every

RAGUSA'S POLITICAL SYSTEM

Ragusa's political system was a variant on that of its rival Venice, though it was somewhat more subtle and complex. The main governing body was the Great Council, which consisted of all the male nobles over the age of 20; their main function was to elect the head of state, the rector, and supervise the Senate. The Senate comprised 45 nobles over the age of 40, though it had a purely consultative mandate. From the Senate, five men over the age of 50 were given a one-year term by the Great Council as Proveditores, keepers of the legal statutes and the constitution.

Executive power was wielded by the Minor Council, which consisted of 11 nobles appointed by the rector, with the youngest taking on the role of Foreign Minister. The rector had a term of office of just one month, during which he lived alone in the Rector's Palace, separated from his family and the rest of society. He was only allowed to leave the palace on state business or to attend church, and couldn't be re-elected within two years. In spite of all these restrictions he was merely a figurehead, wielding no power.

The political system was designed to concentrate power into the hands of a trusted few – in the 15th century there were only 33 noble families – but to avoid any one person or family being able to dominate, and for centuries it worked remarkably effectively.

The class system was rigidly enforced. Inter-marriage between classes was forbidden and social relations between them strongly discouraged – though that doesn't seem to have been necessary, given the divisions even within classes. The nobles defined themselves as Salamancans or Sorbonnais, named after the respective Spanish and French universities, with the former sympathetic to Spanish Absolutism and the latter with a liberal Francophile outlook. Apparently hostility was such that members of the two factions couldn't even bring themselves to greet one another in the street.

two years by envoys who then had to spend the next two years waiting there as effective hostages until they were relieved by the next cash-laden delegation.

In 1588, Dubrovnik joined the Spanish in their '**Invincible Armada**' and lost a dozen of its finest ships. As a result, trade with Britain was interrupted for the best part of two centuries. The battle neatly marks the beginning of the long, slow decline of the republic. New trade routes across the Atlantic made Britain, Spain and Portugal into wealthy nations, and Mediterranean shipping was never to regain its former importance.

Real disaster didn't strike, however, until 08.00 on the morning of 6 April 1667, the Saturday before Easter, when a **massive earthquake** destroyed Dubrovnik. More than 5,000 people – including the rector, the entire Minor Council and more than half the Great Council – were killed. Only the Sponza Palace, the two monasteries, the bottom half of the Rector's Palace and the Revelin Fortress were left standing.

Seizing his opportunity, the Turkish sultan asked for a vast ransom to be paid if Dubrovnik wanted its freedom to continue as before. A delegation was sent in 1673 to the Porte to, well, 'talk turkey' with the Turks. Among the party were Nikola Bono and Marojica Koboga. Bono was to die in prison, but after the Turks were defeated at Vienna in 1683, Koboga came home to a hero's welcome. Dubrovnik had got away without paying the ransom and was still free. It consolidated its position in 1699 by letting the Turks have chunks of land at either end of its territories – which is why, today, Neum is in Bosnia not Croatia, and Sutorina is in Montenegro. This meant that potential attacks from Venice could now only come from the sea and not overland.

Although Dubrovnik would never regain its former glories, the massive programme of rebuilding which went on through the early 18th century was to deliver the harmonious city you see today. Things started to look up for the republic and, by the end of the 18th century, it had regained a considerable amount of its wealth and standing and even boasted some 80 consulates in various cities across the continent.

Unfortunately, however, Napoleon was on the horizon, and on 26 May 1806 – as the only way to break a month-long siege by Russian and Montenegrin forces – the republic allowed a French garrison to enter the town. (Even now, clocks in the city's museums are often set to 17.45, the hour at which the troops entered.) Once installed, the French didn't leave, and on 31 January 1808, the republic was finally abolished. The following year, it was absorbed into the newly created French 'Illyrian Provinces', which stretched all the way up the Adriatic coast to Trieste.

When Napoleon was defeated, Austria sent troops south and took control of Dubrovnik in 1814. Dubrovnik's noble families, in a terminal huff, took a vow of celibacy and swiftly died out. A century later, Dubrovnik became part of Yugoslavia, but when Yugoslavia fell apart, the city came under siege (page 88).

GETTING THERE AND AWAY With no train line, you'll most likely be arriving by plane, boat or bus, or in your own car.

By air Čilipi Airport (w airport-dubrovnik.hr) is about 20km southeast of town (see page 29 for flight details), and there's an airport shuttle (journey time depends enormously on traffic) that coincides with arriving flights (timetable at w platanus. hr/shuttle-bus). It returns to the airport from the Dubrovnik bus station around 2 hours before international departures, 90 minutes before domestic flights, and costs €10. Taxis are available outside Arrivals and cost around €45 – if the meter's off, make sure you've agreed and understood the fare with the driver before you set off.

By sea All **ferries and catamarans** come into the city's port, Gruž, which is about 500m south of the bus station, itself just over 2km north of the old town (catch a local bus, or walk). There are all-year local ferries to the nearby Elaphiti islands and Mljet (see individual islands for details) and, through summer, you also have fast catamarans up the coast to Split, stopping en route at Mljet, Korčula, Hvar and Brač. From spring through autumn, you also have a daytime ferry to Bari in Italy (7½hrs). There are also countless cruises featuring Dubrovnik; these too will bring you into Gruž harbour.

By bus Long-distance **buses** come straight to the bus station [84 C1] (Obala Ivana Pavla II 44a; ✆ 060 305 070; w autobusni-kolodvor-dubrovnik.com), past the port. If you're coming from the north, you'll have driven across the fabulous, modern suspension bridge over the Dubrovačka Rijeka inlet, which cuts a welcome 15km off the journey. From one side, you'll notice it labelled as the Tuđman Bridge, while from the other, it's the Dubrovnik Bridge – telling you something useful about local politics. Through winter, there are two direct buses a day from Sarajevo (in Bosnia & Herzegovina), three from Kotor (in Montenegro), six buses a day from Zagreb (9–10hrs), and eight from Split (4–5hrs). In summer, these services are slightly more frequent but become much more crowded and expensive, and reservations are highly recommended. The bus station has toilets, a café and a left-luggage facility (⏲ 06.30–22.00 daily).

By car   If you're coming in by **car**, be warned that parking in Dubrovnik can be both a problem and expensive. Hotel car parks tend to be overflowing, while street parking, especially in summer, is a non-starter. **Parking** operates in three zones (Zones 1 to 3, with Zone 1 being the closest to the old town), with automated payment possible through one of three corresponding phone numbers: Zone 1 ☎708 200; Zone 2 ☎708 202; Zone 3 ☎708 203 – simply send an SMS containing your vehicle's licence plate number (no spaces) to the number for the appropriate zone; you should receive a confirmation, valid for 1 hour (you'll need to send another SMS for each subsequent hour when the first one is up). Alternatively, you can buy a ticket from parking meters or nearby newspaper kiosks and display these behind your windscreen. The closest car park to the old town is on Iza Grada, alongside the north wall (Zone 1; €10/hr, €2.70 off season), though it will almost certainly be full. A better choice is the larger car park at Gruž harbour (Zone 3; €1.30/hr, €17.30/day). Probably the best option, however, is the huge 24-hour car park at Ilijina Glavica (Zagrebačka ulica; not part of the Zone 1 to 3 parking system; €3/hr, €30/day); there's a bus from there to the Pile Gate, or it's a 10-minute walk down a flight of steps through Baltazar Bogišić Park. More information on the Ilijina Glavica car park is available from Best in Parking (☎020 312 720; w bestinparking.com); for information on parking within Zones 1 to 3, contact the local parking authority (☎020 640 136).

If you park illegally, you can definitely expect your car to be towed away by the ruthlessly efficient 'Sanitat Dubrovnik' (☎020 640 136; w sanitat.hr) tow-away service. The number to call when this happens is ☎020 414 428, 24 hours a day, and the pound, where your car will have been taken, is on Liechtensteinov put, in Lapad. The nearest bus route is #9; take it to the terminus (the hospital) and walk round to the left to find the top end of Liechtensteineov put.

PELJEŠAC BRIDGE

Opened in July 2022, the long-awaited Pelješac Bridge connects Komarna on the mainland to Brijesta on the Pelješac peninsula, making the drive from Split to Dubrovnik quicker and much smoother. Before the opening of the bridge, Southern Dalmatia was cut off from the rest of Croatia by Bosnia & Herzegovina's land corridor to the sea at Neum, and travellers had to undergo passport control upon leaving and re-entering Croatia. When traffic was heavy, this led to long delays at both border crossings, and some travellers even had to obtain visas to pass through Bosnia & Herzegovina.

From Komarna, the spectacular new 2km-long cable-stayed bridge takes drivers to a 22km-stretch of road across Pelješac before returning to the mainland near Ston. The building of the new Ston bypass (opened in April 2023) involved the excavation of two road tunnels and the building of another small bridge over Ston Bay. The new Pelješac Bridge effectively shortens driving time from Split to Dubrovnik by about 1 hour. Eventually, the A1 motorway will run all the way from Zagreb to Dubrovnik, connecting Zadar, Šibenik and Split en route. With 130km of the southern section yet to be built, the estimated completion date is 2030. Pelješac Bridge will be integrated into the A1 route.

GETTING AROUND Flat-fare Libertas **buses** cover the whole of Dubrovnik, and most run from 05.00 to midnight (timetables for city and suburban routes at w libertasdubrovnik.hr). Tickets can be bought in advance from newspaper kiosks at €1.73 apiece or on the bus for €1.99 – and you'll be expected to have approximately the right change. You can also get a day ticket (*dnevna karta*) valid for 24 hours from first use for €5.30 – though the best value is just to get a **Dubrovnik Pass**, which allows free transport on local buses (page 86).

The main bus routes used by visitors are:

#1A and #1B	From Pile to the bus station and on to Gruž; about every half-hour.
#3	From Pile to Gruž; about once an hour.
#4	From Pile to Lapad, passing many of the main hotels and terminating at the Dubrovnik Palace; two to three times an hour.
#5	From Pile to the Lapad post office and on to the Hotel Neptun on Babin Kuk; about once an hour. The return route goes round the one-way system, arriving at the Ploče Gate and then going round behind the old town walls to Pile.
#6	From Pile to the bus station, then up to the Lapad post office, terminating at the Dubrovnik President Hotel on Babin Kuk; about four times an hour.
#7B	From Gruž to the bus station and then up towards Lapad, passing the Hotel Bellevue and the Lapad post office before terminating at the Dubrovnik President Hotel on Babin Kuk; about once an hour.
#8	From Pile to the bus station, then on to Gruž, where it goes into a one-way system, which ends by coming down the hill past the Ploče hotels to the Ploče Gate, and round behind the old town walls to Pile; two to three times an hour, but less frequently at weekends.
#9	From the bus station up to the Lapad post office and on to the hospital before taking a shorter return route to the bus station; about once an hour.
#10	From the bus station to Cavtat; about once an hour. The fare to Cavtat is €4 and you pay on the bus.

Notwithstanding the excellent local buses, Dubrovnik also has plenty of **taxis**, with stands at Pile, Ploče, Gruž, the bus station and Lapad (on Kralja Tomislava, just before the Lapad post office). You can also call taxis from any of the main hotels.

TOURIST INFORMATION The **tourist office** (w tzdubrovnik.hr) dishes out maps and various leaflets and can help you with booking concert tickets, etc. There's an office just outside the Pile Gate [92 B3] (Brsalje 5; ✆020 312 011; ⊕ 19.00 Mon–Sat, 10.00–16.00 Sun) and another at Gruž [84 D2] (Obala Ivana Pavla II br 1; ✆020 417 983; ⊕ 08.00–14.00 Mon–Sat), next door to the Jadrolinija ticket office.

You can also usually pick up maps and flyers from the various local tourist operators and agencies, though of late – particularly when a cruise ship arrives – they've taken to charging a token fee for maps.

🏠 **WHERE TO STAY** Dubrovnik has long been popular with visitors, with the first proper accommodation for them opening in 1347 and private rooms coming on-stream in the second half of the 14th century. The Grand Hotel Imperial, with 70 rooms just up from the Pile Gate, opened for business in 1897, but it was gutted by

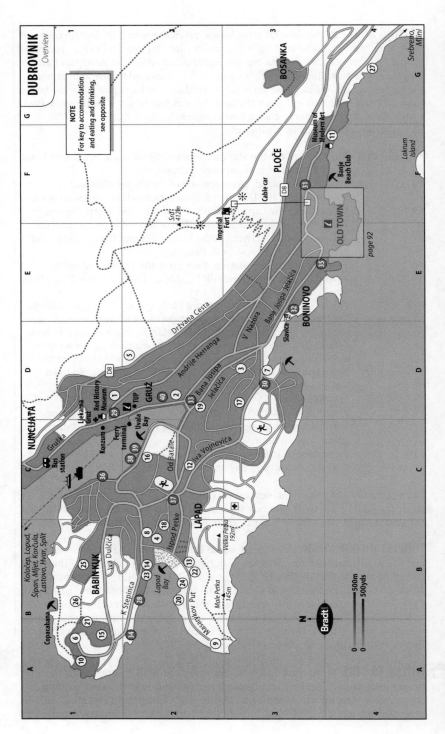

NOTE
For key to accommodation
and eating and drinking,
see opposite

BOSANKA

PLOČE

Museum of
Modern Art

Banje Beach Club

Cable car

D8

Srd
412m

Imperial
Fort

OLD TOWN

page 92

GRUŽ

NUNCIATA

Bus
station

Gruška

Ljekarna
Gruž

Red History
Museum

Konzum

Ferry
terminal

Uvala
Bay

Državna Cesta

Andrije Herranga

Bana Josipa
Jelačića

Bana Josipa Jelačića

V Nazora

Slavica

BONINOVO

Lokrum
Island

Srebreno,
Mlini

BABIN KUK

Copacabana

Koločep, Lopud,
Šipan, Mljet, Korčula,
Lastovo, Hvar, Split

Uva Dulčića

K Stepinca

Lapad
Bay

Iva Vojnovića

Od Bataile

Ispod Petke

LAPAD

Masarykov Put

Male Petke
145m

Velika Petka
192m

N
Bradt

0   500m
0   500yds

84

DUBROVNIK *Overview*
For listings, see from page 83

fire during the war in 1991. It reopened in 2005 as the Hilton Imperial, symbolic of a city once again ready for business.

During the siege of Dubrovnik (page 88), the city lost around half of its total hotel stock, with damage being caused first by bombs and then by refugees flooding in afterwards. The scene improved fast, however, with most of the affected hotels now restored and reopened.

Your main accommodation options in Dubrovnik are hotels or private rooms – of which there is a plentiful and growing supply. Private rooms offer the best value for money, but if you're in the mood to splash out, there's certainly plenty of choice at the top end of the market – in fact, Dubrovnik has Croatia's largest concentration of luxury five-star hotels, but a dearth of low-cost three-star options. If you're coming to Dubrovnik out of season, shop around for serious reductions at almost all the hotels listed here.

Hotel accommodation fills up fast in summer, so it's definitely recommended that you reserve well ahead of time and confirm by email.

In terms of location, Dubrovnik has just a handful of (rather costly) **boutique hotels** in the old town; the rest are distributed around the smart suburb of Ploče just south of the old town (these are Dubrovnik's most opulent historic hotels), while on the Lapad and Babin Kuk peninsulas, a few kilometres away, and in the port area of Gruž, you'll find slightly less expensive options built from the 1960s onwards. A slightly less expensive and quieter alternative, with better beaches but less culture, would be to stay in Srebreno or Mlini, en route to Cavtat (page 114).

Most of Dubrovnik's accommodation is spread out around the **Lapad and Babin Kuk peninsulas** and mainly caters to package tours. It has the advantage of being away from the bustle, and most of the hotels have access to a beach, but you may find yourself further away from the old town than you wish to be. That said, it's only a matter of 5km from the furthest point on Lapad to the old town – it's a pleasant walk, and there are regular buses (page 83). By taxi, you're looking at a 10–20-minute ride, depending on the hotel location and traffic density.

Dubrovnik and Southern Dalmatia **DUBROVNIK**

4

Until recently, accommodation in the **old town** itself was limited to private rooms, but this is gradually changing as new boutique hotels open up for business. Bear in mind if you stay here that it can be noisy and stifling hot in summer, and views will be minimal – but on the other hand, there's atmosphere in spades to be had from being inside the old walls.

If you can afford it, there's a lot to be said for staying in **Ploče**. The hotels overlook the sea and the island of Lokrum and have that view of Dubrovnik's old town walls and port. Seen in the light of early morning or late evening, it's a prospect to die for.

Dubrovnik has a huge supply of **private rooms** (page 46) available, and although they're more expensive here than most places in Croatia, they're still a good deal cheaper than the hotels, with most private double rooms going for around €60–90 a night, even in summer. Private rooms can be booked on the fly, though those in the best locations fill up well in advance. If you are travelling alone, several **hostels** (page 91) do provide reasonable budget accommodation in and around the old town.

Dubrovnik also has a solitary **campsite** (page 91).

Hotels
Old town

Hilton Imperial Dubrovnik [92 A2] (147 rooms) Marijana Blažića 2; ☏ 020 320 320; w hilton.com. It may not technically be in the old town, but it is right by the Pile Gate & offers jaw-dropping views of Dubrovnik's voluminous walls, the shimmering Adriatic & the towering hulk of Lovrijenac. The Hilton renovated this grand old dame in 2018 & she looks every bit as good, if not better, than she did when she first opened back in 1897. Be sure to book a room with a sea-view; some of the rooms & suites on the higher floors have balconies that you could throw a wedding reception on. There's a lovely terrace restaurant & lounge bar in the garden, & facilities include a swimming pool & gym. An executive room is worth the extra as you can take b/fast & enjoy complimentary snacks & drinks, both alcoholic &

non-alcoholic, throughout the day in the lounge that also boasts a terrace overlooking the old city. €€€€€

Hotel Stari Grad [92 D3] (11 rooms, 3 suites) Od Sigurate 4; ☏ 020 322 244; w hotelstarigrad. com. The 4-star Stari Grad (meaning 'old town') is situated between Stradun & Prijeko, only a couple of alleys in from the Pile Gate. What started out as an 8-room boutique hotel in a renovated 16th-century house now has 6 additional rooms in a nearby annexe, a small spa doing Thai massage, & a motorboat for private trips to the islands. You won't have any kind of view from your room (Od Sigurate is a narrow alley), but there is a rather special tiny 5th-floor terrace restaurant affording spectacular views across the rooftops, where you can dine in summer. €€€€€

Pucić Palace [93 E5] (17 rooms, 2 suites) Od Puća 1; ☏ 020 326 222; w thepucicpalace.com.

Fabulously located on the corner of Gundulićeva poljana, the heart of the action in the old city, the 5-star Pucić Palace is situated in a noble's luxuriously refurbished 17th-century home. Rooms are furnished with antiques, & there are 2 restaurants, Lucijan, with tables out front (year-through), & Magdalena, hidden on a 1st-floor terrace (summer-only). Maybe best of all is the Ivan Gundulić junior suite – though it's not the quietest, as it has a balcony overlooking the square, which hosts both the early-morning market & the late-night revelry spilling out from the back door of the Troubadour (page 97). As you'd expect, it's not cheap, with dbls going for well over €500 in summer. €€€€€

St Joseph's [92 C4] (6 suites, 3 rooms) Sv Josipa 3; ☎020 432 089; w stjosephs.hr. Boutique luxury hotel with exposed stone walls & neo-Baroque furnishing in a restored 16th-century property at the heart of the old town. In the main building, there are 6 stately suites, complete with discrete kitchenettes & plush white marble bathrooms. As of 2021, there are 3 additional rooms (slightly less expensive) in St Joseph's Cottage across the street, plus a small guests-only kitchen-restaurant. €€€€€

The Byron [93 F6] (7 rooms) Pobijana 4; ☎020 689 597; w thebyrondubrovnik.com. Opened as a gorgeous 4-room boutique hotel in a carefully restored 17th-century stone building near the cathedral in 2018, as of summer 2024, The Byron will have 3 additional rooms (on the 1st floor). Expect light & airy rooms with wooden beamed ceilings, cool white décor & carefully concealed Culshaw kitchenettes. You'll also get a warm welcome & highly personalised service from the Croatian-Canadian couple who manage it. €€€€€–€€€€

Ploče

Hotel Excelsior [84 F4] (158 rooms) Frana Supila 12; ☎020 353 000; w adriaticluxuryhotels.com. For years after 1991, the 5-star Excelsior enjoyed an uninterrupted reign as Dubrovnik's finest hotel. It may now have a string of competitors, but it has managed to raise its game with a 2017 renovation, & no-one can beat its views of the old town across the water. Just a 5min walk uphill from the Ploče Gate, the Excelsior consists of a stone 1920s building & a largish glass & concrete annexe. It's unashamedly luxurious, with a stone-paved

bathing area affording easy access to the sea, a fitness centre, & a great big indoor swimming pool with 2 jacuzzis. There are 3 restaurants, the nicest being Prora, serving fresh fish on an arched waterside terrace. Front rooms have spectacular sea-views. If you really want to splash out, try 1 of the lavish suites – the corner suites have magnificent views of the old town through mirrored glass in the bathrooms – as well as from the generous balconies. €€€€€

Villa Dubrovnik [84 G4] (56 rooms) Vlaha Bukovca 6; ☎020 500 300; w villa-dubrovnik. hr. Walk 15mins from Ploče Gate southeast along the coast beyond the Excelsior to reach the Villa Dubrovnik, completely renovated in 2009–10. Walk down about 60 steps to get to reception, & you'll find the rest of the hotel below in terraces, dropping down to the rocky shoreline. The public areas are tastefully modern, light & airy, with white linen furnishings & rattan furniture, & the dining room & bar (& all the rooms) have gorgeous views back to the old town. In general, the amenities are excellent (all rooms have sea-views & balconies), & it has its own rocky beaches & a boat to take you into the old town, as well as a lovely outdoor area called the Al Fresco Bar Giardino, which is a perfect place for a pre-dinner drink. €€€€€

Lapad and Babin Kuk

Hotel Bellevue [84 D3] (91 rooms) Pera Čingrije 7; ☎020 330 000; w adriaticluxuryhotels.com. The 5-star Bellevue has long enjoyed 1 of the best locations in Dubrovnik, just 15mins from Pile Gate on a clifftop overlooking a sheltered bay with a beach &, fully refurbished in 2019, is now 1 of the city's finest hotels. Portuguese designer Tereza Prego has given guest rooms a cool, summery Mediterranean look with wooden floors, stylish furnishing & earthy-coloured fabrics. As well as 2 bars (1 offering wine-tasting flights with a sommelier) & 2 restaurants, the hotel boasts a presidential suite. €€€€€

Hotel Dubrovnik Palace [84 A2] (308 rooms) Masarykov put 20; ☎020 430 000; w adriaticluxuryhotels.com. This 1st-rate hotel has to be the classiest place to stay on Lapad. Situated right at the end of the Lapad headland, Dubrovnik's biggest hotel dates from 1972 – its most recent renovation took place in 2014, giving it cool contemporary interiors hung with modern

In October 1991, with the war in full flow, the Yugoslav army laid siege to Dubrovnik, shutting off the water and electricity supplies and raining shells down into the heart of the old town from air, land and sea.

The quick capitulation the Serbs expected never happened, mainly because of determined resistance, but at least in part because Onofrio's fountains – supplied by 15th-century plumbing – continued to function throughout the siege. Nevertheless, for three months there was no water for anything other than drinking and no electricity or telephone service at all.

More than 100 civilians lost their lives in Dubrovnik, either when their houses were bombed or by snipers up in the hills, looking straight down Stradun – people simply didn't believe they were going to be shot in the sunny streets of Dubrovnik's old town. On one day alone (6 December 1991), the Serbs shelled the city from 05.00 to 16.10 with only a 15-minute break. In all, the siege lasted from October 1991 to August 1992, though a ceasefire of sorts was in force at the beginning of 1992.

The material damage caused was enormous, with 70% of the old town's 800 houses sustaining direct hits and more than 50 shells landing on Stradun alone. Many churches and monuments were targeted in spite of being clearly marked with UNESCO flags.

Dubrovnik's newly refurbished airport was completely destroyed, with the brand-new equipment being looted and taken back to Montenegro and on to Belgrade. Many people moved out, and not all have moved back – the old town's population, at 4,000, is still around 20% less than it was in 1990.

The damage sustained to Dubrovnik's reputation as a holiday destination was incomparably worse, and it took a full decade to bring back just half the visitors.

Yet Dubrovnik has made a truly heroic recovery from the war. Today, beyond a few pockmarked buildings and acres of new tiles on the roofs, you'd never know there had been a terrible siege just two decades ago. (Ironically, some of the old tiles pulled off roofs during renovations were sent to villages further north to repair war damage there – only to be caught in the 1996 earthquake, which destroyed much of Slano and Ston at the base of the Pelješac peninsula.)

The only real reminder that the war happened at all – beyond the psychological scars – are the multilingual signs at each entrance to the old town, showing the 'City Map of Damages caused by the aggression on Dubrovnik by the Yugoslav Army, Serbs and Montenegrins, 1991–1992'.

artworks by noted Croatian artists – look out for bold paintings by Edo Murtić & huge tapestry wall-hangings by Jagoda Buić. The 10-floor complex boasts 3 outdoor swimming pools, a choice of rocky beaches & a PADI diving centre, along with 4 restaurants & 2 bars. Every room has a balcony & a sea-view looking out towards the Elaphiti islands, & behind the hotel are lovely paths up into the woods leading to stone belvederes with views out to sea. The hotel is also home to a lavish top-floor health spa, with a big indoor sea-view pool, jacuzzi & sauna, plus a choice of lush face & body treatments, & massages. Bus #4, which leaves from just outside the Pile Gate, takes you to the hotel. €€€€€

Hotel Dubrovnik President Valamar [84 A1] (292 rooms) Iva Dulčića 142; ☎ 020 441 100; w valamar.com. In a similar vein to the Dubrovnik Palace is the 5-star Dubrovnik President Valamar, which dominates the Babin Kuk headland. All rooms have a balcony & a view out across the sea to the Elaphiti islands, & there's a fairly large beach area with a scuba-diving club. It's unashamed upmarket package-tour territory, but the location is excellent & the atmosphere cheerful. It stays open through winter, catering for conferences & events. €€€€€

Hotel Kompas [84 B2] (173 rooms) Kardinala Stepinca 21; ☎020 299 000; w adriaticluxuryhotels.com. Right down by the attractive Lapad Bay beach, which marks the meeting point of the Lapad & Babin Kuk peninsulas, is the 4-star Kompas, reopened in 2015 following total reconstruction. Its minimalist all-white rooms mostly have sea-views, & it has a spa & outdoor sea-view pool. It is under the same management (ALH) as the smart Excelsior, Bellevue & Dubrovnik Palace hotels. €€€€€

Grand Hotel Park [84 B2] (244 rooms) Mata Vodapića 2; ☎020 434 444; w grandhotel-park. hr. Situated between the Kompas & the Komodor, & set back from **Lapad Bay's** beach, is the boxy 4-star Grand Hotel Park. It has a spa with saunas & an indoor pool, plus 2 bigger outdoor sea-water pools with rows of sun beds. Make sure you go for a room in the main building, ideally with a sea-view; those in the annexe are in need of refurbishment. €€€€

Hotel Argosy Valamar [84 A1] (308 rooms) Iva Dulčića 140; ☎020 446 100; w valamar.com. Nearby the Hotel Dubrovnik President Valamar is the 4-star Valamar Argosy. Reopened as an adults-only hotel following renovation in 2018, it has stylish contemporary interiors, a spa, & a lush garden with 2 sea-view infinity pools, as well as access to a beach & tennis courts. There's a big buffet restaurant with a sea-view terrace, but no à la carte. €€€€

Hotel Dubrovnik [84 B2] (22 rooms, 4 suites) Šetalište Kralja Zvonimira 16; ☎020 435 030; w hoteldubrovnik.hr. A nice option is the 3-star Hotel Dubrovnik (not to be confused with the Villa Dubrovnik, the Dubrovnik Palace or the Dubrovnik President) on the pedestrian promenade leading down to Lapad Bay. It has a café-restaurant with outdoor tables, clean, well-appointed rooms, including 4 suites at reasonable rates, & welcoming staff. €€€€

Hotel Komodor [84 B2] (113 rooms) Masarykov put 3E; ☎433 633; w hotelimaestral.com. Across the bay from the Kompas is 1 of the peninsula's

oldest hotels, the 3-star Komodor, dating from 1934 – the 1st in a line of 5 establishments along Masarykov put run by the Maestral hotel chain. €€€€

Hotel Lacroma Valamar [84 A1] (401 rooms) Iva Dulčića 34; ☎020 449 100; w valamar.com. Reopened after renovation in 2018, the 4-star Lacroma stands on Babin Kuk. It is set in grounds with palms, olive trees & a big outdoor pool, & has a spa with an indoor pool. Families have the use of the vast Maro World kids club, opened nearby in 2023. €€€€

Hotel Lapad [84 C2] (163 rooms) Lapadska obala 37; ☎020 455 555; w hotel-lapad.hr. Situated on the Lapad peninsula, facing Gruž harbour, is the Hotel Lapad, which is based around a renovated old building from 1913 with a modern annexe. There's a small outdoor pool in the garden, & the nearest beach is about 600m up the shore. They do (a rather mediocre) buffet b/fast & dinner, & there's an all-day piano bar. €€€€

Hotel Lero [84 D3] (160 rooms) Iva Vojnovića 14; ☎020 341 333; w hotel-lero.hr. Although renovated in 2018, the 4-star Lero still retains something of its 1971 feel – & its location on a busy main road may put some people off. But it's only 15 or 20mins' walk from the Pile Gate, on a bus route, 200m from the nearest beach, & half of the rooms have sea-views. Facilities include an outdoor pool, a piano bar, & 2 restaurants, 1 of which is the Taj Mahal's sister restaurant offering Bosnian cuisine. €€€€

Hotel Splendid [84 B2] (59 rooms) Masarykov put 6; ☎020 433 633; w hotelimaestral.com. Last of the bunch on this street is the 3-star Splendid, which, like the Vis, is right on the beach, a rock-&-pebble affair with sun beds & a beach bar, overlooked by the lovely raised terrace of the hotel's bar-restaurant. €€€€

Hotel Tirena Valamar [84 A1] (308 rooms) Iva Dulčića 36; ☎020 445 100; w valamar.com. The 4-star Tirena Valamar reopened in 2023 following renovation with newly designed rooms & restaurants, an outdoor pool with slides, & the use of the nearby Maro World, an extensive kids club with excellent facilities. It is located on Babin Kuk, between the Argosy Valamar & the Valamar Club Dubrovnik Sunny Hotel, & therefore also within reach of Copacabana beach. €€€€

Hotel Uvala [84 B2] (51 rooms) Masarykov put 5A; ☎020 433 633; w hotelimaestral.com. Opened in 2003, the 4-star Uvala has a Wellness & Spa offering massage, & face & body treatments, & a restaurant doing buffet dining, as well as à la carte Mediterranean fare at lunch & dinner. Guest rooms are spacious & modern, all have balconies, & most have sea-views. €€€€

Hotel Villa Wolff [84 B2] (6 rooms) Nika i Meda Pučića 1; ☎020 438 710; w villa-wolff.hr. Right next door to the Kompas is the 4-star Hotel Villa Wolff. You wouldn't know it walking up the short flight of steep steps from the coastal path (next door to the hotel's waterside Casa Restaurant), but above you is a charming (but slightly dated) boutique hotel, with just 3 dbls, 1 junior suite, 2 suites with balconies & sea-views. It has its own terrace & Mediterranean garden, complete with rosemary bushes, palms, cypresses & ancient olive trees, with a great view across the bay. €€€€

Valamar Club Dubrovnik Sunny Hotel [84 B1] (338 rooms) Iva Dulčića 38; ☎020 447 100; w valamar.com. Further into the Babin Kuk headland & facing the islet of Daksa. Good 3-star family choice, with a big freeform outdoor pool with slides, & the use of the nearby Maro World kids club, providing games, activities & an adrenaline zone with trampolines. It's just 5mins' walk from 1 of Dubrovnik's most popular beaches, the Copacabana, offering water skiing & banana rides. €€€€

Hotel Vis [84 B2] (152 rooms) Masarykov put 2; ☎020 433 633; w hotelimaestral.com. Over on the seaward side of Masarykov is the 3-star Hotel Vis, whose main attraction is being right on a decent-sized pebble beach. Like the Adriatic, it's very often full up. All rooms (comfortable but rather dated) have balconies & either a sea-view or park-view. €€€€

Hotel Ivka [84 C2] (76 rooms) Ulica od Sv Mihajla 21; ☎020 362 600; w hotel-ivka.com. Small, decent value 3-star family-run place on Lapad. Built in 2005, it has sgl, dbl & trpl rooms, most with balconies, & a restaurant doing buffet b/fast & dinner. €€€

Hotel Perla [84 B2] (20 rooms) Šetalište krajla Zvonimira 20; ☎020 438 244; w hotelperladubrovnik.com. On the pedestrian walkway leading down to Lapad Bay, making it ideal for the beach, the 3-star Perla has a ground-floor terrace restaurant & a gym. €€€

Gruž

Berkeley Hotel & Spa [84 D1] (25 rooms & suites) Andrije Hebranga 116a; ☎020 494 160; w berkeleyhotel.hr. Nice, good-value – & very popular – hotel in Gruž, run by a welcoming Croatian-Australian family. Facilities include a heated outdoor pool with jacuzzi & a spa doing massage, sauna, face & body treatments, & manicures. There's no restaurant, but they do a decent b/fast. €€€€

Hotel Adria [84 D2] (118 rooms) Radnička 46; ☎020 220 500; w hotel-adria-dubrovnik.com. On a hillside high above Gruž port, with sunset views over the bay, the 4-star Adria has a restaurant serving buffet b/fast & dinner, & an all-day bar doing light lunches. It lies 2km from Dubrovnik old town. €€€€

Hotel Porto [84 D2] (36 rooms) Hrvatskog crvenog križa 2; m 098 969 7329; w hotelporto.hr. Opened in summer 2021, this newly built hotel stands in Gruž, 10mins' walk from the ferry port & 20mins' walk to the old town. Rooms are modern & comfortable. They serve à la carte b/fast till noon & there's an all-day bar doing snacks. €€€€

Bokun Guesthouse [84 D2] (8 rooms, 3 apartments) Obala Stjepana Radića 7; m 098 969 7329; w bokun-guesthouse.com. Family-run B&B in an old stone cottage, set in a lush walled garden with a pool & barbecue, close to Gruž port. Reasonably priced, but 4 nights min stay in peak season. €€€

Private rooms and apartments

Amoret apartments [93 E5] (19 apartments) Dinka Ranjine 1; m 095 199 9025; w dubrovnik-amoret.com. Amoret started out with 15 cosy self-catering apartments, furnished with antiques & sleeping 2 persons, at 4 locations in the old town. They have now expanded to add 4 more larger apartments at 2 additional locations. €€€

✴ **Van Bloemen apartments** [93 G5] (4 apartments) Bandureva 1; ☎020 323 433 w vanbloemen.com. Formerly known as Karmen apartments but still owned & run by the welcoming Van Bloemen family (who moved here from London in the 1970s), this has to be the most outstanding hideaway in the old town. The apartments, complete with kitchenettes & quirky bohemian artworks, are situated in an ancient stone building in a stunning location right on the old port. They're not cheap – but they're charming,

great value & perfectly located. There is a 20% surcharge for stays of under 3 nights. Nearby, Gianni's ice cream parlour is run by the family's son – ideal for morning coffee & a cake, or a delicious artisan ice cream. €€€
Villa Sigurata [92 C4] (16 rooms) Stulina 4; m 091 572 7181; w villasigurata.com. At 2 separate locations in the old town, Villa Sigurata manage 16 basic but comfortable rooms, including dbls, twins, trpls & 1 sgl. €€€

Hostels
Dubrovnik Old Town Hostel [92 C3] Od Sigurate 7; ☏ 020 322 007; w dubrovnikoldtownhostel. com; ⊕ Mar–Nov. With a total of 22 beds in 4- & 6-bed dorms plus some dbls & 1 sgl. There's a small common room & kitchen – you'll find it in a side alley off the Stradun. €€
Dubrovnik Youth Hostel [84 D3] Vinka Sagrestana 3; ☏ 020 423 241; w hicroatia.com; ⊕ Mar–Nov. Dubrovnik's youth hostel is in a pretty good location, about 20mins uphill from

the bus station, just off Bana Jelačića, & for sgl people on a budget it's as cheap as you'll find in Dubrovnik. 1 dbl, 14 quad & 4 6-bed dorms. €€
Hostel Angelina [92 D2] Plovani skalini 17A; m 091 893 9089; w hostelangelinaoldtowndubrovnik.com; ⊕ Mar–Nov. With rooms & dorms at various locations in the old town, Hostel Angelina offers 12-, 8- & 4-bed dorms, as well as private dbls. €€

Camping
Solitudo Sunny Camping [84 B1] Vatroslava Lisinskog 60; ☏ 020 465 500; w valamar.com. This campsite, close to Copacabana beach on the Babin Kuk Peninsula, 6km from Dubrovnik's old town, is managed by Valamar & offers 300 pitches, newly refurbished bathrooms & laundry areas, & rates start from €38 per pitch. It also has mobile homes, an outdoor pool, a playground, & the Solitudo Beer & Grill all-day restaurant. €€

✖ **WHERE TO EAT AND DRINK** As you'd expect, Dubrovnik is brimming with places to eat, though with a few exceptions there's often surprisingly little to distinguish one place from another. Food in the old town tends universally towards grilled fish, meat and shellfish at the upper end of the spectrum, and pizza and pasta dishes in the mid-tier establishments.

Dubrovnik's busiest **restaurant** district is inside the walls along Prijeko, the street running parallel to Stradun on the landward side for its entire length. Unfortunately, it's managed to get itself something of a bad reputation over the years, which hasn't been helped by the touts along Stradun trying to entice passing trade. While there's no doubt good food to be had, there's a level of unscrupulousness here that probably comes from knowing the chances are you won't be coming back, and tales of poor-quality food and routine overcharging are legion. It's also worth noting that prices

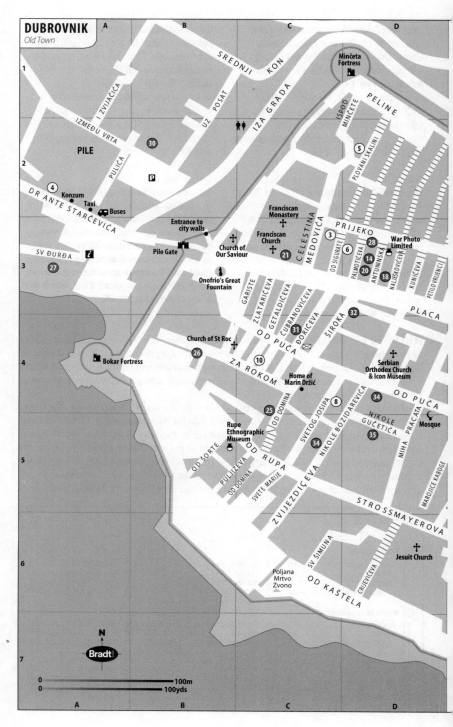

DUBROVNIK
Old Town

SREDNJI KON

Minčeta Fortress

IZA GRADA

UZ POSAT

PELINE

PILE

ISPOD MINČETE

30

PLOVANI SKALINI

IZMEĐU VRTA

5

PULICA

P

Konzum

4

Taxi

DR ANTE STARČEVIĆA

Buses

Franciscan Monastery

PRIJEKO

Entrance to city walls

Franciscan Church

CELESTINA MEDOVIĆA

War Photo Limited

SV ĐURĐA

Pile Gate

Church of Our Saviour

3

6

28

21

OD SIGURATE

PALMOTIĆEVA

14

20

ANTUNINSKA

18

MALJUŠKOVIĆEVA

KUNIĆEVA

PETILOVRIJENCI

27

Onofrio's Great Fountain

GARIŠTE

ZLATARIĆEVA

GETALDIĆEVA

ČUBRANOVIĆEVA

ĐORĐIĆEVA

PLAČA

32

31

ŠIROKA

Church of St Roc

OD PUČA

26

ZA ROKOM

10

Serbian Orthodox Church & Icon Museum

Bokar Fortress

Home of Marin Držić

8

OD PUČA

Rupe Ethnographic Museum

25

OD DOMINA

SVETOG JOSIPA

34

NIKOLE BOZIDAREVIĆA

NIKOLE GUČETIĆA

35

MIHA PRACATA

Mosque

OD SORTE

OD RUPA

PULJIZEVA

OD DOMINA

SVETE MARIJE

ZVIJEZDIĆEVA

STROSSMAYEROVA

MAROJICE KABOGE

Poljana Mrtvo Zvono

SV SIMUNA

OD KAŠTELA

CRIJEVIĆEVA

Jesuit Church

N

Bradt

0   100m
0   100yds

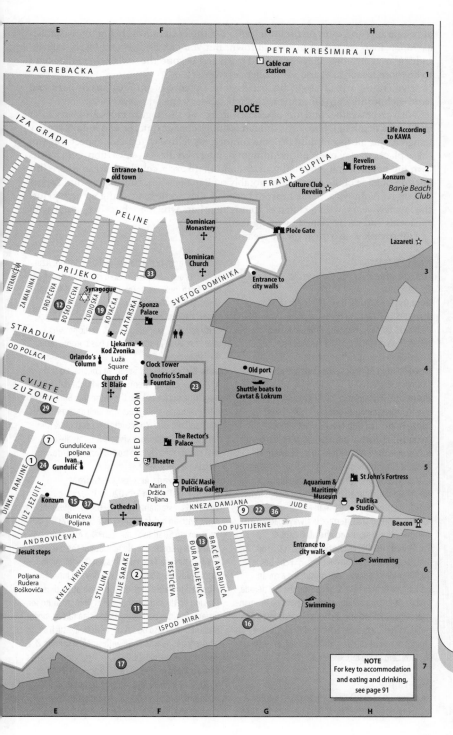

PETRA KREŠIMIRA IV

ZAGREBAČKA

Cable car station

PLOČE

IZA GRADA

Life According to KAWA

Entrance to old town

FRANA SUPILA

Revelin Fortress

Konzum

Culture Club Revelin ☆

Banje Beach Club

PELINE

Dominican Monastery

Ploče Gate

Lazareti ☆

VETRANIĆEVA

ZAMANJINA

DROPČEVA

PRIJEKO

33

BOŠKOVIĆEVA

ŽUDIOSKA

Synagogue

12

19

KOVAČKA

ZLATARSKA

Sponza Palace

SVETOG DOMINIKA

Dominican Church

Entrance to city walls

STRADUN

OD POLACA

Ljekarna Kod Zvonika

CVIJETE ZUZORIĆ

Orlando's Column

Luža Square

Clock Tower

Old port

29

Church of St Blaise

Onofrio's Small Fountain

23

Shuttle boats to Cavtat & Lokrum

7

Gundulićeva poljana

PRED DVOROM

The Rector's Palace

1

24

Ivan Gundulić

Theatre

DINKA RANJINE

UZ JEZUITE

Konzum

15

37

Marin Držića Poljana

Dulčić Masle Pulitika Gallery

Aquarium & Maritime Museum

St John's Fortress

5

Pulitika Studio

Bunićeva Poljana

Cathedral

KNEZA DAMJANA

9

22

36

JUDE

Beacon ☆

ANDROVIČEVA

Treasury

OD PUSTIJERNE

Jesuit steps

KNEZA HRVASA

STULINA

ILIJE SARAKE

2

RESTIĆEVA

ĐURA BALJEVIĆA

13

BRAĆE ANDRIJIĆA

Entrance to city walls

Swimming

6

Poljana Rudera Boškovića

11

ISPOD MIRA

16

Swimming

17

NOTE
For key to accommodation and eating and drinking, see page 91

7

at restaurants and cafés on Stradun itself are usually significantly higher – as much as 50% – than elsewhere in the old town. But you can find several lovely eateries hidden away in stone alleys in the old town and beyond the walls, where they tend to be more reasonable, and some offer sea-views, too.

If you're on a really tight budget there are plenty of **buffets, snack bars and sandwich joints** in town, some with a few tables, some take-away only.

With great weather and lots of visitors, there's no shortage of **cafés and bars** to sit and have a drink in Dubrovnik, though fashions change quickly, and today's groovy hangout can all too rapidly become tomorrow's leftover. You can expect most of these places to stay open until midnight or later. Needless to say, Dubrovnik has its own life beyond that aimed at tourists, and there are a couple of areas where this goes on outside of the town walls, notably on Bana Jelačića, running up into Lapad, and on Iva Vojnovića, in the heart of Lapad. A new scene has sprung up here in just the last few years, with a clutch of trendy new bars which are hugely popular with the locals and rarely visited by foreigners.

Dubrovnik is also great for ice cream.

Restaurants
Inside the old town walls
Expensive
Bota Oyster & Sushi Bar [93 F6] Đura Baglivija 1; m 095 197 7844; w bota-sare.hr; ⊕ May–Oct 15.00–23.00 daily. Near the cathedral, Bota serves fresh oysters from the family oyster beds in Mali Ston Bay, as well as sublime sushi dishes based on fresh Adriatic seafood, notably tuna & shrimp. €€€€€

Proto [92 D3] Široka 1; 020 323 234; w esculaprestaurants.com; ⊕ 11.00–23.00 daily. Proto is 1 of Dubrovnik's most famous landmarks & makes a big deal about having been in business since 1886 & having had Edward VIII & Wallis Simpson to dinner in the 1930s. In spite of the hype there's still a lot to be said for both the traditional Dalmatian fish & meat dishes here, which are probably better than anywhere else in town – & the upstairs terrace is always packed in summer. Worth reserving ahead. €€€€€

Taj Mahal [92 D5] Nikole Gučetica 2; 020 640 123; w tajmahal-dubrovnik.com; ⊕ Feb–Dec 10.00–midnight daily. Once considered a cheap option, prices here have shot up over the last decade. In spite of the misleading name, it serves up Bosnian specialities (not Indian), including Turkish-inspired grilled meats, casseroles & filo-pastry pies, to the sounds of *sevdah* music. It also has a sister restaurant in Hotel Lero (page 89). €€€€€

Mid-range
✳ **Azur** [93 F6] Pobijana 10; 020 324 806; w azurvision.com; ⊕ Mar–Oct noon–22.00 daily.

A change from perennial Dalmatian seafood, Azur serves its own unique CroAsian cuisine, a fusion of local fresh ingredients (mainly seafood) & fragrant Oriental herbs & spices. Informal & fun, you can expect exquisite dishes such as monkfish in black curry sauce, & Szechuan chilli & garlic prawns. Be sure to reserve in advance as it has become rather well known. €€€€

Bura Bistro [93 E5] Bunićeva Poljana; m 091 467 7673; ⊕ Feb–Dec noon–midnight daily. On a busy little piazza behind the cathedral, Bura serves informal tapas-style snacks, as well as some more substantial dishes, to accompany cocktails & fine wines. It's popular with visitors & locals alike & makes a relaxed change from a formal sit-down restaurant meal. €€€€

Gradska Kavana Arsenal Restaurant [93 F4] Pred Dvorom 1; 020 321 202; w nautikarestaurants.com; ⊕ 08.00–midnight daily. With an old-fashioned café (page 97) overlooking Stradun at the front & a restaurant giving views on to the old harbour at the back, Gradska Kavana Arsenal offers reliable dining in a gorgeous location. During the day the interior is geared towards large groups, with other diners soaking up the old harbour views from the outdoor terrace. Besides traditional Dalmatian fare at lunch & dinner, they also do b/fast, with treats such as eggs royale (poached egg with smoked salmon & hollandaise sauce). €€€€

Dundo Maroje [93 E3] Kovačka; m 099 546 5570; w dundomaroje.com; ⊕ summer 10.00–midnight, winter 11.00–22.00 daily. On 1 of the tiny alleys connecting Stradun with Prijeko,

Konoba Dundo Maroje offers a long multilingual menu, including pasta, risotto, & meat & seafood dishes, along with salads, pizzas & burgers. No views whatsoever, but the food is pretty reliable. €€€€–€€€

Rozario [93 F3] Prijeko 1; ☏020 322 015; w konoba-rozario.hr; ⊕ Mar–Nov noon–23.00 daily. Rozario has been open for over 50 years & manages to break the Prijeko mould (page 91), serving up unpretentious local Croatian fare in a nice, homely setting near the Dominican Monastery. €€€€–€€€

✻ **Trattoria Carmen** [93 G5] Damjana Jude 10; m 098 943 8630; w trattoria-carmen-dubrovnik. com ; ⊕ Apr–Oct noon–midnight daily. This welcoming family-run eatery lies hidden in the narrow alley leading to the Aquarium. Come here for tasty Mediterranean fare – the menu changes depending on what's best at the morning market, but regular favourites include the Carmen octopus (octopus casseroled with potato, cherry tomatoes, olives & capers), & homemade pasta with shrimp & truffles. €€€€–€€€

Kamenice [93 E5] Gundulićeva poljana 8; ☏020 323 682; ⊕ May–Sep 07.00–22.00 daily, Oct–Apr 07.00–15.00 daily. Overlooking the morning open-air market in the old town, Kamenice is a great place in a great location. It specialises in inexpensive local seafood. The menu is short but excellent, with the whitebait & squid particularly good, & the house wine affordable. The service can be a little slow & surly, & you'll probably have to queue for a table, but perhaps that's all part of the charm. €€€

Mea Culpa [92 B4] Za Rokom 3; ☏020 323 430; w meaculpa-pizzeria.com; ⊕ Mar–Oct, 09.00–midnight daily. Mea Culpa is located in a long narrow stone alley, serving up large pizzas, pasta, risotto, burgers, & colourful salads. Tables spill out on to the street, & it's a popular place with locals & visitors alike, though the quality of the food can be a bit hit & miss. €€€

Budget

Pizzeria Oliva [93 E4] Lučarica 5; ☏020 324 594; w pizzeriaolivadubrovnik.com; ⊕ 10.00–23.00 daily. Often tipped as the best pizzeria in town, besides doing sit-down cooked-to-order pizzas, Oliva also sells sandwiches (pizza bread slices filled with salami & clotted cream cheese) through a hatch in the wall. €€€–€€

Nishta [92 D3] Prijeko bb; ☏020 322 088; w nishtarestaurant.com; ⊕ May–Oct 11.30–23.00 Mon–Sat. Great little vegetarian option on Prijeko, with plenty of vegan & gluten-free options – mains include smoked seitan burger with sweet potato sticks, fried rice noodles with tofu & ginger, spelt pasta tossed with capers, olives, sundried tomatoes & herbs. Definitely an exception to the general lacklustre quality of many Prijeko eateries. €€€

Spaghetteria Toni [92 C5] Nikole Božidarevićeva 14; ☏020 323 134; w spaghetteria-toni.com; ⊕ Mar–Nov 11.00–23.00 Mon–Sat. Spaghetteria Toni specialises in pasta. Check out the vast homemade lasagne or the various pasta dishes with seafood sauces. Toni feels like an Italian trattoria, only this 1 serves thick Turkish coffee; it's cheerful, informal & popular with locals but not cheap. €€€

Outside the old town walls
Expensive

Maslina Tavern [84 A2] Masarykov put 20; ☏020 430 351; w adriaticluxuryhotels.com; ⊕ Apr–Nov noon–23.00 daily. Fine dining down by the water's edge, with romantic views out towards the Elaphiti islands – & service as smooth & food as mouth-watering as you'd expect from the Hotel Dubrovnik Palace. The house speciality is the Fisherman's Pot, a delicious casserole of mixed Adriatic seafood. €€€€€

Nautika [92 A3] Brsalje 3; ☏020 442 526; w nautikarestaurants.com; ⊕ Mar–Oct noon–midnight daily. For years the ritziest place in town, the Nautika trades heavily on having had Pope John Paul II to lunch on 6 June 2003, though it's hard to imagine the late pontiff scoffing his way through the 5-course menu on display. The emphasis is on fresh Adriatic seafood & Nautika does have an excellent location on the water, right outside the Pile Gate, & a gorgeous pair of terraces, as well as smart dining rooms indoors. The food is excellent, as you'd expect for the price, & the service impeccable. Reservations recommended. €€€€€

Levanat [84 A2] Nika i Meda Pučića 15; ☏020 435 352; w restaurant-levanat.com; ⊕ Apr–Nov 08.00–midnight daily. With an unbeatable waterfront location on Babin Kuk, Levanat is secluded, upmarket & pricey. It's easy to get to by walking along the footpath that starts in Lapad Bay for about 10mins, or from the Babin Kuk hotels; otherwise, you might want to consider getting a taxi, as it's quite a schlep from the old town. The menu focuses on traditional Dalmatian specialities with modern presentation. You can also come here just for a drink. Reservations recommended (not least to check it's open). €€€€€–€€€€

Mid-range

Orhan [84 E3] Od Tabakarije 1; ☎020 414 183; w restaurant-orhan.com; ⏱ noon–23.00 daily. Orhan serves up the same sturdy Adriatic staples – squid risotto, mussels & fish platters – that you find all over Dubrovnik. The real reason to come here, though, are the stunning views over the city walls from the terrace right underneath the Lovrijenac Fortress. There are also a few private rooms available. €€€€

Posat [92 B2] Uz Posat 1; ☎020 421 194; w posat-dubrovnik.com; ⏱ 11.00–23.00 daily. Immediately outside the Pile Gate (just up & to the right) is the Posat fine dining restaurant, which has a large & leafy terrace, making it a good choice for larger groups. They serve well-presented Dalmatian seafood, along with grilled meat dishes. €€€€

☀ **Orsan** [84 C1] Ivana Zajca 2; ☎020 436 822; w restaurant-orsan-dubrovnik.com; ⏱ May–Oct 08.00–midnight daily, Nov–Apr 09.00–17.00 Mon–Sat. In the marina near Hotel Lapad overlooking Gruž port, Orsan specialises in classic Dalmatian seafood, though they do have some very good meat & vegetarian options, too. It's a lovely place to sit, with waterside tables overlooking the boats. In winter they do a very reasonably priced daily set menu, popular with locals. €€€€–€€€

Pantarul [84 C2] Kralja Tomislava 1; ☎020 333 486; w pantarul.com; ⏱ noon–midnight Tue–Sun. Unpretentious but stylish new restaurant in Lapad, popular with locals, serving up creative Mediterranean fare with an emphasis on fresh seasonal produce. €€€€–€€€

Peppers [84 C2] Lapadska obala 20; ☎020 487 578; w pepperseatery.com; ⏱ Apr–Oct noon–15.00 & 18.00–23.00 daily. Near Hotel Lapad, overlooking Gruž port, Peppers serves up creative Mediterranean fare in a stone courtyard – expect sharing dishes such as humus & guacamole, tacos & homemade burgers, along

with cocktails, local beers, & wine by the glass or bottle. €€€€–€€€

Urban & Veggie [84 D2] Obala Stjepana Radića 13; m 095 326 2568; w urbanveggie.restaurant; ⏱ Mar–Oct 08.00–23.00. Close to the ferry port in Gruž, this vegan restaurant serves carefully prepared plant-based dishes at tables shaded by big white parasols on a leafy terrace. They also do a reasonably priced set daily menu. Since opening in 2019, it's become popular with visitors & locals alike. €€€€–€€€

Budget

El Toro [84 D3] Ivo Vojnovića 5; m 098 243 729; ⏱ 09.00–23.00 daily. Just up the road from the Hotel Bellevue, with a nice leafy high-up terrace, you'll find the Café Pizzeria El Toro, which is cheap & cheerful & serves up reasonable pizzas at a good price. €€

FO.RA Focaccia Ragusa [84 F3] Hvarska 6; m 099 681 9263; ⏱ Apr–Oct noon–22.00 Mon–Sat. Lying just outside the walls, close to Ploče Gate, this friendly little eatery serves oven-warm Italian focaccia along with platters of cured meats, cheeses & dips. They also do take-away filled focaccia slices. €€

KIOSK Dubrovnik [84 D2] Dr Ante Starčevića 26; m 099 712 8000; w kioskdubrovnik.com ⏱ Apr–Oct 11.00–22.00 Mon–Sat. Opened in 2022, this sister eatery to Azur (in the old town) overlooks Gruž port. It serves tasty street food, with delights such as tuna poke bowl or Thai green curry, & also hosts occasional after-dark live music. €€

Buffets and snack bars

Here are 3 of the best, all in the old town:

Barba [93 E3] Boškovićeva 5; ⓕ dubrovnik. barba; ⏱ Apr–Oct 10.00–midnight daily. Hip little eatery billing itself as 'seafood street food'. Their speciality is the homemade octopus burger, & they also do daily dishes, such as fried whitebait or squid, depending on what the fishermen bring in. A few nice wooden tables inside, plus several cushions on the stone steps for sitting out. €€–€

☀ **Buffet Škola** [92 D3] Antuninska 1; w buffetskola.hr; ⏱ 09.00–22.00 daily. On the left-hand side heading up towards Prijeko, near War Photo Ltd. Terrific homemade sandwiches filled with local cheese or *pršut*, as well as homemade apple strudel. A few tables outside. €

Presa [92 C4] Đorđićeva 2; ⊕ 10.00–midnight daily. No-nonsense cheapie with sandwiches, grills, & some good, fresh-looking salads. A few tables outside. €

Cafés and bars

The following venues are listed alphabetically.

Inside the old town walls

Buža I [93 G7] Situated on the rocks outside the seaward city walls (but accessed from the old town), Buža is the place to come if you want to watch the sun go down. The only sounds are the sea & the gulls, & it's gloriously informal. The entrance is pretty well hidden – to get there, go up behind the Jesuit Church [92 D6] & out of the square on the opposite corner, & then turn left under the walls along Od Margarite. After a short while you come to a hole in the wall on your right (*buža* means 'hole') that leads out on to the rocks – & there you are. Seats are set out on the rocks that spill down to the Adriatic. This is a great place for taking a dip, too, so don't forget your togs. Only open – you'll see why – when the weather's fine.

Buža II [93 F7] Another hole-in-the-wall establishment, with a slightly different outlook over Lokrum & a slightly more formal set-up, with more chairs, tables & parasols in a main bar area. Again, the bar isn't permanent, so no hot drinks, &, of course, no draught beers. Follow the directions for Buža I (see above) but turn right under the walls along Od Margarite instead of left. Again, you'll quickly come to a hole in the wall, but this time it will be on your left.

D'Vino [92 D3] Palmotićeva 4a; ☎ 020 321 130; w dvino.net; ⊕ 10.00–02.00 daily. Largest selection of wines by the glass in Dubrovnik, accompanied by platters of savoury bites. Also offers guided wine-tasting flights (either 3 reds or 3 whites), so you can learn about quality local wines.

Festival Café [92 C3] Stradun bb; ☎ 020 321 148; w cafefestival.com ; ⊕ 08.00–midnight. Benefitting from a perfect location on Stradun, the rather pricey Festival Café is especially popular through the day & in the early evenings, when it's a great place to see & be seen. Pull up a director's chair & watch the action unfold. €€€€–€€€

Gradska Kavana [93 F4] Pred Dvorom 1; ☎ 020 321 202; w nautikarestaurants.com;

⊕ 08.00–02.00 daily. In arguably the best location in town, next door to the Rector's Palace & opposite St Blaise's Church, the Gradska Kavana (literally 'town café') has a spacious interior & a raised terrace, which is perfect for people-watching. €€€€–€€€

M'arden [92 C4] Od Domina 8; m 099 343 0203; w marden.hr; ⊕ May–Oct 17.00–midnight daily (variable depending on weather). Opened in 2023 by 2 local sommeliers, this slick wine bar occupies a walled garden hidden away near the Ethnographic Museum. Come here to enjoy some of Croatia's finest wines, accompanied by exquisite eats, candlelight, & occasional live jazz. €€€€–€€€

Troubadour [93 E5] Bunićeva poljana 2; m 091 977 3983; ⨍ Troubadourjazzbrasserie; ⊕ summer 08.00–02.00 daily, winter 09.00–23.00 Tue–Sun. Now known as the Troubadour Jazz Brasserie, this little bar is not quite what it used to be. Most of the tables are outside, & they now serve food as well as drinks, but they still host live music most evenings. €€€€–€€€

Outside the old town walls

Cave Bar More [84 B2] Pucića 13; ☎ 020 494 200; w cavebar-more.com. Stylish bar set in a cave under Hotel More, with wonderful views over Lapad Bay from the waterfront terrace built into the rocks.

Dubrovnik Beer Company [84 D1] Obala Pape Ivana Pavla II 15; m 095 356 9620; w dubrovackapivovara.hr. Near the ferry port in Gruž, this popular micro-brewery serves 4 of its own beers on tap. They also offer early-evening tours of the brewery & stage occasional live music.

Fratello's Prosecco Bar [84 E3] Anice Bošković 9a; m 091 201 2345; w fratellos.eu; ⊕ May–Oct 09.00–midnight daily (variable depending on weather). Just a 10min walk from the old town, on the road between Pile Gate & the Lapad peninsula, this open-air wine bar occupies a series of terraces with superb sea-views. Their main thing is Italian prosecco, but they also serve some rather good Croatian sparkling wine along with delicious finger food. They host occasional live music & also do brunch. €€€

Škar Winery [84 C2] Lapadska obala 17; m 098 787 705; w lekri.eu; ⊕ May–Nov

18.00–midnight daily. Close to Hotel Lapad (page 89), overlooking Gruž harbour, this welcoming family-run wine bar serves their own red, rosé & white wine, either by the glass or bottle, along with platters of cheese & cured meats. They also offer early-evening tours of their adjoining winery several times weekly. €€€

Sunset Lounge [84 A2] Masarykov put 20; ☎ 020 430 000; w adriaticluxuryhotels.com. The stylish Sunset Lounge at the Hotel Dubrovnik Palace (page 87) is firmly established as the place to watch sunset in Dubrovnik, through floor-to-ceiling windows that provide spectacular views over the Elaphiti islands & the Adriatic as the day draws to a close – even if prices are fairly high. Bus #4, which leaves from just outside the Pile Gate, will take you to the hotel.

Ice cream

Dolce Vita [92 D3] Nalješkovićeva; m 099 282 0505; ⊕ May–Oct 11.00–23.00 daily. In one of the streets between Stradun & Prijeko, worth checking out is Dolce Vita, which serves delicious cooked-to-order pancakes, along with their own excellent ice cream. €

Gianni [93 G5] Kneza Damjana Jude bb; m 095 392 6323; w gianni-dubrovnik.com; ⊕ Apr–Oct 09.00–22.00 daily (variable depending on weather). There's a flurry of establishments in the old town, with the best being this parlour on Damjana Jude, the narrow alley leading to the Aquarium. It does sublime artisan ice creams & sorbets – favourites include the wild orange ice cream, & the coconut & basil sorbet. €

Self-catering

If you're looking for picnic food, you'll probably be reliant on the Konzum supermarket – there's a branch on Gundulićeva Poljana [93 E5] & another outside each of the 2 main gates. There's also a huge new branch down at Gruž, just past the ferry terminal [84 C2].

If you're planning a hike or a trip to Lokrum Island, a tempting alternative to making your own picnic is to order a day in advance from **Piknik Dubrovnik** (w piknikdubrovnik.com). Their menu includes local specialities & homemade cakes, which come neatly packed in a rucksack, complete with a rug & map. They can also arrange hosted picnics in scenic spots for special occasions.

ENTERTAINMENT AND NIGHTLIFE Dubrovnik has a richly vibrant cultural scene, with its own symphony orchestra, theatre group and dance ensemble. Most performances take place during the season – broadly speaking from May to October – when there's usually something on every night, but most important of all is the annual Dubrovnik Summer Festival (page 98).

Even outside the festival, there are plenty of opportunities to listen to classical music, largely thanks to the tireless **Dubrovnik Symphony Orchestra** (w dso. hr), which puts on an astonishing range of concerts all year round. The two most common venues – outside festival time – are the Revelin Fortress, just outside the Ploče Gate, and the Church of Our Saviour, just inside the Pile Gate, where there are regular candlelit performances.

Dubrovnik also has one of the country's most famous folk-dancing troupes in the form of the 300-strong Lindo ensemble (w lindjo.hr). They're a regular mainstay of the festival and also perform twice a week from May to October at the Lazareti, the old quarantine houses just up from the Ploče Gate. It makes for an amazing and authentic spectacle. Lindo's office is at Marojice Kaboge 12, two streets back from Gundulićeva poljana.

If film is more your thing, check out the **Slavica open-air summer cinema** [84 E3] (w kinematografi.org) in a dreamy location, high above the sea, on the road between Pile Gate and Lapad peninsula. Founded in 1950, it shows European art-house films in the original version (mainly English) with Croatian subtitles. Screenings take place aft er dark from June to September.

Dubrovnik Summer Festival
The Dubrovnik Summer Festival is big, prestigious and serious, with every conceivable space in the old town – indoors and out – being

MARIN DRŽIĆ – DUBROVNIK'S REBELLIOUS PLAYWRIGHT

Born into a large family of merchants in 1508, Marin Držić was originally destined for the Church, and after being ordained at the age of 18, he was sent to Siena to study Church law. He was soon thrown out for his involvement with the theatre and returned home to Dubrovnik, where he wrote his first plays. These weren't popular with the nobles, who rightly saw the Držić comedies for the political vehicles they were – and presumably weren't wild about being portrayed as inbred fools either.

The latter part of the playwright's life is somewhat of a mystery, though we know that he left Dubrovnik and took up something of a crusade against it. He even wrote a series of letters to the Medicis in Florence, asking them to help him overthrow the republic – though he never received an answer and died in Venice in poverty in 1567.

Needless to say, once Držić was safely out of the way his reputation was quickly rehabilitated, and today, his plays – and in particular *Dundo Maroje* – form a central part of the Dubrovnik Summer Festival.

turned into a performance stage. The 45-day festival kicks off on 10 July with the performers being given the keys to the city and closes on 25 August with a fabulous fireworks display.

During the festival, you can find everything from opera and classical concerts to chamber music and soloists, while theatre performances tend to concentrate on Shakespeare and local boy Marin Držić (see above). A festival standard is the traditional performance of *Hamlet* in the Lovrijenac Fortress, a wonderfully atmospheric setting for the play.

Tickets for the main events sell out well in advance, so if you're serious about attending check out the website (w dubrovnik-festival.hr) or contact the organisers (📞020 326 100) as soon as the programme becomes available (usually in April) – and make sure you get your accommodation sorted out way ahead of time, too. If you haven't got tickets in advance, there are usually places available for the lower-key performances on-site – you can buy these from the festival kiosks on Stradun and at the Pile Gate.

Nightlife Though there's plenty of late-evening café activity and drinking going on in the old town, actual nightlife is decidedly thin on the ground in Dubrovnik, with most places closing up by 01.00. However, during peak season the lounge bar at the **Banje Beach Club** [84 F4] (w banjebeach.com), located on the Banje beach just beyond the Ploče Gate, keeps going into the early hours during the summer.

In summer there are more chances to dance, but not a whole lot more. The best place is arguably **Lazareti** [93 H3] (w lazaretihub.com), out past the Ploče Gate on Supila, which features DJs and probably the hippest music you'll find in the area – but Ibiza it ain't, and hours vary. There's also the mainstream dance venue (albeit in a 16th-century tower) **Culture Club Revelin** [93 H2] (m 098 533 531; w clubrevelin.com) on Svetog Dominika, near the Ploče Gate, with similar hours but more commercial music.

In the Gruž port neighbourhood, next to the Red History Museum (page 114), **TUP** [84 D2] is a community-driven cultural centre, promoting local artists and musicians, in a disused factory. It hosts exhibitions, film screenings, workshops and an informal bar year-round and is much loved by the local alternative crowd.

BEACHES The other way of entertaining yourself, of course, is with a trip to the beach. The nicest ones are out on the island of Lokrum, and it's well worth getting out there if you possibly can (page 113) – it's also the nearest naturist beach to the old town.

Dubrovnik's main public beach is at **Banje** [84 F4], just outside the Ploče Gate, facing the old port. It's rather expensive and madly popular in peak season – you can rent parasols and sunbeds here and order yourself cocktails at the summer bar. In spite of being right next to the old port, the water is beautifully clear. But, if you simply fancy cooling off after a hot walk around the city walls, stroll just round the corner at the old port and there's a swimming area off the rocks by the jetty.

Another option is the tiny beach underneath the Hotel Bellevue, half of which is public (the other half belongs to the revamped hotel). It's on a gorgeous little cove facing southeast and hosts Dubrovnik's annual water polo championships – each little beach and cove around the city has its own team.

For pure hedonistic beach games and watersports, you might head for the **Copacabana beach** [84 B1] on Babin Kuk, though it is expensive (two sunbeds and a parasol cost €70 in summer 2024) and in high season it does get mighty crowded with the package tours from the Babin Kuk hotel complex taking up most of the space. Finally, **Lapad Bay beach** [84 B2], sometimes referred to as Sunset Beach, on Lapad, is the locals' beach of choice and offers lovely swimming out to sea between Babin Kuk and Lapad.

ACTIVITIES If lying on the beach is a bit tame for you, there are plenty of more active pursuits on offer. For scuba-diving tuition and trips, the best local company is **Blue Planet Diving** (w blueplanet-diving.com), based at the Hotel Dubrovnik Palace (page 87) on the Lapad peninsula, close to some top dive sites, such as the Taranto wreck and the island of Sveti Andrija (page 70). Alternatively, Dubrovnik-based **Outdoor Croatia** (w outdoorcroatia.com) arranges one-day sea kayaking tours around the nearby Elaphiti islands (page 118), which might also combine snorkelling or cycling. If you prefer land-based activities, **Hiking Dubrovnik** (w hikingdubrovnik.com) does guided hikes up Mount Srđ (page 113) and into rural Konavle, as well as Nordic walking and rock climbing. Keen runners might also keep in mind that Dubrovnik hosts the annual Dubrovnik Half Marathon (w du-motion. com) and the 2.5km Run the Wall race each year in April.

OTHER PRACTICALITIES Dubrovnik's main general **hospital** (Opća Bolnica) is out at Lapad [84 C3] (Dr Roka Mišetića 2; ☏ 020 431 777; w bolnica-du.hr). If you're looking for a list of pharmacies, it's useful to know that there's a **24-hour pharmacy** in the old town, **Ljekarna Kod Zvonika** [93 F4] (☏ 020 321 133) is at the east end of Placa, near Orlando's Column, while the other is **Ljekarna Gruž** [84 C1] (☏ 020 418 990) near the ferry port at Obala pape Ivana Pavla II 9 . One or the other will always be working, though they generally alternate, so call to check. There's a **post office** [92 C4] in the old town at Široka ulica 8 and plenty of other branches, including out at Lapad (Ulica Miljenka Bratoša 21) and on the main road between the old town and Gruž, where you'll find the main post office at Vukovarska 16.

WHAT TO SEE AND DO The main sight is, of course, Dubrovnik itself, and the best way of seeing it is from the city walls, which are among the best preserved and most picturesque in the world. There's a walkway along their entire length, and you should make every effort to circum-perambulate at least once, as it gives you the best possible perspective (physical and historical) of just what Dubrovnik really means. Another wonderful view can be had from the top of Mount Srđ (412m), which looms above the city – walk or take a cable car all the way up (page 113).

Once you've seen Dubrovnik from above, choose your time of day for the city itself with care; after 11.00, there's a predictable tendency towards more visitors and less atmosphere – though early evening is a lovely time, regardless of the crowds, with soft light treating old stone kindly.

There's a lot to see in the old city, but don't be too obsessive – not all of the 48 churches within the walls need a visit (or indeed are open), and the museums are mostly fairly low-key. In any case, make sure you get a **Dubrovnik Pass** (page 86), which will get you free admission to many of the museums and galleries, as well as the walls themselves.

The city is great for walking around – if you want to tap into the knowledge of a local guide consider booking a place on one of the guided walks organised by **Dubrovnik Walking Tours** (✆020 436 846; w dubrovnik-walking-tours.com). All tours leave from Onofrio's Great Fountain [92 B3]; ask at the tourist office for more detailed information.

City walls

(w dpds.hr; ⊕ Jun–Jul 08.00–19.30 daily, Apr–May & Aug–Sep 08.00–18.30 daily, Oct 08.00–17.30 daily, Nov–Mar 09.00–15.00 daily; Mar–Oct €35; Nov–Feb €15) The walls surround the entire old town and run for a whisper under 2km. At their highest they're 25m tall, and at their fattest 12m thick. There are five fortresses and around 20 towers. Work started on the walls in the 8th century and continued more or less continuously until the 16th, though much more than you might imagine is also late-20th-century restoration – even before the Serb shells pounded the city in 1991–92. Since the war, huge amounts of restoration have been done throughout the old city, including the complete repaving of Stradun – not that you'd know – and the replacing of most of the houses' roof tiles.

There are three places where you can get up on to the walls – on Stradun, right next to the Pile Gate (the busiest of the three); on Svetog Dominika, the road leading up to the Dominican Monastery; and on Kneza Damjana Jude, near the Aquarium. The earlier you get up on to the walls, the less crowded you'll find them.

If you stop to take pictures (and you will), the whole circuit takes a leisurely hour or so – at least.

Inside the walls The main sights are all close to one another – the main street, Stradun, is all of 300m long. The following itinerary starts at the Pile Gate and works its way back and forth across the old city, before ending at the Church of St Blaise. At a leisurely pace – and without stopping for any length of time to admire the attractions or visit museums and churches – it would take about 1½–2 hours. If you dip into a handful of the main sights, you should count on a good half-day; if you want a detailed visit to everything on the itinerary, you'll need a couple of full days at least. If you do nothing else, visit the Rector's Palace, the two monasteries and the cathedral treasury.

The **Pile Gate** [92 B3], dating back to 1471, is approached across a wooden drawbridge which used to be pulled up every night. Set into a niche, here is the first of many statues you'll see of St Blaise (Sveti Vlaho), the city's patron saint. Indeed, as you enter the gate, you'll immediately see another – this time by Ivan Meštrović (page 160), Croatia's most famous sculptor.

Once inside the gate you come straight on to Dubrovnik's famous main street, Stradun, which is paved in marble (be careful when it's wet; it can be lethally slippery). This was originally the marshy channel which separated the Roman settlement of Ragusa on one side from the Slavic settlement of Dubrovnik on the other.

On the square inside the Pile Gate stands **Onofrio's Great Fountain** [92 B3], which was completed in 1444 by the Neapolitan architect Onofrio della Cava as part of the city's smart new plumbing. Unfortunately, all the fancy ornamental work from the upper part of the fountain was lost in the Great Earthquake of 1667.

To your left as you come into the city is the tiny **Church of Our Saviour** (Sv Spasa) [92 B3]. It was completed in 1528 as a thank you from the survivors of the 1520 earthquake and itself survived the far more dramatic quake of 1667 – a tribute to the building skills of the Andrijić brothers, from Korčula, who also worked on the Sponza Palace (page 104). The simple Renaissance trefoil façade and rose window are quietly pleasing and hide a Gothic interior mainly used these days as a venue for candlelit concerts.

Franciscan Monastery and Pharmacy [92 C3] (Franjevačkog Samostana; Placa 2; ☎020 641 123; ⊕ summer 09.00–18.00 daily, winter 09.00–14.00 daily; €6)

Next door to Our Saviour is the Franciscan Church and Monastery. The church is entered from Stradun itself, where you'll find the south door crowned by a wonderful *pietà* – evocatively described by Rebecca West in 1937 as 'definite and sensible. The Madonna looks as if, had it been in her hands, she would have stopped the whole affair.'

The pietà survived the Great Earthquake, but the church itself was entirely gutted by fire, and countless treasures were lost forever. What you see today dates from the 18th century onwards, which explains the Baroque nature of it all. The church is famous locally as the final resting place of Ivan Gundulić (page 108), though he's actually interred in a part of the church that is closed to the public – you can still pay your respects at a plaque on the north wall, however.

The rest of the monastery is accessed down a narrow passage next to Our Saviour. At the entrance you'll find the famous pharmacy, self-billed as the oldest in the world. Whether it is or not, it probably was one of the earliest to be open to the public, and it's still operating today, though from a 1901 refurbishment. Besides standard modern medicines, they stock their own brand of Ljekarnica Male Braće natural face creams, such as the lush Krema ruža (rose cream), still prepared to secret medieval Franciscan recipes. The original pharmacy was established in 1317, and in the museum off the cloisters, you can see an interesting collection of jars and poisons from the 15th century on, along with ancient pharmacopoeias.

The museum also contains various religious artefacts, as well as a testy portrait of Ruđer Bošković, Dubrovnik's mathematical genius (see above), painted in 1760 in London. Most interesting of all, however, is a canvas showing the old town before the earthquake – note how much greater Onofrio's Great Fountain was before 1667.

The cloisters themselves are truly exceptional, consisting of rows of double octagonal columns with individualised capitals. They are the work of Mihoje Brakov, a sculptor from Bar (in what's now Montenegro), who died here of the plague in 1348. One of the capitals near the entrance, depicting a medieval man with terrible toothache, is said to be a self-portrait of the sculptor. Inside the courtyard are palm trees and well-trimmed box hedges, and it's a great place to get away from the heat in high summer.

Stradun and Luža Square Stradun itself (also known as Placa – pronounced 'platsa') continues in a widening straight line all the way to the Clock Tower at the far end. As you'll notice, the houses along the street are nearly identical; a result of the careful post-earthquake planning at the end of the 17th century. Note the distinctive '*na koljeno*' single-arched frame that combines the entrance door and window to provide a counter over which goods could be served to customers.

In Luža Square, at the far end of Stradun, you'll find **Orlando's Column** [93 E4], a statue of Roland symbolising the city's desire for freedom (*libertas*), and which has marked the centre of town since its erection in 1418. For centuries, Roland's forearm was Ragusa's standard measure of length (the *lakat*, since you ask), a convenient 512mm long – you can see the reference groove at the base of the statue. All state declarations were read from a platform above the column in the days of the republic and condemned criminals were executed at its base.

Behind Orlando's Column, you can't miss the **Clock Tower** [93 F4], originally built in 1444, which features a complex astronomical clock and a pair of green men (the *zelenci*) who strike the hour. The tower was rebuilt in 1929 (which is presumably when the digital clock was added), so the only thing that's really original now is the bell, dating from 1506, which weighs over two tonnes. The original green men are now in the Cultural History Museum inside the Rector's

Fans of the hit HBO TV series *Game of Thrones*, based on George Martin's epic series of best-selling novels, will know Dubrovnik by another name – King's Landing. Dubrovnik (along with Iceland, Ireland, Andalucía and Morocco) has been a key location for *Game of Thrones* – to the uninitiated, King's Landing is the capital of Westeros, site of the Red Keep and it's hotly (and bloodily) contested Iron Throne – since Series 2 (prior to this, Malta was used as the location for King's Landing). Exact locations include the Bokar and Lovrijenac fortresses, the Minčeta tower (that's the House of the Undying to *Game of Thrones* fans), and the streets and cascading steps outside the Dominican Monastery.

Dubrovnik's city walls, fortresses, streets and palaces are not the only locations in Croatia to be used for filming *Game of Thrones*. Other major locations include the island of Lokrum (as the city of Qarth), Diocletian's Palace in Split (numerous street scenes) including its underground chambers (various scenes in Meereen, including chambers where Daenerys's dragons are kept), the ruined fortress at Klis (Meereen again, including the site outside the city where its former rulers are crucified), a section of old stone waterfront houses in Kaštel Gomilica (a village between Trogir and Split, which forms part of the CGI enhanced city of Braavos), the Arboretum at Trsteno (doubling as the palace gardens in King's Landing), and scenes have also been shot on Biokovo.

It was overseas tour operators who first began capitalising on the *Game of Thrones* connection – indeed by most accounts many local tour guides were initially rather peeved that their city's millennia-and-a-half-long history should have been apparently trumped by a fantasy TV series. But local operators have now waded in as well, and in any case the city's (already staggering) number of visitors has surged further, meaning that unless you visit in the shoulder seasons or off season you're likely to find Dubrovnik full to bursting point.

Palace (page 110). Next to the clock tower is **Onofrio's Small Fountain** [93 F4], dating from 1441.

Sponza Palace [93 F4] (Luža) On the left-hand side of Luža square is the Sponza Palace, which functioned variously as a cistern, the customs house and the state mint. Today, it houses the Memorial Room of the Dubrovnik Defenders, and the State Archives. It's one of the most charming buildings in Dubrovnik, boldly mixing pure Venetian Gothic and late Renaissance into a harmonious whole. It was built in 1522 to plans by the local architect Pasko Miličević and features work by the Andrijić brothers, the master sculptors who were also responsible for much of Korčula Cathedral – as well as the Church of Our Saviour at the other end of Stradun. The Sponza was one of the few buildings to survive the Great Earthquake of 1667.

The entrance is through a wide-arched Renaissance portico, above which there's a lovely Venetian-Gothic first storey, topped with a row of four late-Renaissance windows and a statue of St Blaise in a niche. Inside, there's a courtyard with a double cloister.

The name Sponza comes from the Latin word *spongia*, meaning sponge, as there was originally a cistern on this site. The Sponza's main purpose, however, was to serve as the republic's customs house (which is why it's also sometimes referred to as the Divona or Dogana). On the ground-floor here, goods were measured for duty under the inscription *Fallere Nostra Vetant et Falli Pondera Meque Pondero cum Merces Ponderat ipse Deus* – which translates roughly as 'the scales we use to weigh your goods are the same scales used by God to weigh us'.

The ground-floor rooms originally served as warehouse space, while those on the first floor were used for literary and scientific meetings. Up on the second floor was the state mint, which issued Dubrovnik's currency (*perperae, grossi* and *ducats*) from 1337 until 1803.

After World War II, the Sponza housed the Museum of the Socialist Revolution, though that disappeared following the more recent war. The space is used for concerts during the Summer Festival.

The **Memorial Room of the Dubrovnik Defenders** (☏ 020 321 031; ⊕ May–Oct 09.00–21.00 daily, Nov–Apr 10.00–15.00 daily; free), on the ground-floor, is a commemoration of the tragic events here from 1 October 1991 to 26 October 1992, when more than 200 defenders and 100 civilians were killed. It's a terribly sobering place, with the remnants of the flag from the Imperial Fort on Srđ and the pictures and dates of all the young lives that were snuffed out during the siege. Many of the photos are the work of local photographer Pavo Urban, who was tragically cut down in his prime (aged just 23) by shrapnel just yards from the memorial room in December 1991.

The building also houses the **State Archives** (☏ 020 321 031; call or email e dad@ dad.hr in advance to visit; ⊕ daily), which are among the most complete in the world, chronicling pretty much everything that happened during the 1,000-year history of the republic. Altogether, there are some 8,000m of shelved documents, ranging from the 13th-century city statutes to Marshal Marmont's orders dissolving the republic in 1808.

Dominican Monastery [93 F3] (Dominikanskog Samostana; Sv Dominika 4; ☏ 020 322 200; ⊕ summer 09.00–18.00 daily, winter 09.00–15.00 daily; €4) The winding street Svetog Dominika leads up to the Ploče Gate. On the way, you can't miss the Dominican Monastery. Notice the way the steps on the way up are walled in, up to a height of about two feet, to protect the modesty of travellers and save the monks from impure ankle-related thoughts.

The monastery was used by the occupying French troops from 1808 – you can see from the outside where windows were sealed up to make a Napoleonic prison, and the church itself was used as stables. In the cloisters, you can still see the horse troughs, which were hacked into the retaining walls by the cavalrymen.

The original church here was completed in 1315 but had to be rebuilt after the Great Earthquake of 1667. It was then paved with the coats of arms of all the noble families but, unfortunately, was repaved in 1910 with plain marble. Today, it's a vast, boxy place, and most of the best art has been moved to the museum – though not the greatest treasure of all, a terrific 5m-by-4m crucifixion by Paolo Veneziano, which was installed here in 1358. There's also an interesting painting of St Dominic by local boy Vlaho Bukovac, though it's not, frankly, the artist's best work – you can see some of this at the Museum of Modern Art (page 112) in Dubrovnik, and even more in the painter's home town, Cavtat (page 114).

The cloisters are a late-Gothic masterpiece, built to a design by the Florentine architect Maso di Bartolomeo, but with extra flourishes added by local stonemasons. In the courtyard oranges and lemons grow, and – like the Franciscan cloisters – it's a wonderfully cool, shady place on a hot day.

The monastery also houses an interesting museum and an extraordinary library; with over 16,000 works and 240 incunabula, it was one of the greatest European libraries of the Renaissance. In the museum, you'll find a rare 11th-century Bible, along with a much-reproduced triptych featuring St Blaise with a model of pre-earthquake Ragusa in his right hand – still recognisable as Dubrovnik today, though both the Franciscan and Dominican monasteries sported bigger spires back then. Also of note is a marvellous altarpiece by Titian featuring Mary Magdalene with St Blaise and the Archangel Raphael – the chap on his knees is the member of the Pucić family who commissioned the work.

Up a couple of stairs, there's a room full of votive gold – a fraction of what was here originally, as most of it was sold off after World War II to support the faculty of theology, unfunded in communist times. There's an interesting Flemish diptych here – with Jesus on the left while on the right, there's a reversible panel, with love on one side and death on the other, usefully adaptable according to your moods and whims.

Synagogue [93 E3] (Žudioska 5; ☎020 321 028; ⏰ May–Oct 10.00–20.00 daily, Nov–Apr 10.00–15.00 daily; €7) As you leave the monastery, turn right and you'll find yourself at the eastern end of Prijeko, which is best visited early in the day, before the eager restaurateurs can get their teeth into you, so to speak (page 91). Take a detour down Žudioska, and you'll find one of Europe's oldest (and smallest) synagogues. It's Europe's second oldest (after Prague), and, in spite of restrictions placed on Jews here during World War II, it was the only European synagogue to function all the way through the war.

The synagogue – with original 17th-century furnishings – is on the second floor, while below it, on the first floor, there's a fascinating two-room museum, where you can see richly decorated Torah Scrolls and binders, and ancient Ark Curtains, as well as a copy of the letter signed by Marshal Marmont granting the Jewish community full emancipation from 1808. There's also a chilling selection of documents from 1941, issued by the fascist NDH (page 12), restricting the movement of Jews and ordering them to wear yellow ribbons and badges.

War Photo Limited [92 D3] (Antuninska 6; ☎020 322 166; **w** warphotoltd.com; ⏰ May–Sep 10.00–22.00 daily, Apr & Oct 10.00–17.00 daily, closed Nov–Mar; €10) Continue down Prijeko for most of its length – or if it's already approaching lunchtime consider avoiding the touts by walking along the old city's uppermost street, Peline, which gives great views down the steep-stepped streets crossing Prijeko – and then turn left down Antuninska, where you'll find the extraordinary War Photo Limited.

It's one of Dubrovnik's most emotionally charged galleries and can't be recommended too highly. Specialising in first-rate temporary exhibitions by the world's greatest modern-war photographers, the gallery aims, as the New Zealand-born director, Wade Goddard, says: 'to strip away the Hollywood image of war, to replace the glamour, the heroic bravura, the "only the bad guys suffer" image of war, with the raw and undeniable evidence that war inflicts injustices on all who experience it'.

It would require a heart of stone to come away unmoved by the extraordinary (and often painful) images. Recent exhibitions include *The War in Ukraine* (2023), featuring works by Amnon Gutman, and *War in My Neighbourhood, Lebanon* (2022) by Patrick Baez. There's also a permanent exhibition, *The End of Yugoslavia*, on the upper floor.

To the Orthodox Church and Icon Museum On the other side of Stradun, a short walk along Garište brings you to Za Rokom, where you'll find the little **Church of St Roc** [92 B4]. Round on the right-hand wall of the church is a fine piece of carved graffiti dated 1597 and reading '*Pax vobis memento mori qui ludetis pilla*' – which translates roughly as 'Peace be with you, but remember that you must die, you who play ball here', clearly the work of an irate adult, keen to warn off noisy, football-mad kids.

Continue along Za Rokom until you get to the end of the street, then turn left into Široka. On the right-hand side, you'll find the house where Marin Držić (page 99) once lived [92 C4] – although unless you're a serious fan of the playwright's work, you won't get a great deal out of a visit. Equally, unless you have a lot of time on your hands you probably needn't visit the **Rupe Ethnographic Museum** [92 B5] (Etnografski Muzej; Od Rupa 3; \020 323 013; ☉ Apr–Oct 09.00–18.00 Wed–Mon, Nov–Mar 09.00–16.00 Wed–Mon; €8), a block away – though the former granary building itself is interesting, as you can see some of the vast chambers which were dug into the rock to store grain back in the 16th century, keeping the food dry and cool.

Turning on to Od Puča, you'll find the Orthodox Church on your left and (two doors down) the Icon Museum. This part of town is where most of the small remaining Serbian community lives and works. Just down Miha Pracata, on the left-hand side, you'll also find Dubrovnik's **mosque** [92 D4/5] (☉ 10.00–13.00 daily), established in 1941 for Muslims who arrived from Bosnia & Herzegovina.

The **Serbian Orthodox Church of the Holy Annunciation** [92 D4] (Od Puča; ☉ 08.00–18.00 daily) is one of Dubrovnik's most recent, only being completed in 1877. A plain exterior shelters a rather spare interior, with a traditional iconostasis (with icons from the 15th to 19th centuries) separating the clergy from the congregation. The church was one of the last buildings in the old town – perhaps unsurprisingly – on which restoration work got underway after the end of the siege in 1992. It reopened in 2009 and now serves some 1,500 local Serbian Orthodox believers.

Two doors down is the rarely visited **Icon Museum** [92 D4] (Muzej Ikona; Od Puča 8; \020 323 283; ☉ May–Oct 09.00–14.00 daily, Nov–Apr 09.00–14.00 Mon–Fri; €5), upstairs, on the second floor (past a sign in Cyrillic saying СРПСКА – Srpska, or Serbian). It's a pity as the two-room collection brings together a wide range of icons from the 18th and 19th centuries, as well as some earlier ones from the 15th and 16th centuries. They come from all across the Balkans and Russia, and the differences between the various schools are fascinating – the Russian icons featuring long noses; the ones from the Bay of Kotor having deep, dark shadows. In the second room there are also half-a-dozen dark, dark portraits of local 19th-century Serb notables by Vlaho Bukovac (page 117), quite unlike anything else you'll see by the famous local painter. Note that the Icon Museum is closed for renovation through 2024 but should reopen in 2025.

To Gundulićeva poljana Continuing down Od Puča brings you past the Pucić Palace Hotel and out on to Gundulićeva poljana – literally Gundulić's little field. In the centre of the square stands a **statue of Ivan Gundulić** [93 E5] himself (page 108), which dates back to 1893. There's a marvellous allegorical vignette at the base of the statue; a bethroned Dubrovnik has both Turkey and Venice at her feet – with Turkey represented as the dragon on the left and Venice as the winged lion on the right. A certain irony, therefore, that the city's most expensive hotel, the Pucić Palace, overlooking the very same square, should today be Turkish-owned.

Jesuit Church [92 D6] (Properly the Church of St Ignatius of Loyola, or Ignacija Lojolskog; ⊕ 07.00–19.00 daily) Turn right out of Gundulićeva poljana and head up the great flight of steps – said to be modelled on the Spanish Steps in Rome – leading to the Jesuit Church, a massive structure clearly intended to make a point. It was built to plans by the Jesuit artist Andrea Pozzo, who had already done great works in Rome and would go on to design the cathedral in Ljubljana.

Completed in 1725, the church features a dramatic double-storeyed set of Corinthian columns lifting the façade skywards, and the church behind it is enormous, covering a surface of over 600m². Inside, it feels very big and gloomy, as you'd expect, with the interior modelled on the Gesù Church in Rome and featuring lots of fabulous *trompe l'oeil*, Pozzo's speciality – he was the author of a seminal work on perspective, *Prospettiva de' pittori et architect*, which revolutionised painting in the 18th century and is still used today. The main attraction is the inside of the apse, which features spectacular scenes from the life of Ignatius, the founder of the Jesuit order, by the Sicilian painter Gaetano Garcia.

Altogether less spiritually uplifting – though popular enough with local devotees, it seems – is the 'Grotto of Lourdes', which was added in 1885.

To the Maritime Museum and Aquarium You can leave the big open square in front of the Jesuit Church by the far corner and wind your way all the way along Ispod mira, the alley leading along the inside of the city walls. This is perhaps the quietest and shabbiest part of the town, with lots of buildings still unrestored after being badly damaged in an earthquake in 1979.

At the end of the line, so to speak, you'll find **St John's Fortress** [93 H5], which houses the Maritime Museum upstairs and the aquarium on the ground floor. Spread out over two floors, the **Maritime Museum** [93 H5] (Pomorski Muzej; Damjana Jude 2; ☏020 323 904; w dumus.hr; ⊕ Apr–Oct 09.00–18.00 Tue–Mon, Nov–Mar 09.00–16.00 Tue–Mon; €10) covers the entire history of seafaring in the area, from the Golden Age of the republic through to the arrival of steam-powered ships. It's well worth a visit if you're into ships and sailing, with lots of maps, evocative old photos and models of various types of ship, along with bits of rigging and ships' supplies and cargoes.

Downstairs, you'll find Dubrovnik's seawater **Aquarium** (✆020 323 978; w imp-du.com; ☉ summer 09.00–21.00 daily, winter 10.00–16.00 Tue–Sun; €10), which reopened after renovation in 2022 and now has a *Friend of the Sea* certificate for sustainability. Within its cavernous halls, some 31 tanks display a vast range of Adriatic sea life, including eels, scorpion fish, lobsters, sea urchins, octopus, starfish and tiny seahorses, as well as sponges and corals.

Pulitika Studio [93 H5] (Atelier Pulitika; Tvrđava Sv Ivana; ✆020 323 104; w ugdubrovnik.hr; ☉ 09.00–15.00 Tue–Sun; €5) Hidden away (close to the Maritime Museum), lovers of modern art might like to track down the former studio of local painter Đuro Pulitika (1922–2006), known for his colourful expressionistic landscapes. Everything is left just as it would have been when he was working there, and several of his canvases are on display. You can see more of his works at the Dulčić Masle Pulitika Gallery (page 110) opposite the cathedral.

Cathedral and treasury [93 F5] (Poljana Marina Držića; ☉ Apr–Oct 09.00–17.00 Mon–Sat, 11.00–17.00 Sun; Nov–Mar 10.00–noon & 15.00–17.00 Mon–Sat, 11.00–noon & 15.00–17.00 Sun; treasury €4) Heading back into the heart of the city, the first thing you come to is the cathedral. The former Romanesque number – said to have been bankrolled by a shipwrecked Richard the Lionheart (page 110) – was demolished by the Great Earthquake in 1667, so what you get today is the Baroque replacement, completed in 1713 to plans by the Italian architect Andrea Buffalini. The statues of the saints along the eaves are rather fine, though notice that St Mark has been relegated to an inferior position – perhaps a none-too-subtle snub to Venice.

Surprisingly, for Baroque, the cathedral is a rather spartan affair inside, with a chunky modern altar and acres of whitewash – and it's curious in having a west-facing altar. The compelling attraction is the treasury, though if you're here, it's nonetheless worth having a look at the impressive (school of) Titian altarpiece.

Altogether, there are well over 100 priceless relics in the **treasury** [93 F6], many of which are carried around the town in a grand procession on 3 February, the feast day of Dubrovnik's patron saint. The most important of these is the Head of St Blaise himself, which was bought from Byzantium (along with the saint's arms and a leg) in 1026. The head is housed in a fine casing decorated with 24 Byzantine enamel plaques from the 12th century, featuring austere, intense portraits of the saints.

The treasury also includes one of John the Baptist's hands, a bit of the True Cross incorporated into a crucifix, one of Christ's nappies in a silver box, and a dark wooden lectern which once belonged to England's Henry VIII – after the Reformation, treasures from the dissolved monasteries went up for sale, and a small selection ended up in the hands of enterprising sailors from Lopud.

Over on the right-hand side is an extraordinary painting by Raphael, the *Madonna della Seggiola (Sedia)*, which is almost identical to the 1514 version in the Palazzo Pitti in Florence. Why there's a copy here – painted on what looks like the bottom of a barrel – is a mystery, but the painting itself is a pure wonder.

Last but not least is an extraordinary pitcher and ewer from the 15th century, prominently on display, which is an allegory of Dubrovnik's flora and fauna. Featuring snakes and tortoises, eels and lizards, and some pre-Dalí lobsters, along with alarming amounts of vegetation, it looks like it would be the very devil to clean. It's thought to have been made as a gift for the Hungarian king of the day, Matthias Corvinus the Just, but ended up here as the king died before he could receive the tribute.

Ask anyone about Dubrovnik's cathedral and it won't be long before Richard the Lionheart's name comes up. According to local legend, the English king ran into a terrible storm near here on his return home from the Crusades at the end of 1192, and vowed that if he survived he would build a church on the spot. Miraculously, he was saved, and washed up on Lokrum.

On hearing the news of the arrival of such an important – and apparently loaded – visitor, Dubrovnik sent over a welcoming party, who persuaded King Richard that his money would be better spent on building a cathedral in Dubrovnik. In exchange, the Ragusan nobles would build a votive church on Lokrum at their own expense. Richard agreed, and handed over 100,000 ducats, before continuing on his journey to Italy and – eventually – England.

In all probability, however, the Lokrum part of this charming tale is a Benedictine fabrication. The monks on Lokrum had good cause for inventing – or at the very least embellishing – such a story. Because of it, they enjoyed various privileges in Dubrovnik's cathedral, including the abbot of Lokrum being allowed to hold the Candlemas pontifical mass, which is celebrated on 2 February, the day before St Blaise's feast day. This mass apparently enraged successive bishops of Dubrovnik, who demanded the privilege be rescinded. In the end, in the 1590s, the Ragusan government had to resort to writing letters to the pope, who finally decided in favour of Lokrum's Benedictines – thereby legitimising the Lionheart story.

It's always aroused a certain amount of passion. In 1929, Count Voynovitch, author of a handy little guide to the city, said: 'The basin is delightfully finished'. Just eight years later, however, (the ever-opinionated) Rebecca West was writing: 'Nothing could be more offensive to the eye, to the touch, or to common sense… it has the infinite elaborateness of eczema, and to add to the last touch of unpleasantness these animals are loosely fixed so that they may wobble and give an illusion of movement. Though Dubrovnik is beautiful, and this object was indescribably ugly, my dislike of the second explained to me why I felt doubtful in my appreciation of the first. The town regarded this horror as a masterpiece.'

And it's true; it does.

Dulčić Masle Pulitika Gallery [93 F5] (Galerija Dulčić Masle Pulitika; Držičeva poljana 1; ☎020 612 645; w ugdubrovnik.hr; ☉ 09.00–15.00 Tue–Sun; €8) On the square in front of the cathedral, this small but worthwhile gallery is managed by the Museum of Modern Art Dubrovnik. It focuses on the works of three important local artists, Ivo Dulčić, Antun Masle and Đuro Pulitika. Dubbed the Dubrovački koloristi (Dubrovnik colourists), they founded a 20th-century school of painting known for its use of bold expressive colour and local subject matter, including the city itself and surrounding landscapes and seascapes. In later life, Dulčić became increasingly interested in religious themes, working in paint, mosaic and stained glass – you can see several examples of these works in Dubrovnik's churches and monasteries.

The Rector's Palace [93 F5] (Knežev Dvor; Pred Dvorom 3; ☎020 321 452; ☉ Apr–Oct 09.00–18.00 daily, winter 09.00–16.00 Tue–Sun; €15) Diagonally opposite the cathedral is the Rector's Palace, with the municipal theatre next door.

If you get the chance, pop inside and admire the charming, miniature version of the grand Austro-Hungarian opera houses and theatres – complete with gilded boxes and velvet seating, which date back to 1869.

The Rector's Palace, now housing the **Cultural History Museum,** was the seat of Ragusa's government. It would once have looked more like a castle than a palace, but after the original was accidentally blown up in 1435 (always a mistake keeping your gunpowder next to your government), it was rebuilt in the Venetian-Gothic style by Onofrio della Cava – he of the fountains' fame.

It wasn't to last, as the gunpowder went off again in 1463. This time, the palace was restored by Michelozzo Michelozzi, who also did lots of work on the city's defensive fortresses, and Juraj Dalmatinac, who added various Renaissance touches.

You enter through a fine loggia topped with superb carved capitals on pillars of Korčula marble; the outer pairs are the original Gothic, while the middle three are Renaissance. Most interesting of all is the rightmost capital, thought to portray Asclepius, the Greek god of healing, who was born in Epidaurus (now Cavtat). The main door leads into an atrium, which is the (surprisingly small) venue for summer recitals. In here, you'll find the only statue ever raised to an individual in Ragusa's long history. On dying in 1607, Miho Pracat (page 121), a remarkable ship owner and adventurer from Lopud, left 1,000 shares in the Bank of St George in Genoa to the city. The city was suitably grateful – back then, those shares were worth around 100 lire apiece, at a time when gold was fetching three and a half lire an ounce. The interest on the capital was used by the city to free slaves, and Pracat got his statue.

The ground floor of the palace was formerly a prison, handy for the courtroom off to the right, with a curious marble barrier and wooden bench being about all you can see today. Upstairs are the state offices and rector's chambers – from the day they were elected, rectors were effectively prisoners here, only allowed to leave with the senate's permission. Fortunately, each only served a one-month term.

The main staircase was only used for the rector's inaugural procession on the first of the month, taking him upstairs to his confinement. Nobody ever came down the stairs unless the rector died in office – the hidden staircase behind was the way out. On your way up the main stairs, notice the handrails, supported by realistic (if not entirely tasteful) carved hands.

At the top of the stairs, over the door which originally led into the Grand Council chamber, there's an inscription reading '*Obliti Privatorum Publica Curate*' – a quote from Pericles, reminding councillors to forget their private concerns and think of public affairs instead.

The upstairs rooms are a curious collection – mainly because the palace was plundered, first by the French in the early 19th century, and then again by Yugoslavia's King Aleksandar after World War I, for the Royal Palace in Belgrade. As a result, they're, for the most part, furnished with private donations. You'll find an odd mix of Venetian repro, Louis XV copies, painted wood, Neapolitan ebony and marble veneer, along with an unusual collection of canvases featuring local bigwigs. Note also the keys to the city – the gates were locked every night, and the keys kept in the rector's office – and the candlelit clock.

Church of St Blaise [93 F4] (Sv Vlaho; ☉ usually 08.00–20.00 daily) The original church on this site was built in the 14th century, and although it (mostly) survived the Great Earthquake in 1667, it was subsequently consumed by fire. Miraculously, the 15th-century gold and silver statue of St Blaise (Dubrovnik's patron saint) escaped unharmed.

The new Baroque Church of St Blaise was completed in 1717 to plans by the Venetian architect Marino Grapelli, who based the interior design on the Church of San Maurizio in his hometown. It's even more unusual than the cathedral in its orientation, in having a south-facing altar.

The church is an elegant tribute to the city's patron saint, with a classic Baroque façade. Inside, it's not as austere as the cathedral but not too over the top either. The main attraction is the altar, where you can admire the famous statue of St Blaise holding the city – which shows you what it looked like in about 1485.

Also worth your attention is the painting across the organ loft representing the Martyrdom of St Blaise, which was painted by local boy Petar Matejević in the early 18th century. Spare a moment, too, for the stained-glass windows, which depict Sts Peter and Paul and Sts Cyril and Methodius, the creators of the Glagolitic alphabet (a later variant of which, Cyrillic, is named after St Cyril). These are the work of Ivo Dulčić, one of Dubrovnik's most famous modern artists, who died in 1975.

Ploče and the Museum of Modern Art [84 F3] The Ploče Gate leads out from the old town into the expensive suburb of Ploče. The gate is a complex structure actually comprising several gates and bridges which were built in the 15th century – though the current design dates from 1628. There's the familiar statue of St Blaise and a drawbridge leading out into what used to be a market square.

Just outside the gate, up on the left, **Life According to KAWA** [93 H2] (Hvarska 2; **f** KAWA.LIFE8) is a hip concept store stocking works by up-and-coming Croatian designers and artisans. It's a good place to shop for gifts to bring home, with everything from T-shirts and tote bags to natural cosmetics, jewellery, candles and ceramics.

The main road leads up to the **Lazareti** [93 H3], Dubrovnik's quarantine houses. Dubrovnik was one of the first ports in Europe to introduce quarantine restrictions, and if you wanted to visit, you had to spend 40 days here first before being allowed in. These days, the houses and courtyards are used as artists' studios and performance spaces.

A little further up the hill, on the left-hand side, is Dubrovnik's excellent **Museum of Modern Art** [84 F3] (Umjetnička Galerija Dubrovnik; Put Frana Supila 23; \020 426 590; w ugdubrovnik.hr; ⊕ 09.00–20.00 Tue–Sun; €10). Even if there were no art to see, the building itself is magnificent and well worth a visit. Built in 1939 as the summer villa for a wealthy ship-owner, Božo Banac, it was designed in a Renaissance style reminiscent of the Rector's Palace, and you wouldn't know it wasn't ancient. Since 1950, it has housed the museum's ever-expanding (and excellent) collection.

The permanent collection includes paintings and sculptures from Croatia's greatest artists as well as focusing on the burgeoning local scene. The works are rotated, and there are usually temporary exhibitions, so what's on show at any one time varies. Look out for sculpture from two of Croatia's most representative and best-known sculptors, Ivan Meštrović and Frano Kršnić, as well as landscapes by Mato Celestin Medović and interiors and still lifes from Emanuel Vidović. The show is stolen, naturally, by Vlaho Bukovac (page 117), and the gallery holds some of his very best work, including a number of gorgeous, complex portraits – though they're not always all on show. On the upper floor, the gallery stages temporary summer exhibitions, generally featuring well-known international artists who appeal to foreign visitors – recent solo shows include Francis Bacon (2016) and Andy Warhol (2023).

Mount Srđ [84 E2] Looming large above Dubrovnik, and visible from all over the city, is the mountain of Srđ. Up until 1991, there was a cable car that whisked visitors up to the top for the incredible view over the city and the islands, but it became one of the first victims of the war, dramatically destroyed by a Serb air raid. A new cable car was inaugurated in summer 2010.

A **cable car** runs to the top [93 G1] (w dubrovnikcablecar.com; ⏱ Jun–Aug 09.00–midnight, Sep 09.00–23.00, Oct 09.00–20.00, Mar 09.00–17.00, Apr 09.00–21.00, May 09.00–23.00, Nov–Feb closed; €27/€15 adult/child return); however, if you decide to walk up instead, bear in mind that the serpentine path is long, steep, and entirely without shade for the last two-thirds. At first, it's through pine trees, with butterflies and cicadas – magic and very cool. There's no water to be had on the way up, so take plenty with you. The path climbs up from the main road, running above Dubrovnik – referred to variously as Državna Cesta or Jadranska Cesta (and formerly Put Jugoslavenske Narodne Armije). Starting at the Pile Gate, turn right just after the bus stop and work your way up Zrinsko-Frankopanska. Cross over Zagrebačka and then Gornji Kono, then take the next right and follow this slip road under Jadranska Cesta. After this, the footpath starts off to your left from the highway. From the Pile Gate, it will take you 1 hour to the top of Mount Srđ, depending on how fit you are.

At the top, you'll find the **Imperial Fort** [84 F3], which was built by the French in 1810. In the 1970s, it became a popular discotheque. During the break-up of Yugoslavia, the fort served as command headquarters from the Croatian Army's 163rd Dubrovnik Brigade. Today, it houses the **Museum of the Croatian War of Independence** (Muzej Domovinskog Rata; w mdrd.hr; ⏱ Apr–Sep 08.30–22.00, Oct 09.00–20.00, Nov–Mar 09.00–17.00; €5) tracing both military and civilian events in and around Dubrovnik between 1991 and 1995. However, the main reason to come up here for most visitors is for the magnificent views. There's also a (pricey) bar-restaurant at the top.

There's also a huge stone cross at the top, which now dominates the Old Town, especially when it's illuminated at night. As you come up, spare a thought for the mothers of those killed in the war who come up on foot as a pilgrimage for their sons, walking barefoot to the top and stopping to pray at each of the 13 crosses placed at corners along the way.

Lokrum [84 F4] (w lokrum.hr) When you're in Dubrovnik, keep at least half a day free for a trip to sub-tropical Lokrum, the town's own offshore nature reserve. Said to have been visited unwillingly by Richard the Lionheart in 1192 (page 110) the island is today just a 15-minute boat ride away from the old town quay.

Lokrum remains undeveloped (albeit for an open-air bar-restaurant and a pizzeria) and makes for a wonderful break from the crowds onshore. Even when the boats are arriving full, every half-hour, the 2km-long island can easily absorb all comers, leaving an impression – away from a small central part – of calm and tranquillity, punctuated only by the cries of birds and the fluttering of butterflies.

A network of footpaths criss-crosses the island and provides access to the sea and into the dense woods. There are several rock beaches, and these are cleaner, fresher and less crowded than Dubrovnik's, as well as a warm **saltwater lake** (Mrtvo More, the Dead Sea) on the other side of the island from where the boat arrives. This has a 10m cliff which encourages the local lads to dive off it, apparently without harm. There's a **naturist beach** on Lokrum, too, on the southeastern end of the island, away from prying eyes – follow the FKK signs.

Lokrum's main attraction lies in its enormous variety of vegetation, which is all the more astonishing when you realise there's no freshwater supply – hence the absolute ban on making fires of any kind or even smoking. When you're wandering the paths, look out for numerous species of birds (including peacocks) and butterflies.

In the middle of the island, there's an old **botanical garden**, most of which seems like a series of wonderfully unmaintained secret gardens. Among slightly dilapidated walls, you'll find palms with soft furry trunks, trellises of twisted vines and crippled trees supported on crutches, while broken cloches sprout thyme and basil and lettuce run to seed.

In the heavy silence and deep shade, there's an agreeable air of mystery – which is shattered fairly unceremoniously when you round a corner and discover the restaurant and bar, and a small natural history museum, all within the structure of what was once a large Benedictine monastery. There is also a small *Game of Thrones* exhibition, which includes a replica of the Iron Throne, where many visitors like to have their photos taken.

On the summit of the island – a steepish 20-minute hike – there's the ruined **Fort Royal**. Built by the French in 1808, it gives great views out over Dubrovnik and the nearby coast and the islands.

From the northern tip of Lokrum, it is suddenly clear why Dubrovnik seems vaguely make-believe: it's a film set. So many movies have plundered that fortified look – the big walls, the red-roofed houses nestled between them dominated by a smattering of palaces and churches – that it doesn't seem real. It looks like it's meant to be looked at but could never really have been lived in.

To get to Lokrum, take the half-hourly boat (every day in season, less frequently out of season) from the old harbour, and make sure you know what time the last one is coming back. Tickets cost €27 return, or €5 for children.

GRUŽ [84 D2] Lying 3km west of the old town, Gruž port, besides being the gateway to the islands, has also become something of an up-and-coming neighbourhood over the last decade, with the opening of a handful of hip bars, restaurants and cultural venues. There's the Dubrovnik Beer Company, the Urban & Veggie vegan eatery, and TUP, a community-driven cultural centre in a disused factory. One attraction you shouldn't miss here is the **Red History Museum** [84 D1] (Muzej crveni povjesti; Svetog križa 3; w redhistorymuseum.com; ⊕ Apr–Oct 10.00–20.00, Nov–Mar 11.00–17.00; €9), which examines the reality of life under socialism when Croatia was part of Yugoslavia. Best of all is the reconstruction of a typical family apartment, complete with furniture and various household items from the 1970s and 1980s. It soon becomes apparent that Yugoslav design was far more image-conscious and experimental than some westerners might have thought. There's also a decent gift shop stocking bags, mugs and posters.

SOUTH OF DUBROVNIK

From Dubrovnik, it's 40km south to the Montenegrin border. On the way, there's a string of resorts (Kupari, Srebreno, Mlini, Soline and Plat) collectively known as the Župa Dubrovačka, which leads to the town of Cavtat (pronounced 'tsavtat'), after which there's just Čilipi Airport and the ruggedly beautiful Konavle region (the latter now opening up to tourists, with several agritourism farms serving authentic local food and wine) before you reach the border.

CAVTAT Situated just 16km south, the small, pleasant seaside town of Cavtat makes an excellent and easy excursion from Dubrovnik – and can even be considered as an alternative place to stay, with regular buses and small shuttle-boats between the two and accommodation both cheaper and easier to find here. If you're visiting the area by car, Cavtat makes an ideal base, with nothing like the parking hassles you'll find in Dubrovnik itself. For information about sightseeing and local activities, contact the **tourist office** (☏020 479 025; w visit.cavtat-konavle.com).

Cavtat was originally the Greek and then Roman colony of Epidaurus, though there's nothing left at all from that era barring a few classical fragments built into houses – fishermen, in Rebecca West's nicely turned phrase, having 'taken what they would of sculptures and bas-reliefs to build up their cottage walls, where they can be seen today, flowers in the buttonhole of poverty'.

Getting there and away The #10 Libertas **bus** runs about once an hour from 05.00 to 01.30 from Dubrovnik (last reliable bus back from Cavtat 23.00, for timetables see w libertasdubrovnik.hr and click 'Suburban timetable east'), and costs €4 each way (pay on the bus). The **little shuttle boat** runs until 23.00 in peak season and costs around €20 one-way – and docks conveniently in Dubrovnik's old town harbour. En route, most boats also stop at Srebreno and Mlini, where you have some good pebble beaches overlooked by several modern hotels. There's more than one boat company running to different timetables. Rates are the same for all operators.

⌂ **Where to stay** If you want to stay in Cavtat, there are lots of private rooms available, as well as a number of hotels, including one of Croatia's largest, the five-star Hotel Croatia. Midway between Dubrovnik and Cavtat, there are also several good hotels in Srebreno and Mlini. From Srebreno Bay, a 2km meandering promenade leads past a string of fine pebble beaches to Mlini, a former fishing village made up of houses draped in pink bougainvillaea.

Hotel Croatia (487 rooms) Frankopanska 10; ☏020 475 776; w adriaticluxuryhotels.com. Lovers of 1970s brutalist architecture will adore this stunning multi-tiered 5-star hotel which featured in a 2018 exhibition about Yugoslav architecture at MoMA in New York. The hotel is happily sheltered from view by the headland & has its own beaches (both standard & naturist). It's also home to an extensive spa with indoor & outdoor pools, a rustic steakhouse, & a waterside seafood restaurant overlooking Cavtat's bay. €€€€€
Hotel Supetar (16 rooms) A Starčićeva 27; ☏020 479 833; w adriaticluxuryhotels.com. Fully renovated in 2022, Hotel Supetar occupies a 1920s stone villa right on Cavtat's quayside. Now a slick boutique heritage hotel, it has a fine dining restaurant, a wine bar offering guided wine-tasting, & a garden with a small pool & lounge bar. €€€€€
Castelletto (13 rooms) Frana Laureana 22; ☏020 479 547; m 099 225 5906; w dubrovnikexperience.com. Family-run place in Cavtat with spacious rooms, restaurant & outdoor pool. €€€€

Maistra Select Hotel Mlini (85 rooms) Šetalište Marka Marojice 34; ☏052 800 250; w maistra.com. Overlooking the seafront promenade & beach in Mlini, between Dubrovnik & Cavtat, this hotel makes a fine choice for a relaxing beach holiday, with cultural sightseeing as an option. All rooms have balconies, & the best have sea-views, too. €€€€
One Suite Hotel (18 rooms) Šetalište dr Franje Tuđmana 1; ☏020 222 000; w onesuitehotel.com. Hip design hotel in Srebreno, midway between Dubrovnik & Cavtat, & 10mins' walk to the beach in Srebreno Bay. Facilities include a café with tables in the garden, a gym & a small rooftop pool. €€€€
Villa Pattiera (12 rooms) Trumbićev put 9; ☏020 478 800; w villa-pattiera.hr. Small, welcoming family-run boutique hotel in the old town. The same family also own the nearby Restaurant Dalmacija, overlooking Cavtat's fishing harbour. €€€€
Villa Radović (10 rooms) Ljudevita Gaja 3; ☏020 479 021; w villaradovic.weebly.com. Good-value place with simple, spacious en-suite rooms & use of a communal kitchen. Free airport transfers with direct bookings. €€€–€€

4

✖ Where to eat and drink As well as the restaurants listed, there are several pizzerias – try **Desetka Pizzeria** (Put Tihe 12; 🇫 pizzeriadesetka; €€).

Leut Trumbićev Put 17; 📞020 478 477; w restaurant-leut.com; ⊕ Mar–Nov 11.00–23.00 daily. 1 of the best of Cavtat's many restaurants is at the southern end of the town, right on the water. It's been in the Bobić family since 1971, & the traditional Dalmatian food is excellent, as you'd expect for the price – try their signature dish, the Seafood Selection Platter. €€€€
Taverna Galija Vulčevićeva 1; 📞020 478 566; w galija.hr; ⊕ May–Oct 11.00–23.00 daily. Galija serves 1st-rate seafood & meat, freshly grilled on a big outdoor barbecue. It overlooks the bay at the end of the seafront promenade, where the pinewoods begin. €€€€
Bugenvila Obala A Starčevića 9; 📞020 479 949; w bugenvila.online; ⊕ Apr–Oct 11.00–23.00

daily. A stylish & popular place serving colourful Creative Mediterranean fare (both à la carte & daily set menus) based on fresh seasonal ingredients, wine & cocktails. Nice terrace on the seafront promenade. €€€€–€€€
Ludo More Put Tihe 22; 📞020 432 039; 🇫 ludo. more.restaurant; ⊕ 09.00–23.00 daily. In Tiha Bay, behind the old town, this modern waterside eatery offers a limited & ever-changing menu, depending on what fresh seafood is available that day. Expect treats such as tuna tartar, octopus croquettes & tempura prawns. €€€€–€€€
Little Star Kupalište Kamen Mali; w beachbarlittlestar.com. Summer-only makeshift beach bar built into the rocks near the tip of the old town peninsula, with gorgeous sunset views.

What to see and do Cavtat (the name seems likely to be derived from the Latin word *civitas* (meaning state/citizenship) occupies a peninsula between two bays and has a charming palm-studded front lined with cafés and restaurants. There's not a whole lot to do, though the Franciscan Monastery, at the end of the quay, hides a pair of lovely Renaissance paintings, and the Rector's Palace, at the other end of the waterfront, houses the **Baltazar Bogišić Collection**, part of which is on display there (Obala A Starčevića' 18; 📞020 478 556; ⊕ Apr–Oct 09.00–13.00 Mon–Fri; €2.65) – notable in particular for a selection of excellent works by the local painter Vlaho Bukovac (see opposite).

Many more Bukovac paintings can be found at the artist's house, which is now the **Bukovac House** (Kuća Bukovac, Bukovčeva 5; 📞020 478 646; ⊕ 09.00–17.00 Tue–Sat, 09.00–noon Sun; €5). More than 80 of the artist's oils, spanning his entire career, mainly portraits of well-to-do families, are on show here, as well as several rooms he frescoed when still in his late teens.

Right at the end of the peninsula, in a gorgeous hilltop location overlooking the sea and surrounded by cypresses, is the town cemetery. Here you'll find one of Cavtat's most important treasures, the **Račić Mausoleum** (Trumbićev put 25; 📞020 478 646; ⊕ Apr–Oct 09.00–16.00 Mon–Sat; €4). Its commissioning by a daughter of the ship-owning Račić family seems to have been their downfall. No sooner was the building underway than she, her father and her brother died in quick succession, and just as soon as the mausoleum was completed her mother followed them into it.

The mausoleum is one of the most important works by Croatia's most famous sculptor, Ivan Meštrović, with the white-marble Byzantine sepulchre dating from 1922. Topped with a cupola and featuring sculpted angels, dogs and eagles, along with the four Račić sarcophagi, it's a quite extraordinary work. It excited mixed feelings in Rebecca West when she was here in 1937: 'There are some terrible errors, such as four boy musician angels, who recall the horrid Japaneseries of Aubrey Beardsley… but there are moments in the chapel which exquisitely illustrate the theory that the goodness of God stretches under human destiny, like the net below trapeze acts at the circus.'

VLAHO BUKOVAC – VIRTUOSO PAINTER

Vlaho Bukovac was born in Cavtat in 1855 and showed prodigious talent from an early age. In 1877, he went to the Beaux Arts in Paris to complete his studies and, a year later, became the first Croatian painter to be accepted into the prestigious Paris Salon. Travelling widely around Europe (in the UK, you can see some of his works at the Walker Gallery in Liverpool and the Mercer Gallery in Harrogate), Bukovac nonetheless played a vital part in the development of Croatian art – not just by being enormously prolific himself (he left over 2,000 works), but by supporting younger artists as well.

In his forties, Bukovac spent five years living in Cavtat before accepting the post of Professor of Fine Arts in Prague, though he returned to his childhood home regularly until shortly before his death in 1922.

At their best, Bukovac's paintings are simply marvellous, combining an almost photographic realism with impressionistic touches, and some of his portraits are truly stunning. As a virtuoso painter, he seems to have had a penchant for technically difficult or daring compositions, and there's a wonderful picture of a woman coming in (or going out?) through a doorway, which is in the Museum of Modern Art in Dubrovnik, along with a brilliant portrait of his daughter.

If you're after something a little less esoteric, there's a gorgeous walk around the headland, with plenty of places where you can relax in the shade of towering pine trees and swim off the rocks in limpid turquoise waters. You also have local providers offering scuba diving, **Epidaurum** (w epidaurum.com) and sea kayaking, **Sea Kayaking Cavtat** (w sea-kayaking-cavtat.com).

Rather more strenuous are several local **hikes**. The shorter of these leads from Cavtat to Močiči and Čilipi, taking around 1½ hours. The other involves a 3–4-hour trek up the 'Ronald Brown Pathway' (Pjesačka Staza Ronald Brown) that starts from the main road above the town and leads up into the mountains to the cross commemorating the delegation led by the American Minister of Trade in 1996. There's a useful list of hiking and biking routes, including maps, on the tourist office website (w visit.cavtat-konavle.com).

SOUTH TO THE MONTENEGRIN BORDER Past the airport of the same name you'll find the pretty village of **Čilipi**. After Sunday mass the locals put on a show of folk music and dancing in the main square here, so it's not surprising that it's become something of a Sunday morning excursion from Dubrovnik and the nearby resort hotels.

Alternatively, from Cavtat take the rural road inland from Zvekovica, which runs through the fertile **Konavle Valley**. Half-a-dozen old stone villages are built into its rugged slopes, overlooking the flat valley bottom, planted with vineyards and olive groves and dotted with elegant cypresses. Historically, Konavle supplied Dubrovnik with grain and fresh produce. Visit the 15th-century **Sokol Fortress** (w dpds.hr; ⏲ 10.00–17.00 daily; Mar–Oct €10, Nov–Feb €5), built into a rocky outcrop, complete with crenellated parapets and canons, intended to protect Dubrovnik's lands.

Wine lovers might also visit one of several Konavle wineries producing Dubrovačka Malvasija white wine from an indigenous grape which almost became extinct. Family-run **Crvik** (Kotar 12; ☎ 020 771 230; w crvik-wine.com; ⏲ 09.00–16.00

Mon–Fri), on the main road between Čilipi and Popovići, is probably the best choice – also be sure to taste their award-winning red Vilin Ples, and their orange Blasius fermented naturally on the skins.

Three buses a day (#11; first bus from Dubrovnik 10.00, last bus back 18.30; timetable at w libertasdubrovnik.hr) run from Dubrovnik to Čilipi and on to **Molunat** (40km southeast of Dubrovnik), a sleepy resort which has sprung up around a tiny fishing village in a lovely cove right at the very end of Croatia. With just a handful of private rooms and no hotels nearby, it's within an hour of Dubrovnik, and an utterly charming place to stay. To be honest, however, given the bus times and the minuteness of the place, you'd need to be in Dubrovnik on an extended visit to make the excursion worthwhile. If you do decide to stay a few days in Molunat, **Sea Star Diving** (**f** seastarmolunat) offers scuba-diving trips and tuition, while **Invenium Water Sports** (w inveniumwatersports.com) has sea kayaks and SUPs (stand-up paddle boards) to hire.

✖ Where to eat and drink There are several nice restaurants in the south towards the border, including a number of rustic agritourism eateries:

Kameni Mlin Bistroće 3; **m** 098 309 820; w kameni-mlin.com; ☉ May–Oct 10.00–17.00 daily, Nov–Apr noon–19.00 Sat–Sun. In an old stone mill in Čilipi, everything on offer here is homemade. Through summer, they offer a full 3-course tasting menu, with meat & home-grown vegetables. In winter, they work w/ends only, with occasional live music. €€€€–€€€
Konoba Ivankovi Drvenik 9; **m** 098 184 0948; **f**; ☉ Apr–Oct noon–22.00 daily, Nov–Mar on request. Near Zvekovica, this welcoming family-

run tavern serves rustic local fare, including barbecued lamb, garden salads & homemade desserts. €€€€–€€€
Konoba Vinica Donja Ljuta 44; **m** 099 2152 459; w konobavinica.com; ☉ variable. Inland from the main road in the village of Ljuta, this serves good, traditional local & Dalmatian dishes (including *ispod peka* dishes, *pašticada* & grilled trout) in a rustic setting, with a lovely riverside terrace. €€€€–€€€

THE ELAPHITI ISLANDS (KOLOČEP, LOPUD, ŠIPAN)

The Elaphiti islands lie in a string north of Dubrovnik. These once-quiet islands have seen tourism well and truly arrive, with a growing number of day trip operators allowing much easier access to the islands.

The Jadrolinija (w jadrolinija.hr) ferries and catamarans run up and down the Elaphiti from Dubrovnik four times daily all year round. In summer, tickets from Dubrovnik cost €4.90 one-way, regardless of which island you're going to. There's also a fast TP Line (w tp-line.hr) catamaran calling at Šipanska luka en route between Dubrovnik and Mljet. If you're clever with the timetables, you can also use these services to combine the Elaphiti islands with a trip to Mljet, Korčula and Lastovo, or even onwards up to Split.

Even with more tourism than there used to be, the Elaphiti still make for a great excursion, getting you away from the crowds and into nature; there are no cars on Koločep and Lopud, and barely a handful on Šipan.

KOLOČEP The first inhabited island in the Elaphiti is Koločep, just 7km from Dubrovnik on the Jadrolinija ferry (45mins) or the catamaran (30mins), making it a very easy day trip. The ferry and catamaran both dock at Donje Čelo, and although there's another settlement on the other side of the island, it's here that you'll find the main infrastructure (a post office and a small general store) plus a nice beach.

Outside the tourist season Koločep has an official population of just 150, and the doctor only comes once a week. Indeed, if you come here before May, you'll find nowhere on the island to eat or drink at all – so bring a picnic, and make sure you know what time the last ferry leaves.

Donje Čelo is spread around a gentle bay and has a biggish and reasonably sandy beach. A concrete path heads up from the ferry landing and winds across the island, leading through lovely woods and dry-stone-walled fields to the settlement of Gornje Čelo on Koločep's southeastern shore – where you'll find a nice small hotel and a couple of bars in summer, and nothing whatsoever in winter. Smaller paths head on into the scented woods, and the island's sufficiently large for you to lose sight of anyone else but small enough for most people to avoid getting lost.

Where to stay and eat If you want to stay (from May to Oct), the nicest place is **Kalamota Beach House** (❧ 020 414 616; w kalamota-beachhouse. com; €€€€) in Gornje Čelo. It has ten spacious suites with kitchenettes and balconies and a bar-restaurant serving Creative Mediterranean fare on a palm-lined waterside terrace. The other hotel on the island, the sprawling TUI Blue **Kalamota Island Resort in Donje Čelo**, is now an adults-only all-inclusive. There are also a handful of private rooms available.

LOPUD Fifteen minutes by catamaran or 35 minutes by ferry – and a mere €3.70 beyond Koločep is the larger island of Lopud. Important in Ragusan times, it once had a population of 4,000 and harboured nearly 100 ships, as well as being home to Miho Pracat, the man whose bust sits in the Rector's Palace in Dubrovnik (page 110).

Today, the 4.5km-long island has a population of just 269 (though locals put the figure even lower). Everyone lives in one settlement, the eponymous Lopud, on a curved bay with a decent beach facing the village of Suđurađ on the next-door island of Šipan. There's no traffic, no pollution and no crime – and out of season, nothing much open beyond a bar and a couple of shops. In summer, however, Lopud really comes into its own, and the village positively hums; it's a great place to come for the day or even for a holiday in its own right.

Where to stay and eat If you want to stay on Lopud, there are quite a few private rooms and apartments for rent. There are restaurants and bars all along the front, the most highly regarded being Restoran Obala (w obalalopud.com; €€€€), which serves excellent seafood, plus some vegetarian options, at tables right by the water's edge. Pretty much everything, including all the hotels and most of the island's restaurants, closes from November to April.

RMH Lopud Lafodia Resort & Wellness (156 rooms) Iva Kuljevana; ❧ 020 450 300; w lafodiahotel.com. Located at the far end of the bay from the ferry terminal & harbour, the Lafodia is Lopud's package tour hotel, with a spa & outdoor pool. Refurbished with swish, spacious 156 rooms & suites with balconies & nice views, plus 3 spacious apartments. They also manage the nearby Villa Benessa in a 16th-century stone villa on the seafront promenade, sleeping 8. €€€€

Glavović (12 rooms, 2 apartments) Iva Kuljevana; ❧ 020 759 359; w hotel-glavovic.hr. The 3-star

Glavović was the island's oldest hotel, which opened in 1927 & was renovated in 2004. Even if it's comfortable enough, the accommodation is still fairly basic – though the sandy beach just outside is a bonus. €€€

Restoran Obala Iva Kuljevana 18; m 098 512 725; w obalalopud.com; ◷ Jun–Sep 10.30–midnight daily (depending on the weather). Serves excellent seafood, plus some vegetarian options, at tables right by the water's edge. €€€€

Konoba Peggy w pavlovic-pension-lopud.com. It's worth climbing up the street near the harbour

4

to this place, which does a great grill in summer & boasts breezy views out across the sea to the island of Šipan. It also has 2 rooms & 3 apartments to rent. Try its versions of limoncello & a curiously potent, nameless local drink made from honey & herbs. €€€

What to see and do Historically, Lopud had two monasteries, 33 little churches and a host of villas belonging to wealthy Dubrovnik families who would come here to escape the summer heat, though not a great deal of that former glory remains.

Up on your left as you disembark from the ferry stands the former Franciscan Monastery, commanding a superb site high above the bay. Abandoned for centuries in ruins, as of 2020, it functions as an exclusive vacation property, **Lopud 1483** (w lopud1483.com), which also hosts occasional events. A 20-year restoration project, initiated by art collector Francesca Thyssen-Bornemisza, has seen the former monk's cells turned into five plush suites, complete with contemporary furnishing and eclectic artworks, and the monastery's walled garden replanted with medicinal plants and aromatic herbs, just as it would have been back in the 15th century. Recent guests include the Beckhams.

From here, if you follow the seafront promenade around the bay, you'll see a sign to your left saying *Your Black Horizon*. In a garden set back from the coast, **Your Black Horizon** (☺ Jun–Oct 10.00–18.00 daily; free admission) is a wooden pavilion housing a contemporary lighting installation by Icelandic-Danish artist Olafur Eliasson and Ghanaian-British architect David Adjaye. Commissioned by Thyssen-Bornemisza Art Contemporary, it was originally displayed at the Venice Biennale in 2005, then transferred here in 2007, bringing a quirky international cultural highlight to this castaway island.

Further along the seafront, there's a lovely park with towering pine trees and palms – each one planted, it is said, by grateful sailors who'd avoided shipwreck. Just beyond the park, before the former Grand Hotel, there's a path leading up to the left which crosses the island and comes out half an hour later at **Šunj**, one of the loveliest beaches on the Adriatic. On the crest of the hill, on the left, there's a concrete monument to Viktor Dyk, the Czech poet, author and political journalist, who died unexpectedly of a heart attack while on holiday here in May 1931, aged only 53.

In a sheltered east-facing bay, the sandy beach at Šunj has a lovely shallow descent into the water and several temporary bar-restaurants open in season. It's an ill-kept secret, however, with sizable crowds coming over from the mainland by excursion boats during summer weekends.

The name Šunj provides the clue to Lopud's apparently mysterious use of a snake swallowing a child on its coat of arms – something you're more likely to have seen as the right half of the Alfa Romeo logo. According to the legend, Otto Visconti was shipwrecked here in 1098 on his way back from the Crusades, and so grateful was he to survive that he had a votive church built on the hill above the bay. This was decorated with a copy of a shield which had been used by one of the defeated Saracens – featuring the snake and the child – and which subsequently became the Visconti crest. Over time, the locale became known as *biscione*, the Italian for 'big snake', which was later abbreviated to Šunj.

The present **Church of Our Lady of Šunj** (Gospa od Šunja) above the bay – turn left just after the Dyk memorial, if you're coming from Lopud – dates from the end of the 15th century. If it's open (which, sadly, is not all that often), it's well worth looking in to see the marvellous carved wooden altarpiece featuring Mary and the Apostles. This, oddly enough, is English, from the 16th century. Lopud sailors – arguably among the best in the world at the time – heard that Henry VIII was in

At an altitude of 1,228m, Biokovo Skywalk affords stunning views over the Makarska Riviera PAGE 170

above
(VG/S)

A cable car whisks passengers to the peak of Mount Srđ, for superb views over Dubrovnik and Lokrum Island PAGE 113

below
(C/S)

above
(X/S)
On Dugi Otok, Telašćica Nature Park encompasses plummeting cliffs and a saltwater lake PAGE 6

left
(GS/S)
Chamois, a species of wild goat-antelope, on Mount Biokovo PAGE 168

below left
(GS/S)
Try scuba diving to explore the Adriatic's underwater life, with sights such as this red coral off Lastovo PAGES 63 & 144

below right
(GS/S)
Lake Vrana Nature Park is an ornithological reserve and home to dozens of aquatic bird species, including little egret PAGE 201

Rocky and arid, a large part of the Kornati archipelago
has been proclaimed a national park PAGE 228

above
(X/S)

Dating from the 12th century, St Mary's Monastery sits on a tiny
islet on a saltwater lake on the island of Mljet PAGE 127

below
(RS/S)

above left
(N/S)

Hiking the canyons of Paklenica National Park, in the Velebit mountains PAGE 205

above right
(MPo/S)

The verdant Cetina Gorge, near Omiš, is ideal for rafting, kayaking and canyoning PAGES 72 & 166

left
(Z/S)

Paklenica National Park is a popular venue for rock climbing, with some 590 marked routes PAGES 73 & 202

below
(AA/S)

Sailing boats drop anchor in secluded bays off the Pakleni Islets, opposite Hvar PAGES 185

The lovely Zlatni Rat beach in Bol on Brač is a sought-after
spot for kitesurfing PAGE 176

above
(M/S)

The sea channel between Pelješac and Korčula offers ideal
conditions for windsurfing PAGE 135

below
(GS/S)

above
(JO/S)

Dalmatian a cappella singing, known as *klapa*, is often performed in the domed vestibule of Diocletian's Palace in Split PAGE 19

left
(MPa/S)

A bronze statue of 10th-century bishop Grgur Ninski, by sculptor Ivan Meštrović, in Split PAGE 158

below
(D/S)

You'll hear it before you see it – the *Sea Organ* in Zadar is embedded in the paving on the seafront promenade PAGE 199

The 15th-century Franciscan Monastery on Lopud lay derelict for decades, but has now been restored and provides luxury accommodation PAGE 120

above
(NN/S)

In Zadar, the 9th-century St Donat's has been deconsecrated and is now used for hosting concerts PAGE 198

right
(P/S)

The UNESCO-listed Gothic-Renaissance cathedral in Šibenik is largely the work of architect Juraj Dalmatinac PAGE 212

below
(T/S)

above left (H/D) Hardy little sheep do well in the scanty pastures of Pag Island, where, it is said, there are more sheep than people PAGE 217

above right (BS/D) Made from the milk of the island's free-grazing sheep, Paški sir (Pag cheese) is Croatia's most esteemed cheese PAGE 219

below left (Mi/D) The vineyards on the Pelješac peninsula produce small black grapes of the Plavac mali variety, which does well here to produce potent red wine PAGE 134

below right (D/D) Split's fish market displays an impressive range of Adriatic seafood, delivered fresh each morning by local fishermen PAGE 155

Born into a wealthy family on Lopud in 1528, Miho Pracat sought fame and fortune at sea but twice returned home penniless and in tatters. On the third try, however, he succeeded, and came back to Lopud a fabulously wealthy man – having saved Spain, it's said, from starvation after a bad harvest by using his ships to supply grain (no doubt at a healthy premium).

At an audience with a grateful King Charles V, Pracat was offered gold and a post as a colonial governor, but being wealthy and a patriotic Ragusan to boot he refused both. Instead, he asked for the king's shaving gown – which is why it's in Lopud's Town Museum today.

Pracat's only problem, it seems, was fertility – neither of his two wives produced an heir for him. When he finally died, in 1607, Pracat left his enormous fortune to the republic, mostly in the form of trusts. He was rewarded with the only statue ever raised to one of its own citizens – you can see it today in the Rector's Palace in Dubrovnik.

conflict with the pope and busily dissolving the monasteries, so off they went to go and buy bargain relics and religious treasures. The background to the altarpiece shows the Lopud ship which brought the Madonna here.

There's a direct path leading back from the church into the town; off to the right of this, heading away from Šunj, there's a track leading up to a great ruined **fortress**. Built originally in the 16th century, it was reinforced and expanded by the French between 1808 and 1813. Today, it's soulful and dilapidated, and there's nothing particularly special to see – though the views across to the island of Šipan are undoubtedly fabulous.

ŠIPAN Furthest away, largest and least visited of the Elaphiti, Šipan is lovely. Known as the 'Golden Island', it once had 300,000 olive trees and a sizable population, but centuries of emigration have left it with fewer than 500 inhabitants and – like Lopud – with many more houses than people. During Dubrovnik's Golden Age, it was fashionable for wealthy nobles to spend the summer season on Šipan, and you'll come across their (mostly dilapidated) summer residences all over the island – along with a smattering of Roman ruins and a score of churches from the 11th century onwards, but the main reason to come here is very much to get away from it all.

It takes 1 hour to get to Suđurađ on Šipan from Dubrovnik on the Jadrolinija catamaran or you can take the ferry (1hr 50mins; the standard €4.90 one-way). On the fast TP Line catamaran to Šipanska Luka, this time is reduced to 45 minutes (despite being further away), and tickets are €5.70. The main centres – and the only places where you'll find anything at all to eat or drink – are **Šipanska Luka** (which is where the TP Line catamaran stops) to the northwest at the end of a deep inlet and **Suđurađ**, which is where the Jadrolinija ferry stops, to the southeast, opposite Lopud. The two settlements are about 7km apart and connected by an irregular minibus service, which is (sort of) timed to coincide with the ferries. There's also a handful of other hamlets across the island.

Where to stay and eat Everything on the island is pretty much closed from November to April. In season, there are several private rooms and apartments available at either end of the island. At present, only one hotel is working.

Hotel Božica (26 rooms) Suđurađ; ✎020 325 400; w hotel-bozica.hr. A 4-star hotel with a good restaurant offering stunning views back from Suđurađ towards the Croatian mainland, & a small outdoor pool. €€€€
Eco Apartments Kate (7 rooms) Suđurađ 14; m 092 348 9634; w apartments-kate-sipan.com. In a renovated old stone building near the port in Suđurađ, 7 comfortable apartments, each sleeping 2, with kitchenette & balcony. The owners make their own wine & olive oil & can arrange bicycles for cycling to Šipanska Luka. €€€
✳ **Konoba Kod Marka** Šipanska Luka; ✎020 758 007; w konoba-kod-marka.com; ☼ May–Sep

11.00–23.00 daily. Highly regarded konoba, much loved by sailing crews who moor up to overnight in the bay. No menus, the waiter will tell you what's on offer that day – expect sublime Dalmatian seafood dishes made from whatever the fishermen brought in fresh that morning. A true gourmet experience. Reservations essential several days in advance in high season. €€€€
Stara Mlinica Suđurađ 12; m 098 705 690; ☼ May–Oct 10.00–23.00 daily. Welcoming family-run eatery overlooking the bay in Suđurađ – they serve fresh seafood caught by local fishermen along with their own garden vegetables. €€€

What to see and do An excellent excursion is to start from one end of the island and then walk or cycle across to the other, ie: Šipanska Luka to Suđurađ or vice versa. It takes a leisurely 2 hours by the most direct route, on Šipan's only paved road. The interior of the island is a fertile valley where you'll see grapes, figs and olives being grown, and there are plenty of places to stop and have a picnic and a bottle of wine.

You can also wander up any of the many tracks on the island (though stay well away from any remaining uncleared ordnance – well-marked signs mark the spots), which lead up to the island's two limestone ridges. Here you'll find abandoned olive groves surrounded by crumbling dry-stone walls, though, above Šipanska Luka itself, work is progressing apace on bringing some of the olive trees back into production. You may also come across the rooting marks made by wild boar here. They're a recent arrival on the island and something of a nuisance to the olive farmers, having swum across from the mainland after a forest fire at the end of the 1990s.

As you traverse the island, look out for the ruined Napoleonic fortress on the southern ridge, along with a hospital and barracks dating from the same era. There are also secretive military tunnels which dive into the hillside nearby, though for the time being these are off-limits to the public.

If you're walking from Šipanska Luka to Suđurađ you'll pass a great fortress of a church dating from the 16th century, dedicated to **Sveti Duh** (the Holy Spirit), as you climb up out of the central valley. Just after this the road forks – if you go right, it passes the local clinic and loops down to the port; if you go straight on, it goes directly through Suđurađ itself before emerging at the harbour.

The dominating feature of Suđurađ is the summer residence of Vice Stjepović-Skočibuha, which is the only one of Šipan's 42 original mansions to be entirely preserved. It was built in 1563, with the tower being added in 1577, and is today used for conferences and functions.

If you want to explore further afield, you'll find boats down on the harbour whose owners are happy to take you out to the uninhabited Elaphiti islands as well as to delightful unspoiled coves and beaches on Šipan itself – if there's nobody around, ask at the little bar along the harbour front, which is where most of the fishermen and seafaring types hang out.

MLJET

Mljet is one of the most attractive islands in the whole Adriatic. Despite being unusually beautiful, and entirely unspoiled by deforestation (it was never ruled by

Venice, hence also the lack of towns of any size), it has hitherto remained relatively unvisited – though with the fast connection from Dubrovnik, more people are coming every year. Nonetheless, the island is easily big enough, at over 100km², to absorb many more visitors without getting overcrowded.

The entire western end of Mljet is a national park and features dense pine forests concealing two gorgeous saltwater lakes, the larger of which has an island with a ruined monastery on it. It's easy to visit on a day trip from Dubrovnik, but if you want to stay longer there's a hotel and some private rooms, and the island has great walking, cycling and canoeing, along with a diving school.

HISTORY Legend has it that Ulysses stopped here for seven years on his Odyssey, and while there's absolutely no historical basis for the assertion, it makes a nice story. More credence can be given to the theory that on his way to martyrdom in Rome, St Paul was shipwrecked here, not on Malta. It's not just the name (Mljet used to be called Melina), but also the snakes – St Paul was bitten by one soon after arriving, which would be improbable (then as now) on Malta, whereas Mljet was notoriously snake-infested until the 19th century.

What's sure is the island's use by the Illyrians and the Romans – the remains of the Illyrian fort can still be seen on the summit of Mali Grade, near **Babine Kure**, while the settlement of **Police** is named after the ruins of the 4th- or 5th-century Roman palace there.

The next significant development was in 1151, when Mljet was given to the Benedictines, who built the monastery on St Mary's Island and subjected the islanders to a harsh feudal system and hefty taxes. They stayed on even though Mljet itself was handed over to Dubrovnik in 1333 and lived a reclusive life until the arrival of Napoleon's troops in 1808, after which the monastery was abandoned.

The administrative centre of the island, **Babino Polje**, dates from the Middle Ages, but apart from the monastery, nothing on the western end of the island reaches back beyond the late 18th century, and the new port of **Pomena** wasn't established until after World War II. Pomena is now Mljet's main port and holiday destination, with a hotel and a handful of restaurants. Ferries and catamarans stop here, and its sheltered bay is popular with yachters, who drop anchor to overnight here.

WILDLIFE Mljet is famous for being the only place in Europe where you can find mongooses in the wild. The **Indian grey mongoose** was introduced to Mljet in 1910 by the Austrians in an attempt to eradicate the infestation of venomous snakes. This had been a problem since time immemorial – and was probably why the Benedictines built their monastery on the island in the first place ('Never mind the beauty and the isolation, Brother Jacob, let's get away from those blasted snakes!').

Seven male and four female mongooses were introduced, and they adapted well to the Mljet lifestyle, proliferating and practically eradicating the snake population over the next 20 years. So successful were they, in fact, that they lost their statutory protection in 1949, and excessive numbers have proven difficult to curb. Small animals, as well as both resident and migratory birds, fall prey to the feral hunters, and they're not over-popular with the islanders, either.

Mljet's other fauna used to include the **Mediterranean monk seal**, though none has been spotted here since 1974. You may, however, see the **Turkish gecko**, the **sharp-snouted lizard**, or **Dahl's whip snake** (if the mongooses haven't got to him first), and there are now quite a few **fallow deer** in the forests – following their introduction in 1958. Regarding birds, the European honey buzzard and the tawny

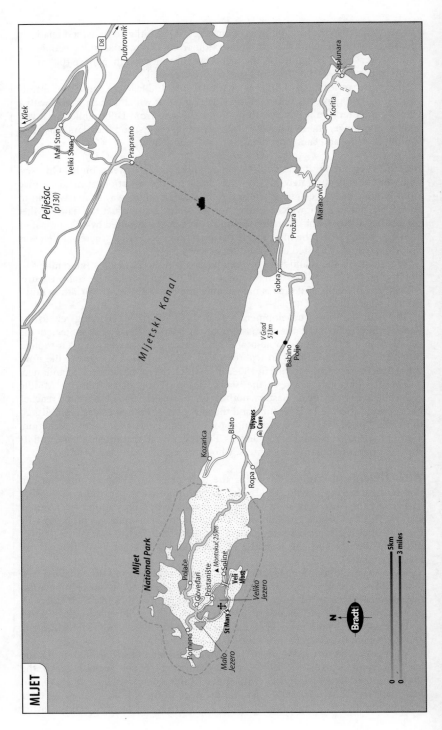

MLJET

Klek

Dubrovnik

D8

Mali Ston
Veliki Ston

Pelješac
(p130)

Prapratno

Mljetski Kanal

Šaplunara

Korita

Maranovići

Prožura

Sobra

V Grad
513m

Babino
Polje

Kozarica

Blato

Ulysses
Cave

Ropa

Mljet
National Park

Polače

Govedari

Pristanište

Montokuc 259m

Soline

Veli
Most

Veliko
Jezero

St Mary's

Pomena

Malo
Jezero

N

Bradt

0   5km
0   3 miles

owl nest in Mljet's forests, while numerous migratory birds also stop here, so you might spot European shag and even peregrine falcons.

GETTING THERE AND AWAY In summer, you can take the Krilo (w krilo.hr) daily fast catamaran from Dubrovnik to Pomena on Mljet (1hr 15mins; €20), which runs all the way to Split, with stops at Korčula, Hvar and Milna (on Brač). Arriving in Pomena is ideal, as it lies within the national park, so you're already where you want to be. This is also where most excursion boats arrive and depart.

Alternatively, TP Line (w tp-line.hr) operates an all-year catamaran from Dubrovnik to tiny Sobra on Mljet's north coast, which runs once daily in winter (1hr 20mins; €5.20), stopping en route at Šipanska Luka, and three times daily in summer (€8.40), when it also proceeds to Korčula and Lastovo. There's also an all-year Jadrolinija car ferry between Prapratno on Pelješac and Sobra (w jadrolinija. hr), which takes 45 minutes. It makes 4 crossings daily in winter (€3.60), upped to 6 daily in summer (€5.60).

Arrivals in **Sobra** are met by the local bus – but be warned that on busy days in summer there can be fewer buses than passengers.

The quickest way of seeing Mljet is by taking an all-inclusive package from Dubrovnik or Korčula, though note that some excursion boats can be a bit rowdy. These go for around €60–110, and include the boat transport, the entry fee to the national park, a trip out to the island on the lake, and (sometimes) a guided tour and/or a light lunch, as well as the chance to swim.

GETTING AROUND Apart from the local buses that run between Sobra and Pomena to coincide with the Jadrolinija ferry arrivals and departures, there's no public transport.

If you want to **cycle** on the island, the obvious place to rent bikes is at the Hotel Odisej (page 126) in Pomena, or by the lakes themselves – the paths around the lakes are absolutely perfect for cyclists. There are several other places which rent out bikes too, such as **Rent-a-bike Baraba** (f mljet.baraba.rentabike) – rates run from around €6 an hour to €24 a day for a regular bike or €15 an hour to €70 a day for an e-bike.

WHERE TO STAY AND EAT The monastery on St Mary's Island served from 1960 to 1988 as the lovely Hotel Melita, but since it was handed back to the Dubrovnik bishopric it's fallen into ruin. Although restoration commenced in 2004, nobody's sure what will become of it – there's no doubt it would make the most wonderful boutique hotel, but there are also plans to turn it into a research or information centre, or to leave it as a visitor attraction. At present, there's just a modest restaurant, Melita (w mljet-restoranmelita.com; ⊕ May–Oct 08.00–20.00 daily), serving the numerous visitors to the islet, to rather mixed reviews.

Although there's only one hotel on the island, in Pomena within the national park, Mljet has a reasonable (and steadily increasing) supply of **private rooms and apartments**, but it's a very good idea to book ahead. Polače, a few kilometres away from the Hotel Odisej but still within easy walking distance of the lakes, has good private rooms on the shore and also has a bakery and a couple of cheerful restaurants.

Half-a-dozen **restaurants** line the harbour in Pomena, which is very popular with people from visiting yachts (as, indeed, is Polače) though food shopping is limited to the early-morning bakery van, a couple of fruit stalls and the absolute basics.

You'll also find rooms, apartments, and several nice waterside restaurants in Saplunara on Mljet's southeast coast. Its main draw is two sheltered bays with beaches – like Pomena, they attract sailing folk who love to overnight there at anchor.

Hotel Odisej (155 rooms) Pomena; 020 362 111; w adriaticluxuryhotels.com; ⊕ Apr–Oct. Next to the ferry port in Pomena, Mljet's only hotel rooms spread across a number of buildings, with sea-view dbls with balconies, plus a restaurant, pizzeria, 2 bars, a small spa & bikes to hire. €€€€€–€€€€
Pine Tree Boutique Apartments (12 apartments) Saplunara 17; m 099 591 0024; w pinetreemljet.com. On Mljet's southeastern tip, near Saplunara beach, a modern 3-storey building combining 12 apartments & the Ante's Place restaurant with a gorgeous waterside terrace. €€€€
Accommodation Mljet (3 apartments) Goveđari 14; m 098 285 697; ◨. In the pinewoods in Goveđari, this renovated old stone house has 3 boho-chic apartments with upcycled furniture & self-catering facilities. It hosts occasional yoga retreats, art exhibitions & open-air summer cinema. €€€

Stermasi (10 apartments) Saplunara; m 098 939 0362; w stermasi.hr. Highly regarded restaurant, serving seafood along with their own garden vegetables & goat's cheese at waterside tables in Saplunara. They also have 10 apartments with kitchenettes. €€€
Villa Radulj (2 rooms, 5 apartments) Kozarica; m 091 517 0012. Lying on the north coast, 5 miles east of the national park, all rooms & apartments have either a balcony or terrace & sea-views. There's also a lovely vine-draped terrace restaurant. €€€
Holiday House Matana (5 apartments, 3 rooms) Pomena 10; m 098 934 0868; w guesthouse-matana-pomena.com. In Pomena, next to the entrance to the national park, Matana offers comfortable accommodation, sea-views & a terrace restaurant. €€€–€€

ACTIVITIES If you're here for more than a day trip, take advantage of the island's excellent **walking and hiking**. From the gentle paths around the lakes to the harder trails into the hills, Mljet's unspoiled beauty is overwhelming, and away from the lakes you'll pretty much have the place to yourself. Even on the lakeshore, you don't have to walk far to have almost total seclusion. There's a good marked trail from near Soline up Montokuč overlooking the lakes (the ascent takes around 40mins), with great views from the top. Rather than retrace your steps, you could return to Pristanište or continue to Polače or Goveđari. Within the park, trails lead to unexplored coves on the island's northwest tip, while even outside the park, the ratio of nature to people is very high. If you're going to be walking or hiking here, or elsewhere in Croatia, it's well worth getting hold of *The Islands of Croatia* by Rudolf Abraham or *Croatia: 9 Car Tours, 70 Long and Short Walks* by Sandra Bardwell, both of which do a great job of covering the country from a walker's perspective. There's a good new hiking map published by the HGSS (page 45).

The **Mljet Hiking Trail**, opened in 2012, is a 43km marked hiking route across the island, from Pomena to Sobra – via Goveđari, Blato, Babino Polje and Veliki Grad – and can be comfortably walked in three days. See w mljet.hr for more details.

If it's watersports you're after, there's plenty of choice. Exploring by **kayak or canoe** makes for a great way of seeing the lakes at your own pace – they can be rented by the little bridge or at the hotel, with prices roughly the same as for bikes. If you prefer a guided tour over going it alone, IDAdventures (w idadventures.hr; m 095 909 9352) arrange half-day kayaking trips, with a light picnic lunch included. For **divers**, the local diving centre (Aquatica-Mljet, based in Pomena; contact Mario Orlandini; m 098 479 916; w aquatica-mljet.hr) can take you out to a Roman wreck, complete with original amphorae, or to a defunct German U-boat, and they also offer scuba-diving lessons at various levels.

WHAT TO SEE AND DO
Mljet National Park (📞020 744 041; w np-mljet.hr; €25 inc the boat ride to St Mary's Island in Jun–Sep, €15 Oct–May) Mljet's main draw is the national park,

and specifically the two saltwater lakes, **Veliko Jezero** (with St Mary's Island and the crumbling monastery) and **Malo Jezero** – literally 'Big Lake' and 'Small Lake'. Established in 1960, the national park is run from the settlement of **Goveđari**, roughly equidistant from both Pomena and Polače. Entry fees go to the upkeep of the park, so don't be tempted to try to avoid paying. Anyway, if you're caught without a ticket, you'll be charged – double. Detailed maps are available from the park office (on the shore of the main lake, at the locality called **Pristanište**) or from the kiosk selling tickets in Pomena. There's another kiosk on the road in from Polače.

The national park is unusual among nature reserves in including the main villages, the hotel and the basic tourist infrastructure within its boundaries, but don't be lulled into a sense of false security. You're in an ecologically fragile area here, and it's important to follow the rules, especially relating to fire – in 1917, an accidental blaze destroyed much of the old forest, and the restoration took decades. So don't light fires, don't smoke, don't camp – and do stay on the paths.

If you're on a day trip you won't have time to see a great deal else other than the lakes. As you'll probably guess – the saltwater's a bit of a giveaway – neither Malo nor Veliko Jezero is actually a lake. The sea feeds into the larger one, and that feeds into the smaller one. The tidal changes allowed the monks to run a useful watermill in the past, and although the mill's long gone you can still easily see which way the tide's headed from the bridge over the shallow channel between Malo and Veliko Jezero.

Probably the most rewarding thing to do is to either hike or cycle the complete 12km perimeter of the **Veliko Jezero**. Happily, the elegant stone **Veli Most** (Great Bridge) spanning the 14m-wide sea channel was reconstructed in 2016, the old one having been demolished in 1958. So doing the whole loop is once again possible.

The boat out to **St Mary's Island** (Sv Marija) runs several times a day (every 30mins during high season), and one ride there and back is included in the price of the national park entry ticket. On the island itself, there's not been much to see in recent years, but the monastery is currently being restored, and the church is now open for services at 11.30 on Sunday. You can visit the monks' gardens, complete with lemon trees, in the original cloisters (if they're open). The island also has a restaurant, which is highly popular as the luncheon venue for excursions.

Take the 10-minute path around the little island, and you'll see two other plain but evocative votive chapels dating from the 17th or 18th century. These were built by grateful sailors who'd survived shipwrecks or storms. If you're here in spring, you'll find lots of wild asparagus, while in summer, you'll be overwhelmed by the noise of cicadas in the afternoon haze.

Beyond the national park Three-quarters of Mljet is forest-covered, meaning good shade in the summer heat (but take plenty of water with you; there are no supplies at all), while the few settlements are rarely visited, and you'll be made to feel welcome by the locals. This is especially true on the 15km-stretch of the island east of Sobra, where the settlements of **Prožura**, **Maranovići** and **Korita** are practically never visited by foreigners. Right at the far eastern tip, at **Saplunara**, are two sandy beaches, the only ones on the island. You'll need a car (or a bike and strong legs) to get here as no buses run beyond Sobra. The first is below the village itself; the other, round the next bay, has a shallow and very sheltered lagoon and is almost deserted. It's a gorgeous place to swim and sunbathe, and there's a beach bar, Hippokampos (🅵 beachbarmljet; ☺ Jun–Sep 09.00–20.00 daily), doing drinks and snacks, and hiring out sea kayaks and SUPs.

The highest point on the island (Veli Grad, 513m) is just above Mljet's diminutive administrative capital, **Babino Polje**, again practically unvisited. Babino Polje sits on the side of the island's largest field system – the endless drystone walls here are the result of centuries of clearing stones from the fields. The main produce is olives and (surprisingly expensive but incredibly tasty) goat's cheese. Much of the island's very drinkable wine comes from the village of Blato, just outside the national park.

Southwest of Babino Polje is **Ulysses Cave** (Odisejeva Špilja), a good half-hour's tough walk across fields and down the cliff, but well worth the effort. It's not suitable for young children, however – if you're travelling with the family, take the boat trip from the Hotel Odisej, as it's a magical cave to explore in calm seas.

TRSTENO

Just 18km up the coast from Dubrovnik is the little village of Trsteno, which would be entirely unremarkable were it not for the wonderful arboretum here. Originally created as the summer residence and gardens of Ivan Gučetić, a Dubrovnik noble, in 1502 and expanded over the centuries, the estate was nationalised by the communists in 1948 and re-branded as the Arboretum of the Yugoslav (now Croatian) Academy of Arts and Sciences. Inexplicably, it was subject to Serb shelling during the 1991–92 war.

Anyway, the gardens here are delightful and make a charming excursion out of Dubrovnik. Buses #12, #15, #22 and #35 from Dubrovnik stop at Trsteno (20mins), and buses going up the coast to Split, etc set down and pick up in the middle of the village, where the first thing you'll see is a splendid pair of huge 500-year-old plane trees. Beyond these, heading towards the sea in a series of terraces, is the **arboretum** itself (❧ 020 751 019; ⓕ trstenoarboretum; ☉ May–Oct 07.00–19.00 daily, Nov–Apr 08.00–16.00 daily; €10).

There's nothing special to do other than to wander round the gardens, which vary from the formality of the oldest part, beneath the villa, with geometrical box hedges enclosing different planted areas, to the wilder areas off to the sides. There's a lovely orchard with citrus fruits, avenues of palms and firs, and all manner of exotic semi-tropical plants, most of them usefully labelled. There's even a rather fanciful 18th-century grotto, where you'll find Neptune with his trident presiding over a water-lily-strewn fishpond and playful water-spouting fountains in the form of dolphins.

If you're looking for a place to eat nearby, **Laptalo agrotourism** (m 099 462 4272; w laptalo-agro.hr; ☉ May–Oct 17.00–23.00 daily) in an old stone building in Gromača on the hillside above Trsteno, comes highly recommended. Everything they serve is homemade, including the wine. Reservations essential, one day in advance.

PLOČE AND THE NERETVA DELTA

Roughly halfway between Split and Dubrovnik lies the industrial port of **Ploče**. Known during the 1980s as Kardeljevo, after one of Tito's pals, it still handles most of Bosnia & Herzegovina's sea-bound freight (the coastal town of Neum, actually in Bosnia's land corridor, is a dreary little resort with no proper port) and acts as a transport hub.

The re-established rail link to Sarajevo (a spectacular journey, passing through the Neretva Canyon) starts from here, running summer-only (early Jun through to late Aug, on Fri, Sat & Sun), stopping en route in Mostar and taking about 3 hours 20 minutes and there are Jadrolinija car ferries across to Trpanj, on Pelješac – three a day in winter, four in summer. Otherwise, there's no reason to break your journey.

South of Ploče is the extraordinary **Neretva Delta**. Long a marshy, malarial swamp, the pancake-flat river delta is now a series of fertile agricultural wetlands, producing Croatia's best citrus fruits (you'll see delicious mandarins for sale along the roadside) and providing shelter to waterfowl and wading birds, as well as spawning grounds for many species of fish, including eels.

Deep in the delta, which is listed under the Ramsar Convention, are five hard-to-find dedicated ornithological reserves. You'll need time, patience and your own transport – in which case you should keep a weather eye on the main road for flying customs squads, on the lookout for Bosnian contraband and speeding tourists.

A total of 310 species of bird have been recorded in the delta, with 115 nesting here, including the pigmy cormorant, coots, crakes, warblers and shrikes, several species of heron and egret, all five species of European grebe and almost every species of European duck, plus the great white pelican and the Dalmatian pelican, which have returned in recent years, after having been thought extinct in these parts. In 1999, a government proposal was initiated to proclaim the entire delta as a nature park, but obstacles include various development and road-improvement plans.

Easily the best way of visiting is to persuade one of the locals to take you around in a punt (the indigenous *trupica* or *lad-a*), poling you along the reedy channels which separate the reclaimed market gardens and giving you a chance to soak up the mysterious atmosphere. Alternatively, join Paddle Surf Croatia (w paddlesurfcroatia.com) for a half-day SUP (stand-up paddle board) tour or a one-day boat and SUP tour of the Neretva Delta. Take insect repellent with you – the mosquitoes here can be fearsome.

The other activity that is big here is kiteboarding. Thanks to stable thermal winds and warm shallow sea, an ever-increasing number of enthusiasts are flocking here. Local providers include Kiteboarding Komin Neretva (w kiteboarding-komin-neretva.com) and Neretva Kiteboarding (w neretvakiteboarding.com).

WHERE TO STAY AND EAT

Hotel Restaurant Villa Neretva (8 rooms) Krvavac II, Metković; ☏ 020 672 200; w hotel-restaurant-villa-neretva.hr. The main reason to stop off here is for the photo safaris that take you by boat to the hotel's sister property, Neretva House, which can only be reached by water.

Dalmatian cuisine dominates the menus at both restaurants, with an emphasis on local freshwater specialities, such as eel & frogs' legs. If you want to stay over, the rooms are simple, well-priced & clean. If you come in Oct–Nov, you can help with the tangerine harvest. €€

PELJEŠAC PENINSULA

An island in all but name, the 65km Pelješac peninsula runs up from the isthmus at Ston to the island of Korčula. Never more than 7km wide, Pelješac is mountainous and rocky, an unlikely home to two of Croatia's best wines, the hearty Dingač and Postup reds, made from the Plavac mali grape (page 134).

Three Libertas buses (w libertasdubrovnik.hr) a day travel up and down the main road from Dubrovnik to Ston (1hr), and one goes all the way to Orebić (2½hrs), the main departure point for Korčula, and buses also hook up with Trpanj, the arrival point for ferries from Ploče, on the mainland. But if you want to explore the dozens of small villages or the myriad hidden bays and beaches, you'll definitely need your own wheels.

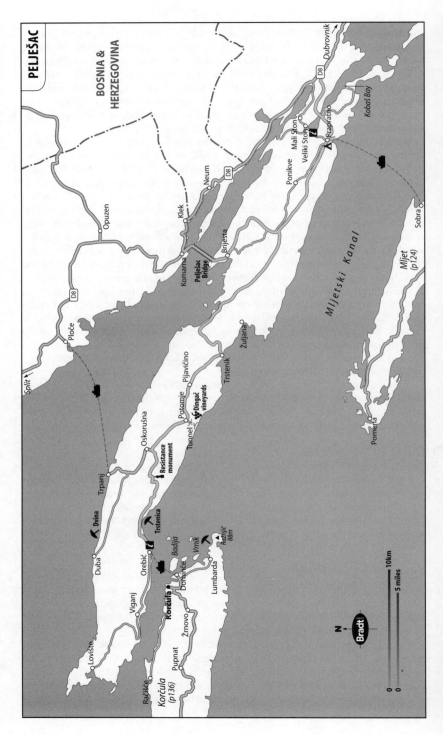

BOSNIA &
HERZEGOVINA

Dubrovnik

D8

Koباš Bay

Mali Ston

Veliki Ston

Prapatno

Ponikve

Neum

D8

Klek

Brijesta

Opuzen

Komarna

Pelješac
Bridge

M l j e t s k i   K a n a l

Sobra

D8

Ploče

Žuljana

Mljet
(p124)

Split

Pijavičino

Trstenik

Potomje

Dingač
vineyards

Oskorušna

Tunnel

Pomena

Resistance
monument

Trpanj

Dvina

Trstenica

Duba

Badija

Vrnik

Razhijić
88m

Viganj

Orebić

Domince

Lumbarda

Lovište

Korčula

Žrnovo

Pupnat

Račišće

Korčula
(p136)

N

Bradt

10km

5 miles

0

0

The opening of the new **Pelješac Bridge** (page 82) between Komarna on the mainland and Brijesta on Pelješac in 2022 has certainly made the peninsula more accessible.

STON The natural land entrance to Pelješac is at Ston, which guards the isthmus with a series of remarkably well-preserved walls from the 14th century on. On the south coast is the village of **Veliki Ston**, while on the northern bay is **Mali Ston**.

The reason for a visit here is twofold – firstly to see (and clamber upon) the walls, which rival Dubrovnik's, and secondly to sample Croatia's best oysters, which are farmed here, as are mussels. The **tourist office** (Gundulićeva poljana 1; ✆ 020 754 452; w ston.hr) in Veliki Ston can supply general information about things to see and do.

The **walls** (w dpds.hr; ⊕ May–Sep 08.00–19.00, Oct–Apr 09.00–15.00; Mar–Oct €10, Nov–Feb €5) and the two settlements they connect, Ston to Mali Ston, were built from the 14th century onwards. Effectively spanning the peninsula, the walls were intended primarily to protect the salt pans – the salt trade was one of the republic's biggest earners, and it's said that Napoleon was even keener to get his hands on Ston than Dubrovnik. Today, 20 of the original 40 towers and some 5km of walls are still standing (they underwent restoration from 2003 to 2009, and sections are occasionally closed for maintenance). You can access the walls in either Veliki Ston or Mali Ston and walk the so-called Big Wall (1.2km; allow 30–45mins) to the opposite side of the peninsula. Along the way, a steep set of steps brings you to Podzvizd Fort (224m) at the highest point above Ston. From here, there are great panoramic views, and you can even see the island of Mljet (page 122).

Each year in September, the **Ston Wall Marathon** (w ston-wall-marathon.com) takes place here, with three races: 4km, 15km and 42km.

The **Ston Salt Works** (Solana Ston; w solanaston.hr; ⊕ May–Oct 08.00–20.00, Nov–Apr 08.00–16.00; €7) are still in use and produce some 1,500–2,000 tons of salt annually. The harvest takes place between mid-July and late August and is done by hand, using wooden rakes and shovels to collect the crystallised salt once the summer sun and wind have caused the seawater to evaporate. Besides the salt pans, there's a small museum and gift shop.

Likewise, if you want to learn more about Ston's oysters, the local **Association of Ston Shellfish Farmers** (w malistonoyster.com) runs boat tours of the oyster beds in Mali Ston Bay so you can see how these aphrodisiacal molluscs are cultivated and taste them raw, plucked straight from the sea.

The area was badly hit by an earthquake in 1996, which destroyed many of the houses in both Veliki and Mali Ston, along with most of the town of Slano, further down the coast towards Dubrovnik – and even today, some of the properties here remain boarded up. Nonetheless, Mali Ston's tourist infrastructure is thriving, and the village is increasingly popular with Croatian romantics on oyster-fuelled weekend breaks. What's more, Ston is the gateway to the Pelješac peninsula, where an increasing number of visitors head specifically for vineyard and winery tours along with wine-tasting. The nearest good winery to Ston, open for tasting, is **Vinarija Miloš** (m 098 965 6880; f) in Ponikve, owned by the Miloš family, who have been making wine here for five generations.

➤ **Where to stay and eat** If you decide to stay over, there are two decent small hotels in Mali Ston, as well as rooms to rent in both Veliki Ston and Mali Ston. Finally, there are lots of restaurants, two of which, on the harbour in Mali Ston, are renowned throughout Croatia for serving fresh oysters and other classic Dalmatian

dishes, and stay open all year: **Kapetanova Kuća** (Mali Ston bb; ✆ 020 754 264;
❶ kapetanovakuca; ⏱ 11.00–23.00 daily; €€€€) and **Bota Šare** (Mali Ston bb; ✆ 020
754 482; w bota-sare.hr; ⏱ 10.00–midnight daily; €€€€).

Ostrea (9 rooms) ✆ 020 754 555; w ostrea.hr.
This is just inside the walls & is somewhat more
upmarket than the Vila Koruna. The same family
run the Kapetanova Kuća restaurant. €€€€

Vila Koruna (6 rooms) ✆ 020 754 999; w vila-
koruna.hr. Just outside the old walls is the
attractive hotel, which has simple dbls with rather
dated décor, & a covered terrace of a dining room
right on the water. €€€

SOUTH OF STON Just 5km south of Ston, there's a flat, highly regarded, tree-shaded
campsite at **Prapratno** (w camping-prapratno.com; €) set back from a wide,
secluded beach giving on to a lovely turquoise bay. Prapratno is also of note for the
Jadrolinija car ferry linking the peninsula with Polače on Mljet, a pleasant hour or
so's trip away, with five crossings daily in summer and four in winter.

Some 8km southeast of Ston, in Kobaš Bay, **Gastro Mare Kobaš** (m 097 796
8008; w gastromarekobas.com) serves truly excellent fresh seafood, much of which
the owner-chef catches himself. Most guests arrive by sailing boat and moor up
directly out front.

Moving west, the small holiday village of **Žuljana** on Pelješac's southern coast
has a decent beach giving on to a stunning emerald-turquoise bay. Here, **Diving
Centre Žuljana** (m 099 216 2510; w divingcentrezuljana.com) offers scuba-diving
tuition and runs trips to six shipwrecks and five sea caves. A further 18km up the
coast brings you to **Trstenik**, which also has a nice sheltered beach and is home to
the renowned **Grgić winery** (✆ 020 748 090; w grgic-vina.com; ⏱ Jun–Sep 09.00–
19.00 daily), open to visitors for tasting.

Resistance monument As you progress up the peninsula, about 40km from
Ston, there's a huge monument to the Resistance, right where the road crests a
hill, near the locality of Pijavičino. If you're under your own steam, stop here by
the abandoned restaurant and take a moment to look at the stylised bronze frieze
depicting scenes from World War II, showing brutal oppression, firing squads,
the first signs of resistance and uprising, and finally, the joy of freedom. On the
back of the curved walls is the seemingly endless list of the local dead, while the
whole is dominated by a pair of curved concrete pillars stretching about 30m into
the sky.

TRPANJ In a sweeping bay on Pelješac's north coast is the small town of Trpanj,
arrival point for the Jadrolinija ferries from Ploče (three a day in winter, four a day
in summer). The cheerful little town has a handful of cafés and restaurants and
a helpful **tourist office** (Zalo 7; ✆ 020 743 433; w tzo-trpanj.hr) on the seafront,
which can arrange private rooms and advise about things to see and do. Opening
hours in winter are sporadic, to say the least. The website has details of some short,
easy local hiking and cycle trails. There are some lovely beaches nearby, the best
probably being Divna (literally meaning 'gorgeous'), 10km west of Trpanj, and
Duba, a further 3km west. Buses connect with the ferries in Trpanj and take you to
Orebić, which leads on to Korčula or back to Ston and Dubrovnik.

Trpanj has one hotel, the **Faraon** (Put Vila 1; ✆ 020 743 408; w hoteli-jadran.com;
€€€€), with around 150 rooms, all with balcony and sea-view, and obligatory full
board. It sits right on the large pebble beach to the west of the harbour, facing across
to the Biokovo massif on the mainland.

Behind Trpanj, in Oskorušna (7km), the highly regarded **St Hills Winery** (020 742 113; w saintshills.com; ⊕ noon–19.00 Tue–Sun) occupies an old stone house and offers various wine-tasting experiences, accompanied by tasty savoury snacks (reservations recommended one day in advance).

OREBIĆ Pelješac's best-known resort, Orebić, is an unpretentious little town with an excellent climate – it's protected by the mountains from the bura wind, giving it mild winters, early springs and long-lasting summers. The town is right across the strait from Korčula, and in summer, 20 Jadrolinija car ferries a day go in each direction (12 in winter), as well as regular little shuttle boats. To get back to the mainland, the easiest routes are to either take the direct bus to Dubrovnik (three a day) or to catch the ferry to Korčula and then go on the next catamaran to Dubrovnik or Split from there. Alternatively, you can catch the bus to Trpanj and the ferry from there across to Ploče.

To the west of Orebić are a series of resort hotels, on a mixture of nice sandy and pebble beaches, giving on to stunning turquoise sea, while 500m to the east you'll find the **Trstenica** beach, which is one of the nicest little stretches of the Adriatic coast – it's backed by pine trees, cacti and palms, and home to a row of fine 18th- and 19th-century villas.

The **tourist office** (Zrinsko Frankopanska 2; 020 713 718; w visitorebic-croatia. hr) has walking maps and a list of **private rooms**, though you'd do well to arrange accommodation in advance in summer.

Where to stay and eat

Adriatic Heritage Boutique Hotel (6 rooms) Šetalište Kneza Domagoja 8; 020 714 488; w hoteladriaticorebic.com. Boutique hotel with plenty of exposed stonework, wooden floors & Persian rugs in a restored 17th-century building. The waterside Stari Kapetan seafood restaurant is part of the property, & they also own the Boutique Winery Mikulić, where they offer tasting. €€€€

Aminess Bellevue Hotel (80 rooms) Šetalište kralja Petra Krešimira IV 13; 020 798 040; w aminess.com. This 4-star hotel is the nearest to the centre & faces on to a rocky beach. Built in 1935 & renovated in 2016, it has a terrace with 2 pools & lovely views of Korčula across the channel. €€€€

Aminess Grand Azur (185 rooms) Šetalište kralja Petra Krešimira IV 107; 020 798 000; w aminess.com. In a sheltered cove with a fine pebble beach, just a 10min walk along the coast from Orebić, this big modern 4-star

hotel has 2 outdoor pools (1 for adults, 1 for children) & a kids club. Choose from B&B or light all-inclusive. €€€€

Guesthouse-Restaurant Mimbelli (5 rooms) Trg Mimbelli 6; 020 713 636; w mimbelli-orebic. com. Nice rooms in a restored 19th-century sea captain's house in the centre of Orebić. Also has a popular terrace restaurant. €€€

Villa Vrgorac (17 apartments) Perna 24; 020 719 152; w villa-vrgorac.com. Located midway between Orebić & Viganj, offers 17 apartments (sleeping 2, 3 or 4), each with kitchenette & balcony, plus a waterside restaurant serving fresh seafood. €€€

Croccantino Obala pomoraca 30; m 098 165 0777; f CroccantinoCRO; ⊕ Apr–Oct 07.00–20.00 daily (depending on the weather). On Orebić seafront promenade, come here for homemade cakes (including gluten-free options) & divine artisan ice cream. €€€

What to see and do From the Bellevue, it's an uphill hike westwards to the 15th-century **Franciscan Monastery,** which houses the icon known as 'Our Lady of the Angels' in a small museum – for centuries, sailors came here with votive gifts, also on display, after being saved from shipwreck, storms or pirates. The terrace of the monastery, at 150m above sea level, looks down across the strait to Korčula town, a lovely view over turquoise waters.

Even finer panoramas can be had from the 961m summit of Mount St Ilija. It's a steep hike, 4 hours up from Orebić including rests, and another two for the descent, but the simply wonderful views from the summit include the whole of the island of Korčula, Mljet to the south, and the gaunt karst mountains of the mainland to the north.

If you're **hiking** up here, wear proper hiking boots (there are reported sightings of vipers), start very early (there's little or no shade), take plenty of water, and use common sense and the route markings as well as the map. Follow the path up to the monastery and then continue to Bilopolje, after which the track bears off to the right, following red-and-white flashes to the summit. For further information, see *Walks and Treks in Croatia* by Rudolf Abraham (page 238).

Some of Croatia's best **red wine** (see below) is produced not far from Orebić, in Pelješac's Dingač region, and some of the vineyards are open for wine tours. In Orebić itself, the upscale **Korta Katarina Winery** (m 099 492 5830; w kortakatarinawinery.com) offers wine-tasting, along with gourmet tapas or dining, and informative tours of their cellars. Otherwise, to taste Dingač on

RED WINES OF PELJEŠAC AND WHITE WINES OF KORČULA

For wine lovers, the Pelješac peninsula and Korčula island make perfect twin destinations, the former being renowned for excellent reds, the latter for whites. Both grow indigenous grape varieties to produce some rather special wines. You'll find a dozen or so wineries open for tours and tasting (listed in the respective regional sections). Note that you should call in advance to agree an exact time for your visit.

Pelješac is known for the indigenous Plavac mali vine, which does well on poor stony soils, to bear small black grapes on low-lying bush vines. If grown in the flat valleys of Pelješac's interior, it produces light easy-going red wine. But the best results come from the Dingač vineyards on Pelješac's steep south-facing seaward slopes, exposed to intense sunlight, near the village of Potomje. Here, the terraced vineyards descend dramatically towards the sea – the slopes are so steep (with inclinations of up to 60 degrees) that the grape harvest has to be done entirely by hand. The result is a powerful full-bodied red wine, regarded by many as Croatia's best.

Across the sea channel, on the island of **Korčula**, local legend has it that the Grk vine was brought here by the Ancient Greeks, who settled in Lumbarda in the southeast of the island in the 3rd century BC. In fact, *Grk* means Greek in Croatian. Grk likes sandy soils, which is why it does so well in Lumbarda. Strangely, Grk vines have only female flowers, so vintners intersperse rows of Grk with Plavac mali in their vineyards to allow for fertilisation. Grk is a refreshing summery dry white wine, with a compact body, a fruitiness and minerality, and a pleasant bitter hint of lemon at the end.

Moving into the fertile valleys of Korčula's rural interior, with its red iron-rich soils, the neighbouring villages of Smokvica and Čara are producers of white Pošip. It is one of Croatia's youngest grape varieties. In 1864, a local farmer found the Pošip grape growing wild in fields between Smokvica and Čara. By 1880, the area was producing wine from single varietal vineyards, and today, Pošip accounts for 85% of Korčula's grape production, while Grk lags behind at 10%. Pošip is a fresh pale-golden wine with aromas of citrus fruits, apple, honey and Mediterranean herbs.

its home territory, call at **Vinarija Madirazza** (m 095 212 1632; w dingac.hr) in Potomje (17km southeast of Orebić).

Finally, if you're a windsurfer you'll want to head a few kilometres further along Pelješac to **Viganj**, one of the top **windsurfing** (page 71) spots in Croatia – contact Water Donkey in Viganj about courses and board rental (w windsurfing-kitesurfing-viganj.com).

KORČULA

Like Hvar, Korčula has a lovely old town and lots of hard-to-reach coves and beaches. Like Hvar, too, Korčula's no secret, but it doesn't have nearly the visitor numbers of its northern neighbour (though Korčula's numbers are growing significantly faster, year on year).

The island is nestled up to the western end of Pelješac (less than 1.5km of sea separates them at the narrowest point) and stretches about 45km west into the Adriatic. On average, it's about 6km across, from north to south, and has a mountainous spine rising to 568m just west of the village of Pupnat.

The main attraction on the island is the old town of Korčula itself, almost opposite Orebić (on Pelješac), though a close second has to be Korčula's powerful white wines (see opposite), notably Pošip and Lumbarda's Grk. Korčula also makes a pretty good base for exploring Pelješac and offers easy excursions over to Mljet (page 122).

HISTORY Korčula's history stretches back as far as anywhere in Croatia, with Neolithic settlements here followed by the arrival of Greek colonists in the 6th century BC. The Greeks co-existed peaceably with Illyrians on the island for several hundred years before the Romans barged in during the 1st century BC, enraged by the island's propensity for harbouring pirates. Most of the population was either killed, exiled or enslaved, setting something of a pattern until the late Middle Ages, when Korčula went through the usual southern Adriatic tussle between Venice, Dubrovnik and the Turks.

In 1298, just off Lumbarda, a total of more than 180 galleys from the rival Venetian and outnumbered Genoan fleets clashed in one of the biggest sea battles of the Middle Ages. Genoa won the day and took 7,000 prisoners, including a certain Marco Polo (page 140), who was back in the Adriatic after more than 20 years in Asia with his father and uncle, and was on that day at the helm of one of the Venetian battleships.

Today, Marco Polo is unquestionably Korčula's most famous son, though some scholars now think he may have been born in Šibenik, further up the Dalmatian coast. Whatever the truth, Korčula does much more for Marco Polo than anywhere else, and the setting of the old town here is suitably evocative of the kind of place where he might have been brought up.

Recent history on Korčula has been dominated by tourism, though there's still a fish-processing factory in Vela Luka, at the western end of the island, and the wine business is increasingly important. Olive oil has also been a valuable source of revenue.

GETTING THERE AND AWAY
By bus Daily buses arrive on Korčula from Dubrovnik and Zagreb, rolling on to the car ferry from Orebić for the last couple of kilometres. The journey from Dubrovnik, up through the Pelješac peninsula, takes a little under 4 hours

4

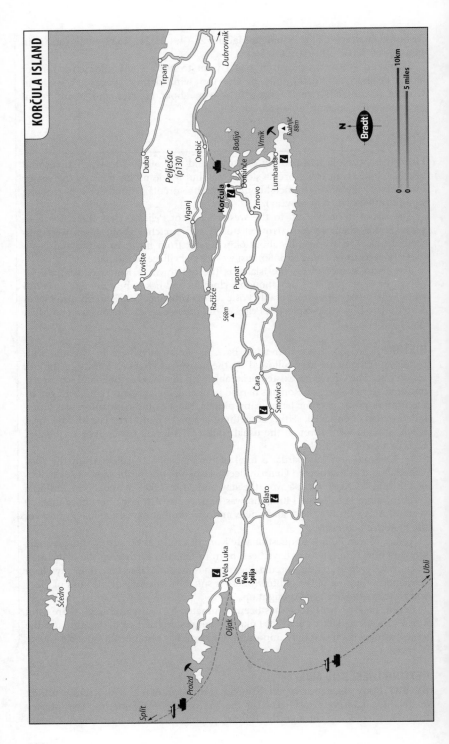

KORČULA ISLAND

Šćedro

Split

Proizd

Ubli

Ošjak

Vela Luka
Vela
Špilja

Blato

Smokvica

Čara

Pupnat

568m

Račišće

Lovište

Viganj

Pelješac
(p130)

Duba

Trpanj

Orebić

Korčula

Žrnovo

Domince

Badija

Lumbarda

Vrnik

Ražnjić
88m

Dubrovnik

N

Bradt

0 — 5 miles
0 — 10km

(alternatively, take the fast TP Line catamaran, 2hrs); from Zagreb it's a 10-hour overnighter, and not particularly recommended (a more comfortable option is taking the bus from Zagreb to Split, then the fast Krilo catamaran to Korčula). From Korčula town to Vela Luka there are half-a-dozen buses a day, though fewer at weekends (timetables at w arriva.com.hr) – the ferries always connect with a bus, however. In summer, there's also a service (one to three times a day) from Drvenik direct to Korčula.

By ferry and catamaran Car ferries from Orebić (arrive early if you're bringing your car) come in at Dominče, 3km south of Korčula town, 12 times a day in winter, 20 in summer. If you're not on the bus already you can avoid the hike into town by hopping on to one of the hourly buses from Lumbarda to Korčula, though don't rely on this service at weekends. As a foot passenger, you're better off taking the smaller boat which runs from Orebić directly to Korčula town's west harbour (7 a day in winter, at least 14 in summer).

A daily Jadrolinija ferry service runs from Split to Vela Luka, at the western end of Korčula (and on to Lastovo), taking around 3½ hours; the same journey can be done in just over 2 hours on the daily catamaran.

There's a daily Krilo **catamaran** (2hrs 45mins; w krilo.hr) from Split to Korčula town itself, departing Korčula early in the morning and returning from Split in the afternoon (the journey is shortened to 2½ hours in winter, when the catamaran doesn't call at Prigradica). The Krilo summer catamaran from Split to Dubrovnik, via Milna (Brač), Hvar and Mljet, also calls at Korčula Town.

GETTING AROUND If you're reliant on **public transport,** you'll be pretty much limited to Korčula town, the sandy beaches of Lumbarda, 6km southeast (roughly hourly buses; flaky weekend service), a few buses to the village of Račišće along the north coast of the island, and the regular bus service along the main road through the rural interior to Vela Luka, via Pupnat, Čara, Smokvica and Blato (timetables at w arriva.com.hr) – for access to Korčula's many hidden beaches and coves, which tend to be at the end of long gravelly roads, you'll definitely need your own wheels.

A great, liberating option is to rent a **bike. Korčula Outdoor** (w korcula-outdoor.com) has mountain bikes for €25 per day and e-bikes for €55. The **tourist office** (Trg 19 travnja 1921; \ 020 715 701; w visitkorcula.eu) has superb maps of the town, the island and its bike routes, and its website has a list of suggested bike routes.

If you don't have your own transport and can't face biking, you might consider taking an **organised tour** with **Korčula Outdoor** (w korcula-outdoor.com) to get more of a feel for the island's hidden charms. They offer hiking and cycling combined with food and wine-tasting, sea kayaking tours, private sailing trips, and one-day speedboat excursions to the nearby islands of Mljet and Lastovo. Alternatively, you can negotiate with one of the **water taxis** at the eastern harbour of Korčula town to take you to one of the local islands or remoter beaches and pick you up a few hours later.

WHERE TO STAY Map, page 139
If you're on a budget or the options listed on page 138 don't suit, there are plenty of good **private rooms** and apartments available – especially along the waterfront west of the town (Put Sv Nikole). Expect to pay at least €80 for a double, with a 30% supplement for stays of three days or fewer.

✴ **Lešić Dimitri Palace** (6 residences) Don Pavle Poše; ☎020 715 560; w ldpalace.com. Luxury boutique option with 6 plush residences, complete with kitchenettes, themed around the life of Marco Polo. It occupies an 18th-century bishop's palace & adjoining medieval cottages in the heart of the old town & has a Michelin-starred restaurant & a small spa doing Thai massage. €€€€€

Aminess Korčula Heritage Hotel (20 rooms) Obala Franje Tuđmana; ☎020 797 900; w aminess. com. The rooms themselves aren't anything to write home about, but the location, right on the old town's western harbour, is perfection itself – so book ahead. This was a popular café in 1871 & became the town's 1st hotel (the Hotel de la Ville) in 1912. €€€€

Hotel Korsal (10 rooms) Šetalište Frana Kršinića 80; ☎020 715 722; w hotel-korsal.com. Smart 4-star at 1 end of the marina, about 5mins' walk from the old town, with sea-views & hardwood floors, & a terrace restaurant. €€€€

Korčula Waterfront Accommodation (5 apartments) Šetaliste Tina Ujevića 33; m 098 937 0463, 098 674 167; w korcula-waterfront-accommodation.com. Beautiful, modern 1- & 2-bedroom apartments sleeping up to 3 & 5 respectively, each with private balcony, just 10mins' walk southeast of the old town. They also have mountain bikes & a motorboat to hire. €€€€

The Fabris (20 rooms) Pelavin mir 1; ☎020 716 755; w thefabris.com. In 2 restored old stone buildings just outside Korčula old town's fortifications, offering dbls & trpls, plus a small ground-floor restaurant. €€€€

Pansion Hajduk 1963 (15 rooms) Ulica 67/6; ☎020 717 267; m 098 287 216; w pansionhajduk1963.com. Small family-run guesthouse a short walk south of the old town, with simple but very good-value rooms, & there's a nice terrace restaurant & outdoor pool. €€€

Hostel Korčula (3 dorms) Don Iva Matijace Opata; m 092 163 9180. In a narrow alley in the heart of Korčula's old town, offering 20 bunk beds spread over 3 dorms, plus a communal kitchen. €

✖ **WHERE TO EAT AND DRINK** *Map, opposite*

While in Korčula town, make sure you pop into the excellent **Cukarin** (🗗 cukarin. korcula), a traditional cake shop with homemade things to buy.

Filippi Šetalište Petra Kanavelića; m 098 275 701; w restaurantfilippi.com; ☉ May–Oct 09.00–midnight daily. On the tree-lined promenade in Korčula's old town, with views of Pelješac across the water, Filippi serves fresh Adriatic fish & local lamb accompanied by quality Dalmatian wines. €€€€€–€€€€

Adio Mare Sv Roka 2; ☎020 711 253; w konobaadiomare.hr; ☉ May–Oct noon–23.00 Mon–Sat, 17.00–23.00 Sun. Since 1974, it has served up delicious traditional Dalmatian dishes in Korčula's old town. €€€€

✴ **Konoba Maha** Vrsi bb, Žrnovo; m 091 605 1207; w konobamaha.com; ☉ May–Oct 17.00–23.00 Mon–Sat. Rustic eatery, run by 2 brothers, serving refined local fare in a romantic farm setting in the hills beyond Žrnovo, 8km southwest of Korčula Town. €€€€

✴ **Konoba Mate** Pupnat; m 099 677 5722; w konobamate.hr; ☉ May–Oct 19.00–midnight Mon–Sat. Small, family-run konoba in the village of Pupnat (11km west of Korčula Town) using fresh, locally grown produce, including vegetables from their own garden. €€€€

Konoba Belin Žrnovo; m 091 503 9258; 🗗 RestoranBelin; ☉ 18.00–midnight daily. Small, rustic, family-run konoba in the village of Žrnovo (4km southwest of Korčula Town). €€€

Massimo Cocktail Bar Šetalište Petra Kanavelića; m 099 214 4568; ☉ May–Oct 10.00–15.00 & 17.00–01.00 daily. The place to enjoy a sundowner atop a stone tower that was once part of the city's fortifications. Not for those with vertigo (or if you've had a few), as you have to climb up/down a ladder to get there. Seeing your drink hauled up on a pulley is all part of the fun. €€€

Maha Bar Ulica prolaz tri saluri; m 092 138 1796; 🗗 komlikomaterino; ☉ 08.00–midnight Mon–Sat, 17.00–midnight Sun. Near Korčula Town port, serves tasty homemade burgers & drinks. Also works through winter, doing a reasonably priced set menu lunch. €€

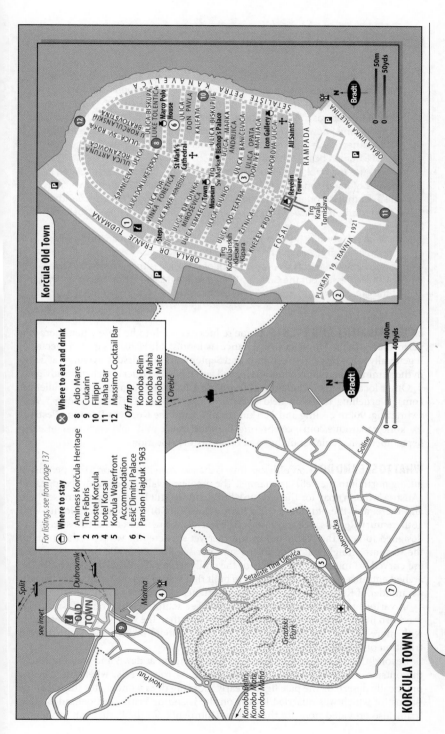

Korčula Old Town

Where to stay

For listings, see from page 137

🛈 Where to stay

1 Aminess Korčula Heritage
2 The Fabris
3 Hostel Korčula
4 Hotel Korsal
5 Korčula Waterfront
   Accommodation
6 Lešić Dimitri Palace
7 Pansion Hajduk 1963

✖ Where to eat and drink

8 Adio Mare
9 Cukarin
10 Filippi
11 Maha Bar
12 Massimo Cocktail Bar

Off map

Konoba Belin
Konoba Maha
Konoba Mate

KORČULA TOWN

IL MILIONE – THE BIRTH OF TRAVEL WRITING

While he was in prison in Genoa, Marco Polo's stories were written down by a Pisan romance writer who was sharing the same cell as the great explorer. Published in Franco-Italian, *Divisament dou Monde* (*Description of the World* – now better known as *The Travels of Marco Polo*) was received with widespread disbelief. But it was too late – modern travel writing had been born. The book soon became known as *Il Milione*, possibly because it was seen as a million fables rather than a travelogue – whoever heard of paper money? Or nuts the size of a human head (coconuts)?

Because the book came out before printing was invented, it circulated as a series of hand-copied manuscripts, and more than 100 different versions still exist (but no original), in several languages, making it even harder than it might otherwise have been to know exactly what Marco Polo actually did or saw.

What's important, however, is that he inspired people to travel and explore foreign lands and was the first Westerner to describe the east in any detail. Controversy still reigns over how much of *Il Milione* is true – how can Marco Polo have missed out the Great Wall, for goodness sake? – but it remains one of the great classics of travel writing all the same.

ENTERTAINMENT AND EVENTS If you're lucky enough to be here when there is a performance of the **Moreška sword dance** (w moreska.hr; €20), it's quite a spectacle. It generally takes place between June and September on Thursday evenings at 21.00 in the summer open-air cinema space, and you'll need to reserve tickets in advance.

Other local events include the **Marco Polo Challenge** (w marcopolo-challenge. com), a gruelling triathlon held over three days in late April, combining 1.9km swimming, 90km cycling and 21.1km running; and the **Korkyra Baroque Festival** (w korkyrabaroque.com), celebrating Baroque music and held each year in early September in Korčula's churches and other historic locations.

WHAT TO SEE AND DO Korčula's top draw is the old town itself, set on a tiny peninsula jutting north into the Pelješac channel. The medieval walls have largely disappeared (Austria wouldn't pay for the upkeep), but there are still towers and buttresses here and there, and the old quarter is a harmonious mix of 15th-century Gothic with 16th-century Renaissance trimmings. The leaf-veined network of narrow streets was designed to keep the place cool in summer yet sheltered in winter – the roads to the west are straight, allowing in the summer sea breezes, while those to the east are curved, to minimise the effects of the chilly winter *bura* (northeast wind). The arched entrances to the old cellars were built that way to ease the passage of barrels, a reminder of Korčula's long-standing importance as a centre of wine production.

In various places around the town, you'll see sculptures by Frano Kršnić, who was born in Lumbarda – they're softer and gentler than the works of Ivan Meštrović, with more than a passing nod to Rodin and a tribute to Korčula's centuries-old tradition of stone-carving.

Beyond the main sights, it's really worth getting up at dawn and walking round the outside of the old town and through the narrow streets, when the place is practically deserted. The pale light of early morning does wonders for the old stone – most of which was quarried locally on the island of **Vrnik**, just behind **Badija**. Vrnik also provided stone for the walls of Dubrovnik, for the Parliament in Vienna, and for Stockholm's Town Hall. To the west of town, just around the headland, are the attractive **Monastery and Church of St Nicholas**.

It's also well worth taking one of the regular taxi boats from Korčula's eastern harbour to the island of **Badija**, just offshore, as it has the best (and closest) beaches to Korčula town. It's a lovely place to wander, with fallow deer and a Franciscan Monastery which hosts religious retreats.

The old town   The obvious access to the old town is through the southern land gate and the 15th-century **Revelin Tower**, which has a small Moreška exhibition inside and excellent views from the top. The sweep of stone steps leading up to the gate was only added in 1907, replacing the drawbridge. On the left-hand side, as you come in through the gate, there's a fine loggia (and a pleasant café). The main street then leads straight to St Mark's Cathedral.

St Mark's Cathedral   (Sv Marko; ⊕ May–Oct 09.00–17.00 daily; €5 gives access to both the cathedral & the treasury in the Bishop's Palace) The cathedral, like Rab's and Hvar's, is actually a church, since the island long ago lost its bishopric, but who's quibbling? It's crammed into a space that's manifestly too small and is one of around 150 churches still used on the island.

Over the main door there's a throned statue of St Mark, flanked by a pair of fine Venetian lions on buttresses, the early 15th-century work of Bonino, the Italian sculptor. Supporting the lions are a wonderfully primitive, cowering Adam and Eve, while the blind pillars feature unusual carved clove-hitches halfway up. Inside, at the end of the curiously skewed nave (look at the ceiling), there's a famous but frankly rather heavyweight altar canopy from the late 15th century and a couple of paintings attributed to Tintoretto – the altarpiece featuring St Mark, and an Annunciation in the southern nave. Also inside, you'll find halberds from a 1483 battle and cannonballs from the Battle of Lepanto in 1571. Near these is a rare and celebrated 14th-century icon which came from the monastery on Badija; it's due for return to the Franciscans there once restorations have been completed.

On the left-hand side of the church is the large chapel dedicated to Roc, the patron saint of the plague; here you'll find a convincing St Blaise by Meštrović and a dusty sculpture over the doorway of St Michael killing Lucifer. If you're in town on 29 July, you'll see the relics of the cathedral's co-patron, St Theodore, being carried in a procession around town.

Bishop's Palace   (⊕ May–Sep 09.00–17.00 daily, Apr & Oct 09.00–17.00 daily; €5 gives access to both the treasury in the Bishop's Palace & the cathedral) Next door to the cathedral is the **Bishop's Palace**, which houses an impressive treasury, though it's really more of a museum. It's an extraordinary collection, covering everything from ancient kitchenware to contemporary art. There are collections of coins, church silver, relics from the Roman catacombs, medieval ballot boxes and a birth register from 1583. Strangest of all is a statue of Mary, Queen of Scots, carved in ivory in the early 17th century – her skirts open to reveal a tiny triptych. The last room is lined with antique ecclesiastical robes, which get an airing on ecclesiastical shoulders during the Easter processions.

Town Museum   (Gradski Muzej; ☏ 020 711 420; w gradskimuzej-korcula.hr; ⊕ Oct–Jun 10.00–15.00 Mon–Fri, Jul–Sep 09.00–21.00 Mon–Sat; €6) Occupying several floors of a nice old building opposite the treasury, the town museum has been carefully renovated and displays sculpture on the ground-floor, where you'll also find the (reproduction – the original's in Zagreb) Greek tablet known as the Lumbarda Stone, which lists the names of the families who lived on Korčula around 2,300 years ago. Upstairs, there's a replica of an old-fashioned kitchen, a section on shipbuilding and a re-creation of an elegant 18th-century salon. On the second floor, there's an exhibition of paintings created on the island between the 17th and 20th centuries, and the reconstruction of a typical old-fashioned Dalmatian kitchen. The third floor is devoted to local crafts such as shipbuilding and stonemasonry.

Other sights Heading away from the centre of town, you'll find the so-called **Marco Polo House**, which has been bought by the town council and now houses the Marco Polo Interpretation Centre (⊕ May–Oct 09.00–21.00 daily, Nov–Apr 09.00–17.00 Mon–Fri; €8). There are great views from the top of the small tower upstairs. There are also plans to build a full-scale reproduction of the galley he used in the famous battle in 1298.

In the southeastern corner of town there's an interesting **Icon Gallery** (Muzej Ikona; ⊕ May–Oct 08.00–15.00 Mon–Sat; €5) – and entry to this also gives you access to **All Saints' Church** (Svih Sveti), across the little bridge which is still used on special occasions by the local Brotherhood, or Guild. Indeed, the Guilds play an important part in Korčula life, with most people belonging to one or another – the Guild of All Saints was founded in 1301, that of St Roc in 1571, and that of St Michael in 1603. In the icon museum, check out the huge candles which are paraded around on feast days, and a fine two-sided cross for use in processions, which dates back to 1430. The church itself was originally the town's cathedral and features an altar canopy similar to the one in St Mark's, along with a fine carved wooden altarpiece.

LUMBARDA Even without your own transport, it's easy enough to get to Lumbarda – there are hourly buses in the week and a restricted service at weekends. But if you're heading for the seaside and not the unassuming village itself, you're much better off either hiring a bike or taking a taxi boat and negotiating to be dropped right at the beach.

MOORISH DANCES – THE MOREŠKA

For around 400 years, the people of Korčula have been dressing up and performing the Moreška, a famous sword dance which continues a tradition once common across the whole of Europe. Few of the dances retain anything remotely Moorish about them (least of all Britain's Morris dancers), but the name has stuck fast. Korčula is special, however, in still using real swords in what is effectively a war dance.

Originally an annual festival, the Moreška is now performed around twice a week (in a much-condensed version – 40mins instead of the original 2½hrs) in Korčula town in summer and makes for a spectacular evening show. The plot's pretty simple – bad king runs off with good king's squeeze; good king's soldiers fight bad king's soldiers; squeeze is saved from bad king's embraces – but nonetheless enjoyable for all that. Mind the flying, broken swords in the front row...

In other villages on Korčula, they perform a similar dance, the Kumpanija (the main difference being that it's sabres rather than swords which are used), particularly in Blato, towards the western end of the island. These are hard to get to without your own transport.

Lumbarda sits on the north shore of Korčula's southeastern peninsula, and the sandy soil here makes not just for the excellent local Grk wines, but also for some of the island's best beaches, all around the Ražnjić headland.

If you're interested in learning more about Grk (page 134), call at the **Bire winery** (w bire.hr; ☺ Jun–Sep 10.00–noon and 16.00–18.00), which offers guided wine-tasting (4 sorts, plus a platter of savoury snacks) and the chance to buy bottles to bring home. Their Grk Defora frequently wins international awards and sells out fast each season. Reservations essential.

The road from Korčula Town to Vela Luka runs the length of the island and passes through the inland villages of **Čara** and **Smokvica**, both renowned for making Pošip white wine. Highly recommended for wine-tasting are the welcoming family-run **Toreta** (f winetoreta) in the centre of Smokvica and **Merga Victa** (w mergavicta. com), aka Black Island Winery, a 10-minute walk from the centre, in the old wine co-operative building. Reservations essential for both.

Where to stay and eat

Hotel Lumbarda (44 rooms) Lumbarda 497; m 095 524 2128; w hotellumbarda.com. A 1970s hotel, refurbished in 2022, with an outdoor pool, restaurant & cocktail bar. €€€

Pansion Lovrić (4 rooms, 9 apartments) m 098 244 109; w lovric.info. Small family-run pansion with dbls & apartments with kitchenettes. The same family has a winery offering tasting. €€€

Pansion Marinka Bire Apartments (10 rooms) m 098 962 2010; w bire.hr. Nice apartments in a vineyard with views down to the sea. The owners

also run the highly regarded Bire winery, nearby & open for tasting. €€€

Villa Nobilo (5 apartments) Rašćiće bb; m 098 909 3119; w villa-nobilo.com. By the sea, 10mins' walk from the centre of Lumbarda, 5 modern apartments with kitchenettes & the use of a lovely vine-draped waterside terrace. €€€

Pizzeria Torkul Lumbarda; m 092 288 6125; ☺ May–Oct 16.00–midnight daily. A sound choice if you are in Lumbarda (4km south of Korčula Town), serves oven-warm pizza & local Grk white wine by the sea. €€

VELA LUKA Right at the other end of the island is Korčula's largest town, Vela Luka. It's much maligned, and in the past was known only for its shipyard and fish-processing factory, but with a great situation at the head of a well-sheltered bay and industry slowing down, the town is increasingly a tourist destination in its own right. It has a cheerful heart, a handful of good places to stay, brilliant beaches on nearby offshore islands, and good transport connections. Direct buses come from Dubrovnik and Korčula town, and it's also on the main ferry and catamaran lines running from Split to Hvar to Vela Luka to Lastovo.

The helpful **tourist office** (☎020 813 619; w tzvelaluka.hr), on the front at Obala 3 br 16, can provide you with maps and local information.

Where to stay and eat
If you want a private room, the place to go is the excellent and very helpful **Mediterano Tourist Agency** (Obala 3; ☎020 813 832; w mediterano.hr), though you'd do well to arrange accommodation in advance in high season – expect to pay around €80 for a double room in summer. Mediterano is also the place to head if you want to rent a car or scooter or arrange an excursion.

Korkyra (41 rooms) Obala 3/21; ☎020 601 000; w hotel-korkyra.com. Modern designer 4-star, with smart rooms, spa & an outdoor pool. Centrally located on the south side of the harbour. €€€€

Hotel Restaurant Dalmacija (14 rooms) m 092 372 8809; w dalmacija-restaurant.eu. Situated right on the waterfront, with clean, rather plain, good-value rooms, & a very nice terrace restaurant serving traditional Dalmatian fare. €€€

Konoba Bata Ul 56/1; ☎020 812 457; ⏰ noon–15.00 & 17.00–23.00 daily. Popular little place hidden away in the backstreets – a reservation might be wise in the evenings. €€€

Pizzeria Alfa Obala 2; ☎020 813 710; ⏰ 11.00–23.00 daily. Best bet in town for a decent pizza, though meals can take a while to arrive. On the waterfront. €€€

What to see and do If you're just passing through, you'll inevitably see the **Mosaic Footpath** (Lula Mosaika; ☐ lukamozaika), which curves around Vela Luka's deep bay and claims to be the world's longest mosaic. It's an ongoing project, and the organisers host mosaic workshops. If you're here for any time, it's well worth making the effort to walk out of town to an impressive **Neolithic cave**, Vela Špilja ('Big Cave' in local dialect; Vela Luka means 'Big Bay'; w velaspila.hr; ⏰ Jun–Sep 09.00–18.00 Mon–Sat), inhabited since prehistoric times and now under archaeological excavation.

If you're feeling more hedonistic, an attractive alternative is to take one of the thrice-daily boats to the lovely little island of **Proizd**, right off Korčula's northwestern tip. This has several pebble beaches, some of which are naturist, and an informal restaurant, operational between the first and last boats. There are also boats from the quayside in Vela Luka out to the even closer island, Ošjak, which is almost within Vela Luka's harbour – it also has some decent beaches.

LASTOVO

A dozen kilometres south of Korčula is the island of Lastovo, barely 10km long. Like Vis (page 188), it was off-limits for half a century and only opened up in 1989. In 2006, Lastovo and its archipelago gained the status of a nature park (w pp-lastovo.hr). Tourists are still comparatively few and far between, though numbers are growing steadily.

It's a low-key destination, with (as yet) only one large(ish) hotel – in Pasadur at the western end of the island – and nothing remotely like nightlife. But if you like lobster, fresh white wine, a chance to meet the local people, peace and quiet, hiking trails and remote chapels, then Lastovo's your place – unless you come during the carnival, when it goes berserk in a small-town sort of way, especially on Poklad's Tuesday (page 146).

The helpful **tourist office** (☎020 801 018; w tz-lastovo.hr) is right where the bus stops. It has some good maps and brochures on the island, including one on the old chapels and churches scattered across the island.

GETTING THERE AND AWAY Lastovo is the last stop for the daily ferry and catamaran from Split via Vela Luka (on Korčula), with boats arriving at Ubli in the early evening and leaving at the crack of dawn (before 05.00), effectively meaning you can't 'do' the island in fewer than two nights. It takes over 5 hours for the Jadrolinija ferry to come from Split (90mins from Vela Luka), but just over 3 hours 15 minutes on the catamaran (55mins from Vela Luka).

A minibus meets the incoming boats in Ubli and takes you the 10km to the village of Lastovo, spread out on a steep hillside facing away from the sea and sheltered from the bura.

 WHERE TO STAY AND EAT If the options below don't suit, the tourist office (see above) can help try to fix you up with a private room or apartment.

Apartments Ladesta (5 apartments) Prežba 26; m 098 984 2041. On the coast in Pasadur, near

Hotel Solitudo (the local minibus from Ubli port to Lastovo Town calls in Pasadur several times daily,

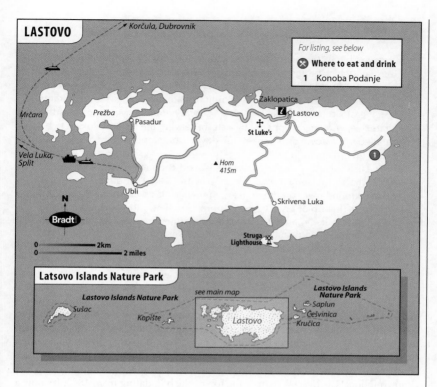

so you're not too isolated). All apartments have sea-view, balcony & kitchenette. **€€€**

Hotel Solitudo (60 rooms, 12 suites) Uvala Pasadur; 020 208 648; w hotel-solitudo.com. Out at Pasadur, the Solitudo is the island's only hotel – they pick up guests from the ferry, & offer bike rental. **€€€**

⛺ Camp Skriveni Skrivena Luka; 020 801 189; m 095 573 4102, 095 817 5481; w campskriveni.com. On the south coast 6km from Lastovo near Skrivena Luka, this has pitches below twisted branches in a small, peaceful olive grove. There are delicious home-cooked meals available, with fresh seafood caught that day by the owner & prepared by his wife. The beach at Skrivena Luka is 500m away, though there's another, more secluded beach slightly closer & only accessible by foot. Highly recommended. **€**

Restaurant & Guesthouse Augusta Insula Zaklopatica 21; m 098 571 884; w augustainsula.com; ⏰ May–Oct 09.00–midnight daily. Serves up excellent dishes in Zaklopatica Bay, much loved by yachters, on the island's north coast. They also have 6 rooms &

apartments to rent (**€€€**), & you can hire scooters from them, too. **€€€€**

Triton Zaklopatica 15; m 091 713 3122; ⓕ TritonLastovo; ⏰ Jun–Sep 14.00–midnight. Also in Zaklopatica Bay & popular with sailing crews, Triton serves freshly caught local fish & lobster. They have 4 rooms & apartments to rent, plus a motorboat to hire. **€€€€**

⛺ Konoba Bačvara Počuvala 14; 020 801 131; ⏰ May–Sep 17.00–23.00 daily. A lovely welcoming little place towards the bottom of the many flights of steps leading down through Lastovo Town itself, with delicious local specialities such as chickpea stew – highly recommended. **€€€€–€€€**

Konoba Podanje [map, above] Prgovo polje; w podanje.com; m 098 920 4821; ⏰ Jun–Sep 17.00–02.00 daily. Set amid olive groves & woodland east of Lastovo Town, this family-run agritourism eatery serves meat & seafood cooked on an outdoor barbecue, along with their own organic vegetables. **€€€€–€€€**

Lastovo's biggest annual festival is Shrove Tuesday (known here as Poklad Tuesday), which brings home expatriates from around the world to take part in the ritual humiliation and slaughter of Poklad.

Legend has it that Poklad was an unfortunate messenger sent by pirates to tell Lastovo to surrender or else. The local people prayed hard, and the pirate fleet was duly scuppered by a storm, leaving the luckless Poklad to be paraded round town on a donkey, run down a long rope, and then burned to death. Charming.

The festival pretty much follows the legend, though it's a luckless puppet rather than a messenger who gets to play the lead. First off, the puppet is paraded round town on the donkey, after which it's slid down a 300m-long rope from the top of town to the bottom, complete with firecrackers going off from its feet. On arrival, it's met by uniformed men brandishing drawn swords before being hauled back up the hill for another two descents. The whole thing ends with Poklad being put back on the donkey before being speared and burned à la Guy Fawkes – though you won't see the Lastovo sword dances on bonfire nights in Britain. It's an extraordinary spectacle.

WHAT TO SEE AND DO Lastovo Town is a cluster of old stone houses built into a hillside, looking inwards on to fertile fields, hidden from view from the sea (in medieval times, the islanders lived in fear of pirates). It's very photogenic, though there are few notable cultural attractions – a handful of small 15th- to 17th-century churches pretty much sums it up. But do make the hike up to the ruined French fort (known to locals as Kašćel) right at the top of the hill, dating from 1810. It's now a weather station with fabulous views.

There are some lovely hiking and cycling trails on the island to several chapels and churches, including the 11th-century St Luke's (Sv Luka), the lighthouse at Struga (the oldest on the Adriatic), a handful of secluded bays with rocky shores where you can bathe, and the summit of Hom (417m). A good way to start exploring is to follow the 6km *Via the Present to the Past* educational trail, which passes through Lastovo Town and introduces the island's cultural and natural heritage.

Lastovo Islands Nature Park (w pp-lastovo.hr) offers a 4-hour tour by boat (reservations essential). An alternative is to try to persuade a local boat owner to take you out to one of the string of islands to the east (the Lastovo archipelago). Here you'll find old lighthouses, pebble and rock beaches, and very, very few other people.

Lying so far from the mainland, Lastovo is virtually free of light pollution at night, and locals have applied to have it recognised as a **Dark Sky** reserve and are promoting astrotourism.

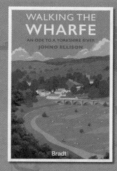
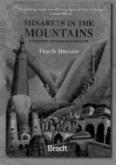
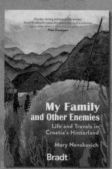

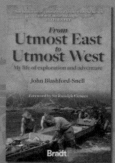

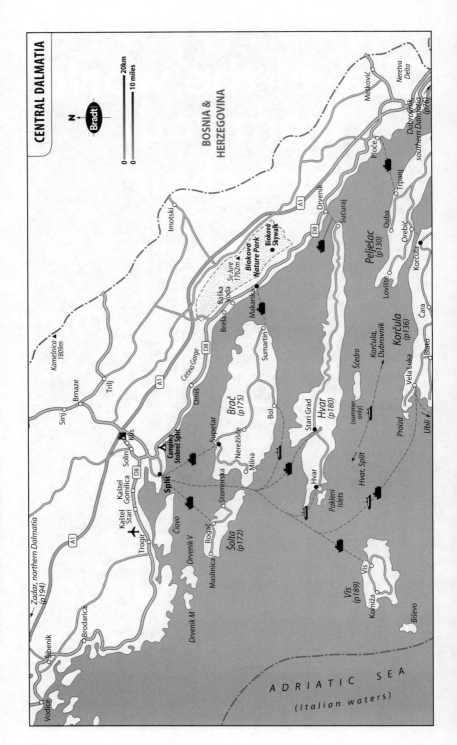

CENTRAL DALMATIA

BOSNIA & HERZEGOVINA

Zadar, northern Dalmatia (p194)

Vodice

Šibenik

Brodarica

Drvenik M

A1

Trogir

Kaštel Stari

Kaštel Gomilica

Solin

Klis

D8

Sinj

Brnaze

Kamešnica ▲ 1809m

Trilj

A1

Cetina Gorge

Omiš

D8

Imotski

Biokovo Nature Park

Sv. Jure 1762m ▲

Baška Voda

Brela

Biokovo Skywalk

Makarska

Drvenik

A1

D8

Sućuraj

Ploče

Neretva Delta

Metković

Split

Camping Stobreč Split

Čiovo

Drvenik V

Rogač

Maslinica

Stomorska

Šolta (p172)

Supetar

Nerežišće

Milna

Brač (p175)

Bol

Sumartin

Stari Grad

Hvar (p180)

Hvar

Pakleni Islets

Šćedro

(summer only)

Hvar, Split

Korčula, Dubrovnik

Pelješac (p130)

Lovište

Orebić

Duba

Trpanj

Korčula

Dubrovnik, southern Dalmatia (p76)

Proizd

Vela Luka

Ubli

Blato

Čara

Korčula (p136)

Vis (p189)

Vis

Komiža

Biševo

ADRIATIC SEA

(Italian waters)

N

Bradt

0   20km

0   10 miles

5

Split and Central Dalmatia

Telephone code 021 (+385 21 from abroad)

Central Dalmatia is wonderfully rich both in cultural sights and the great outdoors – whether it be the stark severity of the **Biokovo massif** above Makarska or the green islands of **Brač**, **Hvar** and **Vis** offshore, with their beaches, bays, coves and fishing villages. Unmissable are Emperor Diocletian's Palace in **Split**, the medieval island town of **Trogir** and the Renaissance elegance of **Hvar** town – along with the extraordinary shingle spit of Zlatni Rat, at **Bol**, and the Blue Cave on **Biševo**, just offshore from the island of Vis, itself only open to tourists since 1989.

SPLIT

Proudly referred to as *'najlipši grad na svitu'* (the most beautiful city in the world) by its inhabitants, Split is indeed exceptional. Overlooking a deep blue Adriatic, with the islands of Brač and Šolta rising into the horizon, and backed by the rugged Dinaric Alps, the city centres on Diocletian's Palace. A monumental limestone edifice combining the qualities of a fortress and a garrison, the palace was built by Roman Emperor Diocletian as his retirement home and completed in AD305.

Through the centuries, people took shelter within the ancient palace walls, later building noble Baroque mansions and quaint churches here so that it became a settlement in its own right. To the west of the palace grew up the neighbourhood of Varoš with its humble stone fishermen's cottages, and to the east, above Bačvice Bay, tree-lined avenues of early-20th-century townhouses. Then came the modern concrete apartment blocks of the 1960s, which make up Split's sprawling suburbs.

Today, Croatia's second biggest city is a brash and captivatingly energetic hub, with a population of just over 160,000 – but the old centre is surprisingly compact and easily manageable on foot. The main draw, Diocletian's Roman palace, lies just along the Riva from the port where you're likely to arrive. It is still stunning after more than 1,700 years of builders' alterations. Diocletian no doubt had a monster ego (being emperor has that effect), but even he could not have imagined his retirement home would be so well worth visiting in the 3rd millennium.

Split's a lively, friendly city, and although it wasn't the victim of a Dubrovnik-like siege during the 1991–92 war (just one casualty was sustained here), it suffered the effects of large numbers of refugees coming in and a huge drop in tourism. Split has also long been a voice of political dissension and was home to the weekly *Feral Tribune*, a bitingly satirical magazine (and regular thorn in the side of politicians) published between 1984 and 2008.

The city is proud of its sporting prowess – if you walk along the seafront promenade west of the old town, you'll see dozens of bronze plaques embedded in the paving, each recording an Olympic-medal-winning athlete originating from Split. In fact, Split claims to have more international-level sportspeople per capita than any other city in the world. Then, of course, there is the fanatically supported local football team, Hajduk Split, which has over 100,000 members – the entire city quakes with suspense when they play their main rivals, Dinamo Zagreb. Sporty Split hosts the annual Split Marathon (w splitmarathon.com), attracting world-class athletes each year in February.

Split is now served by budget airline connections from all over Europe. Besides attracting history and culture enthusiasts, in recent years it has given itself the image of a party destination, due primarily to the fact that it hosts the massive Ultra Europe electronic dance music festival each July. This, in turn, has led to a proliferation of touristy cocktail bars and nightly pub crawls, and problems of drunkenness and antisocial behaviour among groups of younger visitors.

Although the old town was still largely populated by local families in the late 1990s, now the vast majority of residential properties have been converted into holiday apartments. Consequently, the historic centre is plagued by overtourism through summer and almost deserted in winter, when most of the tourist-oriented bars, restaurants and souvenir shops are closed. Nonetheless, the people of Split are a sun-loving bunch, and the café terraces along the seafront promenade buzz all year round.

HISTORY Although previously inhabited, Split only officially came into existence when Diocletian retired here in AD305, after 21 years as Roman emperor. The palace – started halfway through Diocletian's reign, in AD295 – was built on a vast 170m-by-190m ground plan, with walls 2m thick and up to 26m high, making it the largest private residence in antiquity.

Post-Diocletian, the palace continued to be used on and off as a sort of upmarket hotel for the elite until the Roman Empire finally collapsed. After the Avars burned Salona in AD614, refugees moved in permanently, converting chambers into houses and corridors into streets, using the huge defences to good effect against invading hordes from the north.

Byzantium, the Ottomans, the Austro-Hungarians, the Venetians and Napoleon all left their mark on Split, but it was the Scottish architect Robert Adam who practically created it as a tourist destination overnight. Having seen Palladio's drawings, Adam and his team of draughtsmen stopped over in Split for five weeks in 1757, at the tail end of his 'Grand Tour' (tours really were grander then), and made hundreds of drawings and surveys of the palace. Published to huge acclaim in 1764, they came to dominate Georgian architecture and influenced the future shape of whole tracts of London, Bath, Bristol and Edinburgh.

The name Split is itself relatively recent – the town was probably originally called Aspalatos (after the yellow broom still common round here) before metamorphosing into Spalatum, Spalato and Spljet and finally settling down as Split.

GETTING THERE AND AROUND

By air Split's international **airport** is 20km/half an hour west of town, almost at Trogir, and flights are met by airport shuttle buses, which will run you into town for €8 (for details of airlines flying to Split, see page 30). Shuttles return to the airport from Split bus station (in front of the ferry port) 90 minutes before flight departures. For timetables, see w plesoprijevoz.hr. As a cheaper alternative to the shuttle, local bus #37 also runs every 20 minutes from Split to the airport and on to Trogir – buy a four-zone ticket from a kiosk (€2) or on the bus (€4), but be aware that this bus is much slower, making countless stops along the way, so it can take up

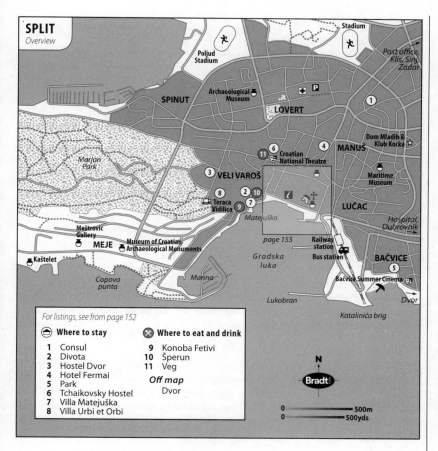

page 155

SPLIT
Overview

Poljud Stadium

Stadium

Post office, Klis, Sinj, Zadar

SPINUT

Archaeological Museum

LOVERT

1

Marjan Park

Croatian National Theatre

6

11

MANUŠ

4

Dom Mladih & Klub Kocka

3 VELI VAROŠ

8 2 10
7
9

Maritime Museum

Teraca Vidilica

LUČAC

Matejuška

Hospital, Dubrovnik

Meštrović Gallery

MEJE Museum of Croatian Archaeological Monuments

Railway station

Gradska luka

Bus station

BAČVICE

5

Kaštelet

Copova punta

Marina

Lukobran

Bačvice Summer Cinema

Dvor

Katalinića brig

N

Bradt

0 ————— 500m
0 ————— 500yds

For listings, see from page 152

Where to stay
1 Consul
2 Divota
3 Hostel Dvor
4 Hotel Fermai
5 Park
6 Tchaikovsky Hostel
7 Villa Matejuška
8 Villa Urbi et Orbi

Where to eat and drink
9 Konoba Fetivi
10 Šperun
11 Veg

Off map
Dvor

to 60 minutes to arrive in busy traffic. A **taxi** to or from the airport will set you back around €40, though some hotels offer to pick up guests from the airport.

By sea Just to the east of the old town, in a row, you'll find the passenger **ferry** terminal, the train station, the bus station and the car ferry terminal.

Ferries and catamarans run frequently from Split not just to the local islands of Šolta, Brač and Hvar but also to Vis, Korčula and Lastovo, as well as down the coast to Dubrovnik, and across the Adriatic to Ancona (overnight services; 11hrs) – see individual islands for details of ferry and catamaran services. If you're planning on taking your car by ferry anywhere in the summer, reserve as far ahead as you can or expect a long wait. There are left-luggage facilities next to the ferry terminal.

By train and bus The **train** station provides a high-speed rail link to Zagreb, though it is certainly not as fast as you might expect (6–8hrs). Through July and August, you also have night trains from Split to Vienna and Bratislava, three times weekly. Timetables are available at w hzpp.hr. Note that there is no railway south of Split.

Split's incredibly well-connected with everywhere by **bus** – at least a dozen a day go to each of Dubrovnik (4–5hrs), Rijeka (8–9hrs) and Zagreb (5hrs). There are

DIOCLETIAN AND THE PALACE

In its heyday the palace must have been extraordinary. At over 30,000m², it included everything from vast reception chambers to temples, arcaded corridors, baths, huge storerooms, extensive private apartments and an entire barracks. No expense was spared in its construction, with materials shipped in from Egypt and Greece, though it was built in a terrible rush, as it had to be ready for the emperor's retirement.

It's thought that Diocletian's wife and daughter never joined him here, in spite of their having lavish residences within the palace, and it's not clear whether he eventually had them killed – or indeed whether or not he himself committed suicide, was murdered, or died a natural death. What is known is that he passed his retirement years in Split having Christians captured, tortured and put to death – so many were martyred, in fact, that Diocletian holds the individual record for saint creation. Fighting Christianity was a losing battle, however – only two years after his death, in AD316, the Milan edict legitimised the religion. Ironically the site of his former tomb is now the city's Christian cathedral.

also international departures several times a week to destinations in Germany and elsewhere in Europe. Again, book ahead if you can, as buses fill up fast, especially in summer. The bus station has timetables on its website (w ak-split.hr), and nearby, there are several booths for left-luggage as well as lockers in the neighbouring train station.

By car If you come in by car, you'll discover that Split has its fair share of traffic problems, and parking (w splitparking.hr, Croatian only) can be a major hassle in summer. The best-located **car park** is right on the Riva in front of the port (€4 for 1hr, then €5/hr after that), but you'll be lucky to find a spot in season. The car parks on Svačićeva and Zrinsko Frankopanska, just north of the old town, are cheaper at €1.20 per hour.

GETTING AROUND Once you've arrived, everything's easily reached on foot, including the beach – the nearest to the old town lies in sandy Bačvice Bay, a 10-minute walk southeast of the centre. If you're not keen on walking, you can use a public bicycle (w splitparking.hr/javne-bicikle, Croatian only) – they are available 24/7 at various locations in the city centre at a cost of €0.66 per 30 minutes for a classic bike, or €1.33 per 30 minutes for an e-bike, payable by credit card through a mobile app. Alternatively, you may end up taking local bus #12 if you're going to the two galleries west of town or to the tip of the Marjan peninsula – Split's huge hilltop park and home to several rock-and-pebble beaches. Tickets cost €2 on the bus or €1 if bought in advance from a kiosk.

TOURIST INFORMATION Split's main **tourist information** office is located on the Riva (Obala Hrvatskog Narodnog Preporoda 9; ☎021 360 1066; w visitsplit.com). There's also a smaller tourist information office inside Diocletian's Palace, on the peristyle by the cathedral in the former 16th-century Church of St Roko (Peristil; ☎021 345 606).

WHERE TO STAY Split these days has plenty of accommodation options, with several boutique-style **hotels** within the walls of the palace, as well as a few larger modern hotels north of the old town. Staying in – or anywhere near – Diocletian's Palace doesn't come cheap, especially in season.

There's a good supply of **private rooms** – expect to pay the usual surcharge of 30% for three nights or fewer. There are no **campsites** in Split itself – the closest is **Camping Stobreč Split** [map, page 148] (w campingsplit.com), complete with a beach and pools, lying 7km east of the city in Stobreč, served by regular buses.

Luxury

Hotel Fermai [map, page 151] (35 rooms) Livanjska 5; ☏021 278 000; w hotelfermai.com. In a Vienna Secession building from 1914, on a rather busy road just 5mins' walk northeast of the old town, the Fermai offers tasteful décor & excellent b/fast. €€€€€

Park [map, page 151] (72 rooms) Hatzeov perivoj 3; ☏021 406 400; w hotelpark-split.hr. If your budget stretches that far, the renovated 5-star Park is one of the nicest & best located of the town's hotels, just round the headland from the ferry terminal, & set above Bačvice beach, 10mins' walk from the old town. The grand dame of Split's hotels, she dates from 1921. €€€€€

Slavija [155 C3] (25 rooms) Buvinina 2; ☏021 323 840; w hotelslavija.hr. Once the sole preserve of backpackers & students, the Slavija has been reborn with a flash new lobby & cleaned-up façade, though the rooms are still relatively basic. Lovely location, but the prices are steep for what you get. €€€€€

Vestibul Palace [155 C3] (11 rooms) Iza Vestibula 4; ☏021 329 329; w vestibulpalace.com. Smart 4-star boutique hotel just up the stairs from the peristyle, with 7 rooms & a small restaurant in the main building, plus 4 in a nearby annexe. 1 of Croatia's only 7 hotels listed on Small Luxury Hotels of the World. High on atmosphere, with stylish, modern, tasteful décor. €€€€€

Jupiter Heritage Hotel [155 C2] (38 rooms) Grabovčeva Širina 1; ☏021 786 500; w lhjupiter. com. A boutique luxury hotel within the palace walls, with a restaurant doing b/fast & a rooftop jacuzzi. €€€€

Peristil [155 D3] (12 rooms) Poljana Kraljice Jelene 5; ☏021 329 070; w hotelperistil.com. A great option tucked within the walls of Diocletian's Palace, right by the Silver Gate, leading from the open-air market to the peristyle. The staff are genuinely welcoming & will go out of their way to help you. €€€€

Piazza Heritage Hotel [155 B2] (16 rooms) Kraj Svete Marije 1; ☏021 553 377; w piazza-

heritagehotel.com. Boutique luxury in the old town, in a Vienna Secession building from 1906, overlooking Pjaca, the main square. €€€€

Mid-range

Divota [map, page 151] (28 rooms) Plinarska 75; ☏021 782 700; w divota.hr. Apartment hotel with rooms & studios at various locations in old stone cottages in Varoš, 10mins' walk west of the palace. Also has a small spa & a Zen garden hosting yoga & meditation. €€€€

Hotel Kaštel 1700 [155 B3] (8 rooms) Mihovilova Sirina 5; ☏021 343 912; w kastelsplit. com. Overlooking the Riva at the southwest corner of the palace, with a side entrance off Voćni trg. Good location but expensive for what you get. €€€€

Consul [map, page 151] (15 rooms) Trščanska 34; ☏021 340 130; w consulsplit.com. 10mins' walk north of the old town & palace, with sgls, dbls & trpls, & a spacious terrace restaurant. €€€

Villa Matejuška [map, page 151] (5 apartments) Tomića stine 3; ☏021 321 086; w villamatejuska. hr. Nice & very good-value apartments just a few minutes' walk from the palace, towards Marijan. €€€

Villa Urbi et Orbi [map, page 151] (5 rooms) Šenoina 2a; m 099 474 0780; 🇫. In Varoš, on the way up to Marjan, small guesthouse with 5 cosy rooms & a leafy terrace. €€€

Budget

With just a few exceptions, those after 'budget' accommodation in Split will need to aim for private rooms & hostels (for a list of officially recognised hostels, see w visitsplit.com/en/hostels).

BASE Rooms [155 C2] (3 rooms) Kraj Svetog Ivana 3; ☏021 317 375; m 098 361 387; w base-rooms.com. Very good value, right next to the Temple of Jupiter, just off the peristyle, in the heart of the palace. €€€

Hostel Dvor [map, page 151] (13 rooms) Radmilovića 71; ☏021 785 908; w hosteldvor.com.

Ideally located in a car-free alley in Varoš, Hostel Dvor offers tastefully designed dorms with bunks, plus 3 dbls. €

Tchaikovsky Hostel [map, page 151] (20 beds) Ulica Petra Iliča Čajkovskog 4; ☎ 021 317 124; m 091 277 7888; w tchaikovskyhostel.com. Popular centrally located hostel with 4- & 6-bed dorms, 20mins' walk from the bus station just beyond the National Theatre. €

✗ **WHERE TO EAT AND DRINK** There are literally dozens of restaurants in Split's tourist-oriented old town, though prices have rocketed, and locals themselves very rarely eat out. If you're self-catering and looking for your own ingredients, see opposite.

Bokeria [155 B2] Domaldova 8; ☎ 021 355 577; ☐; ⊕ 09.00–23.00 daily. Café-restaurant serving all-day drinks & slick Creative Mediterranean fare in the heart of the old town, with occasional visiting guest chefs. €€€€

Corto Maltese [155 B2] Obrov 7; ☎ 021 587 201; ☐; ⊕ 08.00–23.45 daily. Near the covered fish market, funky eatery serving contemporary cuisine & cocktails, with outdoor tables on the street. €€€€

Dvor [map, page 151] Put Firule 14; ☎ 021 571 513; ☐; ⊕ noon–midnight daily. On the coast, east of the old town, Dvor does modern Dalmatian cuisine under the pine trees, high above the sea. €€€€

Pandora GreenBox [155 B2] Obrov 4; ☎ 021 236 120; ☐; ⊕ 08.00–midnight daily. Opposite Corto Maltese & run by the same owner, this vegetarian-vegan eatery serves fancy plant-based dishes. €€€€

✳ **Kod Jože** [155 D1] Sredmanuška 4; ☎ 021 347 397; ☐; ⊕ 10.00–midnight Mon–Fri, noon–midnight Sat–Sun. On the far side of the park behind the palace, hidden down a side street, this homely, well-priced konoba does excellent seafood, as well as other dishes such as rich & authentic gnocchi with game. €€€

✳ **Konoba Fetivi** [map, page 151] Tomica stine 4; ☎ 021 355 152. Family-run eatery doing authentic Dalmatian seafood dishes, just like locals eat at home, including a few old-fashioned specialities rarely seen on restaurant menus. €€€

Šperun [map, page 151] Šperun 3; ☎ 021 346 999; ⊕ 09.00–23.00 daily. Bags of character just off the Riva in Varoš. Choose between the handful of tables outdoors or descend into the main body of the restaurant, which is awash with bric-a-brac. Mainstays include fresh fish simply grilled, seafood risotto & some hearty meat dishes. €€€

Villa Spiza [155 C1] Kružićeva 3; m 091 152 1249; ⊕ Dec–Oct 13.00–22.00 Mon–Sat. Real home-cooking at this informal eatery in the old town, where the menu changes daily depending on what the owner-chef finds at the morning market. €€€

Pizzeria Portas [155 D2] Kod zlatnih vrata 1; m 099 555 5715; w pizzeriaportas.hr; ⊕ noon–22.00 daily. Formerly called Pizzeria Grgur, this is still the place to go for reliable pizzas in the old town, with a lovely terrace. Just around the corner from the Golden Gate. €€€–€€

✳ **Zlatna Ribica** [155 B2] Kraj Svete Marije 8; ☎ 021 348 710; ⊕ Jun–Sep 06.00–23.00 Mon–Sat, 11.00–23.00 Sun; Oct–May 06.00–15.00 Mon–Sat. Next to the covered fish market, this small canteen does platters of fried whitebait, squid & prawns, pulled fresh from the sea that morning by local fishermen. €€€–€€

Veg [map, page 151] Ujevičeva poljana 5; ☎ 021 263 163; ☐ vegst; ⊕ 08.00–23.00 daily. Behind the theatre, informal Veg does plant-based food for vegans, including bowls, wraps & smoothies. €€

Kantun Paulina [155 A1] Matošića 1; ☎ 021 395 973; ⊕ 08.00–23.00 daily. Bosnian-style čevapi (grilled beef rissoles) served in warm bread buns with optional ajvar (red pepper relish) & chopped onions, since 1967. €

✳ **Kruščić** [155 B2] Obrov 6; m 099 261 2345; ☐ Kruscic.Split; ⊕ 08.00–14.00 Mon–Sat. Artisan bakery behind the fish market, doing freshly baked bread, pies, cakes & various daily specials, ideal for a morning snack. €

Rizzo [155 A1] Tončićeva 4; ☎ 021 480 500; w rizzo.hr; ⊕ 09.00–23.00 daily. Sandwich bar doing oven-warm bread buns freshly filled with your choice of cured meats, cheese & salad. €

Luxor [155 C2] Kraj sv Ivane 11; w lvxor.hr; ⊕ 09.00–midnight daily. Arguably the most

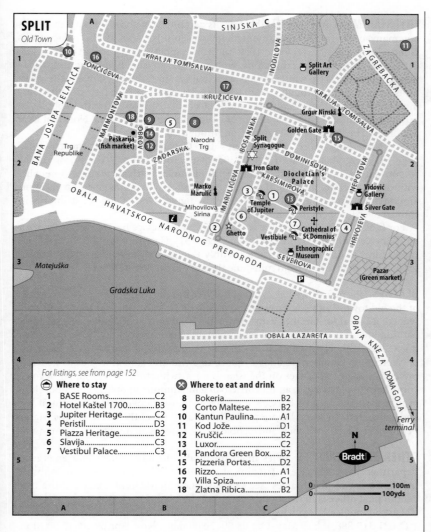

SPLIT
Old Town

SINJSKA

KRALJA TOMISALVA

KRUŽIĆEVA

Split Art Gallery

ZAGREBAČKA

BANA JOSIPA JELAČIĆA

TONČIĆEVA

MARMONTOVA

OBROV

ZADARSKA

Peškarija (fish market)

Trg Republike

Narodni Trg

BOSANSKA

KRALJA TOMISALVA

Grgur Ninski

Golden Gate

Split Synagogue

DOMINISOVA

OBALA HRVATSKOG NARODNOG PREPORODA

Marko Marulić

MARULIĆEVA

KREŠIMIROVA

Iron Gate

Diocletian's Palace

Temple of Jupiter

Peristyle

Vidović Gallery

Silver Gate

NEPOTOVA

HRVOJEVA

Mihovilova Sirina

Ghetto

Vestibule

Cathedral of St Domnius

Ethnographic Museum

SEVEROVA

Matejuška

Gradska Luka

Pazar (Green market)

OBALA LAZARETA

OBALA KNEZA DOMAGOJA

Ferry terminal

Bradt

N

0   100m
0   100yds

For listings, see from page 152

Where to stay

1	BASE Rooms	C2
2	Hotel Kaštel 1700	B3
3	Jupiter Heritage	C2
4	Peristil	D3
5	Piazza Heritage	B2
6	Slavija	C3
7	Vestibul Palace	C3

Where to eat and drink

8	Bokeria	B2
9	Corto Maltese	B2
10	Kantun Paulina	A1
11	Kod Jože	D1
12	Kruščić	B2
13	Luxor	C2
14	Pandora Green Box	B2
15	Pizzeria Portas	D2
16	Rizzo	A1
17	Villa Spiza	C1
18	Zlatna Ribica	B2

atmospheric location for a coffee in Split, with cushions outside on the 2,000-year-old stone slabs of the peristyle itself, & live music (of variable quality) on summer evenings.

Self-catering If you're looking for snacks and picnic food, head for Split's **Pazar** [155 D3] (green market; ⏰ 07.00–13.00 Mon–Sat) immediately outside the palace's eastern wall. Each morning, stallholders display piles of local seasonal fruit and vegetables, as well as cheeses, cured meats, nuts, dried fruit and fresh flowers. Seafood lovers will also enjoy taking a look in the *peškarija* [155 B2] (covered fish market; ⏰ 07.00–noon Mon–Sat), where impressive arrays of glistening Adriatic fish and shellfish are displayed upon mounds of crushed ice. For bread, go direct to a bakery and for more general shopping, you'll find numerous little Konzum, Tommy and Studenac supermarkets around town, plus a useful Ribola supermarket next to the ferry port, opposite the bus station.

ENTERTAINMENT AND NIGHTLIFE Split is certainly not short on bars and clubs, but many of them are now oriented towards tourists. Inside the palace walls, **Ghetto** [map, page 155] (Dosud 10; ⊕ until midnight) is Split's coolest club, staging occasional concerts and exhibitions, with an underground, bohemian feel, and as popular with locals (in winter) as it is with tourists (in summer). Outside the palace walls, from autumn through spring, **Klub Kocka** (Slobode 28; **f**) stages alternative music concerts in the basement of the 1980s brutalist **Dom Mladih** (Slobode 28; w dom-mladih.org) built as the House of Youth in the Yugoslav era. Note that Dom Mladih will be under partial renovation through 2025.

For something more sedate, there's the **Croatian National Theatre** [map, page 151] (Trg Gaje Bulata 1; ⟋021 306 908; w hnk-split.hr). The theatre is also responsible for organising the annual **Split Summer Festival** (w splitsko-ljeto.hr), with opera, theatre, music and dance performances at various open-air locations around town from mid-July through mid-August. One of the most impressive shows is Verdi's opera *Aida* on the Roman peristyle.

For film buffs, under the pine trees, high above Bačvice beach, the lovely open-air **Bačvice Summer Cinema** [map, page 151] (Ljetno Kino Bačvice; **f**; €5) shows films in the original version (mainly English) with Croatian subtitles, with projections after sunset from mid-June through to mid-September.

BEACHES The main town beach lies in **Bačvice Bay**, just a 10-minute walk southeast of the old town. With soft brown sand giving on to warm shallow water and a soft seabed, it's ideal for families with small kids. Bačvice is Split's oldest official public bathing area – it was furnished with changing cubicles back in 1919. Nowadays, it gets unearthly busy with tourists in July–August, but if you come in May–June or September–October, it's a lovely place to swim and sunbathe. Locals generally prefer to escape to beaches on the islands for a swim, though a group of devotees come here to play *picigin*, an eccentric ball game unique to Split, September–June, even if it snows. East of Bačvice, a coastal path, overlooked by a handful of bars and cafés, leads to several more pebble beaches. West of the old town, the Marjan peninsula is laced with rock-and-pebble coves, where you might also swim.

OTHER PRACTICALITIES Split's main **hospital** with an accident and emergency department is at Spinčićeva 1 (Clinical Hospital Firule; ⟋021 556 111; w kbsplit. hr). For a list of **pharmacies**, see w visitsplit.com/en/236/pharmacies. The most central **post office** is in front of the ferry port at Obala kneza Domagoja 3.

Last but not least, if you need a laundrette, there's Modrulj Laundrette, at Šperun 1 (⟋021 315 888; **f**; ⊕ May–Oct 08.00–20.00 daily, Nov–Apr 09.00–17.00 Mon–Sat), just beyond the western end of the seafront at the foot of Varoš, next to the Šperun restaurant.

WHAT TO SEE AND DO
Diocletian's Palace The main draw is clearly the former palace, on the Riva, though what you see now, inside the old walls, is an entire town centred on Diocletian's peristyle. Back in 2011, some 3,200 local people still lived in the historic centre, while by 2023, the number had fallen to about 1,500, with only 500 residing in the palace itself. Until recently, you'd find the cafés and bars catering to a healthy mix of both visitors and residents, but now they are very much tourist-oriented.

Enter the old town from the Riva, which is actually reclaimed land – the gate you go through (known as the Brass Gate) was originally on the sea. It was built to be used as an emergency escape route for Diocletian in case of trouble but may also have seen service as a delivery entrance. The gate leads through a semi-underground corridor flanked by chambers you can visit before climbing some worn steps up into the peristyle.

The peristyle [155 C2] The peristyle (*peristil*), an open, colonnaded square, was the public heart of Diocletian's Palace and is still an extraordinary place to sit and wonder. Everything off to the south (towards the sea, behind you) was originally Diocletian's imperial quarters, while to the north were servants' lodgings and soldiers' barracks.

The pink granite columns are Egyptian, while their capitals are Corinthian. You can see that even originally there were four antique columns too few, with local marble pillars making up the difference. The cracked black sphinx dates back to the reign of Thutmosis III, who ruled Egypt from 1504 to 1450BC and was originally one of ten imported for Diocletian from the land of the Pharaohs. Another four survive in varying states of repair – one in the underground chambers, one at the entrance to the Temple of Jupiter and two in the Archaeological Museum.

The streets out of the peristyle lead to the palace's other three gates – north, to the Golden Gate (the main entrance, coming in from Salona), east, to the Silver Gate (leading to Pazar, the colourful open-air market), and west, to the Iron Gate. On the peristyle itself you'll find the **Vestibule** [155 C3] (above the *podrum*; page 158), the **cathedral** (actually Diocletian's mausoleum), and off down an alley to the other side, the Baptistery of St John (the **Temple of Jupiter** – Diocletian reckoned he was Jupiter's son). Inside the barrel-vaulted temple (also known as the Temple of Aesculapius; €3), you should be able to see a couple of classical statues, an interesting 11th-century baptismal font, and a statue of John the Baptist by Meštrović.

The Vestibule was the grand ceremonial entrance hall to the imperial quarters. The domed roof remains in part, but the ornate mosaics that would have lined it are long gone. Thanks to its exceptional acoustics, this is the place you're most likely to find locals singing *klapa* (Dalmatian plain singing) on a summer evening. It's worth walking through here and circling round to the left (past the Ethnographic Museum), back to the cathedral, for some idea of where Diocletian lived – this was originally the dining halls and Roman baths. There are some floor mosaics here which recently underwent restoration.

Cathedral of St Domnius [155 C2] (Sv Duje; ⏲ May–Sep 08.00–20.00 Mon–Sat, 10.00–18.00 Sun; Apr & Oct 08.00–16.00 Mon–Sat, 09.00–17.00 Sun; Nov–Mar 08.00–16.00 Mon–Sat; €5) In a move that must have had Diocletian whirling in his sarcophagus, the emperor's mausoleum was long ago converted into one of Christianity's smallest cathedrals, honouring one of his own victims, St Domnius.

The main structure, including the dome, is original, dating from AD300, but the choir is a 17th-century addition. The entrance doors, with 28 excellent carved wooden panels describing the life of Christ, by Romanesque master Andrija Buvina, date from 1214. A four-year restoration project, concluded in 2018, revealed that the reliefs would originally have been painted in vibrant shades of blue, red and green and adorned with gold leaf.

At the base of the dome there's a pagan-looking frieze and what are said to be medallions of the heads of Diocletian and his wife. Diocletian's ahead of you as you come in, while his wife is two medallions to the left. Down below, the 13th-century pulpit is a Romanesque masterpiece by Radovan (he of Trogir fame). The Baroque 17th-century chapel is the one housing the Domnius relics; the other two chapels are 15th-century Gothic. Finally, the choir itself may be 17th-century, but the stalls are around the same age as the cathedral doors and are a fine example of early Dalmatian woodcarving.

Take the time to climb up inside the campanile (opening hours same as the cathedral; €7) for dizzying but impressive views over the palace and out to sea – this version dates from 1908, following the collapse of the original, which was built in stages from the 13th to 17th centuries. Reopened in 2020 following a two-year restoration, the proud campanile is considered a symbol of Split and features on the city's coat of arms.

Underneath the cathedral is the spooky circular crypt dedicated to St Lucy, patron saint of the blind (legend has it that Diocletian put her eyes out). The function of this chamber in antiquity isn't known – it's unlikely that it would have been a prison, being under a mausoleum, but large numbers of human bones were found here, and it is the kind of damp, gloomy, airless place you could imagine being used as a dungeon. Ask in the cathedral if you want to see the crypt (€3) – it's not always open, though if you're lucky enough to be here on 13 December, St Lucy's Day, you can enter the crypt for free.

The basement halls (podrum) The walkway from the peristyle to the Riva takes you down through the huge semi-underground chambers that provided the foundations for the imperial quarters above. The only whole rooms remaining from the original palace, they give some idea of the sheer scale and size of Diocletian's ego. Remarkably, these chambers only survive because of sewage – during the Middle Ages, people simply threw their slops down holes in the floor, and it accumulated here, protecting the rooms from future squatters.

After World War II, the western rooms were cleared out and opened to the public, while the eastern wing wasn't excavated until 1997 – at various points you can see the original waste chutes coming in from above, along with the foundations of medieval houses. In recent years, the halls have hosted stands selling jewellery and local artworks, as well as temporary art exhibitions. Sadly, as of January 2024, the city council decreed that the underground chambers should lie empty and be used solely as a tourist attraction (⊕ 09.00–18.00; €7), a move that has understandably irked many locals.

Beyond the palace Just outside the Golden Gate [155 D2], you can hardly fail to spot Meštrović's monumental 1928 statue of **Grgur Ninski** [155 D1]. Originally standing in the peristyle (which looked pretty wild – there's a photo in the first edition of Rebecca West's *Black Lamb and Grey Falcon*), the statue commemorates the 10th-century Bishop Gregorius of Nin, who tried (but failed) to introduce Croatian instead of Latin into the liturgy. According to local tradition, touch his big toe and your wish will come true – which explains why it's been worn golden.

Walk west a block and head down Bosanska, the narrow street separating the palace from the rest of the old town. This is the least well-preserved wall of the palace, with an unbroken row of houses built into the original fortifications. On the left-hand side, unmarked, is Split's first **synagogue** [155 C2] – Europe's third, after Prague and Dubrovnik.

Halfway down the street is the palace's **Iron Gate** [155 C2], which leads out into the old town's main square, Narodni Trg (also known as Pjaca, pronounced piazza). Palazzi from different periods surround the square, with a Venetian Gothic town hall standing on one side and an Austrian Secessionist palace dominating the square's west end. From Pjaca, follow Marulićeva Street to arrive on the next square to the south, just off the Riva. Known to locals as **Voćni trg**, meaning Fruit Square (the open-air market took place here till 1922), it has an excellent statue of

Marko Marulić [155 B2], the father of Croatian literature, who died in 1524 but is still widely celebrated and, indeed, read. Yes, you guessed – it's by Meštrović. Behind the statue stands the 18th-century Baroque Milesi Palace, which hosts some worthwhile art exhibitions through summer.

The old town's western boundary is the wide newly paved shopping thoroughfare of Marmontova, named after Napoleon's Marshal Marmont, the captain of his Illyrian Provinces. Marmont was the man responsible for both the Riva – Narodni Trg had got too small to function as a collective town square – and Trg Republike, now rimmed by open-air café and restaurants and used for summer concerts (during Advent, they sometimes set up an ice rink here).

West of the town, you'll find the popular old quarter of **Veli Varoš**, made up of quaint stone cottages formerly belonging to local fishermen, which leads up the slopes of the 182m **Marjan peninsula**. Marjan (w marjan-parksuma.hr) is a protected forest park, featuring dense pinewoods, cacti and agave, marked footpaths, several delightful little medieval churches, and a number of decent rock-and-pebble beaches – a great place to get away from the crowds, though very popular with the locals at weekends. Stop at **Teraca Vidilica** (which works as a fancy café-restaurant May–Sep and as a basic café Oct–Apr) for a cooling drink on a terrace with a superb view over Split as the city unfolds below and the mountains and islands beckon in the distance.

Museums and galleries

Split has several museums and galleries of particular note, two within the palace, one a 10-minute walk northeast, two about a 15-minute walk north (head up Zrinsko Frankopanska from the top of Marmontova), and two a 20-minute walk west overlooking the coast on the Marjan peninsula – or a short hop on local bus #12 from Trg Republike. Note that a third museum within the palace, the Split City Museum (w mgs.hr), is currently closed for renovation.

Archaeological Museum (Arheološki Muzej; Frankopanska 25; \021 329 340; w armus.hr; ⊕ Jun–Sep 09.00–14.00 & 15.00–20.00 Mon–Sat, Oct–May 09.00–14.00 & 15.00–20.00 Mon–Fri, 09.00–14.00 Sat; €8) Heading north, the secessionist Archaeological Museum houses Croatia's biggest collection of remains from antiquity, and especially is strong (unsurprisingly) on artefacts from Salona (page 165). The Roman findings include excellent glass, jewellery, ceramics and statues, featuring some extraordinarily rich sarcophagi. There's also an extensive collection from very early Christianity.

Ethnographic Museum [155 C3] (Etnografski Muzej; Iza Vestibula 4; \021 344 164; w etnografski-muzej-split.hr; ⊕ Jun–Sep 09.30–17.00 Mon–Fri, 10.00–14.00 Sat; Oct–May 09.30–15.00 Mon–Fri, 10.00–14.00 Sat; €3) Located behind the Vestibule, with a good collection of regional folk costumes, jewellery, lace and embroidery, as well as traditional household furniture and rugs.

Split Art Gallery [155 C1] (Galerija Umjetnina Split; Kralja Tomislava 15; \021 350 112; w galum.hr; ⊕ 10.00–18.00 Tue–Wed & Fri, 10.00–20.00 Thu, 10.00–14.00 Sat–Sun; €5) Has a terrific collection of paintings and sculpture from the 14th century onwards. Unless you're an expert on Croatian art, you won't recognise many of the names, but make the effort to come here and you'll find a rich tradition of painting which is especially strong on late-19th- and early-20th-century works, including a couple of masterpieces by Vlaho Bukovac (page 117). The final room displays contemporary works, including amusing installations and videos. It also hosts some good temporary exhibitions by both local and international artists.

Vidović Gallery [155 D2] (Galerija Vidović; Poljana Kraljice Jelene 1; w emanuelvidovic.org; ⊕ May–Oct 08.30–20.00 daily, Nov–Apr 08.30–17.00 daily; €5) Next to the Silver Gate, just within the palace walls, this gallery displays oil paintings and watercolours by local artist Emanuel Vidović (1870–1953) – mainly hazy seascapes and dimly lit interiors of his homes in Dalmatia and Italy, plus an atmospheric reconstruction of his atelier.

Maritime Museum (Pomorski muzej; Glagoljaška 18; ✆021 347 346; w hpms. hr; ⊕ Jul–Aug 09.00–20.00 Mon–Sat, 09.00–17.00 Sun; Jun & Sep–Oct 09.00–19.00 Mon–Sat, 09.00–14.00 Sun; Nov–May 09.00–16.00 Mon, Wed & Fri–Sat, 09.00–19.00 Tue & Thu, 09.00–14.00 Sun; €3.50) Housed within the 17th-century Gripe Fortress, this museum reflects Split's connections with the sea, displaying six historic ships and boats, some of the first-ever torpedoes (revealing a little-known British-Croatian collaboration), naval uniforms, navigational equipment and ships' engines.

Museum of Croatian Archaeological Monuments (Muzej Hrvatskih Arheoloških Spomenika; Šetalište Ivana Meštrovića 18; ✆021 323 901; w mhas-split.hr; ⊕ Jun–Sep 09.00–13.00 & 17.00–20.00 Mon–Fri, 09.00–14.00 Sat; Oct–May 09.00–16.00 Mon–Fri, 09.00–14.00 Sat; free) Heading west from the old town, a 15-minute walk along the coast will get you to this unusual and fascinating collection of Croatian artefacts from the 7th century on, housed in a wonderfully airy modern building. Around 5,000 items are on display (from a collection of more than 20,000 in total), running from old jewellery and stone inscriptions to a unique series of monuments from early Croatian churches, including gables, friezes, altar canopies and baptismal fonts. Worth buying the English guide for full information. In the grounds, you can see several stone *stećci*, medieval tombstones carved by the Bogumils, a Christian neo-gnostic sect, popular in parts of Bosnia & Herzegovina, south Croatia, Montenegro and west Serbia between the 12th and 16th centuries.

IVAN MEŠTROVIĆ – CROATIA'S GREATEST MODERN SCULPTOR

Born in Vrpolje in Slavonia in 1883 to Dalmatian parents, Ivan Meštrović grew up in the rural village of Otavice (page 214) near Drniš in Dalmatia. After working as an apprentice stonemason in Split, he studied sculpture at the Academy of Fine Arts in Vienna. Influenced by the Vienna Secession movement, he also spent several years in Paris and Rome, where he encountered works by Rodin and Michelangelo. During the interwar period, he worked between his atelier in Zagreb and his villa in Split.

In 1942, he emigrated to Italy, moving to the US in 1947, where he became Professor of Sculpture at Syracuse University and the University of Notre Dame. In 1952, he donated much of his estate to Croatia. He died in the US in 1962. His body was brought back to Croatia and laid to rest in the Meštrović Mausoleum in Otavice, which he had designed.

You can see his sculptures and sketches at the Meštrović Gallery in Split and the Meštrović Atelier in Zagreb. Also of note are his statues of Grgur Ninski and Marko Marulić in Split, the Račić Mausoleum in Cavtat, the Njeguš Mausoleum in Montenegro, and various public works in Belgrade and Chicago.

Meštrović Gallery (Galerija Ivana Meštrovića; Šetalište Ivana Meštrovića 46; 021 340 800; w mestrovic.hr; ⊕ May–Oct 09.00–19.00 Tue–Sun, Nov–Apr 09.00–17.00 Tue–Sun; €12) Five minutes west of the Museum of Croatian Archaeological Monuments is this vast villa built by the sculptor between 1931 and 1939, intended both as a museum and as his retirement home. If you're even remotely interested in Meštrović, then this comprehensive collection is the best anywhere. Outside is the sculpture garden; indoors, the full range of the sculptor's work can be seen, from family portraits to religious tableaux to allegorical works in stone, bronze and wood.

Kaštelet (Meštrovićeve Crikvine Kaštilac; Šetalište Ivana Meštrovića 39; 021 340 800; w mestrovic.hr; ⊕ May–Oct 09.00–19.00 Tue–Sun, Nov–Apr by appointment) The same entry ticket for the Meštrović Gallery is also valid here, just down the road at number 39, which Meštrović bought to house one of his most important works, a series of large wooden friezes dedicated to the life of Christ, and which (pre)occupied the sculptor on and off from around 1916 until its completion in 1950. The courtyard is often used for open-air performances during the Split Summer Festival.

TROGIR

UNESCO World Heritage-listed Trogir – just 26km up the coast from Split – is one of the most attractive stops in Dalmatia, with the old town being not just excellently preserved but also delightfully car-free. Come here to soak up a pleasantly uncorrupted medieval atmosphere, where stone-carved balconies overhang the narrow streets, and Renaissance and Gothic palaces compete for your attention with the ancient cathedral. Be aware, however, that it does get extremely busy in peak season.

The **tourist office** (☎ 021 885 628; w visittrogir.hr), on the front-facing Čiovo, is friendly and has a map for you.

HISTORY Trogir started out in the 3rd century BC as Tragurion, an offshoot of the Greek colony of Issa (on Vis), before being developed as a key port under the Romans. Later overshadowed by Salona (page 165), Trogir grew in importance once again during the 7th century, when Salona was sacked, and its refugees came north to Split.

Relative peace under the Croatians and Hungarians came to a sudden halt in 1123, when the Saracens pretty much demolished the city, but prosperity soon returned, and the 12th–14th centuries were a golden age for the town. From 1420 onwards, Venice ruled, while from 1797 to 1918, the Austro-Hungarians were in charge – with a short break for Marshal Marmont and the French, from 1806 to 1814. The rest, as they say, is Yugoslavia – until Croatia won independence in 1991.

GETTING THERE AND AROUND Trogir is on the main coast road, so it's easy to reach by inter-city **bus** from Split (30mins) to the south or Zadar (2½hrs) or Šibenik (1hr) to the north. It's also the terminus for the local #37 bus from Split – buy a four-zone ticket at a kiosk (€2) or on the bus (€4) – which runs every 20 minutes, making Trogir an easily feasible day trip from Split (40–60mins, depending on traffic) – see w promet-split.hr. (The reverse is also true – if you can get in at one of the private rooms or small hotels in Trogir itself, it's a really attractive option as a base from which to visit Split.) Alternatively, from mid-May to mid-October, Bura Line (w buraline.com) runs a passenger boat service between Split and Trogir (1hr; €8).

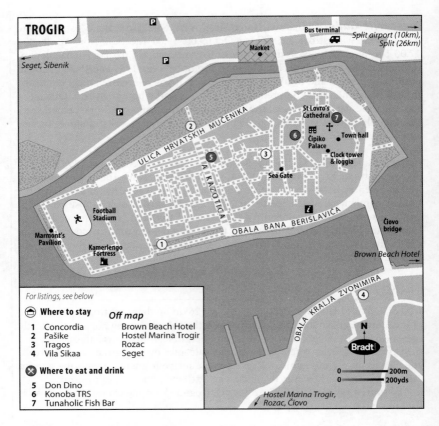

TROGIR

Seget, Šibenik

Bus terminal · Split airport (10km), Split (26km)

Market

St Lovro's Cathedral

Town hall

Čipiko Palace

Clock tower & loggia

ULICA HRVATSKIH MUČENIKA

A KAZOTIĆA

Sea Gate

Football Stadium

Marmont's Pavilion

Kamerlengo Fortress

OBALA BANA BERISLAVIĆA

Čiovo bridge

Brown Beach Hotel

OBALA KRALJA ZVONIMIRA

N

Bradt

0 — 200m
0 — 200yds

Hostel Marina Trogir, Rozac, Čiovo

For listings, see below

Where to stay

Off map

1 Concordia
2 Pašike
3 Tragos
4 Vila Sikaa

Brown Beach Hotel
Hostel Marina Trogir
Rozac
Seget

Where to eat and drink

5 Don Dino
6 Konoba TRS
7 Tunaholic Fish Bar

Split Airport is just 10km east of Trogir. There's a shuttle bus from Split (€8; w plesoprijevoz.hr), and the (somewhat slower) #37 bus will also drop you off in front of the airport. A taxi from the airport to Split will cost around €40. For details of airlines flying to Split, see page 30.

Your only problem might be in leaving if you're heading north in summer – the coastal buses from Split often arrive here full on their way to Zadar. It's not unheard of to take the #37 back to Split, make an onward reservation, and spend some time sightseeing before heading north again.

Trogir's bus station (more of a bus stop; there are no left-luggage facilities) is right by the stone bridge leading on to the island containing the old town. Just beyond the bridge – and indeed on it – you'll find a colourful local market selling everything from fruit, vegetables and flowers to homemade liquor.

Once you're in town, you'll find it charmingly small – the whole place, connected to the mainland by the stone bridge and to the island of Čiovo (where many families from Split have summer houses and an increasing number of properties have rooms and apartments to rent) by a drawbridge, is barely 500m long and under half that width.

WHERE TO STAY *Map, above*

Rooms in or very close to the old town get snapped up quickly, with doubles going for around €80 a night, and there's a 30% surcharge for stays of under five nights here.

Trogir has some excellent small, family-run places – but it's a popular place, and you need to book well ahead.

You can also camp either at **Rozac** (Šetalište Stjepana Radića 55, Okrug Gornji; ✆021 806 105; w camp-rozac.hr; €) on the island of Čiovo or **Seget** (Hrvatskih zrtava 121, Seget Donji; m 098 230 441; w kamp-seget.hr; €), which is a couple of kilometres west of town and has all the usual facilities, including windsurfing.

Brown Beach Hotel (59 rooms) Put Gradine 66; ✆021 355 450; w brownhotels.com. Luxury hotel with garden restaurant, sea-view outdoor pool & spa, 10mins' walk from Trogir old town. €€€€€

Pašike (13 rooms, 1 suite) Splitska 4; ✆021 885 185; w hotelpasike.com. Small, family-run hotel in the old town, with its own restaurant. Free airport transfers with web bookings. €€€€

Tragos (12 rooms) Budislaviceva 3; ✆021 884 729; w tragos.hr. Small, family-run place with lovely stone-walled interior, right in the heart of the old town, with its own restaurant. €€€€

Concordia (11 rooms) Bana Berislavića 22; ✆021 885 400; w concordia-hotel.net. On the southwestern corner of the front, the reasonably priced Concordia is near the fortress, with b/fast on the waterside terrace café included. €€€

Vila Sikaa (10 rooms) Kralja Zvonimira 13; ✆021 798 240; w vila-sikaa-r.com. Across the drawbridge on the Čiovo front, facing back towards Trogir (a lovely view), is the Vila Sikaa, with very nice rooms & a restaurant. €€€

Hostel Marina Trogir (30 beds) Put Cumbrijana 16; ✆021 833 075; w hostelmarina-trogir.com. Next to the sailing marina, hostel with 4 rooms with bunk beds & a common room with basic kitchenette. €€–€

✖ WHERE TO EAT AND DRINK *Map, opposite*

Many of the small hotels have a ground-floor restaurant, and practically every square has its own terrace set up in summer for alfresco dining, but quality is variable and prices steep and it does all feel very touristy. Booking is essential in the high season.

Don Dino Kažotića 8; m 097 705 5560; w dondinotrogir.com; ⊕ 11.00–23.00 daily. Popular family-run restaurant in the heart of the old town. €€€€

Konoba TRS Matije Gupca 14; ✆021 796 956; w konoba-trs.com; ⊕ May–Oct 11.00–23.00 daily. Dalmatian specialties, notably seafood, cooked with a modern twist. €€€€

Tunaholic Fish Bar Radovanov trg 8; m 099 537 6164; w tunaholicfishbar.com; ⊕ Apr–Oct 11.00–23.00 daily. Serving seafood-based street food, such as tuna steak burgers, fried squid & whitebait, in a tiny stone-paved square near the cathedral. €€€–€€

WHAT TO SEE AND DO The old town is entered through a 17th-century gate – hook left and right from here, and you'll find yourself on the pretty main square, Trg Ivana Pavla II, home to most of the famous sights, including **St Lawrence's (Sv Lovre) Cathedral** (⊕ Jul–Aug 08.00–20.00 Mon–Sat, noon–18.00 Sun; Jun 08.00–19.00 Mon–Sat, noon–18.00 Sun; Apr–May & Sep–Oct 08.00–18.00 Mon–Sat, noon–18.00 Sun; Nov–Mar 08.00–noon Mon–Sat; treasury & bell-tower €5).

The cathedral's portal, dating from 1240, is the stunning work of truthful but far from bashful local boy Radovan (look for the inscription above the door: '*per raduanum cunctus hac arte praeclarum*' – 'all of this was made most excellently by Radovan'). Adam and Eve stand apparently appalled at their nakedness, atop two superb Venetian lions. The inner pillars, resting on the shoulders of medieval bugbears (Turks and Jews), frame graphic scenes from the calendar year (labours of the summer and winter months), while above it all sits a superb Nativity.

Inside, the cathedral's a cluttered, sombre place, still used by older local women every morning for prayers. The most important thing to see here is the extraordinary

Ursini Chapel in the north aisle, which is arguably the most beautiful Renaissance monument in Dalmatia. Sculpted by Nikola Firentinac (Nicholas of Florence) at the end of the 15th century, it's here you'll find those torch-bearing cherubs featured in the tourist board's promotional literature. Other sights within the cathedral include the elaborately carved 15th-century choir stalls and an octagonal 13th-century pulpit.

Outside, have a good look at the campanile – the first floor's 15th-century early Gothic, the second's pure Venetian Gothic, and the third is late-16th-century Renaissance. If you have a head for heights, you might climb it too.

Opposite the entrance to the cathedral is the Venetian **Čipiko Palace** complex, now home to the Čipiko tourist agency. Pop into the hallway and check out the giant wooden cockerel on the wall, a trophy from the prow of some long-forgotten Turkish warship. Across the square is the **town hall** – in the courtyard, you'll see the coats of arms of the ruling families of Trogir.

Completing the square are the town's 15th-century **clock tower** and **loggia**. Both feature more work by Nikola Firentinac, while the loggia also has a large Meštrović bas-relief. Behind the loggia is the oldest surviving pre-Saracen church (**St Barbara's**), dating from the 11th century.

It's a short walk south from here to the Riva and the few remaining preserved parts of the city walls – Marshal Marmont, the Napoleonic administrator in the region from 1806 to 1814, had the rest torn down in an attempt to introduce sea breezes as a cure for malaria. Draining the swampy western end of the island a century later was a far more successful strategy.

Along the lovely Riva, you'll find the huge 15th-century **Kamerlengo Fortress** (⊕ 09.00–20.00 daily; €4) which hosts occasional open-air concerts in summer. Beyond that, Trogir's pedestrian-only old town peters out with a football pitch (what a location!), but have a look at **Marmont's Pavilion** if you're up here – it's a small (and sadly graffitied) memorial to the man who really did try to do his best for Napoleon's short-lived Illyrian Provinces.

Finally, if you want to visit the nearby islands of **Drvenik Veli** and **Drvenik Mali** (they both have some nice beaches), you should check the Jadrolinija ferry timetable (w jadrolinija.hr; 3 times daily from Trogir). The highlight, the Blue Lagoon in Krknjaši Bay off Drvenik Veli's east coast, offers translucent turquoise waters for bathing, but it does get very crowded with excursion boats in peak season.

Klis Just 12km north of Split, on the road to Sinj, guarding a narrow mountain pass, rise the magnificent monumental ruins of **Klis Fortress** (Tvrđava Klis; ⊕ 09.00–17.00 daily; €10), perched upon a 340m rocky outcrop. It was captured by the Ottoman Turks in 1537 and remained in their hands for just over a century until the Venetians got their own back in 1648. The ruins are highly atmospheric (the fortress was used as a location for Meereen in *Game of Thrones*) and afford stunning views back down to Split and out across the Adriatic. While in Klis, look out also for the trio of informal restaurants that dish up first-rate local lamb served simply with crusty bread. You can reach Klis from Split by taking the #34 or #36 bus to Klis–Megdan (where you'll find the fortress entrance) or by taking the Sinj bus to Klis–Varoš and hiking up the hill from there. If you have a car, you might also head onwards to **Stella Croatica** (Mihovilovici 21a; m 099 215 0250; w stella-croatica. hr; ⊕ Jul–Aug 10.00–16.00 Tue–Sun, May–Jun & Sep–Oct 10.00–16.00 Mon–Sat daily), a 5-minute drive from Klis. A mini-agritourism centre, it has a Mediterranean garden planted with herbs, an olive oil museum, an informal eatery and a shop selling traditional homemade Dalmatian specialities and natural cosmetics.

If you know your archaeology, a trip out to Salona (now called Solin) might interest you – though be warned that anything which could be carried off has been carried off (some of the best pieces are in the Split Archaeological Museum), meaning you'll need to rely heavily on your imagination if you're going to people the dusty fields here with temples, houses, markets and an amphitheatre capable of seating nearly 20,000 people.

Salona is 5km north of the centre of Split and is best reached on the #1 bus, which drops you off at the Caffe Bar Salona at the entrance to the site. There's a small archaeological museum here (an offshoot of the one in town) called Tusculum, where you can pick up a local map – after which you're on your own to wander across the worn grass and traces of the extensive ruins of the city, home to around 60,000 people in the 1st century AD.

The amphitheatre is the most impressive ruin, though there's very little left beyond the foundations. The Venetians carted off most of the stone in the 17th century and used it for local building works and fortifications, claiming the dismantlement was only to prevent the Turks from using the amphitheatre as a hideout.

If you've come this far, the quickest way back to Split is on the #37 city bus. Cross the new highway using the underpass and walk towards Solin centre until you get to the bus stop.

Sinj Thirty kilometres out of Split is the town of Sinj – half-hourly buses from Split will bring you here in under an hour. Sinj is famous mainly as the scene for the annual **Sinjska Alka**, a festival celebrating the 1715 victory over numerically superior Turks. Taking place over three days leading up to the first Sunday in August, with the main tournament on the Sunday itself, the Alka is a knightly tournament in which metal rings suspended on a wire have to be speared at full gallop by chaps in traditional costume. It's all very noisy and colourful, and one of only two places where the time-honoured Tilting at the Ring still takes place (the other is in the village of Barban, in Istria in north Croatia). The other main event is the huge procession and pilgrimage on the **Feast of the Assumption** (Velika Gospa, 15 Aug) of the Madonna of Sinj – the 15th- or 16th-century painting with which the victory of 1715 is popularly associated.

The friendly and helpful **tourist office** (⟍021 826 352; w visitsinj.com) is at Put Petrovca 12.

Where to stay and eat The **Hotel Alkar** makes a good place to stay in Sinj (Vrlička 50; ⟍021 824 474; w hotel-alkar.hr; €€€), otherwise the tourist office has details of private rooms available. Accommodation can be hard to find during the Alka, so book far ahead if you can. For a town its size, Sinj has a lot of bars and cafés on the cobbled streets around the Church of the Miraculous Madonna of Sinj – and you can expect all of them to be full to bursting point after the Alka.

The two best places to eat are **Konoba Ispod Ure** (Istarska 2; ⟍021 211 311; ⊕ 07.00–23.00 Mon–Sat, 10.00–23.00 Sun; €€€) and **Konoba Potkova** (Alkarsko trkalište 22; ⟍021 822 792; ⊕ 07.00–23.00 Mon–Sat, 10.00–23.00 Sun; €€€), both of which have delicious food and friendly service in a low-key, rustic setting. In the nearby village of Hrvace (7km), **Agroturizam Podastrana** (m 091 619 4723; w podastrana.com.hr; ⊕ Mar–Oct noon–midnight Fri–Sun; €€€) does barbecued meats cooked over an open fire and their own garden salads.

OMIŠ AND THE CETINA GORGE

Lying 26km southeast of Split, **Omiš** sits at the mouth of the **Cetina Gorge**, marked by dramatic rocky cliffs and a small medieval fortress. It was once home to audacious pirates – the marauders would hide their boats upriver, out of sight from the open sea. Today, the River Cetina, which runs from the so-called 'Eye-of-the-Earth' in the foothills of the Dinaric Alps, cutting its way through the mountains and traversing a series of waterfalls and rapids, is a popular venue for adventure sports, including rafting, kayaking, canyoning, rock climbing, ziplining and cycling. Trips are arranged as half-day excursions accompanied by qualified instructors, with all necessary gear provided, plus transport from Omiš (or pick-up in Split). Reliable providers include Adventure Dalmatia (w adventuredalmatia.com), Adventure Omiš (w adventure-omis.com) and Croatia Rafting (w croatiarafting.com). For more general information, visit Omiš **tourist information** (Fošal 1; ☎021 861 350; w visitomis.hr). Music lovers should note that Omiš hosts the three-week **Festival of Dalmatian Klapa** (w fdk.hr) each July.

 WHERE TO STAY AND EAT Accommodation options in Omiš include **Hotel Villa Dvor** (26 rooms; Mosorsko cesta 13; ☎021 863 444; w hotel-villadvor.hr; €€€) built into a rocky outcrop near the mouth of the Cetina, affording views down on to the river, and **Hostel Omiš** (Četvrt kralja Slavca 9; m 091 250 0545; ⧉; €) an ideal inexpensive base for adventure sports enthusiasts.

For eating out in Omiš, try **Arsana Tasting House** (Četvrt kralja Slavca 32b; m 098 133 0917; w arsana-tasting-house.eatbu.hr; ⊕ May–Sep 17.00–midnight Tue–Sun; €€€) offering three tasting menus (including vegetarian) on a leafy terrace, or **Pod Odrnom** (Ivana Katušića 11; m 095 903 3740; w pod-odrnom.hr; ⊕ May–Oct noon–midnight; €€€€) doing barbecued meats and seafood at tables in a stone alley. On the Cetina, 4km upstream from Omiš, romantic **Kaštil Slanica** (Franje Josipa 1, Podašpilje; m 099 314 6220; w kastil-slanica.hr; ⊕ 11.00–23.00 daily; €€€€) serves river delicacies (trout, eel, and frogs' legs) and their own freshly baked bread.

MAKARSKA RIVIERA AND MOUNT BIOKOVO

Twenty kilometres beyond Omiš lies the 60km-long **Makarska Riviera**, a series of cheerfully touristy villages and gorgeous rock-and-pebble beaches sheltered by the solid limestone mass of Mount Biokovo (1,762m) to the northeast.

The first village you'll come to is Brela, known for its turquoise waters giving on to fine pebble beaches shaded by centuries-old Aleppo pines, the best known of which is **Punta Rata**. From Brela, a seafront promenade leads through neighbouring Baška Voda (2.5km), with its lovely Nikolina beach, turning into a footpath to pass a string of small rocky naturist beaches (clothing-optional), then again becoming a well-kept promenade running all the way to Makarska (11km). It's well worth hiring a bike from **Bike Rental Baška Voda** (w ebikerental-baskavoda.hr) in Baška Voda to explore this stretch of coast or take a scuba-diving or snorkelling trip with **Bikini Dive** (w bikinidive.com) in Brela to experience the underwater world.

If you want to stay in Brela, the **Bluesun Maestral** (Filpinska 1; ☎01 3844 288; w bluesunhotels.com; €€€€) is a classic 1960s hotel (it featured in the MoMA exhibition *Toward a Concrete Utopia: Architecture in Yugoslav* in New York), with period design details and artworks, renovated in 2022. Alternatively, **Abuela's Beach House** (Jardula 20; m 091 155 5044; w abuelasbeachhouse.com; €€€) has five spacious, colourfully decorated rooms and apartments with balconies and sea-views, plus a pool, 4km outside Brela. In Baška Voda, the 71-room **Grand Hotel Slavia** (Obala Sv Nikola 71; ☎021 604 999; w hoteli-baskavoda.hr; €€€€) dates from the 1930s and gives directly on to a pebble beach.

MAKARSKA At the heart of the Makarska Riviera is Makarska itself, a small but busy town, tastefully restored in stone after the devastating 1962 earthquake. With a lovely palm-studded front and a 2km beach across the Sveti Petar headland, it's a perfect sunny stop if you're travel-weary and footsore. If you don't have sore feet, then Makarska is also the gateway to some of the most spectacular hiking in Croatia, on the Biokovo massif, home to four rare species of eagle (golden, imperial, grey and snake) and culminating in one of the country's highest peaks, Sveti Jure, at 1,762m.

From the bus station, on Ante Starčevića, the main road running above the town, it's a 5-minute walk downhill to the front, where you'll find everything you need. The **tourist office** (Kralja Tomislava 16; ☎021 650 076; w makarska-info.hr) has maps and information and can put you in touch with any number of agencies handling rooms and excursions.

Getting there and away Without your own wheels, you'll be arriving in Makarska either by bus or ferry. Ferries come in from Sumartin, on the eastern end of Brač, four times a day in winter and five times in summer, while at least ten daily buses stop in on their way from Split (1hr 10mins) to Dubrovnik (3hrs), and vice versa.

🛏 **Where to stay** Most of the big **hotels** in Makarska are on the town's long pebble beach, across the headland to the northeast of town. **Private rooms** (dbls) go for €60–80 depending on the level of comfort and location, with the usual 30% surcharge for three nights or fewer.

Biokovo (52 rooms) Obala Kralja Tomislava 14; ☎021 615 244; w sol.hr. Right on the palm-lined waterfront in the middle of town, with its own ground-floor café-restaurant. €€€€

Maritimo (19 dbls, 1 suite) Put Cvitačke 2a; ☎021 619 900; w hotel-maritimo.hr. Small, beachfront boutique hotel & restaurant towards the northwestern edge of town. €€€€

Osejava (50 rooms) Šetaliste dr Fra Jure Radića bb; ☎021 604 300; w osejava.com. Built on the same waterfront location as what was once Makarska's most famous hotel back in the 1920s, the modern Osejava has a restaurant & small pool. €€€€

Porin Heritage Hotel (7 rooms) Marineta 2; ☎021 613 744; w hotel-porin.hr. Lovely centrally located 19th-century building, once the local library, converted into a hotel in 2002 & renovated in 2021. €€€€

Pension Batešić (3 rooms) Kipara Meštrovića 25; m 095 821 3105; w batosic.com. Small, family-run pansion with a b/fast terrace, all rooms with AC, balcony & en suite. Dinner & boat trips available. Excellent value. €€

Camp Riviera Makarska Roseto degli Abruzzi 10; ☎021 549 542; w campriviera.eu. This **campsite** on the northwestern edge of town also has bungalows & mobile homes which sleep 4 for €252 in peak season. €€–€

Hostel Makarska SubTub Prvosvibanjska 15; m 095 907 7176. Small hostel, centrally located, just 5mins' walk to the seafront, with dorms & private rooms. €€–€

🍴 **Where to eat and drink** Makarska has no shortage of **eateries** along the seafront, where terraces spill out across the pavement and slightly cheaper places sit a block or two back from the sea. There's also an excellent daily market if you're looking for picnic food, just up from the town's only old square, Kačićev Trg.

Arta Larga by Gastro Diva Kalalarga 22; ☎021 330 004; **f** artalargabygastrodiva; ⊕ 09.00– midnight daily. Much loved by locals & visitors alike, this homely eatery serves classic Dalmatian fare with a creative twist. Opened in 2015 by former food blogger, Gastro Diva. €€€€
Konoba Kalalarga Kalalarga 40; m 098 990 2908; **f**; ⊕ May–Oct 14.00–midnight Tue–Sun, Nov–Apr noon–midnight Fri–Sun. Informal eatery serving typical Dalmatian seafood specialities – the menu changes daily depending on what the owner finds at the morning market. €€€
FishDelish Lištun 4; w fish-delish.com; ⊕ May–Sep noon–23.00 daily. Tasty street food in Makarska's old town, with half-a-dozen tables & stools out front – octopus burgers, shrimp rolls with rocket, tuna tartar & avocado bagels. €€€–€€

Activities For scuba diving, **More Sub** (Krešimira 43; m 099 283 6908; w more-sub-makarska.hr) offer basic tuition, PADI courses and diving trips. **Cycling** enthusiasts can hire road bikes, mountain bikes and e-bikes from **Momentum** (Šetalište dr Franje Tuđmana 4; m 091 545 3237; w rentabikemakarska.com), who will also provide information about local routes.

What to see and do Makarska isn't a place you come to for culture – it's a town with a great beach and even better hiking up in the mountains – so the sights can be comfortably counted off on the fingers of one hand. On Kačićev Trg there's the 18th-century St Mark's Church (usually closed), while at the eastern end of town you'll find Croatia's finest **malacological museum** (Franjevački put 1; m 099 463 9293; ⊕ Jun–Sep 09.00–13.00 & 17.00–20.00 daily, Oct–May on request; €6) – that's seashells, to you – housed in the cellars of the Franciscan Monastery. The collection of more than 3,000 shells from around the world was put together by one of the Franciscan monks, Jure Radić, and opened in 1963. Radić also founded the botanical gardens in Kotišina (page 170).

A couple of kilometres along the coast to the north there's a curious shrine at the **Vepric Cave** (Vepric Špilja). Inaugurated in 1908, on the 50th anniversary of the apparitions in Lourdes, the sanctuary was founded by Bishop Carić (who was buried here on his death in 1921) and dedicated to Our Lady of Lourdes. It is popular with pilgrims and is especially busy on 11 February, 25 March, 15 August and 7–8 September.

Finally, if you're here in May, don't miss Makarska's spectacular rowing regatta, which proves the town hasn't entirely forgotten its Venetian legacy.

AROUND MAKARSKA Southeast of Makarska lie several more villages making up the riviera – Tučepi, Podgora, Živogošće, Drvenik, Zaostrog and Gradac, all of which have pleasant beaches and a plethora of rooms and apartments to let. Tučepi is blessed with a long curving pebble beach backed by pines, and a fine place to stay here is the 86-room **Hotel Tamaris** (Slatina 2; ☎021 678 222; w hotel-tamaris.com; €€€€), home to gourmet restaurant Freyja. Similarly, in Gradac you have a marvellous beach and the rather smart 37-room adults-only **Hotel Marco Polo** (Obala 15; ☎021 695 060; w hotel-marcopolo.com; €€€€) with a good waterside restaurant, a hotel boat and bikes to hire. From Drvenik, regular Jadrolinija ferries run to Sućuraj on Hvar's eastern tip, meaning you can combine the riviera and a trip to the islands.

BIOKOVO The Biokovo massif rises up steeply above the Makarska Riviera in three ever-more spectacular shelves, providing hiking at all levels and fabulous views, but if you're coming here to head up into the mountains don't underestimate them, and start out as early in the day as you can. The weather can change very quickly, there's no water or food to be had once you're out, and the karst limestone is hard on even the toughest hiking boots. It's highly inadvisable to go out far if you're alone. If you run into trouble, it's unlikely anyone would find you, and – without wishing to sound alarmist – you should remember that besides chamois goats and mouflon sheep, there are still wolves in the wild up here. A large part of the massif was designated a **nature park** in 1981. To learn more about the terrain and wildlife before setting out, visit the **Adrion Presentation Centre** (Franjevački put 2a; ⊕ May–Sep 08.00–noon & 18.00–21.00 Mon–Sat) in Makarska.

Each year in May, the nature park hosts the gruelling **Absolute Biokovo Challenge** (w absolute-biokovo-challenge.com) fell running competition.

Hiking in the Biokovo Nature Park (w pp-biokovo.hr; 1-day €8, 3-day €16, 7-day €40)

The two main summits reachable from Makarska are **Vošac** (1,420m or thereabouts; a 3½hr hike one-way) and **Sveti Jure** (1,762m; allow a good 5hrs up and 4hrs back).

There are two paths up out of town leading to Vošac and on to Sveti Jure, one going via the village of **Makar** and the other via the village of Kotišina. Once you get to either village the trail is well-signed with red and white flashes, but pick up a map from the tourist office before you head out.

In either case, start off from Kačićev Trg, pass the church and market, and cross the main road, continuing up **Put Makra** until you reach the next main road, Dubrovačka. For the Makar route, you should then stay on the continuation of Put Makra until you reach the village. For Kotišina turn right after 200m up Put Mlinica, which leads to the village of **Mlinice**, from which you'll see signs for the path to Kotišina. Both Makar and Kotišina are at around 200m above sea level and take around 45 minutes to reach on foot from the seafront.

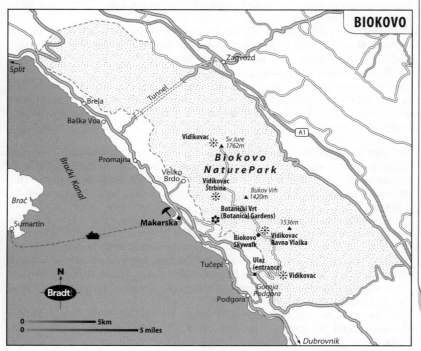

The village of Kotišina was definitively abandoned after the 1962 earthquake, but locals still keep weekenders up here. It's well worth a visit, not just because of the interesting 17th-century **fortress** (Veliki Kaštel, which now hosts a small interpretation centre) built right into the rock here, but also because of the **Botanički Vrt** (w kotisina-makarska.com), the botanical gardens founded by Jure Radić. Radić knew more than anyone about the flora of Biokovo and built the gardens here – more an oversized rockery – as a plant haven.

From Makar or Kotišina it's a tough hike to the summit of Vošac, but the views once you get there are absolutely stupendous, way out across the sea and islands. Beyond Vošac, it's another hour and 45 minutes, the last part of it quite steep, to **Sveti Jure**, the highest point on the massif. At the top, there's a little church completely dwarfed by a TV transmitter.

There are several **mountain huts** on Biokovo, but most are only open by appointment, and you should never assume they'll be open – contact the tourist office for details, or see the list of huts and contacts on the nature park website (w pp-biokovo.hr/en/plan-your-visit/accommodation).

Cycling or driving the Biokovo massif
If hiking's not for you, Sveti Jure isn't necessarily out of the question. There's a narrow road that goes up to the summit from Makarska, making for a 30km white-knuckle ride, best performed by mountain bike or jeep. The road is the highest in Croatia, positively vertiginous, and has no safety barriers.

From Vošac and the road to Sveti Jure, a marked trail heads northwest along Biokovo to **Sveti Ilija** (1,642m), with more wonderful views – but this is further than you'll be able to get in a single day. For more information on hiking, cycling or jeeping up the mountain, contact the tourist office or see Rudolf Abraham's *Walks and Treks in Croatia* (page 238).

High above Tučepi on the Makarska Riviera, at an altitude of 1,228m, the **Biokovo Skywalk** (w pp-biokovo.hr/en/skywalk-biokovo; ⊙ Jun–Sep 07.00–20.00, Apr–May 07.00–19.00, Oct–Nov 08.00–16.00) is a horseshoe-shaped walkway cantilevered over a sheer rock face (opened in July 2020). With a glass floor and glass balustrades, it affords dizzying views down to the Adriatic and over the islands of Brač and Hvar. To get there, drive or cycle up the Biokovo road from the entrance to the nature park, 6km east of Makarska. The skywalk has become a popular spot for marriage proposals. Note that it is closed when the wind is gusty.

Biokovo and Imotski Lakes Geopark
On the far side of the Biokovo mountains, tucked into the border with Bosnia & Herzegovina, near **Imotski**, are two typically strange karstic phenomena, the so-called **Crveno Jezero** and **Modro Jezero** (the Red and Blue Lakes). The area was designated a geopark (w gp-biokovoimotski. com) in 2022.

Each of the lakes was formed by the roof collapsing above a vast cave and even though they're more than 20km from the sea as the crow flies, and on the wrong side of a major mountain range, the lakes are deep indeed – the bottom of Crveno Jezero is a mere 19m above sea level, with the lake depth itself varying between 280m and 320m. Modro Jezero, for its part, really is blue. With less steep sides than Crveno Jezero, it's used by local boys for swimming – when there's water in it at all – or as a football pitch when it's dried up.

If you want to stay overnight in Imotski, try the luxurious new **Emotheo Heritage Hotel** (22 rooms; Ante Starčevića 20; ☏ 021 333 337; w emotheo.hr; €€€€). Alternatively, **Agrotourism Grabovci** (Proložav Gornji; m 095 353 2244;

w agroturizam-grabovci.com; €€€) is a rural hideaway in the hills 6km north of Imotski, with nine stone cottages and a rustic restaurant doing roast meats and their own garden vegetables.

ŠOLTA

The island of Šolta, easily accessible from Split and right next to the much larger Brač, is something of a mystery. It's pretty, it's wooded, it has old stone hamlets (it even has a couple of prehistoric and Roman ruins, and a sprinkling of medieval monuments), it has appealing coves, beaches and bays, and yet it's somehow off the main tourist map – it sees only around a tenth of the visitors of Brač or Hvar, and most of those arrive by sailing boat and put down anchor in Maslinica on the island's western tip. A number of families from Split have weekend homes on the island, accounting for the busy Friday afternoon and Sunday evening ferries.

Šolta is 20km long but less than 5km wide and has a local population of under 1,500, mainly in a handful of settlements along the north coast and in the interior. The south coast, a crenulated maze of steep rocky cliffs, inlets, coves and tiny bays, is almost entirely uninhabited. Olives, figs, honey and fishing still drive the part of the economy that isn't fuelled by tourism. Though tourism itself remains very minimal, and there is little in the way of sightseeing, entertainment or watersports facilities.

The **tourist office** (Šoltanskhi žrtava 14; ☎ 021 654 657; w visitsolta.com) is in Grohote.

GETTING THERE AND AROUND
Four ferries a day make the 1-hour crossing from Split to Šolta's port, **Rogač**, all year round (w jadrolinija.hr); in summer, the frequency increases to six. There's also a fast catamaran service, which cuts journey time down to just 35 minutes (w ksc.hr).

Regular ferries and catamarans are met by the bus which connects all the main settlements – if you miss the bus or want to get around the island at other times your options are limited to walking or calling Šolta Taxi (m 091 393 1303; w taxi-solta.com).

WHERE TO STAY AND EAT
If you're staying here – you could also do a day trip from Split – accommodation is limited to private rooms and apartments, of which there are plenty, plus one boutique hotel. These can be sourced via the tourist office (see above). Private rooms come in at around €60 a night for doubles. Alternatively, you can try:

Martinis Marchi Heritage Hotel Maslinica; ☎ 021 572 768; w martinis-marchi.com. A luxurious 7-suite hotel which even has its own little marina, should you be arriving by private yacht, & a waterside restaurant. €€€€€

Apartments Funda (8 apartments) Nečujam; m 091 505 3560; w apartmani-funda.com. Modern purpose-built apartments in Nečujam, each sleeping 4 & going for €130 in high season. €€€

Villa Šolta (6 rooms & apartments); Rogač; ☎ 021 654 540; w villa-solta.com. A homely & affordable alternative with 5 dbls, 1 spacious 2-room apartment, & a small pool in the garden. €€€–€€

Apartments Salihbegović (5 apartments) Nečujam; m 098 202 638; w salihbegovic.hr. Apartments sleeping up to 3 or 5, from €70 in high season. €€

Šampjer Put Burni gaj 18; ☎ 021 659 107; w restoran-maslinica-sampjer.hr; ⊕ May–Oct 15.00–23.00 daily. A special place to eat just outside Maslinica, serving fresh fish on a terrace with gorgeous sunset sea-views. €€€€

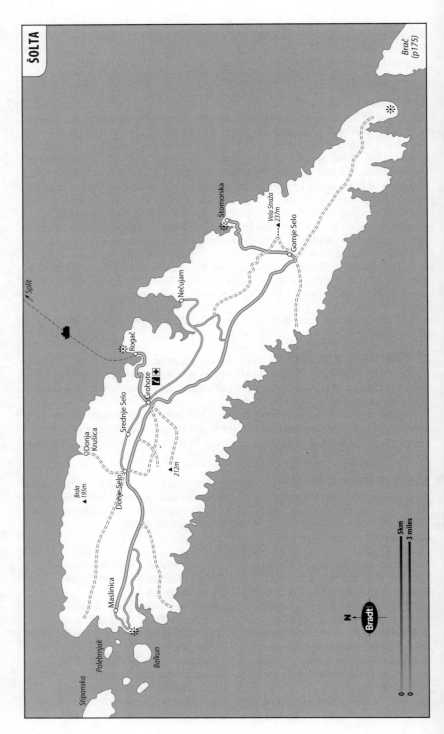

Brač
(p175)

Stomorska

Vela Straža
▲ 237m

Gornje Selo

Nečujam

Split

Rogač

Grohote

Srednje Selo

Donja
Krušica

▲ 212m

Donje Selo

Brda
▲ 195m

Maslinica

Stipanska

Polebrnjak

Balkun

N

Bradt

0   5km
0   3 miles

WHAT TO SEE AND DO If you are walking, make sure you have plenty of water – it's a hot, dry place. It's around 2km up the hill from Rogač to the administrative centre, **Grohote**, which has a shop and pizzeria, as well as a regular market. From here it's the best part of 8km west, passing by the hamlets of **Srednje Selo** and **Donje Selo**, to the sheltered harbour and beaches at **Maslinica**. Heading east from Grohote, it's around 7km to the once-upon-a-time village of Nečujam, now unashamedly a tourist resort.

Also 7km from Grohote, at the foot of the island's high point (Vela Straža, 237m), is the old stone village of **Gornje Selo**, 150m above sea level. There's a paved path from the village to the top of the mountain, where you'll find great views and a large concrete crucifix. There are footpaths down to the south coast, though stock up at the bakery or shop first, as there's nothing on the coast itself.

From Grohote it's a downhill 3km to **Stomorska**, Šolta's other main tourist centre. Stomorska sits at the head of a lovely narrow bay, and although it can get busy (noisy, even) on summer weekends, a short walk along the coastal path in either direction will get you to some lovely little rocky beaches.

BRAČ

Like Šolta, Brač is attractive, hot and sunny, and an easy boat trip from Split – but that's where the similarity ends. Brač is far larger (the third biggest island in the Adriatic, after Krk and Cres) and vastly more popular with tourists. Famous for its white stone from the village of Pučišća – used in Diocletian's Palace in Split in antiquity and more recently in Washington's White House and Berlin's Reichstag – the island today depends mainly on tourism.

Of course, fishing remains important, and the island still has some 60 commercial fishing vessels. Brač is also known for lamb – hardy little sheep graze freely on the island's scanty pastures – which you can taste in the inland villages of Donji Humac and Gornji Humac. The island accounts for some 1 million olive trees, half of which are cultivated in terraced groves rimmed by dry-stone walls. They're visible all over the island, but the nicest way to see them up close is by walking or cycling the 6km circular Olive Trail, which begins and ends in Mirca near Supetar.

Serious hikers might pursue the **Via Brattia** (w supetar.hr/via-brattia), a 140km circular footpath connecting 12 of Brač's top historic and cultural locations.

Away from the two main centres of **Supetar** in the north and **Bol** (a fine base for adventure sports enthusiasts) in the south, Brač can seem quite deserted, particularly in the mountainous interior, where whole villages have been abandoned to time, but also on the large sections of coast not developed or easily accessible by road.

GETTING THERE AND AROUND Nine car **ferries** a day run from Split to Supetar (50mins), rising to 14 a day in summer. There is also a daily catamaran direct to Bol on the southern shore (70mins) all year, with extra services in summer, and catamarans from Split via Milna (1hr), on the western end of the island, to Hvar. Car ferries also run four times a day (five in summer) from Makarska to **Sumartin**, on the eastern tip of Brač (1hr). If you're already in Bol and want to go on to Hvar, there are privately run services across to Jelsa in summer – otherwise, just take the catamaran to Jelsa and get the bus from there. For timetables for all of these services, see w jadrolinija.hr.

Brač also has a small **airport** (w airport-brac.hr), which is used mainly for charter arrivals but receives a once-weekly Croatia Airlines flight from Zagreb in summer as well (⊕ Sat; 50mins). There's usually (but not always) a shuttle to Bol that meets flights. If you're heading onward to Supetar you'll either have to take a bus from Bol or a taxi direct from the airport.

Supetar is the **bus** hub, with most destinations served at least three times a day – once in the morning, once around lunchtime, and once in the late afternoon – and with about ten buses a day to Bol. This makes getting anywhere easy from Supetar but can be a problem if you arrive in Milna or Sumartin and want to move on straight away. The afternoon ferry from Makarska, in particular, doesn't connect with onward transport until the following day, so you'll need to thumb a lift. Buses from Supetar to Bol run six times a day in summer (four in winter).

If you haven't got your own wheels and want to give yourself vastly more freedom to explore Brač, **renting transport** is the way to go. In Supetar, you'll find cycles, scooters and cars for hire, and even motorboats. Hire isn't cheap (though less expensive in Supetar than Bol) but gives you the run of the island and is the only real way of getting away from the crowds in summer. For bike hire, **Big Blue** (w bigbluesport.com) in Bol is a good bet.

Ultimately, a cycle or scooter is the best way of getting around, though if you're relying on pedal power, don't underestimate the summer heat or overestimate your fitness – it's a hilly 40km ride from Supetar to Bol. Cyclists should pick up a copy of the detailed HGSS map of the island, with cycle routes.

SUPETAR The chances are you'll arrive in Supetar. A pleasant cluster of stone houses spreads round the harbour, where you'll find everything you need – the **tourist office** (Porat 1; ☏ 021 630 551; w supetar.hr), the bus station, and a couple of travel agencies. If you're visiting in summer, make sure you have a place to stay arranged in advance – there's a list of private accommodation on w bracinfo.com. The main beaches are west of the town, and being shallow these are good for (and popular with) families. You can hire bikes and e-bikes from **Rent a Roberts** (m 091 534 7575; w rentaroberts.com) near the ferry terminal.

🏠 **Where to stay and eat** Most of the accommodation here is at the big modern touristy **Waterman Resort** complex. A very pleasant alternative is the **Villa Supetar** (Bračka 2; ☏ 021 630 894; w villasupetar.com; €€€), a family-run pansion in the town centre with 20 rooms and five apartments. **Hotel Villa Adriatica** (Put Vele Luke 31; ☏ 021 755 010; w villaadriatica.com; €€€€) offers boutique accommodation and a garden with a pool, restaurant and cocktail bar, but it is now adults-only. For an inexpensive stay, try the welcoming **Rooms Sunce** (Bana Josipa Jelačića 39a; m 091 222 0684; w roomsunce.com; €€) with five comfortable rooms, just a 10-minute walk from the port.

For eating out, favourites in Supetar include the smart **Konoba Kala** (Kala 7; ☏ 021 630 690; w konobakala.com; ⊕ May–Oct 18.00–23.00 Mon, noon–23.00 Tue–Sun; €€€€) for a fancy contemporary take on traditional Dalmatian specialities, and **Pizzeria Peperoncin** (Petra Jakšića 9; m 095 549 1949; ⊕ May–Oct noon–22.00 Tue–Sun €€) doing excellent pizzas. Inland, in the village of Donji Humac (7km), **Konoba Kopačina** (☏ 021 647 707; f; [o] 10.00–23.30 daily (closed Christmas & New Year);10.00–23.30 daily (closed Christmas & New Year); €€€€) is much loved by locals for its succulent roast lamb.

AROUND SUPETAR From Supetar, an interesting side trip can be made to **Škrip**, the island's oldest settlement and home to the **Museum of Brač** (w czk-brac.hr; ⊕ summer 09.00–19.00 Mon–Sat, 10.00–13.00 & 15.00–19.00 Sun; €4). Also

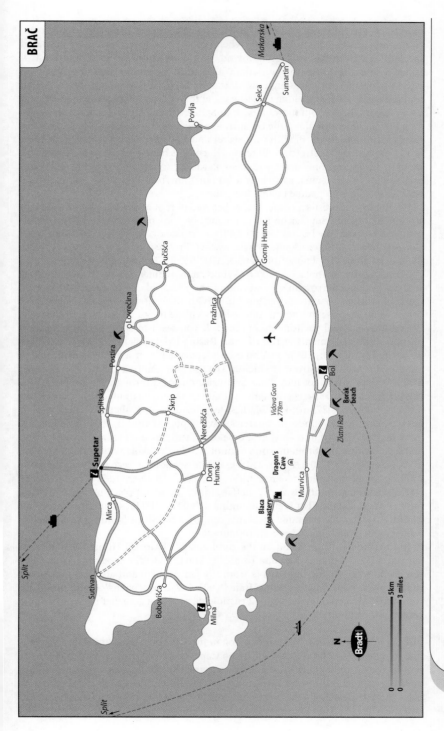

BRAČ

in Škrip is the **Museum of Olive Oil** (Muzej Maslinovog Ulja; w muzejuja.com; ☉ summer 09.00–20.00 daily; €6), where you can taste various olive oil-based specialities. The hilltop village is inland 3km from **Splitska**, itself 6km east of Supetar, and the museum, housed in a fortified old stone building, gives an interesting glance into the toughness of island life in the past; many of the original residents fled to the USA long ago. The usual three buses a day come up here, and it's a pleasant 30–45-minute walk back to Splitska if you fancy a swim afterwards. It's a further 4km east along the coast from Splitska to **Lovrečina**, the only (rather small) sandy beach on Brač. It's no secret and does get rather crowded. A great way of exploring this stretch of Brač's north coast is by sea kayak. **Brač Adventure** (w brac-adventure.com) arrange 3-hour kayaking tours from Supetar to Postira and Postira to Lovrečina, as well as a 5-hour tour from Postira to Pučišća. They offer SUP (stand-up paddle board) tours too.

On Brač's southwestern corner is the sheltered port of Milna, sitting in a wide bay, around 20km from Supetar on a thrice-daily bus. On your way, you might want to come via **Sutivan**, the last settlement on the north coast, which is a charming stone village with access to some good pebble beaches. Private rooms are available through the **tourist office** (Trg Franje Tuđmana 1; ☏021 638 357; w visitsutivan.com).

Milna – the birthplace of 2001 Wimbledon winner Goran Ivanišević – is at the head of a narrow inlet, and one of the nicest places in Brač, within easy reach of beaches that are never too busy. With its well-equipped ACI marina, it comes as no surprise to find this once-sleepy village now a favourite with the well-heeled international yachting community. If you want to stay, there are modern purpose-built apartments at the **Illyrian Resort** (Mala Bijaka 19; ☏021 636 566; w illyrianresort.com; €€€), and nine cosy apartments in a renovated old stone building on Milna's seafront at **Ducina Apartments** (Pantera 26; m 095 775 6968; €€€). Or you might get lucky and find private rooms through the **tourist office** (Riva 5; ☏021 636 233; w tz-milna.hr), though this is not guaranteed in peak season.

East of Supetar (27km), **Pučišća** lies deep inside a long, sheltered, meandering inlet. Since Roman times, its quarries have exported Brački mramora (literally 'Brač marble', though in reality, it's a type of white limestone) far and wide. It's also home to an unusual **Stonemason's School** (Klesarska škola; w klesarskaskola.hr; ☉ Jun–Sep 09.00–13.00, 17.00–21.00), a state school for secondary-aged pupils wanting to specialise in stonemasonry – you can visit their studios and see their works, including fountains and Venetian lions. The nicest place to stay is the 15-room **Puteus Palace** (Trg svetog Jeromina 4; ☏021 381 111; w puteuspalace.com; €€€€€), a waterside boutique hotel in a centuries-old stone building with a lovely walled garden hosting an open-air restaurant.

In the middle of the island, in the rural village of **Gornji Humac** (23km from Supetar, 11km from Bol), **Konoba Tomić** (☏021 647 228; w konobatomic.com; €€€) is a rustic eatery using ingredients from the family farm and also has nine guest rooms and a pool. Nearby, **Nono Ban** (☏021 647 233; w villas-croatia-nonoban. com; €€€€) is a small hotel with 12 rustic-chic rooms, a gourmet restaurant and a garden with a pool.

BOL Brač's biggest draw by far is Bol – or, more accurately, the extraordinary spit of fine shingle called **Zlatni Rat**, the Golden Cape. Featuring in every Croatian tourist promo, the tip of the south-facing 500m triangular spit shifts west or east depending on the season, and the beach attracts around 50,000 visitors a year. It's not the only place to swim near Bol – the town, sheltered by the mass of **Vidova Gora** behind it, is at the heart of a 15km stretch of beaches – but it's certainly the most popular. Bol is also Croatia's top windsurf destination – here the sea channel between Brač and Hvar acts like a wind tunnel, creating ideal conditions for surfing. Each summer, Bol hosts an annual Professional Windsurfers Association (PWA) championship.

Zlatni Rat is a pleasant half-hour stroll along a tree-lined promenade west of Bol, which is a pretty little fishing harbour surrounded by old stone houses. New developments spread up the hill, but the centre itself is compact and charming. It's far too small to accommodate all the people who want to see it, however, so be warned ahead if you're crowd-phobic.

Bol's **tourist office** (☎021 635 638; w bol.hr) has a good supply of maps, which you'll find useful if you're exploring the surrounding area.

Where to stay
Accommodation mainly consists of the big modern Bluesun resort hotels overlooking the seafront promenade between Bol and Zlatni Rat (€€€€€–€€€€): the **Bluesun Holiday Village Bonaca**, **Bluesun Borak** and **Bluesun Elaphusa**. There's not much to choose between them – they're all similarly priced and well located – though the Bonaca was renovated in 2023 and is best for families, and the Elaphusa, with a lavish wellness centre, is a bit more upmarket than the others. All three can be booked through the Bluesun Hotels company (☎01 3844 288; w bluesunhotels.com).

Otherwise, for most of the town's 3,000 or so beds in private rooms and apartments, you'll need to book online in advance. Expect to pay €70 or so for a double in season and a surcharge of 20% for three nights or fewer.

There are also a few smallish hotels and apartments in Bol itself:

Hotels
Villa Giardino (15 rooms) Novi put 2; ☎021 635 900; w villagiardinobol.com. Small, rather plush heritage boutique hotel with a lovely garden. €€€€€

Hotel Kaštil (32 rooms) Radića; ☎021 635 995; w kastil.hr. Nice place right on the fishing port, with sea-view rooms, b/fast on a sunny raised terrace & a ground-floor pizzeria. €€€€

Villa Daniela (30 rooms) Domovinskog rata 54; ☎021 635 959; w villadaniela.com. Centrally located with its own pool but rather dated décor. €€€

Apartments
Zlatni Bol Apartments (6 apartments) Ivana Gundulićeva 2; m 091 224 4700; w zlatni-bol. com. Comfortable modern apartments, each with a terrace, sleeping 2 to 4 people, owned by a welcoming windsurfing enthusiast. €€€€

Alpeza Apartments (9 apartments, 1 villa) Ivana Mažuranića 2; m 098 346 029; w alpeza-apartments.com. A range of stylish, good-value apartments sleeping 2–6 people. €€

Where to eat and drink
There's no shortage of places to eat out in Bol – try **Restaurant Ranč** (Hrvatskih Domobrana 23; ☎021 635 635; ⏰ 18.00–23.00 daily; €€€) with a leafy garden on the hillside above town, or **Taverna Riva** (Frane Radića 5; ☎021 635 236; w tavernariva-bol.com; ⏰ May–Oct noon–midnight daily; €€€€) on Bol's seafront promenade. **Arguola** (Vladimira Nazora 6; €€–€) does good, well-priced sandwiches. Behind Zlatni Rat beach, **Mali Raj** (m 099 426 6162; w maliraj-bol.com; €€€€) does carefully presented Dalmatian specialities in a romantic walled garden with olive trees, while **Konoba Tomić** (☎021 647 228; w konobatomic.com; €€€) in Gornji Humac (11km from Bol, 23km from Supetar) is a family-run agritourism with a rustic restaurant and rooms to rent.

Activities
Besides sunbathing and swimming off Zlatni Rat beach, Bol offers excellent watersports facilities. On Borak beach, **Big Blue** (m 098 212 419;

w bigbluesport.com) provide windsurf tuition and rental equipment, as well as sea kayaks and SUPs for hire. If you want to try scuba diving, their sister company **Big Blue Diving** (**m** 098 425 496; **w** big-blue-diving.hr) are the people to contact.

What to see and do In Bol itself, art lovers should visit the charming **Dešković Gallery** (Trg Sv Petra 1; ☏021 637 092; **w** czk-brac.hr; ⊕ Jul–Aug 09.00–14.00, 17.00–22.00 Tue–Sun; Sep–Jun 09.00–15.00 Tue–Sat; €4) overlooking the fishing harbour. It's named after sculptor Branislav Dešković (1883–1939), who was born in Pučišća (page 176) and created fine bronze figures of animals – several are on display by the entrance. Inside, the gallery showcases paintings by Croatian artists inspired by Brač's rugged landscapes. An entire room is dedicated to Ignjat Job, known as the Croatian van Gogh, for his style and use of colour. The gallery also hosts temporary exhibitions.

Also in Bol, on the seafront promenade, the **Stina Winery** (Riva 16; **m** 099 815 5517; **w** stina-vino.hr; ⊕ Apr–Sep 10.00–midnight daily) occupies a building from 1903, formerly home to Dalmatia's oldest wine cooperative. Now in private hands, Stina offers tours of the cellars and wine-tasting with optional platters of savoury nibbles.

AROUND BOL Beyond Bol, one of the best side trips you can make is to head to the top of **Vidova Gora**. At 778m, it's not just the highest point on Brač but the highest point on any Adriatic island, and the views are terrific – down on to Zlatni Rat far below and across to the islands of Hvar and Vis to the south. The easy way up is to travel by road, either with your own wheels or on a hired bike (e-bikes are available), but the most satisfying way to reach the summit is by hiking up from Bol. It's a good 2½ hours of steady trekking, but well worth the effort – the path is well maintained, though walking boots are recommended.

Another interesting side trip you can make is to the **Dragon's Cave** (Zmajeva Špilja), above the little village of Murvica, to the west of Bol. It's a bit of a mystery as to who carved the wild beasts and mythological creatures here, but they're likely to date back to the 15th century at least. The cave itself is locked, and the once reasonably clear path from near Zlatni Rat has been obliterated with the construction of the new asphalt road to Murvica – so you'll need to contact a local guide (Zoran Kojdić; **m** 091 514 9787).

Finally, there's the extraordinary **Blaca Monastery** (**m** 091 516 4671; ⊕ mid-Jun–mid-Sep 09.00–17.00 Tue–Sun, mid-Sep–mid-Jun 09.00–15.00 Tue–Sun; €7), which underwent restoration work in 2013. This is most easily visited on an excursion, though you can get there on your own (but double-check the opening times at Bol's tourist office) if you have wheels and fancy a hike. There are two routes: either take a boat trip to a bay below the monastery and hike up from there (2.5km, be sure to wear good walking shoes); or get there from the Vidova Gora road – turn right down a gravel track marked Blaca and leave your car at the start of the steep marked footpath around 4km further along (this route's a 3hr round trip).

Set high up under a cliff, the imposing monastery served as a refuge from the 16th century on, and was still inhabited until the last monk, Niko Milčević, died here in 1963. It now houses a curious collection of astronomical instruments, old weapons and watches, and an exceptional library.

HVAR

Smooth, sultry and sexy, Hvar is the undisputed jewel in Croatia's Adriatic crown as far as Europe's cognoscenti and the local smart set are concerned. And indeed, the island, lying south of Brač and stretching finger-like towards the southern end of the Makarska Riviera, is one of the most pleasant in the Adriatic. It has an elegant 16th-century Venetian capital, plenty of beaches and great weather – it boasts 2,700 hours of annual sunshine and averages only eight snowy days a decade. In winter you'll find hotels offering 50% off your room rate for any day on which it rains for more than 3 daylight hours, and free board and lodging if it goes below freezing during the day.

Not surprisingly, along with Dubrovnik it is one of the Adriatic's worst-kept secrets – book well ahead if you want to stay in any of the hotels at the height of the season when the island is quite literally full.

Hvar town sits at the sheltered southwestern tip of Hvar, separated from the other main settlements of Stari Grad, Vrboska and Jelsa by the UNESCO-listed Stari Grad Plain and the 628m bulk of Sveti Nikola, which rises above the island's southern coast. Hvar stretches nearly 70km from west to east, but almost everything that happens here happens in the western third, Sućuraj (on the eastern tip) serving only as an arrival point for car traffic on its way in from the Drvenik ferry.

The island's most unusual crop – it won't take you long to work this out from the number of places it's on sale in Hvar – is lavender, which is cultivated in great purple swathes and makes a spring break here a real treat. There's also a lot of (rather good) wine made, with several wineries open for tours and tasting, and the usual crops of figs and olives. And for sporty types, the island hosts the annual Hvar Half Marathon (w hvarmarathon.com) each year in May.

GETTING THERE AND AROUND Arrival on the island is inevitably by **ferry** or **catamaran**.

From Split there's a **Jadrolinija** (w jadrolinija.hr), car ferry four times a day, all year round, direct to Stari Grad (actually a few kilometres out of town, but buses to Stari Grad, Jelsa and Hvar meet the ferry), with the frequency increasing substantially in summer. The journey takes a couple of hours. Reserve well ahead in summer on this route if you're arriving by car, and also plan your departure carefully, as the queues to get off the island can be pretty intimidating.

Jadrolinija also operates a daily catamaran from Split to Vela Luka (on Korčula) and Ubli (on Lastovo), which stops in at Hvar town, and it's only an hour's journey from the mainland.

In addition, through summer Jadrolinija and two private companies, **Krilo** (w krilo.hr) and **TP Line** (w tp-line.hr), all operate big fast daily catamarans between Split and Dubrovnik, stopping at Hvar town (1hr), Korčula town and the island of Mljet en route. These services offer good onward options for your journey, delivering you to additional islands or directly to Dubrovnik.

In summer there's also a daily Jadrolinija catamaran that runs from Split to Jelsa via Bol, on Brač, and a catamaran from Split to Hvar via Milna, also on Brač (both 1hr 40mins).

If you're travelling by car and want to head onwards to Dubrovnik, you might leave the island via the Sućuraj-Drvenik crossing – the Jadrolinija car ferry runs six times daily in winter (11 daily in summer) and takes 25 minutes.

Public transport is limited to the reliable **bus** service between Hvar, Stari Grad, Vrboska and Jelsa (timetables at w cazmatrans.hr) – all incoming ferries are met, and outgoing ferries fed, by the bus network (with the exception of Sućuraj).

HVAR TOWN Hvar town is Croatia's St Tropez, and one of Dalmatia's most attractive places, rivalling Dubrovnik or Korčula with its Venetian Renaissance charm – though it can get oppressively busy in summer. Besides your regular holidaymakers,

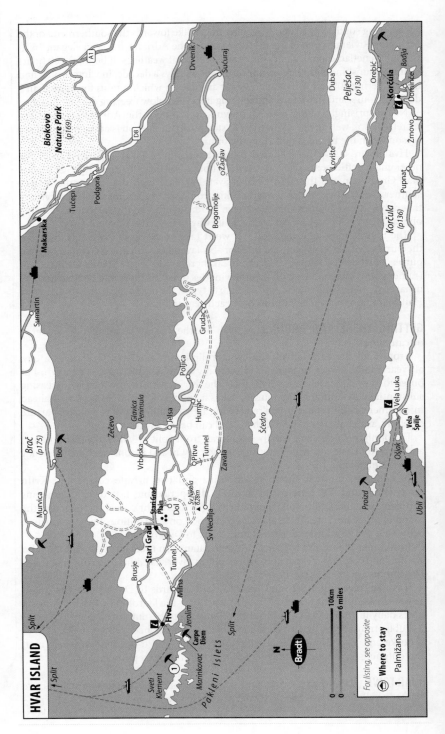

HVAR ISLAND

Biokova Nature Park (p169)

A1

D8

Makarska

Tučepi

Podgora

Šumartin

Brač (p175)

Bol

Murvica

Drvenik

Sućuraj

Zečevo

Glavica Peninsula

Jelsa

Vrboška

Zaglav

Bogomolje

Poljica

Humpac

Pitve

Tunnel

Zavala

Grudac

Šćedro

Stari Grad Plain

Sv Nikola 628m

Dol

Sv Nedilja

Brusje

Tunnel

Milna

Hvar

Jerolim

Carpe Diem

Sveti Klement

Marinkovac

Pakleni Islets

Split

Split

Split

Peljesac (p130)

Duba

Lovište

Orebić

Korčula

Badija

Dominče

Žrnovo

Pupnat

Korčula (p136)

Vela Luka

Vela Spilje

Osjak

Proizd

Ubli

N

Bradt

10km

6 miles

0

0

For listing, see opposite

ⓘ Where to stay

1 Palmižana

180

it's much loved by sailing types, too, and on summer evenings the harbour literally heaves with yachts, moored up several abreast.

The heart of the town is the main square, Trg Sveti Stjepana, billed as Dalmatia's largest piazza, which runs east–west from the cathedral to the harbour. To the north of the square is the swanky old quarter, with the palaces of **Grad** sheltering under the 13th-century city walls and overlooked by the fortress on the hill. To the south is the old residential town of **Burg**.

In the early 15th century, Hvar became the wealthiest town in Dalmatia, under Venice, as all ships to and from the republic stopped in here. What you see today, however (barring the mostly original city walls), is uniformly late 16th century, as the Turks razed it to the ground in 1571.

Where to stay *Map, page 183, unless otherwise stated*

If you're planning to stay in a hotel in Hvar, be prepared to pay the price, which is pretty high in the hotels spread along the coast (most are within 10–15mins on foot) and even higher at one of the few hotels right in town. Count on €160 a night for a decent double room with a view out of town, and anything from €300 to €550 a night in town. Almost every accommodation option in Hvar is owned by (and reserved through) Sunčani Hvar (☏ 021 750 555; w suncanihvar.com) – for a summer visit, book as far ahead as you possibly can.

If the hotel prices have taken your breath away, then you'll need to be looking for a private room online well in advance. Expect to pay at least €100–150 for a one-night stay in a double room during the season; out of season you should be able to do a great deal better than this.

Adriana Hvar Spa Hotel (62 rooms) Obala Fabrika 28; ☏ 021 750 200; w suncanihvar.com. Luxury boutique spa hotel right on the waterfront, with all the facilities you'd expect, including a rooftop pool & bar. €€€€€

Amfora Hvar Grand Beach Resort (324 rooms) Ulica biskupa Jurja Dubokovića 5; ☏ 021 750 300; w suncanihvar.com. This colossal, modern complex round the shore from the old town looks on to gardens with cascading pools, & Beach Club Hvar, an attractive pebble cove & shore colonnade with bathing facilities. €€€€€

Palace Elizabeth Hvar Heritage Hotel (45 rooms) Trg sv Stjepana bb; ☏ 021 750 400; w suncanihvar.com. Sitting in a prime location right across from the Arsenal, the appropriately named Palace has been welcoming guests since 1903 & was fully refurbished in 2019. Upstairs there's a fabulous open terrace giving on to the harbour & main square. €€€€€

Riva Marina Hvar Hotel (46 rooms) Obala Riva 27; ☏ 021 750 100; w suncanihvar.com. Near to where the catamaran docks, the former Slavija hotel is now a swish luxury retreat, renovated in 2022. Oozing understated style, it has a chic bar-restaurant terrace out front. €€€€€

✳ **Palmižana** [map, opposite] Sveti Klement islet; m 099 457 8345; w palmizana.com. A real escape in a botanical garden on the Pakleni islets, 20mins' boat ride from Hvar. Quirky colourful bungalows & villas, filled with modern artworks, plus 2 gorgeous (but rather pricey) boho-chic restaurants. €€€€

Pharos Hvar Bayhill Hotel (202 rooms) Ulica Dinka Kovačevića 10; ☏ 021 750 500; w suncanihvar.com. On the hill above the harbour, set amid pinewoods, this informal hotel appeals to younger visitors, with an outdoor pool & all-day café-restaurant. €€€€

Podstine (54 rooms) Podstine bb; ☏ 021 740 400; w podstine.com. Set in a terraced hillside garden looking towards the Pakleni islets, Podstine has a small spa & beachfront. It lies 25mins' walk along the coast from town. €€€€

Villa Nora (4 rooms) Frane Primija 2; ☏ 021 742 498; 〓. Spacious comfortable rooms in a 14th-century stone house in the town centre, with a courtyard restaurant, where b/fast is served. €€€€

Kuća Hektorović (3 rooms) Petra Hektorovića 8; ☏ 021 718 083; w hektorovichousehvar. hr. Beautifully renovated 13th-century stone house (home to the famous Croatian poet Petar Hektorović in the 16th century), just off the main square in the old town. €€€

Hostel Villa Skansi Domovinskog rata 18; 📞021 741 426. Renovated in 2022, popular hostel offering (big) dorms & 8 private rooms. €€

✗ Where to eat and drink *Map, opposite*

In high summer in Hvar Town, there are literally dozens of restaurants and even more bars and cafés – you'll be choosing between traditional Dalmatian seafood or modern Creative Mediterranean fare, all rather pricey but of variable quality. The biggest challenge may be finding a table at all – many are reserved well in advance by yachting crews and hotel guests. If you come before Easter, you may find only a couple of restaurants open and a mere handful of bars.

Black Pepper Skaline od Gojave 11; m 095 7509 790; w blackpepperhvar.com; ⊕ Jun–Sep 18.00–midnight. Delicious fish & meat dishes, prepared with care & flair, served at tables on the steps going up towards the castle. €€€€€

Giaxa Petra Hektorovića 11; 📞021 741 073; w giaxa.com; ⊕ May–Oct noon–23.00. Creative Mediterranean cuisine served in a romantic late-Gothic courtyard, 1 street back from the main square. €€€€€

✳ Macondo Petra Hektorovića; 📞021 742 850; w macondo.com.hr; ⊕ Apr–Nov noon–14.00 & 18.30–midnight Mon–Sat, 18.30–midnight Sun. With tables in a narrow side alley, Macondo is a firm favourite with the locals for its authentic Dalmatian seafood dishes, which are excellent but pricey. €€€€€–€€€€

Menego Ulica kroz Grodu 26 ; 📞021 717 411; w menego.hr; ⊕ Apr–Nov 11.30–14.00 & 17.00–midnight daily. Homely place specialising in Dalmatian dishes, all made with home-grown produce. €€€€–€€€

Alviž Trg Marka Miličića 2; 📞021 742 797; ⊕ 18.00–23.00. An example of the more reasonably priced eateries in Hvar, popular with locals, Alviz serves good pizzas & Dalmatian fare, near the bus station. €€€

Kogo Trg Sv Stjepana 34; m 098 582 531; w kogohvar.com; ⊕ May–Oct 10.00–midnight. Long-standing pizzeria on the main square, also doing salads, risotto, pasta dishes & grilled meats. €€€

Entertainment and nightlife Hvar offers one of Croatia's hottest party scenes in summer, with a number of bars to choose from, though it is all rather over-hyped. In reality, the jetsetters retire to their private yachts after dinner in town, leaving the mere mortals to drink themselves silly under a starry sky. Stag parties and suchlike had become such a nuisance that, as of 2017, the city council began issuing hefty fines for unruly drunken behaviour, nudity and urinating in public spaces.

For film buffs, in the courtyard of the former Veneranda fortress, on a pine-forested hill above the harbour, Hvar's lovely open-air **Summer Cinema** (Kino Mediteran Hvar; 🏼; €5) shows after-dark films in the original version (mainly English) with Croatian subtitles.

Cafés and bars
Popular cafés & bars in town include:

Central Park Club Bankete bb; 📞021 718 337; w klubparkhvar.com; ⊕ May–Oct 07.00–02.00. Offers a programme of live jazz.
Kiva Fabrika 26; ⊕ May–Oct 21.00–02.00. Classic rock.
Lola Sveti Marak 10; ⊕ May–Oct 10.00–02.00. Cocktails & street food.

Clubs
Carpe Diem Beach Club m 099 446 8468; w beach.cdhvar.com; ⊕ Jun–Sep midnight–05.00. For late-night music & dancing, with occasional guest DJs, try this place on Marinkovac islet, which is served by taxi boat from the harbour in Hvar.

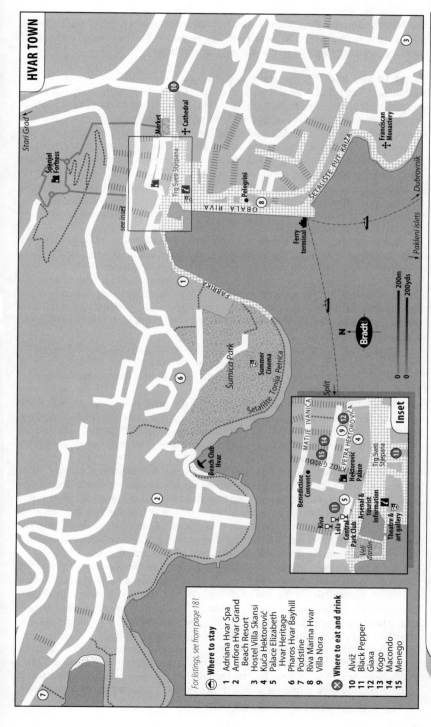

HVAR TOWN

Stari Grad

Španjol Fortress

see inset

Market

✝ Cathedral

10

Trg Sveti Stjepana

ℹ️

● Pelegrini

8

OBALA RIVA

ŠETALIŠTE PUT KRIŽA

✝ Franciscan Monastery

Dubrovnik

Ferry terminal

→ *Pakleni islets*

FABRIKA

1

Šumica Park

Summer Cinema

Šetalište Tonija Petrića

6

Beach Club Hvar

2

7

N

Bradt

0   200m
0   200yds

Split

Inset

MATIJE IVANIĆA

KROZ GROOU

PETRA HEKTOROVIĆA

Trg Sveti Stjepana

Benedictine Convent ●

Hektorović Palace

15 14

9 12

4

13

Kiva

11

5

Lola

Central Park Club

Arsenal & tourist information

Veli Jardin

Theatre & art gallery

For listings, see from page 181

🛏 **Where to stay**
1 Adriana Hvar Spa
2 Amfora Hvar Grand
   Beach Resort
3 Hostel Villa Skansi
4 Kuća Hektorović
5 Palace Elizabeth
   Hvar Heritage
6 Pharos Hvar Bayhill
7 Podstine
8 Riva Marina Hvar
9 Villa Nora

✖ **Where to eat and drink**
10 Alviž
11 Black Pepper
12 Giaxa
13 Kogo
14 Macondo
15 Menego

Split and Central Dalmatia   HVAR

5

183

Activities Aqualis Dive Center Hvar (w hvardiving.com) offers scuba-diving tours and tuition at all levels, while **Hvar Sea Kayaking** (w hvar-seakayaking.com) runs sea kayaking tours, as well as hiking and climbing.

What to see and do The main sights are on or near the main square. The **cathedral** (☏ 021 743 126; ⊕ 09.00–noon & 16.00–18.00) with its Renaissance trefoil façade is attractive enough (and the campanile, with its increasing number of windows on each storey, is lovely), but nothing particularly special inside, barring a fine 13th-century Madonna and Child, in striking contrast to the morbidly graphic Baroque paintings on the other altars. Check out the modern main doors, the work of the sculptor Kuzma Kovačić, the man also behind the design on Croatia's kuna and lipa coins, now replaced by the euro. (If you're around on Maundy Thursday, just before Easter, don't miss the religious processions around the island, maintaining a 500-year-old tradition. The festivities reach a climax on Easter Monday when the six big crosses from the island's main settlements are paraded around town.)

Also on the main square is the great hulk of the **Arsenal** – unusual indeed among naval buildings in having a theatre upstairs, and especially so in this case, as it was one of the first in the Western world open to all comers. The **theatre** (☏ 021 741 009; ⊕ May–Oct, variable hours) was built in 1612, as you can see by the inscription outside saying 'Anno Secundo Pacis MDCXII' – the peace referred to here was the ending of the century-long spat between commoners and nobs throughout the 16th century, following the 1510 uprising by Matija Ivanić, when 19 men were hanged from galley masts here.

Access to the theatre is through an adjoining **art gallery**, which has highly variable temporary exhibitions from Croatian artists. The theatre itself is charming, with just 86 seats and 28 pint-sized boxes, and is finally benefitting from long-awaited restoration.

On the other side of the square, dominating the main town gate, you'll find the so-called **Hektorović Palace**, an ornate but unfinished Venetian Gothic building, which has remained unroofed and overgrown since the 15th century. The 'palace' pre-dates the famous poet, in fact – and a more fitting memorial can be seen at his actual palace in Stari Grad.

Up the stepped street from here you'll find a small **Benedictine Convent** (☏ 021 741 052; ⊕ May–Oct, variable hours), where the few remaining nuns – they never leave the hallowed walls, and are bound to an oath of silence – spend their hours making the extraordinarily intricate lace which you'll find for sale around town (you'll know it's the real thing by the serious price tags). Just below the convent is a small, plain church, remarkable only for the portrait of Cardinal Stjepinac, bearing an even more alarming resemblance than usual to Vladimir Putin.

Continuing straight up the street brings you out into the park above town, and the path eventually winds its way up to the 16th-century **Španjol Fortress** (⊕ May–Sep 09.00–20.00 daily) at the top of the hill. With a wonderful view over the old town and across the Pakleni Islets – especially in the early evening – the place is understandably popular. Inside the fortress there's a collection of amphorae and other bits and pieces fished out from the sea and dragged up here.

South of the town (just follow the quay down past the ferry terminal) is the 15th-century **Franciscan Monastery** (☏ 021 741 193; ⊕ May–Oct 10.00–noon & 17.00–19.00, Nov–Apr 10.00–noon). Just two monks live here now, and the place serves as an endearing little museum, with old oil jars and a comprehensive numismatic collection dating back to Roman times. There are some interesting bits of modern sculpture (some of it by one of the monks) and a collection of mostly Venetian paintings. The biggest of these, taking up most of an end wall, is an especially rowdy Last Supper. It's said to be the work of a Venetian painter who was in quarantine here, with only a cat for company – the cat's on the left and the painter's on the right. On the other side of the cloisters is a curious and rather spooky church, which is a bit of a mish-mash architecturally but has good 16th-century choir stalls and a couple of huge dark altarpieces by Leandro Bassano. Look out among the various tombs for that of the local writer Hanibal Lučić (1485–1553).

Beaches There are several beaches close to town, notably the chi-chi **Beach Club Hvar** (w beachhvar.com), in a bay rimmed by a white stone colonnade with cabanas from 1927, in front of Hotel Amfora. But serious bathers will want to take a trip out to the **Pakleni Islets**, just offshore, which is where all the best beaches can be found (you'll be told that the name Pakleni means 'devils', but it actually refers to the pine resin). To get there, catch a taxi boat from the harbour. The nearest islet, Jerolim, has a couple of peaceful clothing-optional beaches (referred to as FKK beaches, from the German *freikorperkultur*). The next island, Marinkovac, has several waterside bar-restaurants hiring out sun beds, including **Mamato Bar** (f marijamtudor) in Ždrilac bay and **Carpe Diem Beach Club** (w beach.cdhvar. com; page 182) in Štipanska Bay. The furthest and largest island, Sveti Klement, is home to the dreamy **Palmižana** (page 181) with bungalows, villas and a restaurant displaying a collection of modern art, set in an overgrown botanical garden, a short walk from the ACI Palmižana marina.

STARI GRAD
Stari Grad, set around an elongated horseshoe harbour at the head of a long, sheltered bay, was formerly the capital of the island, and the location of the 4th-century BC Greek colony of Pharos (the name Hvar comes from Pharos). These days, you'll find it infinitely less frenetic than Hvar town, though some of Hvar's cool crowd are now looking towards Stari Grad, which has an ever-improving range of hotels and restaurants. Its sheltered waters make it a popular spot for yachters to moor up, too.

The town is on the south side of the harbour, with the northern shore occupied by a string of package hotels (now run by the Valamar chain). If you're driving from Hvar, there are two roads: the new fast route through the tunnel or the picturesque old road over the hills past the village of **Brusje**. Take the high road if you're not in a rush.

Since 1976, each year in late August, Stari Grad hosts the gruelling open-water long-distance **Faros Marathon**, seeing international swimmers tackle the full length of Stari Grad Bay to Cape Kabal and back (16km). The best swimmer usually manages to complete this in just over 3 hours.

For information about sightseeing and local events, head to the **tourist office** (Obala dr Franje Tuđmana 1; \021 765 763; w visit-stari-grad.com) on the harbour.

⬆ Where to stay

Maslina Resort (53 rooms) Uvala Maslinica 11; \021 888 700; w maslinaresort.com. Newly built in 2020, this slick hotel, complete with a tasteful contemporary design, gourmet restaurant, pools & a lush spa, lies in a sheltered bay, near the ferry port, a 20min walk from Stari Grad. €€€€€

Heritage Villa Apolon (8 rooms) Šetalište Don Šime Ljubića 7; \021 778 320; w apolon.hr. Very swish boutique hotel in a beautifully restored 19th-century villa, with spacious suites & its own restaurant, right on the Riva. €€€€
Hidden House (3 suites) Duoljno kola 13; m 091 266 4444; w hidden-house.com. In an old stone

house in a peaceful back alley, this slick hideaway has 3 suites with kitchenettes & funky décor. €€€€
Apartments Marinko (10 apartments) Domobranska 24; m 098 9397 490; w ilovehvar. com. Good-value apartments in the streets north of the harbour, about halfway out to the Valamar hotels. €€€

Oxa Dreamland (3 cottages, each sleeping 4) Put Gospojice 42; ☎ 091 333 3624; w oxadreamland.com. Rustic cottages set in a Mediterranean garden with a pool & olive trees, on Stari Grad Plain, midway between Stari Grad & Jesla. Bikes for guests, ideal for families. €€€

✖ Where to eat and drink

Antika Donja Kola 34; m 099 798 1734; 🄵 antikabarandrestaurant; ⊕ May–Oct noon–15.00, 17.30–23.00. Upmarket creative Mediterranean fare served at a refined little restaurant just off the Riva. €€€€
Jurin Podrum Duoljno kola 11; m 091 755 7382; ⊕ May–Oct noon–23.00 Sat–Thu. Historic eatery (Edward & Wallis Simpson ate here in 1936) in a narrow stone alley, serving homemade pasta & a modern take on traditional Dalmatian fare. €€€€
Kod Damira Trg Stjepana Radića 5; m 091 573 6376; ⊕ 09.00–23.00. Owner-chef Damir

will give you a warm welcome & feed you on authentic Dalmatian seafood, just like locals eat at home – 1 of the few eateries to stay open all year. €€€€–€€€
Hora Hvar Starigradsko polje; m 091 531 8781; w horahvar.com. Visit the Žuvela family's agritourism to better understand the significance of Stari Grad Plain's UNESCO-listed status – have a quick tour of their fields, followed by lunch made from their produce, including Bogdanuša white wine, unique to the island. €€€

Activities If you want to get out of town, it's well worth picking up one of the good local booklets from the tourist office that detail various **walks and cycle routes** in the area, including ones up to Svete Nikola and to Glavica, the hill overlooking the town. You can also rent bikes in Stari Grad from **Hvar Life** (Vukovarska cesta 31; m 091 315 5591; w hvar.life), and the cycling round here is excellent, with quite flat terrain and very little traffic – in fact, Stari Grad makes a better base for hiking and cycling on the island than Hvar town.

What to see and do Little that is visible has survived from antiquity, barring a small section of the original walls, a few paving slabs, and some Greek gravestones in the museum at the monastery. However, as of 2020, archaeologists have unearthed further traces of Greek and Roman settlements, including a beautifully preserved mosaic floor and some graves, but for now, these finds remain hidden from public view. Today, the town is nevertheless a small but agreeable hodgepodge of little streets and small squares, and if you're lucky you might discover more about its ancient past at a temporary exhibition at the **Stari Grad Museum** (☎ 021 766 324; w msg.hr; ⊕ Jul–Aug 10.00–13.00 & 19.00–21.00 Mon–Sat, 19.00–21.00 Sun; May–Jun & Sep 10.00–13.00 Mon–Sat; Oct–Apr on request). Afterwards, head for the **Tvrdalj** (☎ 021 765 068; ⊕ May–Oct, variable hours), the summer house of one of Dalmatia's most famous poets, Petar Hektorović (1487–1572). The fortified house has undergone numerous facelifts since being started in 1520 but features interesting inscriptions on the walls from Hektorović's work, in Croatian, Italian and Latin, and a heavy cloister surrounding a fishpond – a memorial to the poet's love of fish, fishing and fishermen. There's also a **Dominican Monastery** (Dominikanski samostan; ☎ 021 765 442; ⊕ May–Oct 09.00–13.30 daily) to visit, with an interesting museum off the cloisters.

Stretching between Stari Grad and Vrboska is the UNESCO-listed **Stari Grad Plain**, where the ancient Greek system of land division is incredibly well-preserved, and the cultivation of grapevines and olive trees appears to have changed remarkably little over the past two-and-a-half thousand years. You might cycle to

Jelsa this way, taking the 'old road' and then passing through waterside Vrboska en route. Afterwards, you could head into the inland villages of Pitve, Vrisnik, Svirče and Vrbanj to make a loop before returning to Stari Grad.

In the opposite direction, in the hilltop village of Selca (7km southwest of Stari Grad), wine lovers might call at the **Lacman Family Winery** (m 091 943 8675; w lfw.hr; ⊕ May–Oct 10.00–21.00 Mon–Sat). Lacman specialise in natural wines (grapes fermented on the skins, without artificial yeast) and offer tasting on a terrace with spectacular views, plus occasional live music.

JELSA AND SURROUNDINGS The small town of **Jelsa** is made up of modestly 19th-century houses, sitting on a pretty port on Hvar's north coast. It's an attractive place in itself, surrounded by pine forests (hiding a couple of big modern hotels, one to each side of the bay) and giving easy access to a number of beaches, including by taxi-boat to the best ones on the Glavica Peninsula, and across to the naturist island of **Zečevo**.

The **tourist office** (Trg Tome Gamulina 1; ☏021 761 017; w visitjelsa.hr; ⊕ May–Oct 08.00–20.00 Mon–Sat, 09.00–noon & 17.00–20.00 Sun) is on the main square behind the harbour.

Where to stay and eat Hotel accommodation in Jelsa is at the two big modern (but rather dated) all-inclusive hotels that make up the Jelsa Resort complex, hidden amid pinewoods at each side of the harbour – the **Fontana Resort** (☏021 761 810; w jelsaresort.hr; €€€€) and the **Hotel Hvar** (☏021 761 024; w jelsaresort.hr; €€€€). Private rooms, however, are in good supply and considerably cheaper here than in Hvar town. There are also two nice little family-run B&Bs – the seven-room **Pansion Murvica** (Sv Roka; ☏021 761 405; w murvica.net; €€), near the bus station (they also have a ground-floor restaurant, plus a nice stone house available in the village of Humac) and the six-room **Villa Rosa** (Jelsa 551; m 092 374 4295; €€), which offers a shared kitchen and a garden with a barbecue. In neighbouring Vrboska, the eight-room **Villa Welcome** (Vrboska 237; ☏021 774 110; w villawelcome.com; €€) is a similar family-run option.

Two lovely places for rustic dining in Jelsa's rural interior are **Konoba Humac** (Humac, 7km east of Jelsa; m 091 523 9463; ⊕ May–Sep noon–22.00 Mon–Sat; €€€) and **Konoba Vrisnik** (Vrisnik; ☏021 768 016; ⨍; ⊕ May–Sep 17.00–01.00 daily; €€€).

In **Zavala** on the south coast, you might stay at the excellent **Villa Stella Mare** (Zavala 112; ☏021 767 128; w stellamare-hvar.com; €€€€–€€€). There are five apartments, a restaurant and pool, and the friendly staff will rent you a bike or a boat if you want to explore the hidden coves along Hvar's south coast. Nearby, you can eat fresh seafood on a waterside terrace at **Restaurant Davor** (Zavala 129; ☏021 767 214; ⨍; ⊕ Jun–Sep noon–23.00 daily; €€€€).

What to see and do If wine is your thing, Jelsa has two highly regarded **wineries** open for tours and tasting: **Tomić** (☏021 762 015; w vina-tomic.com) and **Duboković** (m 099 441 0110; ⨍).

Jelsa also offers one of the very few routes across the island to the glorious south coast. You'll need wheels, as the route winds 4km up to the old village of **Pitve** before entering the Vratnik Gorge and a long tunnel, which comes out above the tiny fishing village of Zavala (around 7km from Pitve). Wine lovers might stop in Pitve to visit the **Viticulture Collection** (w muzejopcinejelsa.hr), presenting traditional and modern winemaking techniques and hosting wine-tasting.

From Jelsa, a pretty 45-minute walk west along the coast brings you to **Vrboska**, a charming old village set along both sides of an inlet. Stone bridges connect the two halves, which are dominated by the fortified 16th-century **Church of St Mary** (Sv Marija), built after the Turks destroyed the place in 1571. You can climb up to the battlements for a nice view over the village.

Three kilometres offshore from Zavala is the island of **Šćedro**. Protected since 1972, the island doesn't see many visitors (though there are a couple of sheltered bays, with seasonal eateries, where yachters drop anchor to overnight) and has a resident population of around 15. It makes for a lovely day trip from Zavala (or Jelsa), with its dense woods, sheltered inlets and the remains of a 15th-century monastery.

East of Jelsa, Hvar becomes very empty indeed, and although there's plenty to explore if you have your own wheels, it's pretty much impossible otherwise.

VIS

The lovely hilly island of Vis is Croatia's farthest-flung possession, and its oldest recorded settlement, having been colonised by the Greeks (from Syracuse, on Sicily) at the beginning of the 4th century BC. The colony of Issa then went on to found its own colonies (notably at Trogir and Salona) before succumbing to Roman rule, and following much the same historical fate as most of the rest of Dalmatia – Venetians, Austrians, the French, Austrians again, and then Yugoslavia – with the notable exception that Vis was also a British possession, from 1811 to 1814.

The British came back here in 1944, when the island was briefly Tito's headquarters – after the war, when Vis was a Yugoslav naval base, the only foreigners allowed on the island for decades were British veterans, who came back every September for their annual reunion.

For centuries, the islanders lived mainly from fishing (local waters are particularly rich in sardines) and winemaking (producing whites from the indigenous Vugava grape and reds from Plavac).

Since 1989, Vis has been open to foreigners, and despite the growth in tourism over the past decade, remains pleasantly less busy than Hvar or Brač. As the few hotels that were built here during the Yugoslav era were very modest, the majority of visitors have been sailing folk who arrive on private yachts. The island is the jumping-off point for trips to the famous Modra Špilja (Blue Cave) on nearby Biševo, but it's well worth visiting in its own right.

The capital, Vis town, is in a sheltered inlet on the spectacular north side of the island (the cliffs at Gradac, nearby, rise 100m out of the sea), while Komiža, in a large bay facing west, is the other main settlement, closer to the island of Biševo.

Founded in 2019, the **Geopark Vis Archipelago** project aims to highlight local geology and its relationship to the natural environment and human settlement – call in at the visitor's centre in Komiža to learn more. They have devised four geotrails, complete with explanatory information panels, which criss-cross the island and can be followed on foot or by bike.

Note that there are plans to build two big new luxury hotels, one in Vis Town and one in Komiža (tentatively scheduled to open in 2026), which will undoubtedly change the image of the island. One can only hope that they will respect both the gorgeous natural environment and the local way of life.

GETTING THERE AND AROUND Two or three **ferries** a day come from Split all year round (2½hrs), stopping twice a week in Hvar, while in summer there's also

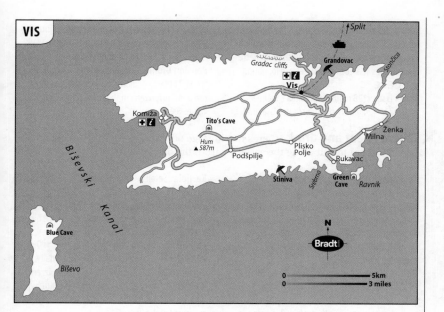

a daily catamaran, which takes around 1½ hours from Split. Don't even think about trying to bring your car here in summer – rent a scooter or mountain bike on the island.

Public transport on Vis consists of the **bus** which runs several times daily between Vis town and Komiža, a short (15mins) but fairly spectacular ride along the northernmost of the two main roads across the islands. Another, less regular bus service covers the other, southern, road. There's also a great network of tracks and **hiking** trails across the island, including to Tito's Cave (Titova Špilja), used as a base by the Partisan leader towards the end of World War II. Several hiking routes are described in detail in Rudolf Abraham's *The Islands of Croatia* (page 238), and there's an excellent detailed map of the island published by the HGSS. Adventure sports activities can also be arranged through **Alternatura**, a group of local enthusiasts specialising in hiking, cycling, sea kayaking, climbing and abseiling, as well as culinary history and Yugoslav military tours, with a maximum group size of 12 persons (Hrvatskih mučenika 2, Komiža; 021 717 239; w alternatura.hr).

VIS TOWN Ferries arrive in Vis town, the diminutive capital, which consists of Luka to the west and Kut to the east, though the whole place is a lovely, easy 20-minute walk around the bay from end-to-end. The **tourist office** (021 717 017; w tz-vis.hr) has some local information and maps, while **Ionios** (m 091 255 5545; w ionios.hr) is the place to go to rent bikes and scooters – a wonderful way of seeing the island.

Where to stay

Pomalo Inn (10 rooms) Trg Patija 4; m 099 393 7260; w pomaloinn.com. In a stone building from 1810 in Kut, this hip B&B opened in 2022. There's no restaurant but they do b/fast & have bikes for guests. €€€€€

San Giorgio (10 rooms) Hektorovića 2; 021 607 630; w hotelsangiorgiovis.com. Beautiful little boutique hotel in Kut, with its own gourmet restaurant, Boccadoro, in a tumbledown building across the alley. €€€€€

Nautic Apartments (4 rooms), Vladimira Nazora bb; ☎021 711 711; w nautic-apartments.com. In Kut, 4 comfortable apartments with kitchenettes & a spacious shared sea-view terrace for eating out. €€€€
Hotel Issa (128 rooms) Apolonija Zanelle 5; ☎021 711 124; w vis-hoteli.hr/hotel-issa. Built in 1984, the Issa offers dated but functional interiors, with a pebble beach out front, just a 10min walk from the ferry landing station. €€€
Pansion Dionis (8 rooms) Matije Gubca 1; ☎021 711 963; w dionis.hr. Nice little family-run pansion/pizzeria in the town centre. Good value. €€

✕ Where to eat and drink

There's no shortage of places to eat in Vis – but for the best, head out to Kut along the eastern part of the bay.

✳ **Pojoda** Don Cvjetka Marasovića 8, Kut; ☎021 711 575; ⏲ summer noon–midnight daily, winter 17.00–23.00 (on request). Truly lovely seafood restaurant in a beautiful courtyard with lemon trees. Much loved by sailing crews, possibly the best restaurant on Vis. Highly recommended. €€€€€
Villa Kaliopa Vladimira Nazora 34; m 091 271 1755; ⏲ May–Sep 17.00–midnight daily. Swanky place with tables below the palms in the romantic walled garden of the 16th-century Renaissance Garibaldi Palace. Pricey but good, popular with well-heeled Italians. €€€€€
Konoba Vatrica Petra Krešimira IV 13, Kut; ☎021 711 574; f; ⏲ summer 09.00–01.00 daily, winter 17.00–23.00 daily. Consistently good konoba on the waterfront in Kut, with specialities including lobster pasta. €€€€–€€€

Karijola Šetalište Viškog Boja 4; ☎021 711 358; w pizzeria-karijola.com; ⏲ Jul–Aug noon–midnight daily, May–Jun & Sep 17.00–23.00 daily. Nice terrace, & the best pizzas on Vis, with a bigger sister restaurant in Zagreb. €€€
Lambik Bar Bistro Trg Podloža 2, Kut; m 095 222 4221; f; ⏲ summer 08.00–02.00 daily, winter 10.00–21.00 daily. Friendly café-pizzeria & informal eatery on the main square in Kut, with wicker sofas out front & a wonderful vine-covered courtyard at the back. €€€
Mvsevm Vis Korso 5; m 091 598 7893; f; ⏲ Jun–Sep 08.00–noon, 18.00–midnight daily. Cosy bar furnished with antiques, serving morning coffee & evening wine & cheese, popular with sailing crews. €€€

What to see and do

There's not much to see in the way of Greek and Roman heritage, though the **Archaeological Museum** (Arheološki Muzej; ☎021 711 729; ⏲ Jun–Sep 10.00–13.00 & 17.00–20.00 Mon–Fri, 10.00–13.00 Sat; out of season visits by appointment; €4) housed in the old fortified battery (Gospinoj batariji) has a few treasures on show, including the famous 4th-century BC bronze head of a Greek goddess. There is also a useful leaflet detailing the sites of local ruins, though there isn't that much to see on the ground – the remains of the Greek cemetery and walls are really just vestiges, while what was once the Roman theatre has been firmly overbuilt by a Franciscan monastery.

More immediately evocative – especially to students of English history – are the remains of the imperial forts. Head up the hairpins behind the town then along the headland on the eastern side of the bay to the ruins of the **Wellington Fort** – though unfortunately, the route takes you past the huge local rubbish heap, all going into landfill (a sobering reminder of the negative impact of buying plastic bottles of mineral water). On the northern headland, the once even more dilapidated **King George III Fort** was restored and converted into a (very expensive) bar-restaurant and wedding reception venue in 2013 (w fortgeorgecroatia.com) – which would have been great aside from the fact that you can now hear the music, quite loudly, even in the otherwise quiet neighbourhoods of Kut and Lučica on the opposite side of the bay. Heading out past Kut takes you past a small **British cemetery**, just before the popular pebble beach, **Grandovac**. There are nicer beaches not far from town, however – rent a bike and head out of town to **Stončica**, which is great for kids.

Finally, if you want to base yourself somewhere more remote than Vis town or Komiža, try **WearActive** in **Rukavac** (m 098 1314 179; w wearactive.com). Run by a Welsh couple, they offer a week's bed and breakfast, including five days of activities (kayaking, hiking, cycling, etc), three evening meals and four picnic lunches, together with transfers to/from Vis town (and restaurants when eating out), for €1,280–1,430 per person (late May–late Sep).

Note that the **Geopark Vis Archipelago** have devised a well-marked **Geotrail Vis-Rukavac**, which leads to some of the finest natural attractions on the south coast, including the islet of Ravnik with its Green Cave, the sandy bay of Milna, Srebrena Bay with its smooth white rocks, and the tiny beach hidden within Stiniva Bay. However, some of these sites are incredibly difficult to reach without appropriate transport and the Geopark is still working on how to make them more accessible.

KOMIŽA

Komiža, at the other end of the island, is a strong rival for Vis. Set under the bulk of Hum Mountain (587m), the town stretches in a lovely palm-studded sweep round the bay and has plenty of appealingly run-down 16th- and 17th-century houses, as well as a fine 16th-century Venetian fortress, dominating one end of the harbour.

Komiža's **tourist office** (Riva Sv Mikule 2; ☏021 713 455; w tz-komiza.hr) can fill you in on local sights, while **Alternatura** (Hrvatskih mučenika 2; ☏021 717 239; w alternatura.hr) can arrange visits to the Blue Cave on Biševo (page 192).

Where to stay and eat

Plenty of eating and drinking goes on around Komiža's attractive main square, Škor, which is home to a handful of bars, cafés and restaurants, though the better and less touristy places tend to be those further north along the waterfront around Pol Kalafotovo beach.

Insulae Apartments (3 apartments) Dr Ante Starčevića 27; ☏021 713 029; w eco-insula-vis.com. In an 18th-century stone house in a peaceful alley with a small garden, the architect-owner offers homely modern apartments. €€€

Villa Kuljiš (3 apartments, 2 rooms) Pape Aleksandra III 4; m 098 268 452; w vis-apartments-kuljis.com.hr. Old stone house doing cosy accommodation with a guests-only dining room, just a few steps from a pebble beach. €€€

Villa Nonna (7 apartments) Ribarska 50; ☏021 713 500; m 098 380 046; w villa-nonna.com. On the edge of the bay, this offers studio apartments set in a renovated 400-year-old stone house. €€€

✻ **Bako** Gundulićeva 1; m 098 360 469; w konobabako.hr; ⏱ May–Sep 16.00–02.00 daily, Oct–Apr 17.00–midnight Fri–Sat. In a pebble bay with tables right up to the water, Bako's specialities include shrimp risotto & barbecued fresh fish. €€€€

Konoba Jastožera Gundulićeva 6; m 091 984 2513; w jastozera.eu; ⏱ Apr–Oct noon–02.00 daily. In a wood-&-stone lobster house built over the water, Jastožera specialises in lobster & other seafood. €€€€

Fabrika Riva Svetoga Mikule 12; ☏021 713 155; w fabrikavis.hr; ⏱ Jun–Sep 09.00–midnight daily. On the seafront promenade, overlooking the harbour, hip eatery serving pizza, pasta, bruschette, salads & smoothie bowls, with vegan options. €€€

Cukarin Hrvatskih mučenika 8; ☏092 422 5300; ⓕ cukar.komiza; ⏱ May–Oct 08.00–20.00 Mon–Sat, 08.00–14.00 Sun. Delicious cakes & biscuits made from traditional local ingredients, such as figs, almonds, lemon & carob flour. €

What to see and do

Behind the town, up the hill, is the austere fortified Benedictine **Monastery of St Nicholas** (Sv Nikole). On the saint's feast day, 6

December, the local fishermen drag a fishing boat up here and then set fire to it in a display that certainly has nothing whatsoever to do with pagan rites.

Wandering along local beaches, you'll likely note pebbles of many colours and types, some clearly of volcanic origin. To learn more, call in at the **Geopark Vis Archipelago** (**m** 091 271 3023; **w** geopark-vis.com) visitor centre, occupying a modernist pavilion by architect Ivan Vitić from 1961. The geopark aims to highlight the synergy between people and nature on the island and promote education and sustainable development. From here, you might walk the well-marked **Geotrail Komiža**, which begins and ends in the village and is certainly the most accessible of the park's four geotrails.

Scuba-diving enthusiasts should note that the seabed around Vis has many fascinating dive sites, notably wrecks, both ships and planes from World War II. Two reliable providers, both based in Komiža, are **ISSA Diving Centre** (**w** scubadiving.hr) and **B-24 Diving Centre** (**w** diving-croatia.hr).

A lovely way to spend an evening here is to attend an after-dark film screening at Komiža's **Summer Cinema** (Kino Mediteran Komiža; **f**; €4) on the roof terrace of the Memorial Centre from 1964. Films are shown in the original version (mainly English) with Croatian subtitles.

BLUE CAVE (*MODRA ŠPILJA*)

No trip to Vis seems to be complete without the obligatory visit to this cave on the island of Biševo, 5km southwest of Vis (the island is now uninhabited, though families still tend the vines here, travelling back and forth by boat). And indeed, if you get there at the right time of day (between 11.00 and midday), and you have a moment in the cave to yourself, then it is surely one of the most beautiful sights on the planet. Sunlight filters down through the water and reflects off the pale sea floor, giving a vibrant blue and turquoise shimmer to the cave.

Unfortunately, that's not the experience most people have. Out of season, access to the cave is often made impossible by choppy seas, while in July and August, on calm days, the cave gets almost as crowded as its namesake on Capri, and you'll be briskly ferried out to make room for the next boatload coming in. Swimming and diving here are now prohibited due to extreme visitor numbers.

The cave was discovered – and the entrance enlarged to allow boats in and out – in the 1880s. You can access the cave most easily via an excursion from either Vis or Komiža. After a quick peep in the cave, excursions usually then take you on to one of Biševo's many coves and beaches, and often feature the obligatory fish picnic. Some also take a look in the informative **Modra Špilja Visitor Centre** (**w** bluecave-bisevo.com) on Biševo.

Finally, spare a thought while you're here for the terribly endangered Mediterranean monk seal, the world's rarest pinniped; the islet of Brusnik, off to the west, near Svetac, is one of the very few places where it's recently been sighted in the past decade or so. Brusnik is also home to a charming endemic subspecies of the Dalmatian wall lizard, *Podarcis melisellensis melisellensis*.

6

Zadar and Northern Dalmatia

Northern Dalmatia is a region of extreme contrasts – you'd never dream, gazing at the thundering torrents of the Krka waterfalls, that the most barren islands of the Kornati archipelago were only a few kilometres offshore. Just as you'd never guess, confronted by a wall of heat on dry and dusty **Pag**, that the island of **Pašman** offered such sweet shelter on its wooded southern bays.

Zadar, the region's economic and transport capital, offers a wealth of things to see in a cultured old town, while Šibenik's Renaissance cathedral is one of the highlights of Dalmatia. The region is home, too, to three near-perfect national parks and a dedicated nature park: **Paklenica**, where you can hike serious summits and still go swimming on the same day; **Krka**, where you can visit a 14th-century monastery on an island between waterfalls; **Kornati**, where 89 islands, islets and reefs offer the true desert island experience; and **Lake Vrana** (Vransko Jezero), privileged home to 100,000 wading birds. Add in the islands of **Ugljan** (Zadar's quiet holiday retreat) and **Dugi Otok** (a sailor's heaven), and you could spend all your holidays here.

Phone codes vary across the region – they're included with each listing.

ZADAR

Zadar, with a population of around 71,000, is the cultural, economic and transport centre for northern Dalmatia. While its suburbs sprawl along the coast and inland, at its heart you'll find an unpretentious, partially walled old town on a narrow peninsula, full of fine churches and excellent museums.

HISTORY Zadar was first settled by Liburnian Illyrians the best part of 3,000 years ago, but from as early as the 3rd century BC onwards the Romans had their eye on it, naming it Jadera and finally making a Municipium of it in 59BC, then giving it colony status 11 years later.

On the partition of the empire, Zadar became the capital of Byzantine Dalmatia and had a period of some prosperity until the rise of Venice. Locals today are still proud of the fight Zadar put up against the Venetians, but despite four revolts in the 12th century and further uprisings over the next 200 years, Zadar went the same way as the rest of Dalmatia, ceding to Venice in 1409.

The Venetians' endless feuds with the Turks did nothing special for Zadar, though they did leave the city with a fine set of 16th-century defensive walls. Austria picked up the reins on the fall of Venice, with a brief French interlude, and allowed Italian immigrants to take care of the city – something that continued after World War I, with Zadar not joining the nascent Kingdom of the Serbs, Croats and Slovenes, but becoming Italian (Zara) instead. Indeed, some older people still speak Italian,

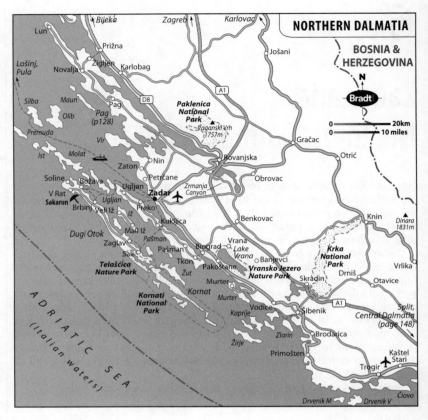

though you'll find the younger generation more switched on to German or English as a first foreign language.

When Italy capitulated in 1943, Germany took over Zadar, and the Allies practically bombed it into oblivion, a fate many feared might happen again during the winter of 1991, when the Serbs laid siege to the city. People went hungry and thirsty during the siege, but the old town remained intact, something that cannot be said for the inland suburbs, some of which still show the scars of warfare three decades after it ended. What the UN termed 'low-level warfare' continued as late as 1995.

GETTING THERE AND AROUND Zadar is a transport hub, with regular **bus** arrivals and departures (half-a-dozen a day, for the most part) to and from Zagreb (3½hrs), Rijeka (4–5hrs), Split (2½–3½hrs) and Dubrovnik (8–8½hrs), as well as several weekly runs to and from places like Frankfurt and Munich. If you want to reserve a seat in advance (recommended in peak season) and save yourself a trip to the bus station, you can also buy long-distance bus tickets online at GetByBus (**w** getbybus.com).

Note that Zadar train station is currently closed – the city is no longer served by **train** and this looks unlikely to change in the near future.

Zadar Airport (**w** zadar-airport.hr) is about 10km away to the southeast, with daily Zagreb flights with Croatia Airlines (40mins), and Ryanair also flies direct to Zadar from the UK. There's a **shuttle bus** running into town from the airport (w zadar-airport.hr/en/public-transport; €4.65), as well as direct shuttle buses to the island of Pag (w plesoprijevoz.hr/en/zadar-croatia) or if you want to take a **taxi** you can find one in front of the airport – expect to pay around €26 to town.

In summer (Jul–Aug) you have a twice-weekly ferry (w jadrolinija.hr) running between Ancona in Italy and Zadar (daytime crossings 7hrs, night crossings 9hrs). There are lots of **ferries** out to the islands of the Zadar archipelago (notably Ugljan and Dugi Otok; w jadrolinija.hr, w gv-zadar.com), as well as regular excursions to the Kornati archipelago – see the relevant sections later in this chapter for details. There is a ferry up to Lošinj (w jadrolinija.hr), and the same company runs an overnight service to Ancona in Italy once weekly through summer. Finally, there's a catamaran running up to the island of Silba (w miatours.hr) in summer, and there's a fast catamaran that runs four days a week up to Pula via Mali Lošinj (w krilo.hr).

Zadar's bus station is 1km southeast of the old town and port, while most of the hotels and beaches – and the town's marina – are 3km northwest of it, at Borik. There's a bus about three times an hour from the bus station up to Borik, via the harbour. Local ferries and catamarans (to Ugljan, Dugi Otok, etc) depart from Liburnska obala, the waterfront by the old town; longer routes (eg: Mali Lošinj and Ancona) depart from Gaženica, a short bus ride (3.5km) southeast of town (buses depart from beside the Jadrolinija office on Liburnska obala).

TOURIST INFORMATION The **tourist office** (Jurja Barakovića 5; ☎ 023 316 166; w zadar.travel), near the main square, Narodni trg, in the old town, has good maps and other documentation, and friendly staff. You'll also find lots of agencies which can organise excursions for you, of which there are any number from Zadar, including trips up to the Plitvice Lakes, down to the Krka River and waterfalls, or out to the Kornati archipelago.

WHERE TO STAY *Map, page 196*
The bulk of Zadar's hotels are out towards Borik, which has a swanky campsite (w falkensteiner.com; €) and a clutch of mostly package-oriented hotels (take bus #8). There's also accommodation a bit further along the coast at Zaton, Petrčane and Nin, all of which are on a regular bus service to Zadar (see opposite). However, a few lovely places have opened up in the old town itself in recent years, including the charming Almayer Art and Heritage Hotel and the Boutique Hostel Forum.

Private rooms can be booked online and should be reserved well in advance during peak season. You'll be lucky to get away with paying under €80 for a double in summer, plus the usual 30% surcharge for short stays.

Zadar centre

✴ **Almayer Art & Heritage Hotel** (16 rooms) Braće Bersa 2; ☎ 023 335 357; w almayer.hr. In Zadar's old town, this charming hotel offers superb rooms & a lovely courtyard restaurant, aptly named Corte. It also hosts occasional art exhibitions & a pop-up fashion store. Highly recommended. €€€€
Art Hotel Kalelarga (10 dbls) Majke Margarite 3; ☎ 023 233 000; w arthotel-kalelarga.com. Boutique 4-star in the centre of the old town, has a good restaurant, Gourmet Kalelarga, popular with locals. €€€€

Bastion (28 rooms) Bedemi Zadarskih Pobuna 13; ☎ 023 494 950; w hotel-bastion.hr. Top-notch boutique 4-star in the centre of town, incorporating part of the remains of the medieval fortifications – plush, efficient, with a truly wonderful spa & lovely rooms. €€€€
Kolovare (207 rooms) Bože Peričića 14; ☎ 023 203 200; w hotel-kolovare.com. The Kolovare is large, modern & functional, & has a small pool plus access to a beach out front. It is located halfway between the old town & the bus station. Some rooms have views across to Ugljan. €€€€–€€€

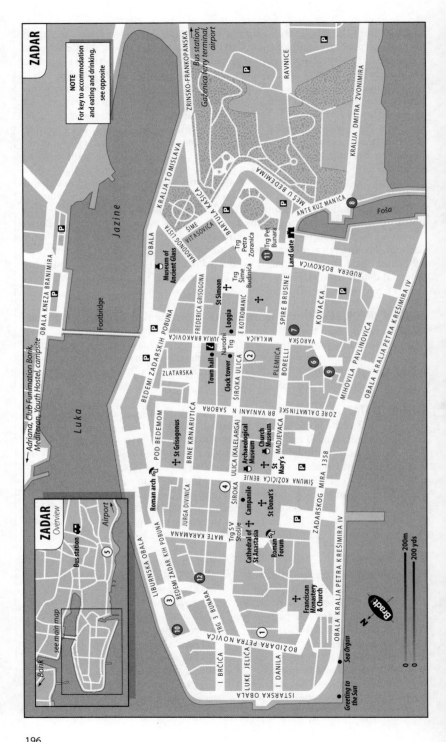

ZADAR

NOTE
For key to accommodation
and eating and drinking,
see opposite

ZADAR
Overview

Borik

see main map

Bus station

Airport

Jazine

Luka

Footbridge

Adriana, Club Funimation Borik,
Mediteran, Youth Hostel, campsite

Zrinsko-Frankopanska
Bus station,
Gaženica ferry terminal,
airport

RAVNICE

KRALJA DMITRA ZVONIMIRA

OBALA KNEZA BRANIMIRA

OBALA

KRALJA TOMISLAVA

NARODNIH LISTA

ŠIME VITASOVIĆA

BARTULA KAŠIĆA

MES U BEDEMIMA

ANTE KUZMANIĆA

Fošа

Museum of
Ancient Glass

FREDERICA GRISOGONA

St Simeon

Trg
Petra
Zoranića

Trg Pet
Bunara

Land Gate

RUĐERA BOŠKOVIĆA

BEDEMI ZADARSKIH POBUNA

JURJA BIAKOVIĆA

ZLATARSKA

Town hall

Clock tower

Narodni
Trg

Loggia

E KOTROMANIĆ

ŠIROKA ULICA

Trg
Šime
Budinića

SPIRE BRUSINE

VAROŠKA

KOVAČKA

POD BEDEMOM

BRNE KRNARUTIĆA

SABORA

BR VANJANI N

ZORE DALMATINSKE

PLEMIĆA
BORELLI

MIHOVILA PAVLINOVIĆA

OBALA KRALJA PETRA KREŠIMIRA IV

St Grisogonus

Roman arch

Archaeological
Museum

St
Mary's

Church
Museum

MADIJEVACA

ŠIMUNA KOZIČICA BENJE

ZADARSKOG MIRA 1358

ULICA (KALELARGA)

JURGA DIVINICA

ŠIROKA

Campanile

St Donat's

Roman
Forum

Cathedral of
St Anastasia

Trg S V
Stošije

MATE KARAMANA

LIBURNSKA OBALA

BEDEMI ZADAR KIH POBUNA

TRG 3 BUNARA

BOŽIDARA PETRA NOVIĆA

I BRCICA

LUKE JELIĆA

I DANILA

ISTARSKA OBALA

Franciscan
Monastery
& Church

OBALA KRALJA PETRA KREŠIMIRA IV

Sea Organ

Greeting to
the Sun

Bradt

N

0   200m
0   200 yds

1

2

3

4

5

6

7

8

9

10

11

12

196

Central Apartments [not mapped]
(9 apartments) Several locations; ☎023 380 717;
w centralapartments.hr. Good selection of nice
apartments in central Zadar. €€€

✳ **Boutique Hostel Forum** (111 beds) Široka
ulica 20; ☎023 250 705; **w** hostelforumzadar.com/
en. Excellent modern hostel in the centre of the
old town (quads, twins & dbls), with good b/fast.
Friendly, efficient, good value & supremely stylish, &
hands-down the best location in Zadar, overlooking
the Forum. Highly recommended. €€€–€€

Borik

Adriana (48 rooms) Majstora Radovana 7; ☎023
555 600; **w** falkensteiner.com. Falkensteiner's
adult-only offering in the area, with its own
spa. €€€€€
Club Funimation Borik (306 rooms) Majstora
Radovana 7; ☎023 206 100; **w** falkensteiner.com.
Large, smart, family-friendly, all-inclusive 4-star,
with oodles of swimming pools & plenty to keep
kids entertained. Well worth getting HB. €€€€€
Mediteran (30 rooms) Matije Gupca 19; ☎023
337 500; **w** mediteran.hr. One of the better
hotels in Borik, with nice dbls with balconies &
sea-views. €€€
HI Youth Hostel (294 beds) Obala Kneza Trpimira
76; ☎023 331 145; **w** hicroatia.com. Located
between Borik marina & Borik beach. €€–€

WHERE TO EAT AND DRINK *Map, opposite*

The city boasts lively cafés and bars, with terraces spilling out on to the pavements,
as well as a handful of good restaurants. This is the place to try Zadar's most famous
speciality, Maraskino, a cherry liqueur first made by monks at the Dominican
Monastery in the 16th century and produced here commercially since the 1820s. It
was long Austrian royalty's most popular tipple, and apparently, Ernest Hemingway
and Alfred Hitchcock were partial to it, too. Even if it's a touch *démodé* now, that
shouldn't stop you from trying it. Once. Široka ulica – more commonly known as
Kalelarga – is lined with a whole string of ice-cream shops (particularly as you get
closer to the Forum), serving some stupendously good flavours.

✳ **Corte** Braće Bersa 2; ☎023 335 357;
🕐 08.00–23.00 daily. Romantic restaurant
serving refined contemporary Mediterranean
specialities, in a courtyard garden at the Almayer
Art & Heritage Hotel (page 195) in Zadar's old
town. €€€€
Kornat Liburnska 6; ☎023 254 501;
w restaurant-kornat.hr; 🕐 noon–midnight Mon–
Sat. Old-fashioned fine dining on the waterside
promenade in Zadar's old town. Worth a splurge
for the classic Dalmatian fish & meat mains infused
with a Mediterranean twist. €€€€
✳ **Foša** Kralja Dmitra Zvonimira 2; ☎023 314
421; **w** fosa.hr; 🕐 noon–midnight daily. Dine

on fresh seafood on the terrace of the restaurant
at the eponymous gate. The grilled squid & Swiss
chard (*blitva*) are highly recommended. €€€€
Dva Ribara Blaža Jurjeva 1; ☎023 213 445;
w 2ribara.com; 🕐 noon–23.00 daily. Very good
place serving a modern take on Dalmatian fish &
seafood dishes. €€€
Gourmet Kalelarga Majke Margarite 3; ☎023
233 000; 🕐 07.00–23.00 daily. Expect carefully
presented Mediterranean fare at the restaurant of
the Art Hotel Kalelarga (page 195), much loved by
locals & visitors alike. €€€
Pet Bunara Stratico 1; ☎023 224 010;
w petbunara.com; 🕐 noon–22.00 Wed–Mon.

Zadar and Northern Dalmatia ZADAR

6

197

Slick restaurant serving Creative Mediterranean cuisine, with an emphasis on local, seasonal organic ingredients & quality Dalmatian wines. €€€

Bistro Pjat Stomorica 10; ✎023 213 919; ⓕ bistropjatzadar; ⏱ Dec–Oct 10.30–23.00 Mon–Sat. Cosy, welcoming eatery doing authentic homemade meals based on whatever the owner finds at the morning market. €€

Konoba Stomorica Stomorica 5; m 099 488 3694; ⓕ konoba.stomorica; ⏱ Mar–Oct noon–midnight daily. Informal eatery serving traditional Dalmatian fare at outdoor tables in Zadar's old town. €€

✳ **Pizzeria Tri Bunara** Jurja Bijankinija 8c; w pizzeria-tri-bunara.com; ⏱ 08.30–23.00 Mon–Fri, noon–23.00 Sat–Sun. Good-value, unpretentious pizzeria, serving tasty pizzas, salads & lasagne, behind Hotel Bastion. €€

WHAT TO SEE AND DO All of Zadar's sights are in the old town, within a few hundred metres of each other. They're ordered in the text from the northwestern corner, working back towards the southeast. To get to the start, either walk along the tree-lined, sea-facing promenade (a nice place for a picnic) or walk around the remains of the town walls facing the harbour – these are mostly 16th-century Venetian, though you'll see Roman fragments, particularly near the footbridge across the harbour. Note that Zadar's fortifications are part of the UNESCO-listed 'Venetian Works of Defence between the 16th and 17th centuries: Stato da Terra – Western Stato da Mare', along with five other fortification systems in Italy, Croatia and Montenegro.

The **Franciscan Monastery and Church** (Franjevački Samostan i Crkva; ⏱ 10.00–14.00 Mon–Fri; €5) dates back to the 13th century, but it's been much remodelled since and you wouldn't know it wasn't entirely 18th-century Baroque these days. The choir stalls inside are late 14th century, however, and the treasury – rarely open – houses some important works, including a big 12th-century crucifix. The monastery's fine cloisters are mid-16th-century Renaissance.

From here it's a stone's throw (if they haven't finished tidying up the piles of Roman rubble) to the site of the **Roman Forum**. Originally 90m by 45m, the forum would have made a decent-sized football pitch. Until the 19th century, criminals were tied to the pillar here, and… well, pilloried, I suppose.

Many of the original bits of Roman stonework ended up in the solid church that dominates what's left of the forum today. The Church of the Holy Trinity (deconsecrated) was started in the 9th century by Bishop Donat and has been known as **St Donat's** (Sv Donata) ever since. It's a 27m-high structure, built on a circular ground plan, and each summer its tall interior is used for classical music recitals during the Musical Evenings at St Donatus (w donat-festival.com) rather than religious worship. Look out for everything from upside-down capitals to gravestones to altars to whole pillars within the structure of the walls – all Roman. Parts of the floor, too, are the original Roman flagstones. You can walk upstairs to the gallery, looking down into the church, but don't lean on the handrails, as they're not very sturdy and it's a long way down.

Round the corner from St Donat's is the triple-naved Romanesque **Cathedral of St Anastasia** (Sv Stošije) dating from the 12th and 13th centuries (⏱ Apr–Oct 09.00–18.00 Mon–Sat, Nov–Mar 08.00–17.00 Mon–Sat). Badly bombed during World War II, it was painstakingly rebuilt afterwards. The façade features an attractive series of blind arches and two rosette windows. Inside there are some 13th-century frescoes, a 14th-century altar canopy (sheltering an altar containing bits of 9th-century stonework), some 15th-century choir stalls and the marble sarcophagus commissioned by Donat in the 9th century to house the mortal remains of St Anastasia herself.

Behind the cathedral, the bottom half of the lovely **campanile** (worth the climb for superb views; ☉ same hours as cathedral; €3) dates from the 15th century, though it wasn't completed until the 1890s, to a design by the British architect (and sometime writer of ghost stories) Sir Thomas Graham Jackson. Given the centuries-old rivalry between the bishops of Zadar and Rab, and Rab having lost its bishopric in 1828, it can only have been professional irony that made Jackson model his campanile on Rab's most famous bell tower. Or perhaps simply he was very good at copying things – his most famous work in England is the Bridge of Sighs, in Oxford. He did get away – for a while – with one amusing prank, however, which was to make the bell tower play 'God Save the Queen'.

Across the forum is **St Mary's Church** (Sv Marija) – the squat, 16th-century Renaissance front hides a church originally consecrated in the 11th century, along with a few more bits of the Roman forum. Behind it stands yet another Rab-like campanile, though this one's original, dating back to the early 12th century.

Next to this is Zadar's excellent **Church Museum** (Crkva Muzej; ☉ summer 10.00–13.00 & 17.00–19.00 Mon–Sat, 10.00–13.00 Sun; winter 10.00–12.30 & 17.00–18.30 Mon–Sat; €5), which houses a wonderful collection of reliquaries, paintings and sculpture, presented in a dazzling permanent exhibition, *The Gold and Silver of Zadar*. Nearby, in a modern building, there's the **Archaeological Museum** (Arheološki muzej; Trg opatice Čike 1; ☏023 250 542; w amzd.hr; ☉ Jul–Aug 09.00–21.00 daily, Jun & Sep 09.00–20.00 daily, Apr–May & Oct 09.00–15.00 Mon–Sat, Nov–Mar 09.00–14.00 Mon–Fri; €5), a fine collection, carefully displayed and labelled, from Liburnian times on, including some of the finest medieval sculpture in Croatia.

Continue from the Forum to the waterfront (Obala Kralja Petra Krešimira IV) and turn right, which will bring you to Zadar's two large outdoor art installations, the **Sea Organ** (Morske orgulje) and **Greeting to the Sun** (Pozdrav suncu). Both designed by local architect Nikola Bašić, these are, for many visitors, the city's most memorable attractions. The *Greeting to the Sun*, on the tip of the peninsula, is *the* place to watch the sun set over the islands. Installed in 2008, it is a circle of 300 glass plates set into the stone paving – solar-powered light-sensitive modules activate a multi-coloured light display come sunset. The white stone steps down to the water by the *Sea Organ* are a popular spot for swimming. Installed in 2005, the organ is made up of 35 pipes set inside the steps. They open out to the sea to create slightly haunting humming and moaning sounds powered by the ebb and flow of the tide and the prevailing wind. You can't see anything as the pipes are hidden within the stonework, but you will surely hear the organ from afar.

Heading towards the harbour, the 12th-century Romanesque **Church of St Grisogonus** (also called Chrysogonus – Krševan in Croatian) is all that's left of one of Croatia's oldest monasteries, founded in AD908. The outside, with its rows of blind arches and a pretty Tuscan-inspired colonnade on the back of the church, is more endearing than the rather shabby 13th- and 14th-century frescoes inside.

The town gate leading on to the harbour, down from St Grisogonus, contains all that's left of a **Roman triumphal arch** from Trajan's time. Back inside the walls, head towards Narodni trg, the heart of business life in medieval times, now overlooked by an impressive clock tower. The **town hall** features fine reliefs of Šibenik Cathedral and Diocletian's Palace in Split, while the 16th-century **loggia** across the square, with unusually tall pillars, does service these days as a gallery.

Heading towards the city gate leading to the footbridge over the harbour, turn right up a flight of steps to reach Zadar's excellent **Museum of Ancient Glass** (Muzej Antičkog Stakla; Poljana Zemaljskog odbora 1; ☏023 363 831; w mas-zadar.hr; ☉ May–Oct 09.00–21.00 daily, Nov–Mar 09.00–16.00 Mon–Sat; €6).

Opened in 2009, it has a magnificent collection of glassware from the 1st century BC to the 5th century AD from the surrounding area, well displayed and labelled, and is one of the best museums in Croatia. On the ground floor, it hosts glass-blowing demonstrations (🕐 09.00–14.00 Mon–Fri, 09.00–13.00 Sat) and has a marvellous gift shop stocking replicas of ancient glass jugs, bottles, beakers and jewellery.

A block east of Narodni trg is the **Church of St Simeon** (Sv Šimeon). The Baroque building itself can't compete with Zadar's other churches, but **St Simeon's Sarcophagus**, inside, certainly can. Commissioned in 1377 and delivered in 1380, it's an impressively chunky burnished silver and gold coffin, with dramatic reliefs on the front and a life-sized portrait of the saint on the lid, complete with swept-back hair and bushy eyebrows. For more detail come on the saint's feast day, 8 October, and you'll find even more silverwork and some fine reliquaries on the inside, when the sarcophagus is opened up for its annual inspection. (If you don't see it here, there's a very good copy in Zagreb, in the atrium of the building that houses the Strossmayer Gallery.)

Trg Pet Bunara ('the square of five wells'), nearby, was the town's main water supply for centuries – the Romans, of course, had proper running water, but from medieval times until the arrival of the businesslike Austrians, the underground cistern here was as good as plumbing got.

From here the easiest way out is through the **Land Gate** (Kopnena vrata). On the outside of this there's a big relief of a no-nonsense Venetian lion – the open Bible tells you that Venice was at peace at the time. The miniature harbour nearby is all that's left of the defensive moat that once protected the city.

Note that the once very popular Garden Festival no longer takes place near Zadar in Petrčane, but has moved to the 'Garden Resort' in Tisno (page 229).

AROUND ZADAR

NIN, ZATON AND PETRČANE When you've run out of things to do in Zadar, an excursion can be made up to the gorgeous little town of **Nin**, north along the coast from Zadar beyond Petrčane and Zaton.

Nin was an important settlement already in Roman times, and even more so as a religious centre in the Middle Ages – witness Meštrović's enormous statue of **Gregorius of Nin** in Nin and Split (and the far smaller version of the same, in Varaždin).

These days (and for most of the past thousand years, if truth be told), Nin's a quiet town on its own little island, connected to the mainland by a pair of bridges. There's not a whole lot to see and do, but the tiny and rather perfect **Church of the Holy Cross** (Sv Križa) is Croatia's oldest (from around AD800), and you can absorb some more history at the local **Archaeological Museum** (Muzej Ninskih Starina; ☎023 264 160; 🕐 Jul–Aug 09.00–14.00 & 18.00–22.00 daily, Sep 09.00–19.00 daily, May–Jun & Oct 09.00–14.00 Mon–Sat; €4). When you're done, there are several sandy beaches nearby in the lagoon and at **Sabunike** (though you have to wade out a long way before getting knee deep!), with views across to the Velebit massif nearby. Nin's waters offer popular venues for windsurfing and kitesurfing – a reliable provider is **Kiteboarding Croatia** (w kiteboarding-croatia.com).

On the road out from Zadar to Nin, you'll pass the beach destinations of **Petrčane** – home to slick new family-oriented resorts out at Punta Skala – and **Zaton**, where there's also a colossal modern resort and one of northern Dalmatia's best beaches, if sea and sunshine are your thing.

There's a regular bus service to Nin/Zaton from Zadar's main bus station, running every hour or so (timetables at w liburnija-zadar.hr).

Where to stay and eat

Iadera Hotel & Spa (210 rooms) Punta Skala, Petrčane; ☎023 555 911; w falkensteiner.com. Falkensteiner's top-end offering at Punta Skala. Slick & stylish with excellent spa facilities & impressive sunset views. €€€€€
Falkensteiner Family Hotel Diadora (230 rooms) Punta Skala, Petrčane; ☎023 555 911; w falkensteiner.com. Upmarket family-oriented

hotel with plenty of activities & entertainment for kids. €€€€
Zaton Holiday Resort (Over 600 units) Zaton; ☎023 280 280; w zaton.hr. Apartments, mobile homes & glamping by Zaton's great swath of sandy beach, surrounded by shady pine trees. Restaurants, supermarket. Great for kids, with outdoor pools & playgrounds. €€€€–€€€

SOUTH TO VRANSKO JEZERO South of Zadar are a string of unpretentious resort towns leading to the island of **Murter**, connected to the mainland by a bridge and the best jumping-off point for the Kornati archipelago (page 225).

On the way, just past **Biograd** (where you can catch the ferry to Pašman; page 224), is Croatia's largest natural lake, Vransko Jezero – turn left as you approach Pakoštane, 5km south of Biograd, and then right after just under 2km.

Already an ornithological reserve since 1983, **Lake Vrana Nature Park** (Park Prirode Vransko jezero; w pp-vransko-jezero.hr; €5/€2.50 adult/child) was declared as a nature park in 1999 in a bid to reinforce the protection of its unique habitat and birdlife, and was declared a RAMSAR site (Wetland of International Importance) in 2012. The lake is nearly 14km long and between 1.5 and 3.5km wide and has a surface area of over 30km², but it's never more than 4m deep. A channel that was dug at the end of the 18th century, in an attempt to drain the lake, now provides it with an occasional top-up of saltwater at high tide, and it's also partly connected with the sea by underground fissures in the limestone.

A total of 260 bird species have been recorded here, while 87 species over-winter in the park and 102 nest here – including a small colony of rare purple herons. You can also expect to see marsh harriers, ducks, terns and white egrets, and 100,000 coots, which over-winter here.

The nature park offers guided tours by kayak or bike (both available for hire), as well as a range of educational birdwatching and biodiversity programmes. There are six well-marked thematic hiking trails and cycle trails around the lake (though some sections are apt to be fairly rough, so a decent mountain bike is advised), and bird hides are in place in the ornithological reserve at the northern end of the lake.

There's a road running behind the hills on the lake's northeastern shore that goes from the village of Vrana to the settlement of **Banjevci**. If you turn up the gravel road to the right here, it leads steeply up a Križni Put (Way of the Cross) to a small chapel on top of the hills, built as a memorial to the people who were thrown into a deep sinkhole here by the partisans at the end of World War II. There's a café (very welcome in the summer, when it gets seriously hot up here) and souvenir shop, and a good path beyond leading up to Kamenjak, a rocky hilltop with unrivalled views out west over the lake and the Kornati archipelago.

For more information, contact the park office (Kralja P Svačića 2, Biograd; ☎023 383 181; ⊕ 07.00–15.00 daily) or to learn more about Lake Vrana and the region's other nature parks, call at the Multimedia Visitor Centre BioSfera Biograd (Trg Kralja Tomislava 1, Biograd; ⊕ May–Sep 08.30–21.30 Wed–Mon).

In the village of Vrana, a superb but rather expensive place to stay is **Maškovića Han Heritage Hotel** (Vrana Marina 1; ☎023 333 230; w maskovicahan.hr; €€€€€), the 17th-century summer home of an Ottoman admiral, designed as a sturdy fortress, which has been carefully restored and turned into a 16-room boutique hotel with a restaurant and spa.

PAKLENICA NATIONAL PARK

(w np-paklenica.hr; ⊕ Jun–Sep €10, Oct–Apr €4–6; a 3-day climbing pass is €5.30–20, inc entrance ticket, or €7.90–30 for 5 days) Situated halfway between Karlobag and Zadar – an hour from either, by bus – is Paklenica National Park, a pair of wonderful limestone gorges running up from the sea, deep into the Velebit massif. Popular with Croatian walkers and climbers, it is truly spectacular, offering everything from a gentle stroll to a seriously strenuous trek, and pitches for rock climbers of every level.

The park was opened in 1949 and is unusually interesting for both climatic and physical reasons. Situated under the highest peak of the Velebit massif (Vaganski Vrh, 1,757m), the area experiences three distinct climates – coastal, continental and sub-alpine. The rock is Velebit karst (page 4), and walking is possible from sea level up to the top of the massif.

Most of the lower reaches are heavily forested with deciduous trees, while higher up mountain pastures support sub-alpine flowers and herbs. One of the most attractive features of the park, however, is the more than 100 species of butterfly found here, making it a lepidopterist's paradise.

There are also lots of beetles and several reptiles (you'll see snakes slithering off the path as you approach) and amphibians, and an extraordinary 260 species of bird to watch out for. In the remoter parts of the park, you might spot rare species such as peregrine falcons, golden eagles and eagle owls, as well as various types of woodpecker.

On the other hand, you're equally certain not to come in contact with the bears that live in the furthest reaches of the park – they're extremely discreet.

GETTING THERE AND AWAY All buses up the coast from Zadar towards Rijeka make three Paklenica-related stops. From south to north, the first stop is at Seline (closest to the southern gorge, Mala Paklenica), the second is at the Bluesun Holiday Village Alan (the closest stop to the main entrance to the park), and the last is at Starigrad Paklenica.

Although there are lots of buses up and down the coast, leaving in the middle of summer can be harder than arriving, as it depends on the passing buses not being full already. Early mornings are generally better than other times of day, but it's not a guaranteed recipe for success.

WHERE TO STAY *Map, opposite*
The stretch of coast along here is one of the easiest places in Croatia for accommodation, though not one of the most luxurious.

You can't **camp** within the park itself, but there is a staffed mountain hut and several unstaffed mountain shelters along the massif. The main campsite, Camping Paklenica, is across the road from the entrance to the park, next to the Bluesun Holiday Village Alan, and is actually attached to the hotel (page 204). Other smaller campsites are along the road north and south of town.

There are any number of **private rooms** in the area, including some on the trail up into the park. No official agency handles these, so your best bet is to book in advance online or alternatively (but risky in peak season) wander up and down

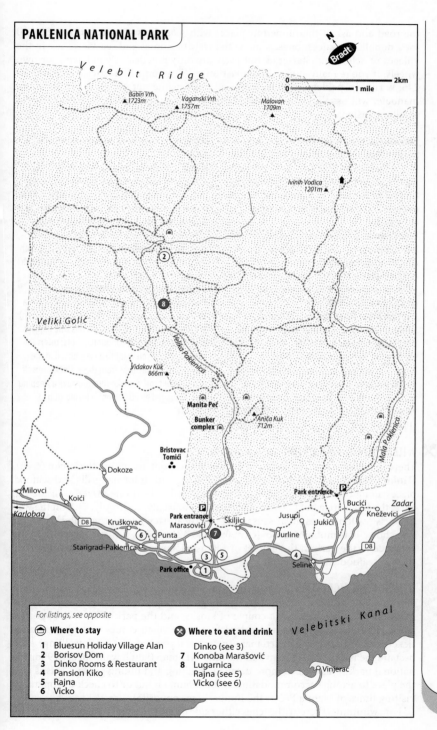

PAKLENICA NATIONAL PARK

For listings, see opposite

🛏 **Where to stay**

1 Bluesun Holiday Village Alan
2 Borisov Dom
3 Dinko Rooms & Restaurant
4 Pansion Kiko
5 Rajna
6 Vicko

🍴 **Where to eat and drink**

   Dinko (see 3)
7 Konoba Marašović
8 Lugarnica
   Rajna (see 5)
   Vicko (see 6)

the road and ask at the numerous places with *sobe* signs – expect to pay €60–80 for a double. The nicest ones, some with lovely balconies and sea-views, are in the villages of Seline and Starigrad, but these are only practical if you have your own wheels. If you're really stuck, the **tourist office** (Trg Tome Marasovića 1; ✆023 369 245; w rivijera-paklenica.hr) in Starigrad itself, while not having a private-room mandate, will usually help you out. There are also three hotels and a number of smaller pansions.

Bluesun Holiday Village Alan (187 rooms, 34 mobile homes) Dr Franje Tuđmana 14; ✆023 209 050; w bluesunhotels.com. Out on the main coast road is this 1970s high-rise hotel, now revamped & part of the Bluesun chain & with a great location on the beach & good views. Also has a campsite (€). €€€€

Dinko Rooms & Restaurant (6 apartments, 2 rooms) Paklenička 1, Starigrad-Paklenica; m 098 402 007; w dinko-paklenica.com. Much loved by rock climbers since 1965, family-run Dinko (€€€) has been welcoming diners, as well as overnight guests, since 2013. €€€

Pansion Kiko (10 rooms) Ante Starčevića 7, Seline; m 098 1643 743. Good-value, family-run pansion, peaceful location by the sea, 5mins' drive southeast of Starigrad Paklenica. €€€

Vicko (23 rooms) Jose Dokoze 20; ✆023 369 304; w hotel-vicko.hr. Small, cheerful & family-run, with nice rooms in the main hotel & lovely sea-view rooms. Also has a 4-star annexe, **Villa Vicko** (16 rooms, 2 apartments), just across the street. In

addition, the hotel has a good restaurant (€€€). €€€

Rajna (10 rooms) Dr Franje Tuđmana 105; ✆023 359 121; w hotel-rajna.com. Good-value family-run place right by the entrance to the park, with its own restaurant (€€€). They offer hiking, biking & kayaking tours, & also have renovated stone guesthouses at Varoš (3 interconnected houses sleeping up to a total of 10, €420/night), & within the national park itself at the hamlet of Marasovići (sleeps 4, €115/night). €€

Borisov Dom (aka Planinarski Dom Paklenica) (50 dorm beds) Starigrad-Paklenica bb; ✆023 301 636; m 097 755 7654 (Irena Šaran); ☉ Jun–Sep daily, Oct–May w/ends. The biggest & best equipped of the mountain huts, this is the place to stay if you want to base yourself in the valley & make day trips from there. Book yourself in ahead of time, & make sure you have a sleeping bag. Managed by PD Paklenica hiking club in Zadar. €

✖ WHERE TO EAT AND DRINK   *Map, page 203*

There is a whole clutch of places where you can eat out, including the **Vicko** (€€€), **Dinko** (€€€) and **Rajna** (€€€; see above), along with informal grills and seafood places along the main road and on the shore, and at least one pizzeria. Inside the park, the **Lugarnica** hut (☉ May–Oct 10.00–17.00 daily; cash-only; €€), on the way to Borisov Dom, does great sausages, grah (bean stew) and other food. Another fine choice is **Konoba Marašović** (m 091 588 4213; €€€), a rustic tavern near the entrance to the park in the hamlet of Marasovići, serving typical Dalmatian fare, such as seafood and roast lamb.

OTHER PRACTICALITIES Everything you need is within easy reach of the park entrance, including a supermarket with good long opening hours and all the makings of a decent picnic, a couple of kiosks, and the park office (see opposite) itself. Here you'll be given a standard free map which comes with the entrance ticket, and you can buy detailed maps (essential if you're doing much walking) – the best are the national park map and the SMAND map (you'll want sheet #19 for the national park) – as well as more detailed climbing and hiking guides. This is also the place to arrange accommodation at the mountain hut or to check the opening/visiting times of Manita Peć or the Bunkers (see opposite).

For swimming, there are beaches either side of the Bluesun Holiday Village Alan.

EXPLORING THE NATIONAL PARK The national park's geomorphology consists primarily of a horizontal plateau running between the Velebit massif and the sea. Two gorge valleys, Velika and Mala (large and small) Paklenica, with cliffs over 400m high in places, cut through this to the sea, and there are also several networks of subterranean caves. The most famous of these is Manita Peć, which has been explored for nearly 200m of its depth into the mountain and contains two enormous halls.

Because of its triple climate, the weather is unusually variable. It's one of the few places where you might be drenched by rain, then sunburned and finally hailed on, before going for an afternoon swim in the sea. Prepare for all weathers, especially in May and early June, when there's still snow on the north-facing slopes above 1,500m. In high summer the inner parts of the park can be fearsomely hot, but even when the sun's shining on the coast, localised storms can see you hailed on.

There are two official routes into the park, up the two canyons. The main entrance is up a clearly marked road 300m south of Bluesun Holiday Village Alan. A brisk kilometre up here brings you to the park office, where you buy your ticket and maps, after which it's a further 2km to the end of the road and the car park. You'll come across the entrance here to what used to be one of Paklenica's greatest secrets, the enormous **bunker complex** (🕐 Apr–Oct 09.00–15.00 daily) built for Tito in the 1950s as a crisis headquarters in times of war. For decades nobody was allowed to even mention its existence, but you can now visit parts of the huge complex, and it's a fascinating glimpse into the paranoia of power. Since July 2022, there has been a visitors' centre and café here; contact the park administration for more details (Paklenička ulica, Starigrad; 📞023 369 155; w np-paklenica.hr).

The other entrance to the park is up Mala Paklenica, 4km south, just after and opposite the Church of St Mark. Turn inland and it's nearly 2km to the clearly visible canyon entrance, where you can park.

Anića Kuk
This is easily the most-climbed peak in the national park. There are something like 25 routes up the sheer west and north faces, and these are all serious climbs that shouldn't be attempted without ropes and proper climbing equipment and experience. There's also a good walking route to the 712m summit, which makes for a fine 6-hour return trip from Bluesun Holiday Village Alan (4½hrs if you have a car).

Anića Kuk is not high, but it's an isolated, exposed peak and the nearest major summit to the sea. The side facing into the gorge is a near-vertical drop of over 400m; don't stray too close to the edge.

The walking route follows Velika Paklenica upstream from the car park on a well-made erosion-avoiding paved road until you reach a sharp uphill left-hand bend, hard on the river, after half an hour. Cross the river here at the sign and follow the faded red and white markers towards the base of the cliff, and then up to the left below the cliff in a wide sweep up through woods and scrub before emerging on to naked karst, where a path continues to the summit.

It's a bit of a scramble and can be hard on the hands, but another half an hour brings you to the airy, vertiginous summit, which is easily worth it for the fabulous views out across to the barren island of Pag.

Manita Peć
(2hrs) This trail takes in the dramatically beautiful cave at Manita Peć. The walk is sometimes steep but never difficult, taking around 2 hours from Bluesun Holiday Village Alan, with beautiful views out over the gorge. Manita Peć

itself can only be visited with a guide. It should be open (⊕ Jul–Sep 10.00–13.00 daily, May–Jun & Oct 10.00–13.00 Mon, Wed & Sat; €3.90) – check at the park office before you head up here, to avoid disappointment.

From the car park, head up the gorge for around 30 minutes until the path levels out (turning from paved to grit). After a short while there's the sign to Anića Kuk to the right, and indicators to Lugarnica (30mins) and Planinarski Dom (Borisov Dom, 50mins). It's not far from here to the path heading off to the right, which eventually leads to Mala Paklenica (page 207), after which you soon reach the sign saying 40 minutes to Manita Peć, and that's about how long you should allow to cover the long zigzags heading uphill to the left, to the cave at 550m.

The cave itself – like most caves – is nothing special outside, but inside it's marvellous. A tunnel-like entrance leads through to two huge chambers, some 40m long and 40–65m wide, with a height of over 30m. The atmospheric artificial lighting shows off the stalactites and stalagmites, and the weird dripstone pillars. Nature's a wonderful thing.

Blinking outside in the daylight, there's an unmarked (and very hard to find) path up to Vidakov Kuk, which heads off to the left (with your back to the cave). However, despite Vidakov Kuk having splendid views, following the trail up from Manita Peć is really *not* advised. For a start, it's poorly marked, rough and largely overgrown. Secondly, the section where it climbs steeply uphill a few minutes beyond Manita Peć has been used as an open toilet by less considerate visitors. Bear in mind that you'd need to scramble up through this section, using your hands and probably slipping on the loose rock and scree a few times, and any interest in

STAYING ON THE RIGHT TRACK

Within the park, the trails marked on the map in red are marked in reality with red and white flashes on rocks and trees, and it's very rare that you can't easily see from one mark to the next. Some of the least-used paths may have faded markings, but others will impress you with their fresh brightness. There are also lots of paths used by local people that aren't guided on the ground; these are marked with dotted lines on the map. On the steeper paths you may well appreciate the use of a stick or walking poles, especially if it's been raining, as some of the trails can be pretty slippery.

A word of warning: it's highly inadvisable to leave the marked paths – high up in the park there are still minefields, while lower down you'll have to cross naked karst. And believe me, wild karst is awful stuff to cross – you'll find it extremely wearing, both mentally and on your clothes and hands. The shallowest slopes will confront you with jagged rocks, and even 2m climbs or drops are difficult.

Assistance in case of an emergency depends, in the first instance, on members of your party or other walkers and climbers – there is a mountain rescue service (w hgss.hr; in case of emergency in the mountains call ☏112), but they need to be alerted. It's a good idea, therefore, to let people know where you're headed before you set out.

Good, detailed local maps (published by the National Park Office and by SMAND; w smand.hr) are available through the park office or some of the larger bookshops in Zagreb and other cities. Rudolf Abraham's book *Walks and Treks in Croatia* (page 238) has details of hiking in Paklenica and other mountain areas in the country.

climbing Vidakov Kuk from this side should sensibly evaporate. Truly, there's no shortage of nicer walks in the national park!

Veliki Golić (10hrs) Some of the more spectacular views in Paklenica can be had from the long ridge of Veliki Golić, and an excellent 10-hour walk (8½ if you have a car) takes in this ridge and returns via Borisov Dom.

The walk starts exactly as if you were going to Manita Peć (page 205), but heads straight on when the path branches up and left to the cave. After half an hour you'll come to a water trough and a sign saying 'Borisov Dom 30 minutes'. The main path branches up to the left here, and 10 minutes further on you need to take the path branching steeply uphill, away from the river. Follow this up its zigzags for about 40 minutes, after which you'll come to a straighter section, with markings on the dry-stone wall leading to the farm at Ramići (not the only place named Ramići in the immediate vicinity, unfortunately).

The main marked trail leading through the farm leads up to Vidakov Kuk – the path you want, to Veliki Golić, is a hard right-hand turn, almost behind you as you arrive at the farm. From here, after skirting between a series of dry-stone walls, the path rises steadily, and you're soon a long way above the farm. The ground becomes rougher as the path skirts the 903m summit of Čelinka and crosses a rocky wood before surfacing on an open pasture. This leads directly to the corner of the ridge, level with the top of Čelinka. It takes about 2 hours from the river to this point, from which there are fine views down on to the refuge below, across to the peak of Anića Kuk and over to the sea.

The ridge is an extraordinary formation, consisting of a series of parallel broken limestone ridges at an angle of about 40 degrees. The valley side is nearly a sheer drop, but the side from which you've approached is relatively shallow, as is the line of the ridge itself, which takes the best part of 2km to rise from 900m to 1,285m. There are endless false crests to this, but the summit is superb, with spectacular panoramic views making the 4–5-hour ascent well worthwhile. Make sure you have appropriate clothing, however – this is where I was once caught in a late-May hailstorm.

The best way down is to continue along the ridge, scaling a secondary summit of 1,160m, before the path curves back on itself to bring you down to Borisov Dom. This takes around 2 hours, after which it's an easy 1½ hours back to the car park.

Mala and Velika Paklenica (10hrs) This is a terrific circular walk, including both gorges and some very fine views. It runs from Bluesun Holiday Village Alan to Seline, up Mala Paklenica, across the broad ridge between the two canyons and then down Velika Paklenica. It can be done in reverse, but with Mala Paklenica being the tougher walk, you're better off tackling it while you're fresh, preferably before it gets too hot.

If you take your time and aren't in a hurry, the walk takes around 10 hours, including the hour between the two villages, which you can't avoid unless someone gives you a lift, as you end up where you started. It's a pretty long, tough day out, so be prepared, but it's well worth the effort.

At the entrance to the Mala Paklenica gorge, the dirt road peters out and you're on the trail upstream. It's very rustic and empty compared to Velika Paklenica, and less well-marked at first, but the route is clear enough, starting on the left-hand side of the gully before crossing over to the other side. Unless there's been exceptional rain, the gully is dry from May to September.

As you enter the canyon proper the walls steepen, and the path becomes clearer and better marked. At the first big boulders on the valley floor the path climbs to the right, crossing the first of three assisted sections, with steel cables and well-secured pitons to help you up.

The next 2 hours are hard, ascending sharply, but the way the rock's been sculpted by flowing water, the small flowers and trees growing tenaciously from pockets in the cliffs, and the fine views should cheer you up. After a while you'll notice puddles on the valley floor, which gradually become a rivulet and eventually turn into a bubbling, refreshing stream. The path criss-crosses this on well-marked boulders.

When the gorge forks, take the left-hand one, following the stream. Some 20 minutes later, the path definitively leaves the stream, but only after a couple of false alarms, and then heads steeply uphill, zigzagging until you're at 650m. At the top there's a dry-stone wall clearly marked Sv Jakov, though there's no obvious church. This junction is easy to pinpoint on the map.

Take the left-hand of the two paths, marked Starigrad. The path is a bit indistinct here, running across pastures, but there are markers. If you lose these, head west-northwest until you join the marked path coming in from your right. At this point the trail starts down a rocky gully. It divides fairly often, but the correct path is always well-marked, eventually coming out at a small farm.

Leave the farm on the leftmost track, and then fork immediately right on the marked path. From here it's easy to find your way to the valley floor – even if there aren't signs, you can follow the donkey droppings, as you're now on the farm's access road. The path comes out suddenly and unexpectedly to the top edge of Velika Paklenica, and it's an ideal picnic spot – it's almost all downhill from here, and the views are great.

The path down is a steep, knee-testing zigzag – you might be grateful for walking poles here – until you reach the valley floor, after which it's an easy walk back to the entrance of Velika Paklenica.

Other walks The walks described from page 205 are only a fraction of what you can do in the area, particularly given that none of them even take you up on to the spectacular Velebit ridge.

You can also wander happily around at lower altitudes to the west of the park, discovering the abandoned and near-abandoned villages in the hills. One of these, **Bristovac Tomići** (the locals leave off the Bristovac), is the start of a good walk up to Vidakov Kuk and provides a poignant look at a world where electricity supplies, running water and central heating never quite caught on.

The more ambitious, however, will want to scale the region's highest peak, **Vaganski Vrh**, just 73m lower than Croatia's highest point, Dinara. Bear in mind, however, that the ridge hasn't entirely been de-mined, so discuss your route with the park staff before heading off and stay on the marked trails.

While an ascent of Vaganski Vrh is possible to complete within a day from the park's entrance, the 14-hour minimum round trip isn't for the faint-hearted, and you need to set off very early in the morning indeed and be extremely well-equipped – friends who've done it reckoned that 2 litres of water per person was nothing like enough.

Better by far is to stay overnight at Borisov Dom or one of the other mountain huts and start the 5–6-hour climb to the summit from there. On a clear day they say you can see Italy on one side and a good 100km into Bosnia on the other, but those days do tend to come in winter, when a combination of snow and a vicious *bura* (northeasterly wind) are likely to dissuade you from making the ascent at all.

Best of all is a three-day circuit covering the **Velebit ridge** – again, discuss your route in detail with the park staff before heading out, and remember there are still mines in the ground. On the first day head up Mala Paklenica, going straight on instead of left at Sv Jakov (page 212), and then right instead of straight on at the junction for Borisov Dom. The route then skirts left of the 999m summit of Martinovo Mirilo, eventually reaching the Ivine Vodice hut at 1,200m, where you can stay the night (check it's open, of course, before you start out).

Day two then starts with the climb up to the ridge and the chance to reach the summits of Malovan (1,709m, around 4hrs from the refuge) and Vaganski Vrh (1,758m), among others, before coming down at Borisov Dom for the second night out. Bear in mind that it's a lot further on to Babin Vrh (1,723m) than you might think – count on 14 hours just from the Ivine Vodice hut – and that you don't want to get caught out at this altitude at any time of year.

Zrmanja Canyon Immediately south of Paklenica National Park, the emerald green **River Zrmanja** runs down through a dramatic rocky canyon to meet the sea at Novigrad. Various adventure sports companies organise half-day rafting and kayaking trips, taking you down a 12km route (generally from Kaštel Žegarski to Muškovci) over a series of spectacular waterfalls and rapids. Bring a bathing suit and trainers – you'll be given a wetsuit, life jacket and helmet. Rafting here is suitable for all ages, from 6 years and upwards. Reliable providers include **Adventure Dalmatia** (w adventuredalmatia.com), who also offer transfers from Zadar and back.

ŠIBENIK

Šibenik is something of an odd man out on the Dalmatian coast, firstly because it has no classical history – it was founded by the Croats and doesn't show up until the 11th century – and secondly because it's never really been considered a tourist town. Indeed, until the 1990s and the war with Serbia, it was a light industrial hub with a moderately busy port and nothing much in the way of either beaches or visitors.

It's well worth stopping here, however, not just for the cathedral – the most important piece of Renaissance architecture in Croatia (and classified by UNESCO as a World Heritage Site in 2000) – but also for its charming medieval old town, with three hillside fortresses and a fourth fortress guarding the sea channel, and its position as a springboard for trips into the Krka National Park and to the Kornati archipelago (pages 215 and 225).

By the end of the war in 1995, Šibenik's industrial base was in ruins, and during the second half of the 1990s, the town found it hard to recover, with high unemployment and consequently very little money around for spending. The past two decades seem to have brought with them new optimism, however, with the opening of several very good hotels plus a Michelin-starred restaurant, considered by many to be the best in all Croatia. It would be no exaggeration to say that Šibenik is now a discrete up-and-coming destination.

HISTORY After first being mentioned in 1066, Šibenik was tossed back and forth between Venetians, Hungarians, Byzantines, Croats and Bosnians, before knuckling definitively under Venice (1412–1797) and the Austro-Hungarian Empire (1797–1918). Italy was very briefly in control (only until 1920) before the city became Yugoslav and, finally, in 1991, Croatian.

The Venetians built the defensive walls (best preserved on the north side of town) running all the way up to the three recently restored hillside fortresses, and it was also under Venice that St Jacob's Cathedral was built, in fits and starts, over more than a century.

GETTING THERE AND AROUND Šibenik is easy to reach. The **bus** station is 200m south of the old town – there are regular buses up and down the coast, including several daily to Zadar (90mins) and Split (90mins). The train station (only serving local routes inland to Knin and Drniš) is a further 300m to the southeast. Both the bus and train stations have left-luggage facilities. Nearby, on the coast, a new port facility is under construction, which should open in late-2024. From Šibenik, a local Jadrolinija (**w** jadrolinija.hr) ferry sails several times daily up the coast to Vodice, stopping en route at the tiny car-free islands of Zlarin and Prvić. A second Jadrolinija ferry (☺ twice daily in summer; once daily in winter) sails to the island of Žirje, stopping at Zlarin and Kaprije en route.

Šibenik's old town is entirely pedestrianised, which is excellent, so once you've arrived you'll be on foot – it's all perfectly manageable, though the narrow streets running up to the fortresses are pretty steep.

TOURIST INFORMATION The friendly **tourist office** (Obala palih omladinaca 3; ☎ 022 214 411; **w** sibenik-tourism.hr), with town plans, etc is on the seafront promenade, at the foot of the old town. For those exploring the surrounding area, head for the **Šibenik County Tourist Office** (Nikole Ružića bb; ☎ 022 219 072; **w** dalmatiasibenik.hr).

WHERE TO STAY *Map, opposite*
If you're here for just a couple of nights, you'll probably want to stay in the old town to soak up the medieval atmosphere – you'll find a handful of cosy boutique hotels and a couple of hostels here. If you're looking for a hotel with extra facilities, such as a spa and pool, you'll need to stay out of town at one of several modern resorts. Alternatively, you might go for one of the slew of private rooms in shamelessly touristy **Vodice**, just 12km up the coast, which is enormously popular with Croatians and eastern Europeans and is connected to Šibenik by regular buses and the Jadrolinija ferry that stops at the tiny islands of Prvić and Zlarin.

D-Resort Šibenik (69 rooms) Obala Jerka Šizgorica 1; ☎ 022 331 452; **w** dresortsibenik. com. On Mandalina peninsula, 1.5km east of Šibenik's old town, this luxury hotel was designed by local architect Nikola Bašić (also responsible for Zadar's *Sea Organ*; page 199). Expect funky details, contemporary artwork & good eco-credentials. €€€€€

Amadria Park Šibenik (5 hotels) ☎ 022 361 001; **w** amadriapark.com. Formerly known as Solaris Beach Resort, this slick, modern resort lies outside town, on the waterfront facing the island of Zlarin. Hotels range from the large, upscale Ivan to the family-oriented & very child-friendly Andrija. Spa, pools, beach, campsite, restaurants, clubs & bars. €€€€

Panorama (20 rooms) Šibenski most 11; ☎ 022 213 398; **w** hotel-panorama.hr. The best alternative to staying in Šibenik itself is the smart, modern Panorama – 4km northwest of town, perched above the gorge of the River Krka by the

Šibenik Bridge, with great views. You can get here on the local bus to Zaton, or inter-city buses will drop you off (though they're unlikely to pick you up). €€€€

Heritage Life Palace Hotel (17 rooms) Ulica Kralja Tomislava 12; ☎ 022 219 005; **w** hotel-lifepalace.hr. Charming boutique hotel in a 16th-century palazzo, with a terrace restaurant on the square out front in the old town. €€€€–€€€

Jadran (57 rooms) Obala dr Franje Tuđmana 52; ☎ 022 454 488; **w** rivijera.eu. The old town's oldest hotel (built in 1961) is rather boxy & in need of a good makeover – but it has a lovely terrace café out front, where locals like to drink morning coffee overlooking the harbour. €€€

Hostel Sveti Lovre (30 beds) Andrije Kačića Miošića 11; ☎ 022 212 515; **w** hostelsvlovre.com. Hostel next to the Medieval Mediterranean Garden in Šibenik's old town. The 4 rooms, each sleeping 6–8 in bunk beds, are themed around medicinal herbs & decorated accordingly. €€

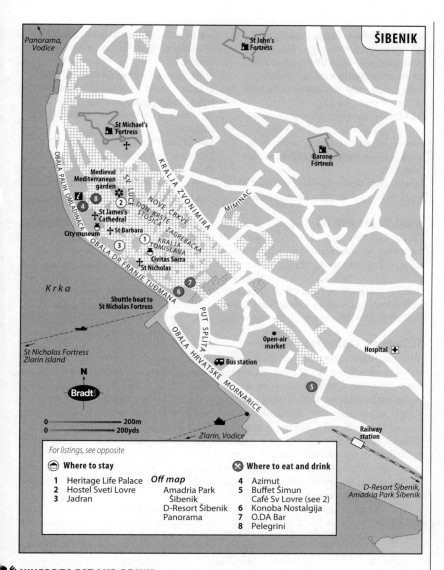

ŠIBENIK

Panorama, Vodice

St John's Fortress

St Michael's Fortress

Barone Fortress

KRALJA ZVONIMIRA

MIMINAC

NOVE CRKVE

DON KRSTE STOŠIĆA

SV LUCE

Medieval Mediterranean garden

8
4
2

St James's Cathedral

City museum

St Barbara

3

1

KRALJA TOMISLAVA ZAGREBAČKA

Civitas Sacra

St Nicholas

6
7

OBALA DR FRANJE TUĐMANA

OBALA PALIH OMLADINACA

Krka

Shuttle boat to St Nicholas Fortress

St Nicholas Fortress Zlarin island

PUT SPLITA

OBALA HRVATSKE MORNARICE

Open-air market

Hospital +

Bus station

5

Railway station

N

Bradt

0 ———— 200m
0 ———— 200yds

Zlarin, Vodice

D-Resort Šibenik, Amadria Park Šibenik

For listings, see opposite

Where to stay
1 Heritage Life Palace
2 Hostel Sveti Lovre
3 Jadran

Off map
   Amadria Park
   Šibenik
   D-Resort Šibenik
   Panorama

Where to eat and drink
4 Azimut
5 Buffet Šimun
   Café Sv Lovre (see 2)
6 Konoba Nostalgija
7 O.DA Bar
8 Pelegrini

Zadar and Northern Dalmatia   ŠIBENIK

6

✖ WHERE TO EAT AND DRINK *Map, above*

Like most Dalmatian towns, Šibenik's favourite food is fish, and, like everywhere else, it doesn't come cheap. If you want to splash out on one really outstanding meal while in Dalmatia, you might do it here, at Pelegrini. For more modest fare, Šibenik's also well supplied with pizzerias and snack bars, plus a succession of cheerful cafés and ice-cream parlours along the seafront.

✳ **Pelegrini** Jurja Dalmatinac 1; ✆ 022 213 701; w pelegrini.hr; ⊕ Apr–Oct 18.30–22.00 Mon–Sat. The nicest restaurant in town, & possibly the best in Croatia, overlooking the façade of the cathedral from a flight of stone steps , with additional tables in a walled courtyard. Serves truly delicious & creative cuisine, made from local seasonal ingredients. The holder of 1 Michelin star. €€€€€

Konoba Nostalgija Biskupa Fosca 11; ☎022 661 269; 🅵 konobanostalgija; ⊕ May–Sep 18.00–22.00 Mon–Sat. Highly regarded family-run restaurant using local seasonal produce to create a modern take on Dalmatian cuisine in the old town. €€€€

O.DA Bar Trg Ivana Gorana Kovačića 1; 🅼 091 592 3607; 🅵 O.DA.bar; ⊕ 09.00–15.00 Mon–Fri. Tiny vegetarian eatery, serving vegan salads, hummus wraps, smoothies & homemade cakes. €€€

Azimut Obala palih omladinaca 2; 🆆 azimut.art; 🅵; ⊕ 09.00–midnight daily. Alternative venue near the cathedral, hosting concerts & exhibitions, with tables on the seafront promenade serving drinks. €€

Buffet Šimun Fra Jerolima Milete 17; ☎022 212 674; ⊕ 08.00–22.00 Mon–Sat. Reasonably priced authentic Dalmatian meals, just like locals eat at home, at this friendly eatery near the train station. €€

Café Sv Lovre Andrije Kačića Miošića 11; ☎022 215 515; 🆆 hostelsvlovre.com; ⊕ Apr–Oct 09.00–21.00 daily. In the Medieval Mediterranean Garden, this romantic café serves light meals plus local wine, herbal teas & ice cream. €€

WHAT TO SEE AND DO Šibenik's must-see is the wonderful cathedral – a UNESCO World Heritage Site. The old town itself is also a joy to explore, with its three imposing hillside fortresses, which you can arrive upon by way of any number of narrow flagged streets, medieval archways and a mix of Gothic, Renaissance and Baroque buildings. Otherwise, the rest of the old town is really its own attraction, though there are several other churches worth visiting (notably **St Nicholas** and **St Barbara**), as well as a small **City Museum** (Gradski Muzej; 🆆 muzej-sibenik.hr; ⊕ 08.00–20.00 Mon–Fri, 10.00–20.00 Sat; €5).

St James's Cathedral

(Sv Jakov; ⊕ summer 08.30–20.00 daily, winter 08.30–noon & 16.00–20.00 daily; €5) This triple-aisled basilica with three apses and a cupola, was started in 1431 but not completed until 1536, and reflects the transition from Venetian Gothic to Tuscan Renaissance. What makes it unique, however, is the extraordinary barrel vaulting, consisting of stones chiselled to fit together snugly using carpentry techniques, and leading to the cathedral's exterior being almost identical to its interior – something you won't see in any other church. It's difficult to get a good look at the roof from outside, as the town crowds up to the cathedral, but postcards – or a hike up to the St Anne Fortress – will give you a good idea. A result of the design is also that the façade is the only one in Europe able to reflect the true shape of the triple-aisled church behind it – all the others are effectively stage scenery, stuck on for effect.

The cathedral is largely the work of Juraj Dalmatinac (George the Dalmatian), a sculptor who was born in Zadar but rose to fame in Venice (perhaps under the tutelage of Donatello). He was chief architect here, on and off, from the early 1440s until his death in 1473. The extraordinary frieze on the outside of the cathedral of 74 individual heads running round the apses (a fabulous glimpse of 15th-century life), along with the stunning baptistery inside the big echoing church, are his finest works. In front of the cathedral, you'll find a Meštrović statue of him.

The north side of the cathedral makes up one side of the elegant Trg Republika Hrvatske; the other is occupied by a fine loggia, built between 1533 and 1542. Originally the town hall, the version you see today is mostly a post-war reconstruction, following the 1943 bombing of the town – though no less lovely for that.

Nearby, at **Civitas Sacra** (Kralja Tomislava 10; 🆆 civitassacra.hr; ⊕ Jun–Oct 08.00–20.00 Mon–Sat, Nov–May 08.00–16.00 Mon–Sat; €5), you can discover how the cathedral was constructed, through an interactive presentation and augmented reality.

St Michael's, Barone and St John's fortresses Be sure to hike up through town to see St Michael's Fortress, Barone Fortress and St John's Fortress (**w** tvrdjava-kulture.hr), each affording magnificent views over Šibenik's terracotta rooftops and out across the bay. St Michael's Fortress has a rooftop stage hosting open-air summer concerts – Einsturzende Neubauten and Bryan Ferry have both played here.

Walking up to St Michael's Fortress takes you past the pretty **Medieval Mediterranean Garden** (Andrije Kačića Miošića 11; ⊕ summer 08.00–23.00 daily, winter 09.00–16.00 daily) of the Franciscan Monastery of St Lawrence, well worth popping into. Laid out in the shape of a cross with a gurgling fountain at the centre, its borders are planted with lavender, rosemary, sage and roses, plus olive, fig and pomegranate trees, creating a meditative escape from worldly woes, just as the monks intended. It's also home to a lovely café.

Around Šibenik Back down on the seafront promenade, through summer you have a shuttle boat several times daily to **St Nicholas Fortress** (Tvrđava Sv Nikole; ☏ 022 338 343; **w** kanal-svetog-ante.com; ⊕ May–Oct daily, see website for boat departures). Tickets should be bought in advance at the St Nicholas Fortress Info Centre (Obala Franje Tuđmana 4; €15). Built in the 16th century to protect Šibenik against the Ottoman Turks, this triangular-shaped fortress sits on a tiny islet at the entrance to St Anthony's Channel. Originally armed with 32 cannons, its vaulted halls were primarily gunpowder stores. It is part of the UNESCO-listed 'Venetian Works of Defence between the 16th and 17th centuries: Stato da Terra – Western Stato da Mare', and was used as a film location for *Game of Thrones*.

Another worthwhile half-day trip from Šibenik is **Zlarin** (**w** tz-zlarin.hr), served by Jadrolinija ferry (25mins) from the port. Nowadays home to some 280 residents, in the 1830s, this tiny island had a thriving community of over 1,600. While the women worked the fields, cultivating grapes and olives, their menfolk were sailors and fishermen, especially known for coral hunting. Learn more about this at the excellent **Zlarin Coral Centre** (Centar Koralja Zlarin; Niz Bebana 16; **m** 091 495 5500; **w** hckz.hr; ⊕ May–Oct 09.00–21.00 Mon–Sat, 09.00–15.00 Sun; Nov–Apr 10.00–16.00 daily; €7). Besides tracing the history of coral hunting, it examines humankind's impact on the marine environment and introduces Zlarin without Plastic, a campaign to ban single-use plastic on the island. While on Zlarin, you might also have a swim from the beach near the harbour, and for supper, try **Konoba Prslika** (**m** 099 691 7026; ⨍ konoba.prslika; ⊕ May–Oct 17.00–01.00 daily; €€€€), a welcoming rustic restaurant serving Dalmatian seafood in a courtyard garden.

About 7km from Šibenik, near the village of Dubrava, there is a **falconry centre** (Sokolarski Center Dubrava; Škugori bb, Dubrava; **m** 091 506 7610; **w** sokolarskicentar.com; ⊕ 09.00–19.00 daily; €10). As well as informative 45-minute presentations on birds of prey, the centre runs environmental education programmes and one- and five-day falconry courses, and has a small hospital where sick or injured birds are cared for and rehabilitated. Larger groups are asked to call in advance.

PRIMOŠTEN A little over 25km south of Šibenik the coast road passes Primošten, the old town of which occupies a photogenic, teardrop-shaped peninsula covered in stone houses with a church-spire protruding above them. The 'peninsula' was originally an island connected to the mainland by a wooden bridge (hence its name, from *pri mostu*, meaning 'at the bridge'), though the bridge was later replaced by an embankment. Adjacent to this is a second, slightly larger peninsula, mainly covered with pine forest and separated from the old town by a lovely long, curving, pebble beach.

The **tourist office** (☎022 571 111; w tz-primosten.hr), at the entrance to the old town, has details of private accommodation and other useful information.

🏠 **Where to stay and eat** Kamenar (Rudina Biskupa Arnerića 5; ☎022 570 889; w restaurant-kamenar.com; ⊕ May–Oct noon–midnight daily; €€€; €€€), near the entrance to the old town, has nine clean, pine-furnished rooms above the restaurant of the same name. There's one large hotel here, the 324-room **Zora** (Raduča 11; ☎022 581 111; w zora-hotel.com; ⊕ Mar–Nov; €€€€) on the forested peninsula just north of the old town. **Konoba Mediteran** (Put briga 13; ☎022 571 780; w mediteran-primosten.hr; ⊕ Apr–Oct 13.00–midnight daily; €€€€–€€€) serves Dalmatian seafood specialities and reliable house wine in the old town.

NORTH TO DRNIŠ AND KNIN From Šibenik the road runs north along the eastern border of Krka National Park (see opposite) to **Knin**, some 60km distant, passing through **Drniš** (w tz-drnis.hr) on the way.

Drniš is renowned for its *pršut* (similar to Italian prosciutto), though strangely, there's nowhere you can actually buy it here – local producers live in villages outside town. But it's still well worth a wander up to the medieval hilltop **fort** (*gradina*), with a defence tower, a 16th-century minaret (Drniš was ruled by the Ottoman Turks between 1522 and 1683), and dramatic views down on to the rocky Čikola Canyon. You might also look in the **Town Museum** (⊕ 08.00–10.30 & 11.30–14.00 Mon–Fri; €4), exhibiting local archaeological finds and a collection of sculptures, paintings and sketches by Ivan Meštrović (1883–1962), Croatia's greatest 20th-century sculptor, who hailed from the area. In the town park, you can see Meštrović's *Spring of Life* fountain, sculpted in 1906 when he was just 23.

However, the main attraction, the **Meštrović Mausoleum and Church of the Holy Redeemer** (Meštrovićev Mauzolej i Crkva Presvetog Otkupitelja; Otavice; ☎021 340 800; w mestrovic.hr; ⊕ May–Oct 10.00–18.00 Tue–Fri, 10.00–14.00 Sat–Sun; Nov–Apr 08.00–16.00 Tue–Sat; €5) lies 10km east of Drniš, in Otavice. A 10-minute walk up a tree-lined avenue brings you to the mausoleum reception, and from here a flight of 121 stone steps leads up to this cubic hilltop building, capped by a dome. The interior is octagonal and flooded with natural light through an opening above the altar, illuminating a relief depicting Christ being carried upwards by an angel. There are also two alabaster windows, and four niches bearing reliefs of the Evangelists. Designed by Ivan Meštrović and completed in 1936, it was intended as both a family mausoleum and a village church. Meštrović and his close family are buried in the vault below. The hilltop location affords panoramic views over Petrovo Polje (a long flat karst plain) and down to the Meštrović family home (designed by the sculptor in 1912) in Otavice.

Continuing from Drniš towards Knin, the scars of the Croatian War of Independence (1991–95) are still very much in evidence. Several properties in the area remain devastated, windowless and roofless, and while some of the older Serbs who'd lived here for generations have clearly returned, there are few if any young people around. Houses that weren't destroyed by shells were gutted by fire, and the torched wrecks of cars still stand in their driveways. The farming villages of **Kaldrma** and **Kosovo** in particular are a dreadful reminder of the awfulness of war.

Knin (w tz-knin.hr), which played a significant role in the conflict of the 1990s as the short-lived capital of the Serb enclave of Krajina, is an uninspiring place, and its population is nothing like what it was 30 years ago. If you stop in Knin (and it's easy, with so many onward buses, and trains to Šibenik and Split), then make the effort to climb up the hill to the terrific **medieval fortress** (w fortressofknin.hr; ☺ Mar–Oct 08.00–19.00 daily, Nov–Feb 08.00–15.00 Mon–Fri) which dominates the town. It's the way fortresses are meant to be, with great big walls, ramparts, buttresses, towers and a sturdy central keep, and panoramic views out over the surrounding countryside.

East of Knin, close to the border with Bosnia & Herzegovina, the **Dinara Nature Park**, designated in 2021, encompasses Dinara (1,831m), Dalmatia's highest peak, as well as the source of the River Cetina, which runs down to meet the sea at Omiš (page 166) in Central Dalmatia. Various marked hiking paths lead up Dinara for astounding panoramic views over the surrounding landscape.

KRKA NATIONAL PARK

(w npkrka.hr; winter/summer €7/40) The 72km Krka River and waterfalls are a popular rival to the Plitvice Lakes further north and are essentially a result of the same travertine process. Krka makes a great excursion from Šibenik (by boat or bus) and is offered as a day trip by any number of tour operators all the way from Zadar to Split, though it's easy enough to visit under your own steam, too.

Krka is the most popular national park in Croatia after the more famous Plitvice, with a huge number of visitors annually. In fact, there's arguably more to see here than at Plitvice, and a far greater water flow. The biggest falls, Skradinski buk (where you used to be able to swim, though that has been prohibited since 2018), see an average of 55m³ per second all year round, rising to a splashy 350m³ per second after heavy rains inland.

After much wrangling between the proponents of hydroelectricity and conservationists, the middle and lower parts of the Krka River were finally declared a national park in 1985, and the park's recently been extended pretty much all the way to the river's source, near Knin. The two most impressive waterfall systems are Roški Slap to the north and Skradinski buk to the south, separated by a wide section of river on which you'll find the islet of Visovac and a Franciscan monastery. There are also archaeological remains to be seen at Burnum. For the last 20km downstream from Skradinski buk, the Krka is at sea level, with a mix of salt and fresh water.

GETTING THERE AND AWAY If you're not on an excursion, you can easily reach Krka National Park on the **bus** that runs half-a-dozen times a day from Šibenik to the western entrance at Skradin, stopping on the way at the eastern Lozovac entrance (timetables at w atpsi.hr). If you have your own wheels, there's plenty of parking at both. Out of season you can usually drive the 4km into the park from the Lozovac entrance, while in summer you have to take the park bus.

Access from Skradin to the waterfalls is by national park **boat**, included in the entrance fee, which leaves the quay every hour on the hour and takes around 25 minutes. Both the park bus from Lozovac and the boat from Skradin only run from April to October, so if you're on public transport in winter you need to factor in a good 45-minute walk at either entrance – the entry fee is reduced as compensation. You can also sail straight to Skradin from the sea, tying up just downstream from the Skradin bridge.

Inside most of the park itself – from the Skradin bridge upstream – you're restricted, quite properly, to the national park boats and footpaths. If you want to see the **Krka Monastery** (Orthodox Monastery of the Holy Archangel;

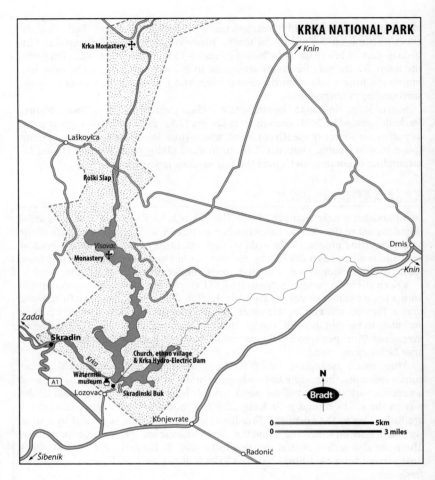

Krka Monastery ✝

Knin

Laškovica

Roški Slap

Visovac
Monastery ✝

Drniš

Knin

Zadar

Skradin

Krka

Church, ethno village
& Krka Hydro-Electric Dam

Watermill
museum

Lozovac

Skradinski Buk

N

Bradt

Konjevrate

0 ——————————— 5km
0 ——————————— 3 miles

Šibenik

Radonić

⊕ Apr–Oct; €15) towards the northern end of the park, or Visovac island with its 15th-century Franciscan monastery (⊕ Mar–Nov; €15), you can join one of the organised boat trips which can be booked through the national park office. For further information, contact the **national park office** in Šibenik (◌022 201 777; **w** npkrka.hr) or the **information centre** in Skradin (◌022 771 688). Reservations on any of the boat rides upstream of the first waterfalls – highly recommended in summer – can be made online.

🏠 **WHERE TO STAY AND EAT** Skradin – a pretty, leafy town with cafés along the waterfront – is worth visiting in its own right now that it has recovered from being pummelled by both sides during the homeland war. Nice places to stay in Skradin include **Guesthouse Ankora** (Mesarska 5a; **m** 095 910 7068; **w** guesthouseankora.com; **€€€**) and **Wine Garden Rooms** (Ribarska 7; **m** 099 651 5866; **w** winegardenskradin.com; **€€€**). In Lozovac there's the **Hotel Vrata Krke** (Lozovac bb; ◌022 778 092; **w** vrata-krke.hr; **€€€**). A little further east, on the road from Šibenik to Drniš, **Kalpić B&B** (Kalpići 4, Radonić; **m** 099 584 5520; **w** kalpic. com; **€€€**) offers eight cosy rooms and an outdoor pool, while the highly regarded rustic **Konoba Vinko** (Konjevrate; ✆022 778 750; ◼; €€€) serves barbecued meats and garden salads.

Contact the **tourist office** for more information, including a list of private accommodation (Trg Male Gospe 3; ✆022 771 329; w skradin.hr).

WHAT TO SEE AND DO The national park has a rich variety of plant life (some 1,197 species and sub-species), as well as 31 different kinds of fish, including 10 species endemic to the Krka River. A diverse range of amphibians and reptiles, some 142 species of bird, and 9 species of bat – some practically extinct elsewhere in Europe – make the park an important wildlife sanctuary. Dragonflies and butterflies are spectacular – 38 species of the former, and 81 of the latter have been recorded here.

In terms of attractions for the visitor, the first and most obvious sight is **Skradinski buk**, the largest of a series of waterfalls dropping down towards Skradin in 17 steps. As at Plitvice, wooden walkways and forest paths lead you around the waterfalls, in this case from bottom to top and back again, with a full leisurely tour taking a couple of hours. At the bottom, there are a couple of open-air café-restaurants. After crossing the long footbridge below the thundering Skradinski buk, follow the trail up to the small **church** and **ethno village**. Here you'll find interesting ethnographic displays, including a blacksmith's workshop, an interactive area for kids and a **watermill museum** – in the past the power of the falls was harnessed for milling, rolling and pounding, and there are demonstrations during the season, included in the park entry fee. There's a small café here, too. Before reaching the church you'll pass the former site of the **Krka Hydro-Electric Dam**, which went into operation here in 1895 and was only the second such hydroelectric power station in the world (the first, at Niagara Falls in the USA, went into operation just two days earlier). After the watermill museum, follow the road for a short distance (towards the Lozovac entrance) then turn left and follow boardwalks through the forest and across water channels and pools, before descending on the far side of Skradinski buk to the base of the falls again.

From April to October, you can also take a variety of national park boat excursions – buy your ticket on arrival if you haven't reserved ahead, and then visit Skradinski buk while you're waiting. The most popular excursion is the 2-hour boat ride up to the ridiculously picturesque island of **Visovac**, where you'll be given half an hour to explore the Franciscan church and monastery. Started in the 14th century, it now houses a small museum and a precious library.

A bigger excursion (4hrs) takes in Visovac and then heads upstream through a gorge to the **Roški Slap** waterfalls, which may not quite be a match for Skradinski buk but make for a delightful hour's wander all the same.

From the upper end of Roški Slap, it's a further 2-hour excursion by boat (€15) up to the fine Orthodox Krka Monastery, dating from 1359, though much rebuilt over the succeeding 400 years.

Also within the confines of the national park are some excellent ruined medieval castles and important archaeological remains; ask for directions and a map when you buy your entry ticket, if you're interested.

PAG

Pag, stretching some 60km alongside the coast north of Zadar, is one of the most barren of the Adriatic's big islands. It supports fewer than 8,400 people (and rather more sheep) in a handful of villages, and it can be a torpid, stifling place in the dog days of August, with the general lack of trees (barring some ancient olive groves in the north, and some stunted figs) being maddening and oppressive.

Nonetheless, it's stunningly photogenic (which is why it has been used for photo shoots for Porsche and *Vogue*) as well as being very popular as a holiday destination, with an interesting old town and some fine sandy beaches, and the wonderful lace-making tradition of Pag town, which remains charming rather than touristy. Tourism is Pag's sole source of real prosperity, but apart from a few weeks at the end of July and the beginning of August in Novalja – Croatia's answer to Ibiza, with club owners and entire clubs coming down from Zagreb for the season – Pag is still far from crowded.

Pag's reputation in the past was tied to salt, and there are still big saltpans in the centre of the island, but today its fame rests primarily on *Paški Sir* (Pag cheese), the distinctive hard cheese that is one of the highlights of Croatia's indigenous cuisine. Pag lamb is also a local speciality.

HISTORY It's hard to believe now, but Pag was covered with woods when it was first settled by the Illyrian tribes, and was still forested through its Roman occupation, the arrival of the Slavs in the 7th century, and the feuding of the bishops of Zadar and Rab (back when Rab had a bishop) over the island's saltpans in the late Middle Ages.

It was the Venetians who did the damage, here and throughout northern Dalmatia, cutting down the trees wholesale for shipbuilding (it has to be said that the locals were usually quick enough to sell the precious wood). The scrub grasses

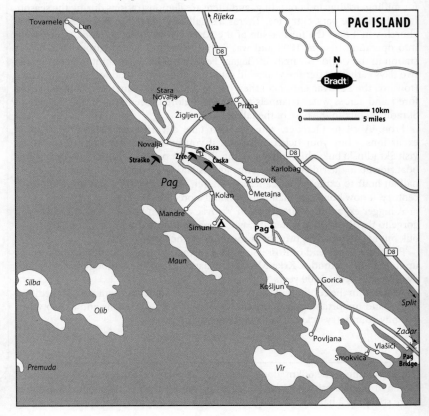

Pag cheese (Paški sir) served sliced on a platter with *pršut* (prosciutto) is a classic starter in restaurants throughout Dalmatia (Croatia). Similar to Italian *pecorino*, Pag cheese is made from sheep's milk, obtained from hardy free-grazing sheep, which feed on Pag's scanty salt grasses and aromatic wild sage, contributing to its unique flavour. It is matured for up to two years, during which time it is rubbed with olive oil and ash and regularly turned over. The oldest and largest producer, **Paška Sirana**, on the main road on the southeast outskirts of Pag town, was founded as a cooperative in 1946 (in former Yugoslavia, with its socialist system, cooperatives were worker-owned), providing employment for dozens of local families. In Kolan, Pag's slickest dairy, **Gligora**, was built in 2009. Here, the Gligora family offer tours of their dairy (w gligora.com/tours-tasting/cheese/production-facility-guided-tour) – you can see the cheesemaking process and the maturing room, and then sample a platter of six cheeses. There's also a farm shop where you can buy cheese to bring home. As of 2019, the EU has recognised Pag cheese as PDO (Protected Designation of Origin).

and roots that were left behind were then over-cropped by sheep, and the *bura* winds blew away whatever topsoil was left. The land has never recovered, even now supporting little more than a few herbs and salt grasses.

Pag fell under Austro-Hungarian control after the fall of Venice and became Yugoslav after World War I, though neither left much of a mark on the island until the bridge connecting it to the mainland was built in 1968.

GETTING THERE AND AROUND Access to Pag from the south is across the road bridge, while from the north you're better off taking the **ferry** from Prižna to Žigljen (6km across the island from the main resort of Novalja), which runs hourly in winter and continuously in summer (day and night). Note that when the bura's a-blowing, however, especially in winter, the ferry might not be running at all. There's also a daily **catamaran** from Rijeka to Novalja via Rab during summer (w jadrolinija.hr).

Six **buses** a day run from Zadar to Pag town and Novalja during the summer, slightly fewer off season, and two daily Rijeka–Zadar buses run via the island rather than along the coast, stopping at Novalja and Pag town on the way. Three buses a day run from Zagreb to Novalja and Pag, and there's also a daily bus from Novalja and Pag to Split. Most of these routes are run by **Antonio Tours** (w antoniotours. hr) or **Arriva** (w arriva.com.hr). Pag town is under an hour from Zadar, 3½ hours from Rijeka, and 5½ hours from Zagreb.

PAG TOWN The attractive, partially walled old centre of Pag you see today is in fact the new town – the original Pag was on a hillside 3km south of here, and you can still see some of the ruins, including an elegant Romanesque church at Stari Grad Pag. The new town was founded in 1443 and built according to designs by Juraj Dalmatinac, the man behind Šibenik's lovely cathedral. The bus stops just west of the old town, near the Pagus Hotel.

Tourist information (Od Špitala 2; ☏ 023 611 301/286; w tzgpag.hr) is on the southern side of the old town, towards the bridge across to the old salt warehouses, and has a good reversible map of the town and the island.

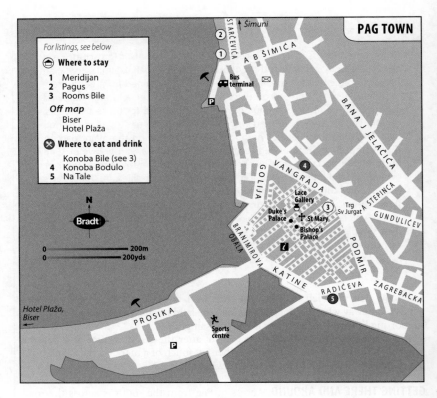

You can book excursions from the usual agencies – the best of these are the day trips out to the Kornati archipelago.

🏠 Where to stay and eat *Map, above*

The nearest **campsite** is 8km away, at Šimuni (☎023 697 441; w camping-simuni.hr; **€€€–€€**), on an attractive bay on the western side of the island, halfway to Novalja, which offers wooden bungalows as well as pitches – buses stop here, and there's a popular marina, too. Rooms are available to rent across the island.

Hotel Plaža (38 rooms) Marka Marulića 14; ☎023 600 855; w plazahotel.hr. Comfortable 4-star hotel with a restaurant & infinity pool, plus bikes, kayaks & SUPs to rent. **€€€€**

Pagus (117 rooms) A Starčevića 1; ☎023 666 000; w hotel-pagus.hr. All-inclusive 4-star family hotel, right by the bus stop, with a concrete beach & sea-view dbls with balconies. **€€€€**

Biser (20 rooms) A G Matoša 10; ☎023 611 333; w hotel-biser.com. Across the bay, a 30min walk from the old town, the 3-star Biser looks on to a rather nicer sand & pebble beach. **€€€**

Meridijan (45 rooms) Ante Starčevića 16; ☎023 492 200; w meridijan15.hr. Centrally located, with rooms decorated in vintage Biedermeier style. Restaurant & pool. **€€€**

Rooms Bile (4 rooms) Jurja Dalmatinac 35; ☎023 611 127. Above the informal Konoba Bile in Pag's old town. Stay here for a warm welcome & authentic island experience. **€€€**

Konoba Bile Jurja Dalmatinac 35; ☎023 611 127; ⊕ 19.00–midnight daily (depending on the weather). Tiny informal wine bar in the old town serving platters of Pag cheese & *pršut* (prosciutto), popular with locals. **€€€**

Konoba Bodulo Vangrada 19; \023 611 989; ☺ noon–midnight daily. Low-key, family-run konoba with tables in a courtyard shaded by vines just outside the old town. €€€

Na Tale Stjepana Radića 4; \023 611 194; ☺ Feb–Dec noon–midnight Mon–Sat, noon–22.00 Sun. Popular bistro on the seafront promenade serving Pag lamb & a range of Dalmatian seafood specialties. €€€

Activities

For adventure sports enthusiasts, the best way to explore this wild rocky windswept island is on foot or by mountain bike. **Pag Outdoor** (w pag-outdoor.com) have devised a series of hiking paths and cycling trails, which can be done with a guide or solo using an app. The project centres on Pag town, but there are also routes beginning from Novalja – they are all well-maintained and graded easy, average or difficult. Leading through extraordinary karst landscapes speckled with wild sage, these paths take you to tumbledown churches, a lighthouse, a Byzantine fortress and several remote beaches – you might spot Pag's hardy sheep and rare vultures, too. Be sure to wear proper hiking boots and carry plenty of water. If you're lucky enough to be here in summer when there's a full moon, you might join a guided night-time trek. Pag Outdoor also offer guided sea kayaking and rock climbing.

What to see and do

A regular grid of old narrow streets meets at the town's main square, Trg Kralja Krešimira IV, which contains the **Church of St Mary** (originally intended to be a cathedral), the **Duke's Palace**, and the unfinished **Bishop's Palace** – Pag never quite got its act together on becoming a bishopric.

The church has a fine, simple front, with a carved Gothic portal, four unfinished-looking saints, and a Renaissance rosette window. Inside, there are lovely Romanesque arches with Corinthian capitals (at the far right-hand end check out the cavorting dolphins), while on the ceiling there's a huge plaster relief of St George and the Dragon. The solid bell tower, behind and to the left, looks firmly rooted in the 16th century.

Given the town's heritage, it would be madness not to pop into the tiny **Lace Gallery** (Galerija paške čipke; ☺ May–Oct 10.00–noon, Jul–Aug 20.00–22.30), on one side of the square, which has a small collection of intricate work. Pag has been famous for its lace for centuries, with each piece being unique; after being closed for decades the lace school here was reopened in the late 1990s. If you want to buy genuine lace, your best bet is to purchase directly from the lace museum or the women making it – you'll see them dressed in black in the old town in the mornings, with their hair distinctively braided. The asking price reflects the considerable amount of time it takes to make. Pag lace (Paška čipka) was inscribed on the UNESCO List of Intangible Cultural Heritage in 2009.

Also revived has been the **Pag Carnival** in February, a cheerful affair with lots of dressing up, folk music, dancing, parades and processions, and performances of the local play *The Slave Girl of Pag*. It's so much fun that the carnival is repeated at the end of July – and why not? On **Assumption Day** (Velika Gospa, 15 August), a statue of the Virgin Mary is carried in a solemn procession from a shrine in the old church in Stari Grad Pag down to the Church of the Assumption of the Virgin Mary in the town centre.

NOVALJA AND NORTHERN PAG

Much busier and far more developed than Pag is the resort of Novalja, 20km north. Within reach of a whole load of good beaches (notably **Zrće**, **Časka** and **Straško**), it's understandably popular, and well-equipped for visitors. For more information on Novalja, contact the **tourist office** (Trg Briščić 1; \053 661 404; w visitnovalja.hr).

The **bus station** is on the edge of town. From here it's a 15-minute walk to the waterfront from where the catamaran departs for Rab and Rijeka (there's also a shuttle bus service covering the route).

⌂ **Where to stay and eat** There are thousands of private rooms available, and an enormous campsite (Straško; ☎053 661 226; w campingstrasko.com; €€), which used to be partly given over to naturists but is now textile-only. The sleepier old town, Stara Novalja, is a few kilometres to the north. For something decidedly more upmarket, go for the boutique **Hotel Boškinac** ✱ (Škopaljska ulica 220; ☎053 663 500; w boskinac.com; €€€€€) in a lovely location about halfway between Novalja and Stara Novalja, with its own Michelin-starred restaurant and winery. Hotels in Novalja itself include **Villa Marija** (Bok bb; ☎053 662 155; w sanko-novalja.com; €€€), which has six modern apartments and a pool, while the 12-room **Villa Mediteran** (Sonjevi stan 28; ☎053 669 020; w villa-mediteran. com.hr; €€€) lies in a quiet cove on Pag's southwest coast, and has a restaurant plus bikes, kayaks and SUPs to hire. For accommodation contacts, go directly through the Novalja **tourist office** (page 221). Expect to pay around €60 for a double room in summer.

What to see and do Some 2km south of Novalja, just off the main road to Pag town, is the beach of **Zrće** (w zrce.eu), a kilometre or so of shingle that has become Croatia's top venue for summer open-air music festivals, with clubbing until dawn. There are three main bars/clubs operational through the summer; the original is **Kalypso**, but offshoots of well-known Zagreb clubs – and notably **Aquarius** – have long been setting up camp here, too. There's a shuttle bus from Novalja if you don't fancy the walk.

Also close to Novalja are the meagre ruins of the Roman town of **Cissa** (now Časka), with the best bits being underwater, as the coast sank here. The main attraction is the underground Roman aqueduct, constructed in the 1st century AD, and visitable for around 150m of its length – further excavations are underway.

The island of Pag ends in the narrow 20km-long **Lun Peninsula**, famous for its ancient olive groves (the few trees not cut down by the Venetians) and ending in the quiet fishing village of **Tovarnele**.

SILBA, OLIB AND PREMUDA

North of Dugi Otok and Ugljan and west of Pag, the Zadar archipelago ends in the cluster of small islands including Silba, Olib and Premuda. Though little visited by overseas tourists they are a lovely area, far from the madding crowds of Hvar, Brač and other better-known islands, but easily accessible by catamaran and ferry from Zadar.

SILBA Silba is the nicest of the three, a lovely, traffic-free oasis home to clean seas and sandy beaches, with a good range of private rooms and apartments to choose from, including plenty of eco-friendly options. Silba, the main village, is a small place pinched at the centre of the island's hourglass shape, with only a 5–10-minute walk to the ferry dock and the beaches on either side of the island. Which side of the island you choose to swim on depends as much on the weather as anything else – if the seas are slightly rough on one side, you'll probably find them calm on the other. The **tourist office** (☎023 370 010; w tzsilba.hr) can supply you with a small map and other information.

Getting there and away Silba is connected to Zadar by once-daily fast catamaran (1½hrs; w miatours.hr) all year and by slower ferry departing from Zadar's Gaženica terminal and continuing to Mali Lošinj (4hrs; w jadrolinija.hr). Another fast catamaran connects Silba with Zadar (1hr 10mins; w krilo.hr) several times weekly, and continues north to Pula in Istria.

Where to stay and eat The village has everything you really need for a week's stay, including a small supermarket, a well-stocked fruit and vegetable stall, and several restaurants and cafés. If you reserve accommodation online, the owner of your apartment will usually arrange to meet you from the catamaran or ferry with a small hand-pulled cart on which they'll transport your bags and show you to your accommodation. As well as private accommodation, there's one small pansion.

✳ Fregadon (6 rooms) Silba bb; ☎023 370 104; w pansion-silba.com. This small pansion provides an alternative to the private accommodation on the island. Also houses a decent restaurant (€€€) – it is open to non-guests, but you need to make a reservation the previous day. €€€

Silba Blu B&B Silba bb; ▪. Friendly B&B with 3 rooms, set in a walled garden with pine trees overlooking the sea. €€€

Restoran Vila Velebit Silba bb; m 098 175 6409; w vilavelebita-silba.hr; ⊕ Jun–Sep 10.00–23.00 daily. Welcoming family-run restaurant serving local seafood specialities, generally considered the best on the island. €€€€

Konoba Žalić Silba bb; ☎023 370 105; ▪; ⊕ Jun–Sep 13.00–23.00 daily. Nice little konoba, serving pasta dishes plus barbecued fish & meat. €€€

UGLJAN AND PAŠMAN

Just a few kilometres offshore from Zadar are the pretty neighbouring islands of Ugljan and Pašman. They were originally a single island, until a channel was dug between them during the 19th century to help sea traffic on its way.

Most visitors are locals, as neither island has yet been really developed as a package destination. As a result, Ugljan and Pašman are better geared up for individual visits rather than groups, though they're far from empty, with Ugljan being the most densely populated island in the Adriatic (it's practically a suburb of Zadar).

GETTING THERE AND AROUND There are frequent car **ferries** over to Preko on Ugljan from Zadar's Gaženica ferry terminal (25mins), with passenger services also running from Zadar's old town (25mins) and from Biograd to Tkon on Pašman (20mins) (all w jadrolinija.hr). A regular **bus** service runs the length of the two islands – timetables can be found on the Ugljan Tourist Office website (w preko.hr) and at w liburnija-zadar.hr/en/island-transport.

UGLJAN The island of Ugljan is largely dedicated to the cultivation of olives, and some of Croatia's best olive oil comes from here, although it's rarely commercially available. Many of the rest of the inhabitants work in Zadar, while there are lots of mainlanders' second homes on the island, meaning it can get pretty busy on summer weekends.

Preko Just half an hour away from Zadar, Ugljan's main settlement is Preko, an unpretentious little town focused more on day-to-day life than anything like a tourist industry. Ferries come across roughly every hour all year round, and alternate ones are met by buses heading north up to the town of Ugljan or south to Pašman, passing through Kali and Kukljica on the way (page 224).

The **tourist office** (Magazin 8; ✆ 023 286 108; w preko.hr), towards the far (northern) end of town if you're arriving by ferry, is cheerful enough and has a list of private rooms (expect to pay around €60 for doubles). Otherwise, for private rooms and apartments, contact **NavAdriatic Travel** (Magazin 5; m 095 592 2593; w navadriatic.com), from where you can also rent out bicycles and boats – great ways of getting yourself around the island. **Villa Eden** (Jaz 18; m 098 1652 165; w eden.hr; €€€) has apartments by the beach at Jaz, around 500m from town. For something luxurious, stay at **Dunatovi Dvori Heritage Hotel** (✆ 023 681 753; w dunatovi-dvori.hr; €€€€), a renovated waterside villa from 1912 in Preko, with 14 rooms, a restaurant and pool.

Worth the 90-minute uphill hike is the trip up to **St Michael's Fortress**. At 250m it's one of the highest points on either island, and the views across to Pag to the north, Dugi Otok to the west, the Kornati archipelago to the south and over to the Velebit massif on the mainland can be absolutely breathtaking. Built by the Venetians in the early 13th century, the fortress is very much ruined, mostly by time, but there are tentative plans to restore it and open an interpretation centre, presenting the natural and cultural heritage of the islands of the Zadar archipelago. Most of the walking is on asphalt road, and it can get extremely hot, so take a hat and water. The nicest hike on the island is the rocky path to the top of the tongue-twisting Šćah, the highest point on the island at 286m, from the village of Turkija.

After your exertions you'll definitely deserve a swim, and Preko has a nice enough town beach, but under 100m offshore is the lovely little wooded island of Galovac, with a 15th-century monastery and the best local beaches. In summer it's easy enough to find a taxi boat to whisk you across.

Ugljan village

The village of Ugljan, 10km north of Preko, is a forgotten sort of place, though it has a lovely beach and a Franciscan monastery you can visit. Ask at the **Preko tourist office** (see above) about private rooms, or stay at **Villa Stari Dvor** (✆ 023 288 8699; w staridvor.hr; €€€) in Batalaža Bay, with a pool plus a good restaurant serving Dalmatian seafood. Alternatively, try **Apartmani Galius** (Gaj 9; ✆ 023 288 314; w apartmaniugljan.com; €€€), which also has its own restaurant and offers boat trips. A decent spot for eating out in Ugljan is rustic **Restoran Apollo** (m 095 850 0207; ☉ Jun–Sep 17.00–midnight; €€€), doing fresh local seasonal specialities.

Kali and Kukljica

Heading south from Preko, it's not far to the active fishing village of Kali and a further 5km on to Kukljica, which is a fishing village as well, but also the nearest thing Ugljan has to a holiday resort. The **tourist office** (Svetog Lovre 2; ✆ 023 282 406; w kali.hr) can help you find private accommodation. In Kali, an authentic place to eat is family-run **OPG Pierini** (m 099 214 5713; f pierini. kali; ☉ Jun–Sep 17.00–23.00 Mon–Sat; €€€), serving locally caught seafood and homegrown vegetables. In Kukljica, you might try **Konoba Udica** (m 098 919 7269; w konoba-udica.com; ☉ Jun–Sep 11.30–midnight; €€€) doing a wide range of classic Dalmatian fare. From here it's barely 2km to the bridge leading over to Pašman.

PAŠMAN

Pašman is a smaller, less densely populated, even less developed version of its northern neighbour, and although the number of visitors has been growing every year, that's from a pretty low base.

The island is a popular weekender for locals from Biograd on the mainland. Nine ferries a day all year round (13 in summer) head across to **Tkon**, the main settlement in the south of the island (20mins). Tkon has apartments to rent, a couple of reasonable beaches and a naturist campsite, **Sovinje** (m 098 314 045; w fkksovinje.hr), 2km to the south, with one of the few sandy naturist beaches in Croatia.

Not far from Tkon, on Mount Ćokovac, is the **Monastery of Kuzma i Damjan** (⊕ 16.00–18.00 Mon–Sat). Originally a Venetian fortress, built in 1125, it became an important Glagolitic centre and is today the only active Benedictine monastery in Croatia. The church here was built from 1369 to 1419 and has a fine 14th-century crucifix.

A few kilometres north, on the way to the village of Pašman, at **Kraj**, there's a solid, defensive Franciscan monastery dating from 1390, though much remodelled in the 16th century. The Renaissance cloisters here are lovely, and there's an interesting little museum housing several valuable religious works.

The village of **Pašman** itself, 6km north of Tkon, is the last place of any significance heading towards Ugljan – after that it's one sleepy fishing hamlet after another. There are a handful of private rooms available – there's a list on the website of the **tourist office** (☏ 023 260 155; w pasman.hr) – and a couple of pleasant beaches from which to swim. A good spot to eat is family-run **San Marko** (Pašman 87; ☏ 023 260 328; w san-marko.com; ⊕ Jun–Sep 15.00–midnight daily; €€€) serving barbecued fish in a cheerful courtyard.

Between Ugljan and Dugi Otok lies the sheltered island of Iž, which is little more than two harbour settlements – **Mali Iž** and **Veli Iž** – connected by what passes for a road in these parts. There's one hotel on the island, in Veli Iž, the **Korinjak Vegetarian Hotel & Camp** (☏ 023 277 064; w korinjak.com; €€€€–€€€), which has 76 fairly simple rooms, serves vegetarian meals and hosts occasional yoga retreats.

In the past Veli Iž was famous for its pottery, supplying large parts of the coast with clay cooking pots. Local lore has it that potters threw unsold goods into the sea on the homeward voyage, rather than face the shame of having failed to sell them. There's a daily ferry to Iž from Zadar (40mins) – don't bother bringing the car.

DUGI OTOK AND THE KORNATI ARCHIPELAGO

Dugi Otok (literally 'long island') and the Kornati archipelago, stretched in a 75km line marking the outer ridge of the Adriatic's submerged mountains, are among the most dramatic and spectacular places in Croatia.

The endless indentations and extraordinary shapes of the islands are a magnet for sailors in summer, and although there's almost nothing as such to do, the wild scenery alone makes for a remarkable visit.

It's easiest to visit the Kornati archipelago as part of an excursion – these are offered from Zadar and Šibenik but are best from Murter (page 229), which is home to the park office. Bear in mind that some excursions – from Zadar in particular – only go as far as Dugi Otok's Telašćica Bay (nevertheless a very beautiful nature park), not into Kornati National Park itself. Far and away the finest way to see them, however, is from the deck of your own boat, and the archipelago is understandably popular with nautical tourists, although the sheer number of islands means you'll never find them too crowded.

DUGI OTOK Dugi Otok is nearly 45km long but never as much as 5km wide. All the attention goes to the two lobster-clawed ends of the island. The tiny resort and harbour of **Božava** is in the northwest, while the island's capital, **Sali**, is in the southeast – this is the closest town to the remarkable Telašćica Bay, a nature park which blends imperceptibly into Kornati National Park at its southern end.

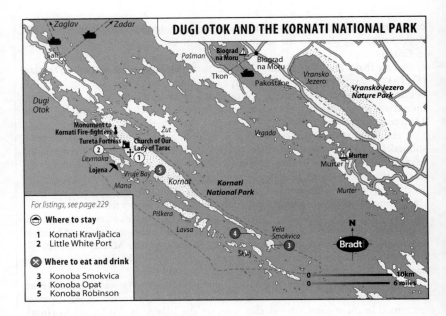

DUGI OTOK AND THE KORNATI NATIONAL PARK

For listings, see page 229

🖰 **Where to stay**
1 Kornati Kravljačica
2 Little White Port

❌ **Where to eat and drink**
3 Konoba Smokvica
4 Konoba Opat
5 Konoba Robinson

The island has no freshwater supply at all, so it relies on collected rainwater, and in hot summers drinking water has to be ferried over from the mainland; it's not a place to leave taps running. The north is moderately fertile, while the southern end of the island (like most of the Kornati archipelago) is more dramatically barren.

There are a few diving schools on Dugi Otok, including **Kornati Diving Center** in Zaglav (**f** KornatiDC) and **Diving School Božava** (**m** 099 594 2264, 099 537 5459; **w** bozava.de) in Božava – see the Dugi Otok **tourist office** website (**w** dugiotok.hr).

Getting there and around
There are two different ferry routes to Dugi Otok from Zadar. The **car ferry** runs three or four times a day, all year round, and takes 1 hour 40 minutes to reach Brbinj. There's really nothing much here, in spite of the sometimes-busy port and surrounding olive groves, so if you're not driving yourself, try not to miss the connecting bus which meets the ferry and makes the 15km run north to Božava. There's no bus south from Brbinj to Sali, around 20km distant. There is, however, a small **passenger ferry** running three times daily, all year round, from Zadar either to Sali or Zaglav (**w** gv-zadar.hr; approx 1hr 5mins), 3km north – when it goes to Zaglav there's a bus onwards to Sali – and a catamaran (approx 45mins) running the same route. In summer there are also various privately operated hydrofoil and ferry services from Zadar to the island.

Dugi Otok's settlements are connected by a single road, although if you're here without your own wheels you'll soon discover there's only one bus a week which connects north with south; and if you do bring your own car, remember there's only one petrol station (at Zaglav). If you want the flexibility to visit both ends of the island and you don't have your own wheels (car or bike), you can call on the services of a local **taxi** operator – Taxi Frka (**m** 098 891 036; **w** taxidugiotok. com) can be highly recommended, and they also have bikes and kayaks to hire. Alternatively, begging, borrowing or renting a boat is still one of the best ways of visiting.

Božava and around

The fishing village of Božava, with just 112 residents, is a (very) quiet place most of the time, though it's increasingly popular with Italian **yachtsmen and women** at the height of the season. There's even a mid-sized hotel complex, the eponymous Božava (☏ 023 291 291; w hoteli-bozava.hr; €€€€–€€€), which consists of four hotels: the Maxim (the most upmarket), Agava, Lavanda and Mirta. Private rooms can be booked through the **tourist office** (☏ 023 377 607; w dugiotok.hr).

A couple of kilometres northwest of Božava is the even smaller village of **Soline**, at the head of **Soliščica Bay**, which has plenty of swimming opportunities on mostly rocky beaches, heading up towards **Veli Rat**, the northernmost settlement on the island. From here it's a few hundred metres north to the lighthouse and some popular rocks from which to bathe. If you turn left down a gravel road halfway between Soline and Veli Rat, it's a kilometre or so south to **Sakarun**, a half-kilometre stretch of big smooth white stones on a truly lovely turquoise bay, facing south and popular with sailing boats, which drop anchor here.

Sali

Sali, with over 1,000 inhabitants, is Dugi Otok's social and economic hub. It still derives a good deal more of its revenue from fishing than tourism, though that balance is surely set to change as more people are visiting every year. The town is understandably popular with sailors, who come here on their way to or from Telašćica Bay, the Adriatic's largest and most dramatic natural harbour, and the Kornati islands.

Sali's **tourist office** (Sali II 49; ☏ 023 377 094; w dugiotok.hr) will help with finding you private rooms and will also point you in the right direction for one of the dive centres here, as well as organising boat trips for you around the island and into the Kornati archipelago – by far the best way of seeing the dramatic scenery.

Where to stay and eat

✳ **Villa Nai** Žman 199; ☏ 023 643 520; w villanai.com. An absolutely gorgeous (but very expensive) place to stay & eat in Žman, a short distance north of Zaglav. Designed by local architect Nikola Bašić, it has 8 rooms, 2 restaurants & a pool, set amid olive groves on a hillside high above the sea. €€€€€

Hotel Sali Sali IV 32; ☏ 023 377 049; w hotel-sali.hr. 300m across the headland to the north & set in pine woods. Rents out bikes – just what you need to cruise over to Telašćica Bay, around 8km each way. €€€

Apartmani Šoštarić (4 apartments) Sali II 89; ☏ 023 377 050; w apartmanisostaric.com. The pink building right beside where the ferry/catamaran from Zadar sets down passengers in Sali is clean, comfortable & good value. €€

Konoba Trapula Sali I 74; m 095 713 7297; w konoba-trapula-sali.eatbu.hr; ⏱ Jun–Sep noon–midnight. Serves Dalmatian risotto & pasta dishes plus barbecued fish & meat. €€€€–€€€

What to see and do

Before you let yourself be whisked off to the Kornati islands, don't miss the spectacular **Telašćica Bay** (w pp-telascica.hr; €4–7, valid for 1 day), a nature park which is just as beautiful (and more easily accessible, if you're already on Dugi Otok) as its more famous neighbour. Be sure to see the **Grpašćak Interpretation Center** (w grpascak.hr), hosting an interactive multimedia presentation of the park's flora and fauna, opened in 2022 in a renovated fort with superb sea-views. If you're arriving by sea with your own boat, you can find ticket prices on the park website. Although you can walk the 3km west to the head of Telašćica Bay, it is the farther end of the bay you really want to get to – and most of the walking is on asphalt, so it's really more pleasant to hire a bike or take a taxi (see opposite). Taxis also take passengers from Sali out to the beach at Saharun and pick them up at the end of the day.

In the southwestern pincer, about 8km from Sali but still within Telašćica Bay, there is a small string of cafés, and just south of these, a 5-minute walk up through the trees, are some spectacular sea cliffs, some of the highest on the Adriatic. Beyond the cafés is **Mir Bay** ('bay of peace'), which harbours a saltwater lake connected to the sea by underground karstic channels. The rocks around here are popular with naturists. Donkeys roam this area, but you are advised not to feed them – they have been known to become quite aggressive and bite.

KORNATI NATIONAL PARK (Kornati National Park office: Butina 2; ☎022 435 740; w np-kornati.hr; entry per boat per day: €65 up to 11m, €95 11–18m, €160 18–25m; per boat for 3 days: €130/190/320; per boat for 5 days: €190/290/480) Of the 140-odd islands, islets and reefs of the Kornati archipelago, 89 were declared a national park in 1980, with the boundary also including the spectacular Telašćica Bay on Dugi Otok. It's understandably popular with yachting types and a great place to learn to sail.

The park is managed from the town of **Murter**, on the island of Murter, connected to the mainland at Tisno by a drawbridge. As it's the closest place to the national park it's also the best starting point for an excursion – you'll see much more if you're not spending most of the day schlepping your way up the coast from Split or down from Zadar.

Murter is also the place to start if you want to stay on one of the Kornati islands and experience so-called 'Robinson Crusoe tourism' (see opposite).

Even if you're only here on a day trip, you'll see some of the most extraordinary scenery in Europe. Most of the islands are covered in sage and feather grasses, or low scrub, turning the grey karst green, though some also permit the cultivation of figs, grapes and olives.

Where the islands face the open sea, to the southwest, dramatic cliffs plunge into the water. Known locally as 'crowns' (you'll have your wrist slapped if you say 'cliff'), they rise up to around 80m tall and extend underwater almost as far. The crowns are the most obvious sign of the fault zone running down the Adriatic, the result of sudden tectonic movements in the past.

The highly varied submarine flora and fauna, along with the unusual geomorphology, also make for excellent diving and snorkelling.

The largest island, after which the archipelago takes its name, is **Kornat**. If you sail down its south coast, you'll spot 12 enormous crosses traced into the landscape as dry-stone walls. A fine piece of land art by local architect Nikola Bašić, this is the **Monument to Kornati Firefighters**, in remembrance of 12 Croatian firemen who died fighting a wildfire here in summer 2007.

Further down Kornat's south coast, the waterside **Church of Our Lady of Tarac** combines the ruins of a 6th-century Christian basilica and a small 17th-century church and was probably intended as a place of thanksgiving for sailors during storms. Each July, the Bishop of Zadar holds a service here, attended by local fishermen in their boats, to bless the land and the sea. Nearby, the hilltop **Tureta Fortress** was built by the Byzantines in the 6th century – it's worth a climb up for superb panoramic views over the surrounding seascape. South from here lies **Vruje Bay**, a deep sheltered inlet with a handful of houses, including a couple of seasonal restaurants and a small shop selling basic provisions for yachters.

West of Kornat, in a southwest-facing bay on **Levrnaka** island, lies **Lojena**, a lovely sandy beach. South from here, on **Mana** island, you'll see a cluster of tumbledown stone cottages, high upon a cliff. In fact, these are fake – they were built as a film set for a German film in the 1950s. More recently, they featured in the Croatian film *Murina*, which won the Camera d'Or at the Cannes Film Festival 2021.

⌂ Staying and eating in the national park *Map, page 226*

This represents quite an investment; as you can't normally stay for less than a week, you need to pay for transport as well as accommodation, and it doesn't make much sense not to have your own boat while you're out there.

On the other hand, there are few places in Europe that offer you this much isolation or privacy with such a great climate. In some cases, there's no electricity, let alone shops or restaurants, and the cottages have just the bare essentials, though twice a week a supply boat will come and deliver you staples (food, not office supplies), as well as the gas which powers the fridge, cooker and lights. Catching your own fish, grilling it over an open fire, and watching the sun plunging into the sea on a sultry evening is a sure cure for urban stress.

Local house owners with a contract from the national park office authorising them to provide private accommodation are listed on the national park website. These include the lovely six-bed **Kornati Kravljačica** (w kornati-kravljacica.com; €€) and the five-bed **Little White Port** (w littlewhiteport.com; €€), both on the largest island, Kornat, and both of which come with the use of a small motorboat, at extra charge.

Otherwise, you could try talking to the locals in Murter and negotiating your way out to one of their own houses on the islands – the archipelago is actually the property of the people of Murter, and there's still a certain amount of fishing and agriculture that goes on. Your chances with this particular strategy will be greatly enhanced if you speak Croatian and can handle your rakija.

If you sail the Kornati by private boat, you'll find a dozen or so seasonal **eateries** (⊕ Jun–Sep) in sheltered bays across the islets, most with moorings out front. Top choices include **Konoba Smokvica** (Vela Smokvica island; m 091 333 0044; w smokvica-kornati.com; €€€€€), much loved for its beautifully presented fusion seafood dishes; **Konoba Opat** (Kornat island; m 091 224 7878; w opat-kornati.com; €€€€€) near Kornat's southern tip, serving fresh seafood, with an adjoining cocktail bar; and **Konoba Robinson** (Vrulje Bay, Kornat island; m 091 583 6474; w restaurantrobinson.com; €€€€) doing classic Dalmatian seafood on a waterside terrace.

Murter

Murter The island of Murter is about 25km up the coast from Šibenik and is served by half-a-dozen daily buses (timetables at w atpsi.hr) – change in Vodice if you're coming from the north. The island is joined to the mainland by a bridge at Tisno, a small waterside town best known for **The Garden Resort** (w thegardencroatia.com), which hosts a programme of open-air music festivals through July and August.

Murter has some pretty good beaches, though most visitors come here as a starting point for exploring the Kornati. One attraction worth seeing is the **Betina Museum of Wooden Shipbuilding** (Vladimira Nazora 7, Betina; w mbdb.hr; ⊕ Jun–Aug 09.00–21.00 Mon–Sat, May & Sep–Oct 09.00–19.00 Mon–Sat, Nov–Apr 09.00–15.00 Mon–Sat; €5) where you can learn about the *gajeta*, a traditional boat used by Murter's farmers and fishermen to sail the Kornati.

The **Kornati National Park office** (see opposite) in Murter Town will sell you entry tickets, a one-day fishing licence (€10), a diving permit (€15 pp, which includes the entrance fee – note that diving is strictly controlled, and you can only dive as part of an organised diving tour) and good maps, as well as letting you know who's authorised to offer excursions into the park.

There are a number of **agencies** in town who can arrange both day trips and longer stays on the islands, and costs generally include the park entrance fee. **Coronata** (Zrtava ratova 17; m 098 211 140; w coronata.hr) and **Tureta Tours** (Trg Rudina 6; ☎022 434 472; w tureta-tours.hr) are both reliable.

Appendix 1

LANGUAGE

The official language is Croatian, written using the Latin alphabet. Croatian is a tough language to learn, but words are nothing like as difficult to pronounce as you'd think since every letter always has a unique pronunciation – albeit often not the same as in English. Although you're unlikely to have time to learn much Croatian, grab at least a handful of words and phrases to take with you – the effort will be richly rewarded.

The language comes from the group usually described by linguists as Serbo-Croat, meaning that Serbs, Montenegrins, Croats and Bosnians can readily understand each other – not that you'd necessarily know this, judging by the strife of the past 30 (or even 200) years. Within Croatia itself, there are also regional variations and dialects. In Dalmatia, Italian speakers will notice some words borrowed from Italian or, more specifically, the Venetian dialect of Italian. Historically, much of the Dalmatian coast came under Venice from 1420 to 1797, and especially on the islands, many Venetian words have remained, incorporated into the local dialect. Even in Split, for example, you'll hear *šinjorina* (from the Italian *signorina*) rather than *gospođica* (official Croatian) when someone is talking about a young lady.

The use of the Latin alphabet is largely to do with religion and the east–west division of the Roman empire – it was in Croatia in the 9th century that Sts Cyril and Methodius invented the Glagolitic alphabet (see Glagolitic Alley, in Istria), which was converted by St Clement, in Ohrid (now in the Former Yugoslav Republic of Macedonia), into the Cyrillic alphabet, variants of which are now used throughout the Orthodox world. You won't see Cyrillic – unless you happen into an Orthodox or Greek Catholic church, or you're travelling on into neighbouring Bosnia or Montenegro.

Most people – especially in tourist destinations along the Dalmatian coast – speak at least one foreign language, with English very widely spoken. Italian is understood by many on the coast and islands. In inland Dalmatia, German is the more widespread third language, after Croatian and English.

PRONUNCIATION Croatian words aren't anything like as hard to pronounce as you might expect them to be – just concentrate on pronouncing each letter the same way every time, and you won't go far wrong.

A	as in **pa**rty	Đ, đ	as in **G**eorge, **j**am (sometimes
B	as in **b**ed		written Dj, dj, to help non-natives)
C	as in fa**ts**, ba**ts**	E	as in **pe**t
Č, č	as in **n**ur**t**ure, cul**t**ure	F	as in **f**ree
Ć, ć	as in **ch**ew, **ch**ump	G	as in **g**oat
D	as in **d**ote	H	as in **h**at
		I	as in f**ee**t, p**i**zza

J	as in **y**et	S	as in **s**and
K	as in **k**ept	Š, š	as in **sh**ovel, **ch**ampagne
L	as in **l**eg	T	as in **t**oo
M	as in **m**other	U	as l**oo**k
N	as in **n**o	V	as in **v**ery
O	as in h**o**t	Z	as in **z**oo
P	as in **p**ie	Ž, ž	as in trea**s**ure
R	as in ai**r**		

WORDS AND PHRASES
Courtesies

Hello/Bye (informal)	*bog*
Cheers!	*živjeli!* [**zhi**-vel-ee]
Good morning	*dobro jutro* [**dob**-ro you-tro]
Good day	*dobar dan* [**dob**ber dan]
Good evening	*dobra večer* [**dob**-ro vetch-air]
Good night (on leaving)	*laku noć* [**la**koo notch]
Good luck (as a salutation)	*sretno* [**sret**-no]
How are you?	*kako ste?* [ka-ko stay]
I'm fine, thank you	*dobro, hvala* [**dob**-ro, hfar-la]
please/thank you	*molim/hvala* [mo-**leem**/hfar-la]
Thank you very much	*hvala lijepo* [hfar-la lee-**ye**po]
Excuse me	*oprostite/sori* [o-pros-ti-te/sorry] (*skužajte* [**skoo**-zhay-teh] is also sometimes used in Dalmatia)
goodbye	*doviđenja* [**doe**-vee **jen**-ya]

Basic words

yes/no	*da/ne* [dar/**nay**] (*nema* = emphatic no) [nay-ma]
that's right	*tako je* [ta-ko yay]
OK	*OK* [okay]
maybe	*možda* [mozh-da]
large/small	*veliko/malo* [veli-ko/mar-lo] (*velika/mala* are feminine forms)
more/less	*više/manje* [vee-sh/man-ye]
good/bad	*dobro/loše* [**dob**-ro/lo-sh]
hot/cold	*toplo/hladno* [top-lo/hlad-no]
toilet	*toalet* [toe-a-let], *WC* [vay-say]
men/women	*muški/ženski* [moosh-kee/zhen-skee]

Numbers

1	*jedan*		12	*dvanaest*
2	*dva*		20	*dvadeset*
3	*tri*		30	*trideset*
4	*četiri*		40	*četrdeset*
5	*pet*		50	*pedeset*
6	*šest*		60	*šezdeset*
7	*sedam*		70	*sedamdeset*
8	*osam*		80	*osamdeset*
9	*devet*		90	*devedeset*
10	*deset*		100	*sto*
11	*jedanaest*		1000	*tisuća*

A1

Questions

how?	*kako?* [ka-ko]
how much?	*koliko?* [ko-lee-ko]
what's your name?	*kako se zovete?* [ka-ko say zov-et-e]
when?	*kada?* [ka-da]
where?	*gdje?* [gud-ee-ya]
who?	*tko?* [teko]
why?	*zašto?* [**za**-shto]
do you speak English?	*govorite li engleski?* [gov-**or**-itay lee en-gleski]
how do you say in Croatian?	*kako se to kaže na hrvatskom?* [ka-ko say toe ka-zhay na hair-vat-skom]
can you tell me the way to…?	*možete mi reći put do…?* [mo-**zhet**-e mee retchi put doe]
how do I get to…?	*kako mogu doći do…?* [ka-ko moe-goo **do**-tchi doe]
is this the right way to…?	*je li ovo pravi put do…?* [yay lee ovo **prar**-vee put doe]
is it far to walk?	*je li daleko pješice…?* [yay lee dal-ecko **pyay**-shee-tzay]
can you show me on the map?	*možete mi pokazati na karti?* [mo-zhet-ay mee pocka-zarti na **kar**-tee]

Getting around

bus/bus station	*autobus/autobusni kolodvor* [out-o-**boos**/out-o-**boosnee** kolo-dvor]
train/express train	*vlak/brzi vlak* [vlack/berzee vlack]
main train station/ railway station	*glavni kolodvor/željeznički kolodvor* [glav-nee kolo-dvor/zhel-**yez**-neetchki kolo-dvor]
plane/airport	*avion/zračna luka* or *aerodrom* [av-ion/zratch-na **loo**-ka or air-o-drom]
car/taxi	*auto/taxi* [out-o/taksi]
petrol/petrol station	*benzin/benzinska stanica* [ben-zin/ben-zinska **stan**-itza]
entrance/exit	*ulaz/izlaz* [oo-laz/iz-laz]
arrival/departure	*dolazak/odlazak* [do-laz-ak/odd-laz-ak]
open/closed	*otvoreno/zatvoreno* [otvo-ren-o/zatvo-ren-o]
here/there	*ovdje/tamo* [ov-**dee**-ye/**tar**-mo]
near/far	*blizu/daleko* [bleezu/dal-ecko]
left/right	*lijevo/desno* [lee-**yeh**-vo/des-no]
straight on	*ravno* [rav-no]
ahead/behind	*naprijed/iza* [nap-ree-**yed**/eeza]
up/down	*gore/dolje* [go-reh/dol-yeh]
under/over	*ispod/preko* [iz-pod/precko]
north/south	*sjever/jug* [syeh-vair/yoog]
east/west	*istok/zapad* [iz-tok/zap-ad]
road/bridge	*cesta/most* [tzesta/most]
hill/mountain	*brežuljak/planina* [breh-**zhul**-yak/plan-**eena**]
village/town	*selo/grad* [**seh**-lo/grad]
waterfall	*slap* [slap]

Accommodation

reservation	*rezervacija* [rez-air-vatz-eeya]
passport	*putovnica* [put-ov-nitza]
bed	*krevet* [krev-et]
room	*soba* [**so**-ba]
key	*ključ* [kl-youtch]
shower/bath	*tuš/kada* [toosh/ka-da]
hot water/cold water	*topla voda/hladna voda* [top-la **vo**-da/hlad-na **vo**-da]

Miscellaneous

tourist office	*turistički ured* [tooris-**titch**-kee u-red]
consulate	*konzularni ured* [kon-zoo-larnee u-red]
doctor	*liječnik/doktor* [lee-**yetch**-nik/doktor]
dentist	*zubar* [**zoo**-bar]
hospital/clinic	*bolnica/klinika* [bol-**nitza**/klin-icka]
police	*policija* [**pol**-itz-ee-yah]

Time

hour/minute	*sat/minuta* [sat/min-**oota**]
week/day	*tjedan/dan* [**tjeh**-dan/dan]
year/month	*godina/mjesec* [god-eena/mee-**yeh**-setz]
now/soon	*sada/uskoro* [sa-da/oos-koro]
today/tomorrow	*danas/sutra* [da-nas/**soo**-tra]
yesterday	*jučer* [**you**-tchair]
this week/next week	*ovaj tjedan/slijedeći tjedan* [ov-eye **tyeh**-dan/sli-**yeh**-detchi tyeh-dan]
morning/afternoon	*jutro/poslije podne* [**you**-tro/poz-**lee**-yeh pod-nay]
evening/night	*večer/noć* [**vetch**-air/notch]
Monday	*ponedjeljak* [pon-ed-**yeh**-lee-yak]
Tuesday	*utorak* [**oot**-or-ak]
Wednesday	*srijeda* [sree-**yeh**-da]
Thursday	*četvrtak* [**tchet**-ver-tak]
Friday	*petak* [**pet**-ak]
Saturday	*subota* [**soo**-bo-ta]
Sunday	*nedjelja* [ned-yeh-lya]
January	*siječanj* [**si**-yeh-tchan-yeh]
February	*veljača* [**vel**-ya-tcha]
March	*ožujak* [o-zhu-yak]
April	*travanj* [trav-anya]
May	*svibanj* [svee-banya]
June	*lipanj* [lip-anya]
July	*srpanj* [ser-panya]
August	*kolovoz* [kolo-voz]
September	*rujan* [**roo**-yan]
October	*listopad* [lis-toe-pad]
November	*studeni* [**stoo**-den-ee]
December	*prosinac* [pro-seen-atz]

spring	*proljeće* [pro-**lyeh**-tcheh]
summer	*ljeto* [lyeh-toe]
autumn	*jesen* [yeh-sen]
winter	*zima* [zeema]

Food and drink

bon appetit!	*dobar tek!* [**dob**-bar-tek]

Essentials

breakfast	*doručak* [do**roo**-tchak]
brunch	*marenda* [ma-**ren**-dah] (in Dalmatian dialect)
lunch	*ručak* [roo-tchak]
dinner	*večera* [**vetch**-air-a]
water	*voda* [**vo**-da]
beer	*pivo* [**pee**-vo]
draught beer	*točeno pivo* [totch-**ay**-no **pee**-vo]
wine	*vino* [**vee**-no]
white wine	*bijelo vino* [bee-**yello vee**-no]
white wine and tap water	*bevanda* [be-**van**-dah]
white wine and mineral water	*gemišt* [gem-**isht**]
red wine	*crno vino* [**tzair**-noe **vee**-noe]
rosé wine	*roze vino* [rozay **vee**-no]
house wine	*domaće vino* [dom-**atch**-ay **vee**-no]
spirit (generic)	*rakija* [**rak**-ee-ya]
spirit (from herbs)	*travarica* [trav-**are**-itza]
cold	*hladno* [**hlad**-no]
hot	*vruće* [**vroo**-tchay]
bread/bakery	*kruh/pekarnica* [kroo/pek-**are**-nitza]
jam	*džem* [d-zhem] (some say *pekmez* [**peck**-mez])
coffee	*kava* [ka-va]
tea	*čaj* [tchai – rhymes with 'try']
tea with milk	*crni čaj s mlijekom* [tzair-nee tchai soo mil-yeh-kom] (ask for black, otherwise you get fruit tea with milk...)
tea with lemon	*čaj s limunom* [tchai soo lee-**moon**-om]
sugar	*šećer* [**shetch**-air]
salt	*slan* [slun]
cheese	*sir* [seer]
soup	*juha* [**you**-ha]
bean soup	*fažol* [**fa**-zhol] (not a vegetarian dish!)
egg (eggs)	*jaje (jaja)* [**ya**-yay/(ya-ya)]
ham	*šunka* [**shoo**nka]
air-dried ham	*pršut* [per-**shoot**]
fish	*riba* [**reeba**]
chips	*pomfrit* [pom-freet]
meat	*meso* [**may**-so]
vegetables	*povrće* [pov-air-tchay]
fruits	*voće* [**vo**-tchay]
homemade	*domaće* [dom-**a**-tchay]
grilled	*sa roštilja* [sar rosh-til-ya]
baked	*pečeno* [petch-**ay**no]

fried	*prženo* [per-**zay**no]
boiled	*kuhano* [**koo**-hano]
stuffed	*punjeno* [**poon**-yayno]

Fish Note that names of fish and shellfish get really complicated as they vary from place to place along the Dalmatian coast, with even the locals getting confused and disputing what names are correct where.

sardines	*srdela* [sr-**de**la]
anchovies	*inćuni* [in-ch**oo**-nih]
mackerel	*skuša* [skoo-sha]
bass	*lubin/brancin* [loo-ben/bran-tsin]
grey mullet	*cipal* [tzi-pal]
red mullet	*barbun* [bar-boon] or *trilja* [**tree**-ljah]
bream	*zubatac* [zoo-ba-tatz] or *orada* [or-**rah**-dah]
tuna	*tuna* [toona]
trout	*pastrva* [pas-ter-va]
salmon	*losos* [loss-oss]
squid	*lignje* [lig-nyeh]
cuttlefish	*sipa* [**see**-pah]
mussels	*dagnje* [dag-nyeh] or *mušule* [m**oo**-shoo-leh]
oysters	*oštrige/kamenice* [osh-trig-eh/kam-en-itz-eh]
shrimps	*škampi* [shkampi]
prawns	*kozice* [**koz**-it-seh]
crab	*rak* [rak]
lobster	*jastog* [yah-stog]
fish stew	*brudet* [br**oo**-det]

Meat

beef	*govedina* [**gov**-ed-eena]
pork	*svinjetina* [**svin**-yet-eena]
lamb	*janjetina* [**yan**-yet-eena]
mutton	*ovčetina* [**ov**-tchet-eena]
veal	*teletina* [**tel**-et-eena]
chicken	*piletina* [**pil**-et-eena]
wild boar	*divlja svinja* [**div**-lee-yah **svin**-yah]
braised beef in sweet wine	*pašticada* [pash-ti-tsada]
stuffed cabbage leaves	*sarma* [sar-ma]

Vegetables and side-dishes

potatoes	*krumpir* [krum-**peer**]
rice	*riža* [**ree**-zha]
green peppers	*paprika* [pap-**reeka**]
onion	*luk* [look]
garlic	*češnjak* [tchesh-nyak] or *bili luk* [bee-lee look]
asparagus	*šparoge* [shpar-o-gay]

Salads

salad	*salata* [sal-ata]
green salad	*zelena salata* [**zel**-ena sal-ata]
cucumber	*krastavac* [krasta-vatz]

cabbage	*kupus* [koo-poos]
tomato	*rajčica* [rai-tch-itza] or pomidor [po-**mee**-dor]
	(*paradajz* [para-dize] is sometimes used)
mixed	*miješana* [me-**yeh**-sha-na]
olive oil	*maslinovo ulje* [mas-lin-ovoh ool-yeh]

Fruit

orange	*narandža* [na-**rand**-zha]
	(or *naranča* [na-rand-tcha])
lemon/s	*limun* [lee-**moon**]
plums	*šljive* [shl**yee**-vay]
melon	*dinja* [din-ya]
pears	*kruške* [kroosh-kay]
peaches	*breskve* [**bresk**-vay]
cherries	*trešnje* [tresh-nee-yeh]
strawberries	*jagode* [yag-o-deh]
apples	*jabuke* [ya-**boo**-keh]
bananas	*banane* [ba-na-neh]
water melon	*lubenica* [**loo**-ben-itsah]

Appendix 2

FURTHER INFORMATION

BOOKS Many of the books listed here are long out of print, but most can be found second-hand – either by trawling through old bookshops or online at places like AbeBooks (**w** abebooks.com).

History and politics

Bracewell, Catherine Wendy *The Uskoks of Senj: Piracy, Banditry and Holy War in the Sixteenth-Century Adriatic* Cornell University Press, 1992. The definitive account of the history of the Uskoks.

Curta, Florin *Southeastern Europe in the Middle Ages 500–1250* Cambridge University Press, 2006. Good regional account of the medieval period.

Glenny, Misha *The Fall of Yugoslavia* Penguin, 1996, 3rd edition. Former BBC correspondent's account of how it all fell apart – compelling, if depressing, reading.

Goldstein, Ivo *Croatia: A History* C Hurst & Co, 1999, 2nd edition. Well-balanced Croat historian's view of Croatian history from Roman times to the present day. Hard to find, however, in spite of its relatively recent publication.

Harris, Robin *Dubrovnik – A History* Saqi, 2003. Solid doorstop of a tome with a wealth of fascinating insight and wonderful illustrations – hardly a dent in the wallet at 20 quid.

Hawkesworth, Celia *Zagreb: A Cultural and Literary History* Signal Books, 2007.

Macan, Trpimir, and Šentija, Josip *The Bridge – A Short History of Croatia* Journal of Croatian Literature, Zagreb, 1992. Notwithstanding the rather fanatical introduction by Yale professor Ivo Banac, this is an excellent history of Croatia in two sections, the first up to 1941 and the second from 1941 to 1991, with semi-official status. Hard to find, however.

Mesić, Stipe *The Demise of Yugoslavia: A Political Memoir* Central European University Press, 2004.

Morris, Jan *Venice* Faber & Faber, 1993. Traces the history and aspirations of the Venetian Empire, casting light on its cultural, social and economic effect on Dalmatia.

Rheubottom, David *Age, Marriage and Politics in 15th-century Ragusa* Oxford University Press, 2000. Intriguing – if at times weighty – insights into the inter-relationships between politics, kinship and marriage in the republic. Expensive, however, even second-hand.

Silber, Laura et al. *The Death of Yugoslavia* Penguin, 1996. Tie-in with the BBC series, and while it's not wholly successful without having seen the programmes, it's still a frightening blow-by-blow account of the events of the war.

Tanner, Marcus *Croatia: A Nation Forged in War* Yale University Press, 1997. An excellent and detailed history of Croatia, by the *Independent*'s correspondent during the conflict – probably the best book currently available.

Vale, Giovanni *Republic of Venice* Extinguished Countries, 2021. Examines the impact of 400 years of Venetian rule in Dalmatia.

Travel and travel literature

Abraham, Rudolf *Walks and Treks in Croatia: 30 Routes for Mountain Walks, National Parks and Coastal Trails* Cicerone, 2019. The most detailed and comprehensive guide to hiking in Croatia available in English, covering the main ranges (Velebit, Biokovo, etc) as well as islands and areas further inland.

Abraham, Rudolf *The Islands of Croatia* Cicerone, 2014. Award-winning guide to hiking on Croatia's islands, including in-depth coverage of Krk, Rab, Korčula, Hvar, Vis and others, and detailed local hiking maps and information on wildlife, etc.

Bardwell, Sandra *Croatia: 9 Car Tours, 70 Long and Short Walks* Sunflower, 2016. Excellent guide aimed at walkers and hikers and covering the coast and islands as well as the Plitvice Lakes.

Bridge, Ann *Illyrian Spring* Chatto & Windus, 1935. Rather fey (very 1930s) novel about a painter working her way down the Adriatic coast in search of inspiration and love – but great descriptions of Pula, Split, Dubrovnik, etc.

Coyler, William *Dubrovnik and the Southern Adriatic Coast from Split to Kotor* Ward Lock & Co, 1967. Delightfully dated mini hardback with lots of black-and-white photos.

Cuddon, J A *The Companion Guide to Jugoslavia* Collins, 1986, 3rd edition.

Delalle, Ivan *Guide to Trogir* Trogir Tourist Board, 1963. Brilliant black-and-white pocket guide to the city first published in 1936; full of words like 'historiography'.

Goldring, Patrick *Yugoslavia* Collins Holiday Guides, 1967. Marvellous pocket guide featuring mainly Croatia – and a splendid farmer smoking a roll-up on the cover.

Gray, William *Travel with Kids* Footprint, 2012. Great source of inspiration for family travel.

Kaplan, Robert *Balkan Ghosts* Picador, 1994. The author uses his 1990 odyssey through the Balkans to explain the conflictual politics across the region in-depth. Relatively easily available second-hand.

Kastrapeli et al. *Dubrovnik Tourist Guide* Minčeta, 1967. Classic 1960s mini guide – gushing prose, black-and-white photos.

McClain Brown, Cody *Chasing a Croatian Girl. A Survivor's Tale* Algoritam, 2014. Often hilarious anecdotes on life in Croatia by this popular blogger, an American expat living in Croatia. Particularly amusing for those with some familiarity with Croatian habits and customs.

Murphy, Dervla *Through the Embers of Chaos – Balkan Journeys* John Murray, 2002. Brilliant account of a long cycle tour through the Balkans, including Dubrovnik, Split, Zagreb, etc. Truly a wonderful, inspirational book.

Thompson, Trevor and Dinah *Adriatic Pilot: Croatia, Slovenia, Montenegro, East Coast of Italy, Albania* Imray, 8th edition, 2020. Benchmark sailing guide.

Voynovitch, Count Louis *A Historical Saunter through Dubrovnik (Ragusa)* Jadran, 1929. Nearly impossible to find, but marvellous short guide to the city from a 1929 perspective. It's amazing how little has changed in spite of both a world and a local war.

West, Rebecca *Black Lamb and Grey Falcon* Canongate Books, 1993. Without question, the most comprehensive (1,200pp) and best-written account of Yugoslavia in the 1930s. Rebecca West travelled widely in Croatia (and the other republics of the former Yugoslavia) in 1936 and 1937 and spent five years researching and writing this book. Fatally flawed in places and terribly naïve in its conclusion, it's nonetheless by turns funny, passionate and tragic – and always brilliantly opinionated. If you come across the original two-volume hardback from the 1940s, go for it; there are excellent black-and-white photographs.

Natural history

Gorman, Gerard *Central and Eastern European Wildlife* Bradt, 2008. Excellent all-round introduction, well-illustrated.

Mitchell-Jones, A J et al. *The Atlas of European Mammals* Academic Press, 2002. Heavyweight guide to nearly 200 species, with distribution maps and a real wealth of detail.

Polunin, Oleg *Flowers of Greece and the Balkans* Oxford, 1980. The definitive guide to the flora of southeast Europe.

Still, John *Butterflies and Moths of Britain and Europe* Collins, 1996. Handy guide for lepidopterists.

Svensson, Lars; Killian, Mullarney; and Zetterstrom, Dan *Collins Bird Guide* Collins, 2023, 3rd edition. Simply excellent guide to European birds, with truly wonderful illustrations. The many Collins field guides (trees, flowers, etc) are also highly recommended.

Tolman, Tom and Lewington, Richard *Collins Butterfly Guide* Collins, 2009. The definitive guide to the butterflies of Europe.

Art and culture

Beretić, Dubravka *Art Treasures of Dubrovnik* Jugoslavija Guides, 1968. Obscure guide dating back to the communist heyday – still remarkably accurate, however.

Čošić, Stjepan et al. *Croatia: Aspects of Art, Architecture and Cultural Heritage* Frances Lincoln, 2009. Large coffee table book with essays on various aspects of Croatian art and history, and an introduction by John Julius Norwich.

Pavičic, Liliana and Pirker-Mosher, Gordana *The Best of Croatian Cooking* Hippocrene Books, 2007, expanded edition. You're back home and missing those Croatian dishes? This is the book for you.

Salter, Alicia *Four Emperors and an Architect* Lexicon Publishing, 2013. Beautifully illustrated book examining how Roman building under the Tetrarchy (most notably Diocletian's Palace in Split) inspired Scottish architect Robert Adam's neoclassical masterpieces.

Susnjar, Ante *Croatian-English/English-Croatian Dictionary and Phrasebook* Hippocrene, 2000. Good, helpful reference guide to the language.

WEBSITES There's a mountain of information and a wealth of resources concerning Croatia on the web. Here's a selection:

General

W croatia.hr The National Tourist Board's exemplary website, with a huge amount of practical information and the phone numbers of most hotels, travel agencies and campsites across the country.

W croatianmiscellany.wordpress.com Croatia in black and white.

W dalmatia.hr Central Dalmatia county, official regional tourist information site.

W diving-hrs.hr Croatian Diving Federation. Small (the English part, anyway) but useful site listing the rules and regulations for scuba diving.

W eudict.com Excellent English-Croatian and Croatian-English dictionaries, though you need to have some idea of context as the responses are provided without separate definitions (the word 'set' gives you 41 different responses, for example).

W hr The so-called 'Croatian Homepage,' an English-language site featuring 7,500 links in hundreds of categories, all about Croatia. You can spend many hours here.

W mdc.hr Muzejski dokumentacijski centar, with details of most museums in Croatia.

W meteo.hr Croatian Meteorological Service. Click on the flag for English and find out everything you ever wanted to know about Croatia's weather, including forecasts.

W tportal.hr/imenik Croatia's online phone directory (including an English-language option). Just what you need when it turns out the phone number listed in this guide has already changed.

W uhpa.hr Association of Croatian Travel Agencies. A good way of finding out what can be organised for you.

Transport

w akz.hr Zagreb bus station, mostly in Croatian. Nonetheless, an excellent site with all arrivals and departures if you're flying into the capital and want to head down to Dalmatia, including costs and the facility to buy tickets online – go to Vozni red (timetable) from the homepage.

w ak-split.hr Split bus station, with times for arrivals and departures.

w libertasdubrovnik.hr Dubrovnik city buses, plus intercity services.

w hak.hr Hrvatski Autoklub (Croatian Automobile Club). In Croatian only, though it does have an interactive traffic snarl-up area in English.

w hzpp.hr National Railway. Even in Croatian, you'll be able to find your way round the timetables, and the standard fares are displayed when the times come up – online booking is a bit trickier.

w ina.hr The state-owned oil company. Complete with fuel prices and the locations and opening hours of every petrol station in the country.

w jadrolinija.hr, w krilo.hr, w miatours.hr, w snav.it, w tp-line.hr The main ferry and catamaran companies plying the Dalmatian stretch of the Adriatic.

Government and media

w dzs.hr Croatian Bureau of Statistics. Everything you ever wanted to know.

w hic.hr/english/index.htm Another news portal (also available in Croatian and Spanish).

w hrt.hr Croatian national TV and radio (in Croatian).

w mint.gov.hr Ministry of Tourism & Sport. More statistics and all the forms you'll need if you're planning on starting a business in the Croatian tourist industry.

w mvep.gov.hr Ministry of Foreign & European Affairs. Everything you need to know about visa requirements, etc.

w tportal.hr Big customisable portal in Croatian from the main telecoms provider, with daily news bulletins, weather, traffic, entertainment, etc.

Hiking and cycling

w hps.hr Hrvatski planinarski savez (Croatian Mountaineering Association).

w trail.viadinarica.com Via Dinarica, a long-distance hiking and cycling trail, launched in 2024, connecting Slovenia, Croatia, Bosnia & Herzegovina, Montenegro, Serbia, Kosovo and Albania, which in part runs through Dalmatia.

Sailing

w aci-marinas.com Adriatic Croatia International Club homepage, with full details of everything ACI offers.

w navily.com A Europe-wide sailing app with plenty of useful information about marinas and anchorages in Dalmatia, including a facility for booking berths.

Index

Page numbers in **bold** indicate main entries; those in *italics* indicate maps

INDEX OF ADVERTISERS